London

Selection of
Restaurants
& Hotels

2007

CENTRAL LONDON
GREATER LONDON

Commitments

"This volume was created at the turn of the century and will last at least as long".

This foreword to the very first edition of the MICHELIN Guide, written in 1900, has become famous over the years and the Guide has lived up to the prediction. It is read across the world and the key to its popularity is the consistency of its commitment to its readers, which is based on the following promises.

The Michelin Guide's commitments :

Anonymous inspections

Our inspectors make regular and anonymous visits to hotels and restaurants to gauge the quality of products and services offered to an ordinary customer. They settle their own bill and may then introduce themselves and ask for more information about the establishment. Our readers' comments are also a valuable source of information, which we can then follow up with another visit of our own.

Independence:

Our choice of establishments is a completely independent one, made for the benefit of our readers alone. The decisions to be taken are discussed around the table by the inspectors and the editor. The most important awards are decided at a European level. Inclusion in the Guide is completely free of charge.

Selection and choice:

The Guide offers a selection of the best hotels and restaurants in every category of comfort and price. This is only possible because all the inspectors rigorously apply the same methods.

Annual updates:

All the practical information, the classifications and awards are revised and updated every single year to give the most reliable information possible. Consistency: The criteria for the classifications are the same in every country covered by the Michelin Guide.

...And our aim :

to do everything possible to make travel, holidays and eating out a pleasure, as part of Michelin's ongoing commitment to improving travel and mobility.

Dear reader

We are delighted to introduce our new Michelin Guide for London.

It is the third city in our new collection, which began in 2005 with the publication of our New York City Guide and was followed in 2006 by San Francisco.

We hope you like our new look. By introducing photographs, more text and an easy-to-follow layout, we have modernised our appearance while retaining the professionalism and independence for which we are known. We make this guide for you and value your opinions, so let us know what you think about this guide and about the restaurants we have recommended.

All the restaurants within this guide have been chosen first and foremost for the quality of their cooking. You'll find comprehensive information on over 420 dining establishments within these pages and they range from gastropubs and neighbourhood brasseries to internationally renowned restaurants. The diverse and varied selection also bear testament to the rich and buoyant dining scene in London, with the city now enjoying a worldwide reputation for the quality and range of its restaurants.

You'll find that Michelin Stars are not our only awards – look out also for the Bib Gourmands. These are restaurants where the cooking is still carefully prepared but in a simpler style and, priced at under £28 for three courses, they represent excellent value for money.

As well as the restaurants, our team of independent inspectors have also chosen 50 hotels. These carefully selected hotels represent the best that London has to offer, from the luxurious and international to the small and intimate. All have been chosen for their individuality and personality.

Look out for other great cities to follow in this series.

Consult the Michelin Guide at www.viamichelin.com
and write to us at themichelinguide-gbirl@uk.michelin.com

CONTENTS

S. Ollivier/MICHELIN

SIME/PHOTONSTOP

GREATER LONDON

WHERE TO STAY

How to use this guide

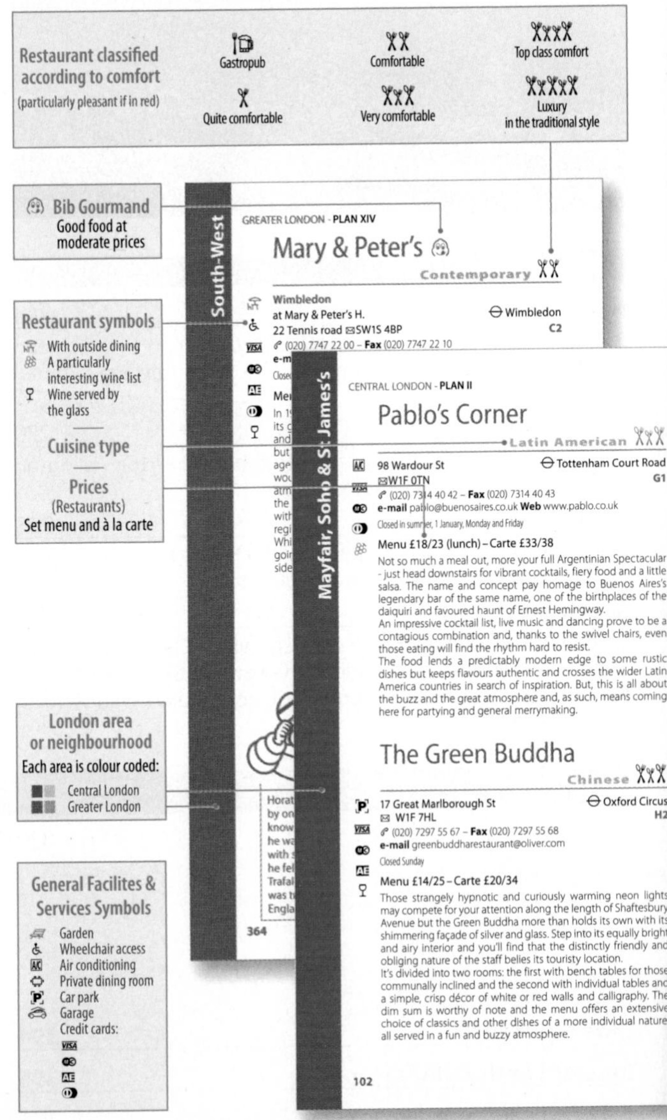

Restaurant classified according to comfort
(particularly pleasant if in red)
Gastropub
Quite comfortable
Comfortable
Very comfortable
Top class comfort
Luxury in the traditional style
Bib Gourmand
Good food at moderate prices
Restaurant symbols
With outside dining
A particularly interesting wine list
Wine served by the glass
Cuisine type
Prices
(Restaurants)
Set menu and à la carte
London area or neighbourhood
Each area is colour coded:
Central London
Greater London
General Facilites & Services Symbols
Garden
Wheelchair access
Air conditioning
Private dining room
Car park
Garage
Credit cards:
South-West
GREATER LONDON - PLAN XIV
Mary & Peter's
Contemporary
Wimbledon
at Mary & Peter's H.
22 Tennis road SW1S 4BP
Wimbledon
C2
(020) 7747 22 00 – Fax (020) 7747 22 10
364
Mayfair, Soho & St James's
CENTRAL LONDON - PLAN II
Pablo's Corner
Latin American
98 Wardour St
W1F 0TN
Tottenham Court Road
G1
(020) 7314 40 42 – Fax (020) 7314 40 43
e-mail pablo@buenosaires.co.uk Web www.pablo.co.uk
Closed in summer, 1 January, Monday and Friday
Menu £18/23 (lunch) – Carte £33/38
Not so much a meal out, more your full Argentinian Spectacular - just head downstairs for vibrant cocktails, fiery food and a little salsa. The name and concept pay homage to Buenos Aires's legendary bar of the same name, one of the birthplaces of the daiquiri and favoured haunt of Ernest Hemingway.
An impressive cocktail list, live music and dancing prove to be a contagious combination and, thanks to the swivel chairs, even those eating will find the rhythm hard to resist.
The food lends a predictably modern edge to some rustic dishes but keeps flavours authentic and crosses the wider Latin America countries in search of inspiration. But, this is all about the buzz and the great atmosphere and, as such, means coming here for partying and general merrymaking.
The Green Buddha
Chinese
17 Great Marlborough St
W1F 7HL
Oxford Circus
H2
(020) 7297 55 67 – Fax (020) 7297 55 68
e-mail greenbuddharestaurant@oliver.com
Closed Sunday
Menu £14/25 – Carte £20/34
Those strangely hypnotic and curiously warming neon lights may compete for your attention along the length of Shaftesbury Avenue but the Green Buddha more than holds its own with its shimmering façade of silver and glass. Step into its equally bright and airy interior and you'll find that the distinctly friendly and obliging nature of the staff belies its touristy location.
It's divided into two rooms: the first with bench tables for those communally inclined and the second with individual tables and a simple, crisp décor of white or red walls and calligraphy. The dim sum is worthy of note and the menu offers an extensive choice of classics and other dishes of a more individual nature, all served in a fun and buzzy atmosphere.
102

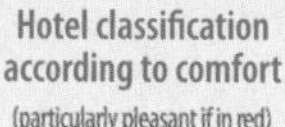

Hotel classification according to comfort

(particularly pleasant if in red)

Quite comfortable

Comfortable

Very comfortable

Top class comfort

Luxury in the traditional style

Hotel symbols

39 rm Number of rooms

Breakfast included (or not)

Prices for a single/double room

With restaurant

Quiet hotel

Swimming pool

Spa

Sauna

Tennis

Exercise room

Lift

WIFI

Satellite TV

Equipped conference room

Areas - Map number and coordinates

⊖ Underground station

CENTRAL LONDON – **PLAN III**

Hotel Bloomsbury

26 Chesham Pl ⊖ Knightsbridge
SW1X 8HQ **C2**
(020) 7235 65 40 – **Fax** (020) 7235 66 42
e-mail hotelbloomsbury@quiethotels.co.uk
Web www.bloomsbury.com

56 rm – £95/124 £150/224

The Window (See restaurant listing)

...ns certainly knew how to build hotels. The ...as originally called the Great Central and was ...of the great railway hotels; the façade today still ...itectural style of that age. Once inside, however, ...lise you're in the company of an international ...ion, where size, comfort and facilities fit the ...ards demanded by your average 21st century

...ing feature of the hotel is the vast glass-roofed ...hich the Window restaurant serves breakfast and ...l menu at lunch and dinner. Those after some-...ore traditional should head downstairs to the ...Cellar Bar, while the Mirror Bar is an altogether ...ated spot for cocktail hour. ...many of which face inwards into the atrium, are ...proportioned and have every mod con you need. ...also a good size and the majority have separate ...uble washbasins. Those looking for even greater ...ion will be more than happy with the well equip-...o.

WHERE TO STAY **397**

WHERE TO STAY Belgravia & Victoria

CENTRAL LONDON - **PLAN II**

Rob's Cafe ✿

British XX

33 Romilly St ⊖ Leicester Square
W1F 0TN **H1**
(020) 7518 22 00 – **Fax** (020) 7518 22 10
e-mail Robscafe@lindahouse.co.uk **Web** www.robscafe.com
Closed 25-26 December, 1 January, Monday and Bank Holidays
Menu £21/35 (lunch) – Carte £27/55

Linda House is a handsome four storey 18th century building in the heart of Soho. To gain entry, you ring the doorbell and you'll then be ushered into one of the two dining rooms. Regulars may have their favourite but there's little to choose between them – they're both warm and welcoming, although the first floor room is slightly larger than the ground floor.

There is something about being cosseted in a characterful house that makes dining here such a pleasure and it provides the perfect antidote for those feeling bruised and buffeted by the bigger, more boisterous places.

The cooking is modern in its approach and presentation but flavours are far more vigorous and full bodied than one expects and the marriages of various ingredients bear testament to real talent. Evidence of Rob's Welsh roots pops up here and there, from the laver bread to the Welsh cheeses and his homeland provides much of the produce. Tasting and Garden menus are available for those making it an occasion and there are some interesting small producers featured on the wine list.

A LA CARTE

FIRST COURSE	MAIN COURSE	DESSERT
· Ravioli of shellfish with Champagne and chives	· Roast sea bass with black olives, baby squid and creamed fennel	· Lemongrass jelly with pineapple and coconut
· Loin of tuna wrapped in basil with soy, avocado and a salad of radish	· Assiette of lamb with new season garlic, borlotti beans and rosemary	· Vanilla yoghurt parfait with blueberries

103

Mayfair, Soho & St James's

Stars for good cooking

✿ to ✿✿✿

Sample menu for starred restaurant

A culinary history of London

For 2,000 years London has been one of the greatest commercial centres of the world. It owes this success in no small part to the Thames, which links the city to the sea and thus trading routes across the globe: this not only accounts for London's prosperity, it also says a lot about its relationship with food.

S. Ollivier/MICHELIN

Successive waves of invaders, immigrants and merchants have introduced new foods to the city's menu – from Roman olive oil to Norman wine. By the 16C the London docks were bursting with exciting new smells and tastes from the New World: corn and rice from North America, and rum, coffee, sugar and cocoa from the West Indies.

Protein and Politics

With so much on offer it is little surprise that Londoners have long been preoccupied by food. Medieval London was chock full of dining options, with cook-shops and eating-houses competing with street traders to keep Londoners well fed. Pepys' diary gives a vivid insight into a 17C diet, which seems to have been heavy on the protein – one dinner contained "a brace of stewed carps, six roasted chickens, and a jowl of salmon" – but also included more exotic ingredients such as nutmeg. More importantly, the diaries paint a picture of a city where eating and drinking were an integral part of socialising.

Nowhere is this clearer than the coffee houses that evolved during the 18C. These were grubby but fragrant spaces where everything from politics to poetry would be discussed over a cup of coffee or chocolate. They were also important centres of business, serving as counting houses and auction rooms before the development of the stock exchange.

The city developed, perhaps unfairly, a reputation for bad

food during the 19C; Henry James famously describing London eating places "whose badness is literally fabulous". However, the opening of the first big restaurants soon put paid to this slur: Monsieur Ritz helped to pioneer a revolution, replacing the communal benches of the cookhouse with tables where small groups could eat in relative seclusion. By the beginning of the 20C, everyone from big spenders at glitzy hotels to the humbler clientele at a Lyons Corner House could enjoy the private dining experience.

From coupons to coriander

The Second World War may have compromised the quality of food on London plates, but eating out remained defiantly popular, even during the Blitz. After the austerity of rationing, London got more adventurous in the 1950s; immigrants from the Caribbean, Africa and Asia created demands for specialist food stores, while the arrival of new cooking styles finally began to percolate through to the culinary imagination.

Today the world is London's mollusc of choice with world-renowned restaurants throughout the city. Although fusions of different styles and ingredients are still popular, in the last few years there has been a return to home-grown fare, with the emphasis on quality and sustainability prompting an explosion of farmer's markets across the city: these days even bangers and mash can be cordon bleu if you source it right.

Roger-Viollet

Practical London

Arrival/Departure

Getting to the UK's first city from abroad can try the patience of even the most eager Londonophile, but at least you have plenty of options to choose from.

Planes...

Heathrow, the UK's busiest airport, can suffer from its popularity, but is conveniently located on the Piccadilly Line and so is marvellous for southwest London. But those wishing to be whisked to the centre shouldn't hesitate to board the popular Heathrow Express to Paddington - more expensive than the tube, but you're sped to Zone One four times quicker. Getting a taxi is a much riskier strategy - depending on traffic, the journey can take an hour or more and is correspondingly pricey.

Gatwick to the south is further out in the sticks, but has some convenient rail links from the south terminal. The Gatwick Express runs to Victoria Station taking 30 minutes, although other services get there almost as fast. The Thameslink line, meanwhile, runs through London Bridge and King's Cross, before going up to burgeoning Luton Airport, the original EasyJet hub.

...and trains

Stansted was also a cheap flights trailblazer and is known for Norman Foster's modern terminal building. Trains and coaches go to Liverpool Street, convenient for east London. Business travellers, however, should consider flights to London City Airport, with the prospect of amazing views from the plane and a speedy transfer onto the Docklands Light Railway (DLR).

S. Ollivier/MICHELIN

Eurostar

Of course, those travelling from Paris or Brussels need not take off at all; the glamour of Eurostar train travel is still intact after more than a decade of faithful service. Expect even greater convenience when the Channel Tunnel Rail Link completes in 2007 and the London terminus switches from Waterloo to St Pancras.

Getting Around

You know you're a true Londoner when you've mastered how to use the Tube, but those on a flying visit should not despair - it's easier than it looks.

Tube and oysters

Travelcards go a long way on London's transport system, since unlimited journeys within the zoned areas will work out cheaper than numerous single fares, and the cards can also be used on buses and the DLR. However, those here for a while (or who just want the thrill of swiping their wallet on the little yellow gate pads) would be well-advised to get an Oyster card, which electronically stores travelcard or pre-pay credit. These contactless smartcards have become beloved by Londoners in a very short time - not least because they offer savings on fares.

A bit of nouse can save you a lot of hassle. Remember that tube trains will be packed with commuters during rush hour periods and that platforms can be a long escalator away from ticket barriers. Also be aware that sometimes (especially in central London) a Tube journey isn't necessary at all. Leicester Square, for instance, is but 250m from Covent Garden. Check your A-Z and if the journey looks relatively straightforward, walk - you'll get a much better view.

Drivetime

Buses provide another alternative and from the top of a double decker you'll get a sight-seeing tour for the price of your fare. The night bus service has improved immeasurably in the past couple of years (a good thing too, since the Tube still stops not long after midnight). But London life would not be complete without the occasional black cab ride home. Look for the illuminated sign on the roof before hailing and make sure you're in the mood for banter.

For those brave enough to drive themselves, the Congestion Charge may have helped to clear your way, but you'll pay a price for it - £8 each day you drive within the charge zone (£10 if you pay the day after). The good news for motorists is that the charge doesn't apply at the week ends, or before 7:00am or after 6.30pm during the week. However, in February 2007 the zone will be extended further west into Kensington and Chelsea, although the charging period will stop half an hour earlier at 6pm.

Living London Life

There is something for everyone in London and finding out what's here for you is part of the fun. The trick is to realise that everyone's London is different and it's okay to think outside of the box.

So by all means head to Oxford Street to revel in London shopping at its most frenetic, but know you'll find similar stores on the (quieter) Kensington High Street and you may prefer to try your luck in the local markets. The West End has an international reputation as a theatrical powerhouse, but the most daring work is often found on the fringe, in poky venues above pubs. Likewise, the superclubs of Clerkenwell and Shoreditch are famous the world over as party palaces, but you may prefer to embrace the Latin rhythms of a salsa evening, and belly dancing classes are also becoming a phenomenon.

Tips and tipping

And when it comes to the important bit - eating - there are a few tips to ensure a good old time. Those on a budget need not miss out on fine dining experiences, with many good value lunch menus to be had. Conversely, in the City and with restaurants popular with business folk, dinner is often the cheaper option, while West End pre- and post-theatre menus are ideal for cut-price gourmets. Keeping tabs on water and wine refills should avoid nasty surprises coming with the bill - but note there is no standard procedure for tipping, and although some restaurants leave the amount open, others add a service charge of anything up to 15%. If you're unhappy, speak up. Finally, it can be pretty frustrating when the perfect restaurant says it can't fit in your cosy table for two until mid-way through 2008. Invite some friends and ask for a table for four and you may have better luck - less romantic, but the food will taste just as good. Bon appétit!

Stubbing it out

There's one thing, however, that everyone will be doing in enclosed public spaces: not smoking. Following parliamentary approval, the smoking ban comes into effect in summer 2007 and, among other things, covers restaurants, clubs and pubs. Many of these are expected to provide outdoor areas for smokers - but English winters are a good incentive to give up.

"SCARY AND HILARIOUS"
JAMES KING - RADIO 1
Metroline
AS
514
OPEN

Where to **eat**

Alphabetical list of restaurants

A – B

G – H – I

J – K – L

M – N – O

P – Q – R

S – T – U – V

W – Y – Z

Starred restaurants

Within this selection, we have highlighted a number of restaurants for their particularly good cooking. When awarding one, two or three Michelin Stars there are a number of factors we consider: the quality and compatibility of the ingredients, the technical skill and flair that goes into their preparation, the clarity and combination of flavours, the value for money and, above all, the taste. Equally important is the ability to produce excellent cooking not once but time and time again. Our inspectors make as many visits as necessary, so that you can be sure of the quality and consistency.

A two or three star restaurant has to offer something very special in its cuisine; a real element of creativity, originality or personality that sets it apart from the rest. Three stars – our highest award – are given to the very best.

Cuisines in any style and of any nationality are eligible for a star. The decoration, service and comfort have no bearing on the award.

We will also point out any restaurants that we feel have the potential to rise further and already have an element of superior quality. These rising stars, along with the existing stars, will continue to be closely watched.

Let us know what you think, not just about the stars but about all the restaurants in this guide.

The awarding of a star is based solely on the quality of the cooking.

Exceptional cuisine, worth a special journey

One always eats extremely well here, sometimes superbly.
Distinctive dishes precisely executed, using superlative ingredients

Gordon Ramsay	XXXX	202

Excellent cooking, worth a detour

Skilfully and carefully crafted dishes of outstanding quality

Capital Restaurant, The	XXX	205
Gavroche, Le	XXXX	39
Pétrus	XXXX	102
Pied à Terre	XXX	139
Square, The	XXXX	42

A very good restaurant in its category

Offering cuisine prepared to a consistently high standard
Name in red *the 2007 Rising Stars for* ✿✿

Amaya	XXX	104
Angela Hartnett at The Connaught	XXXX	40
Arbutus	X	76
Assaggi	X	158
Atelier de Joël Robuchon, L'	X	95
Aubergine	XXX	208
Benares	XXX	49
Chez Bruce	XX	335
Club Gascon	XX	172
Escargot, L'	XXX	50
Foliage	XXX	206
Glasshouse, The	XX	325
Gordon Ramsay at Claridge's	XXXX	41
Greenhouse, The	XXX	45
Hakkasan	XX	143
Ledbury, The	XXX	239
Locanda Locatelli	XXX	121
Maze	XXX	47
Mirabelle	XXX	46
Nahm	XX	108
Nobu	XX	59
Nobu Berkeley St	XX	64
Noisette, La	XXXX	203
1 Lombard Street	XXX	168
Orrery	XXX	120
Rasoi	XX	214
Rhodes Twenty Four	XXX	167
Richard Corrigan at Lindsay House	XX	63
River Café	XX	320
Roussillon	XXX	107
Savoy Grill, The	XXXX	89
Sketch (The Lecture Room and Library)	XXXX	43
Tamarind	XXX	51
Tom Aikens	XXX	207
Umu	XX	58
Yauatcha	X	77
Zafferano	XXX	103

Rising Star

Galvin at Windows	XXXX	44

Bib Gourmand

Establishments offering good quality cuisine for under £28

(price of a 3 course meal not including drinks).

Restaurants by cuisine type

French Mediterranean

French traditional

Gastropub

Restaurant	Rating	Page
Noura Brasserie	XX	112
Noura Central	XX	68

Malaysian

Restaurant	Rating	Page
Awana	XXX	212
Champor-Champor	X	185

Mediterranean

Restaurant	Rating	Page
Aurora (Soho)	X	82
Cru	X	278
Ditto	X	336
11 Abingdon Road	XX	244
High Road Brasserie	XX	311
Lock, The	XX	286
Moro	X	183
Portal	XX	179
Salt Yard	X	149
Sam's Brasserie	X	311
Snows on the Green	X	322

Modern European

Restaurant	Rating	Page
Addendum	XXX	171
Alastair Little	X	78
Angela Hartnett at The Connaught	✿ XXXX	40
Arbutus	✿ X	76
Aurora (City)	XXX	166
Avenue, The	XX	69
Axis	XXX	90
Bank (Strand and Covent Garden)	XX	93
Bank (Victoria)	XX	112
Belvedere	XXX	240
Berkeley Square	XXX	55
Blandford Street	XX	129
Bluebird	XX	216
Blueprint Café	X	181
Bonds	XXX	166
Brackenbury, The	X	322
Bradley's	XX	266
Café, The	X	80
Caprice, Le	XX	57
Chancery, The	XX	173
Chapter Two	XX	292
Clarkes	XX	242
Drones	XXX	210
Embassy	XXX	48
Fifth Floor	XXX	210
Fig	X	274
Flâneur	X	187
Frederick's	XX	280
Glasshouse, The	✿ XX	325
Gordon Ramsay at Claridge's	✿ XXXX	41
Hoxton Apprentice	X	279
Hush	XX	62
Island	XX	156
Kensington Place	X	247
Lanes	XX	175
Medcalf	X	191
Mirabelle	✿ XXX	46
North Pole	XX	295
Odette's	XX	263
Origin	XXX	140
Oscar	XX	123
Oxo Tower (Brasserie)	X	180
Oxo Tower (Restaurant)	XXX	170
Patterson's	XX	60
Plateau (Grill)	XX	294
Plateau (Restaurant)	XXX	292
Portrait	X	84
Prism	XXX	169
Quaglino's	XX	67
Ransome's Dock	X	309
Redmond's	XX	315
Richard Corrigan at Lindsay House	✿ XX	63
Savoy Grill, The	✿ XXXX	89
Searcy's	XX	176
Smiths of Smithfield	XX	178
Sonny's	XX	306
Tate Modern (Restaurant)	X	182
Village East	X	184
Vinoteca	X	187
Wapping Food	X	299
Wharf, The	XX	330
White Swan, The	XX	177
Whits	XX	244
Wolseley, The	XXX	48

Moroccan

Restaurant	Rating	Page
Momo	XX	66
Pasha	XX	221

North African

Restaurant	Rating	Page
Azou	X	323

Polish

Wódka	X	249

Seafood

Bentley's (Oyster Bar)	X	79
Bibendum Oyster Bar	X	230
Chamberlain's	XX	176
Deep	XX	317
Fish Hook	X	312
Fishworks (Chiswick)	X	312
Fishworks (Regent's Park and Marylebone)	X	133
J. Sheekey	XX	91
One-O-One	XXX	209
Poissonnerie de l'Avenue	XX	216
Rudland Stubbs	X	190
Wright Brothers	X	186

South-East Asian

Cicada	X	188
Cocoon	XX	73
Crazy Bear	XX	145
E & O	XX	243
Eight over Eight	XX	226
Great Eastern Dining Room	XX	277
Taman Gang	XX	65

Spanish

Cambio de Tercio	XX	222
Cigala	X	148
Fino	XX	145
L Restaurant and Bar	XX	246
Tapas Brindisa	X	186

Thai

Bangkok	X	230
Blue Elephant	XX	318
Chada	XX	308
Chada Chada	X	133
Mango Tree	XX	111
Nahm	✿ XX	108
Nipa	XX	157
Oh Boy	X	331
Saran Rom	XXX	316

Traditional

Ambassador, The	X	190
Bedford and Strand	X	96
Bellamy's	XX	69
Bentley's (Grill)	XXX	56
Brew Wharf	X	189
Butcher and Grill, The	X	309
Konstam at the Prince Albert	X	191
Langan's Coq d'Or	XX	219
Ritz Restaurant, The	XXXXX	38

Turkish

Ozer	XX	126

Vietnamese

Au Lac	X	276

Restaurants with outside dining

Amici	XX	336
Anglesea Arms	🍺	324
Aquasia	XXX	213
Aurora (Soho)	X	82
Aventure, L'	XX	129
Babylon	XXX	240
Bank (Victoria)	XX	112
Barnsbury, The	🍺	283
Belvedere	XXX	240
Berkeley Square	XXX	55
Bertorelli (Soho)	X	85
Bevis Marks	XX	175
Boisdale	XX	111
Bollo, The	🍺	306

S. Olivier/MICHELIN

CENTRAL LONDON

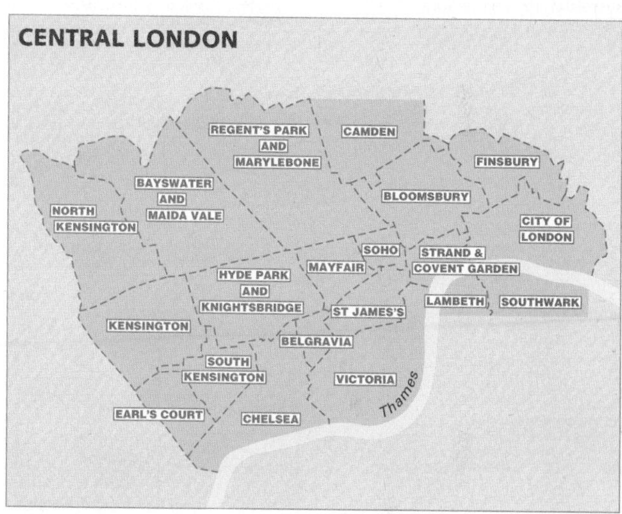
CENTRAL LONDON
REGENT'S PARK AND MARYLEBONE
CAMDEN
FINSBURY
BAYSWATER AND MAIDA VALE
BLOOMSBURY
NORTH KENSINGTON
CITY OF LONDON
SOHO
STRAND & COVENT GARDEN
MAYFAIR
HYDE PARK AND KNIGHTSBRIDGE
LAMBETH
SOUTHWARK
ST JAMES'S
KENSINGTON
BELGRAVIA
SOUTH KENSINGTON
VICTORIA
Thames
EARL'S COURT
CHELSEA

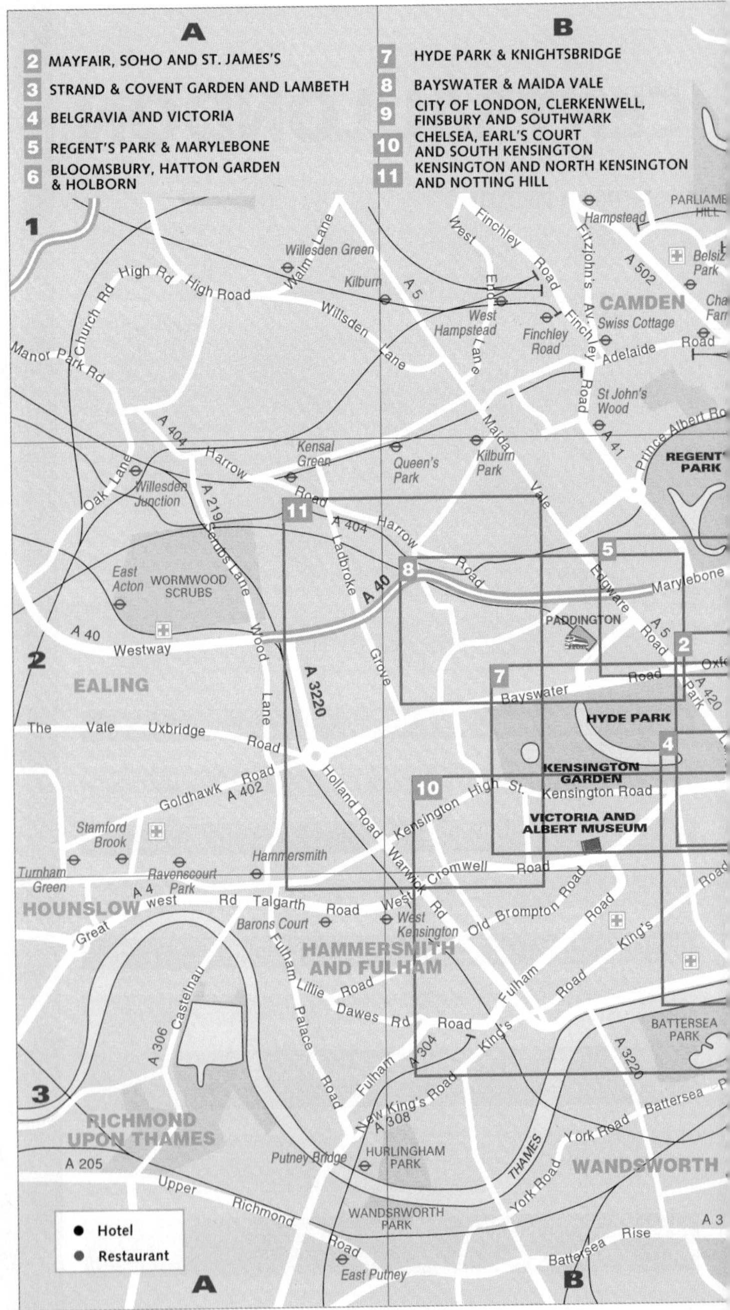

A
B
2 MAYFAIR, SOHO AND ST. JAMES'S
3 STRAND & COVENT GARDEN AND LAMBETH
4 BELGRAVIA AND VICTORIA
5 REGENT'S PARK & MARYLEBONE
6 BLOOMSBURY, HATTON GARDEN & HOLBORN
7 HYDE PARK & KNIGHTSBRIDGE
8 BAYSWATER & MAIDA VALE
9 CITY OF LONDON, CLERKENWELL, FINSBURY AND SOUTHWARK
10 CHELSEA, EARL'S COURT AND SOUTH KENSINGTON
11 KENSINGTON AND NORTH KENSINGTON AND NOTTING HILL
CAMDEN
REGENT'S PARK
PADDINGTON
HYDE PARK
KENSINGTON GARDEN
VICTORIA AND ALBERT MUSEUM
WORMWOOD SCRUBS
EALING
HOUNSLOW
HAMMERSMITH AND FULHAM
RICHMOND UPON THAMES
HURLINGHAM PARK
WANDSRWORTH PARK
BATTERSEA PARK
WANDSWORTH
THAMES
Hotel
Restaurant

Central London Plans
(Plan I)

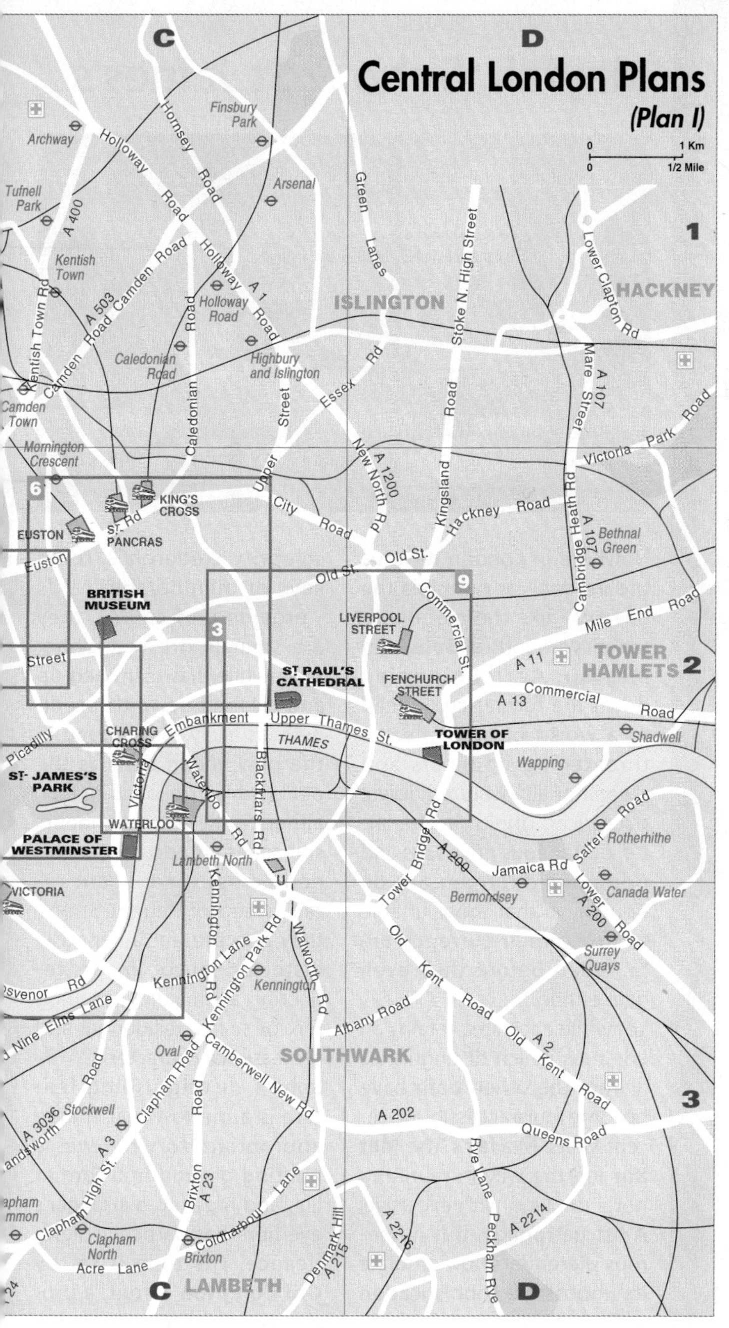

CENTRAL LONDON - **PLAN II**

Mayfair, Soho & St James's

C. Eymenier/MICHELIN

Nowhere in London rewards the insider - or punishes the unwary - like the metropolitan playgrounds of **Soho** and **Mayfair**. A wrong turning down the former could lead to a world of neon sleaze, threatening bouncers and - worst of all - watered down, overpriced drinks. In the latter, outrageous price tags and pompous doormen are de rigueur, so that those unable to prove their currency are humbled before they even gain entrée.

Yet while each area retains an edginess which distinguishes it from the other, both have become more accessible in recent years. Mayfair's **The Met Bar** led the way in reuniting hotel drinking with exclusive, A-list patronage, but numerous pretenders now emulate its impossible sophistication while admitting those without celebrity credentials, room keys or membership cards - provided, of course, they are smartly dressed. Soho, meanwhile, has glammed up and cleaned up, with 'seediness' as likely to be found in the new vegan delis as the old tawdry strip joints. In fact, although the two neighbours still seem an odd couple joined across the elegant retail sweep of Regent Street, they also present a curiously distorted mirror image, reflecting a similarly intriguing mix of social, residential and professional character.

Soho's distinguishing feature is a metrosexual charge appropriate to what was a hunting ground in a former life, and meeting a stranger's eye here has particular significance. The tone is set by **Old Compton Street**, a promenade flush with the pink pound and along which gay bars mingle with welcoming brasseries and coffee shops, perfect for al fresco people gazing. In contrast to Mayfair - where if one doesn't own a Rolls, one gets a taxi - Soho's narrow streets are designed for the flâneur and in summer crowds spill from drinking dens onto the roads, the occasional rickshaw doing well to squeeze by. Authentic dim sum eateries in **Chinatown** repay you knowing them well, while hip lounge bars quickly fill with the advertising execs and dotcom stalwarts working nearby; often, they appear not to close. A trick is to set your sights low - basement-level Soho is a revelation from which to emerge many hours later, blinking into the daylight, having sung through till dawn in a private karaoke venue few others know exists.

By comparison, the attraction of Mayfair is more apparent on the surface - although it can be equally tricky to find the way in. Here, the designer emporiums of **Bond Street** attract boutique investment bankers, welcomed by security men who also keep the riff-raff out. Even for those asked to 'window shop', however, Mayfair offers a fascinatingly grand milieu of plush hotels, eccentric galleries and lovely public spaces. While you'd be lucky to spot a single blade of grass under the sprawling masses in **Soho Square** on a sunny day, Mayfair's **Grosvenor Square** is perfect for champagne picnics and **Mount Street Gardens** provide a lovely shaded hideaway in which the occasional tuxedoed visitor can be seen enjoying a sneaky aperitif. Like Soho, Mayfair also has its secrets and the enchanting Georgian enclave of **Shepherd Market** comes as a surprise against the backdrop of **Park Lane** hotels, its human scale and casual air an unexpected find at the end of the Monopoly board.

But if Mayfair keeps a strong hold on London's monied heart, cross **Piccadilly** and you may find **St James's** has a claim to its class. This, after all, is clubland - and not of Soho's G-A-Y variety but of the **Pall Mall** gentleman's kind. With blackballing and family pedigrees still in vogue, it would be wrong to suggest this stately area is loosening up like its neighbours, and the haughty mix of auction houses, elite institutions and royal abodes seems designed to resist change. Yet many of the clubs now admit women, implying a degree of onward progress - and as anyone familiar with the Second Earl of Rochester's ramble round **St James's Park** will suspect, all sorts of intrigue perhaps lies behind the charming fustiness.

Mayfair, Soho and St James's
(Plan II)

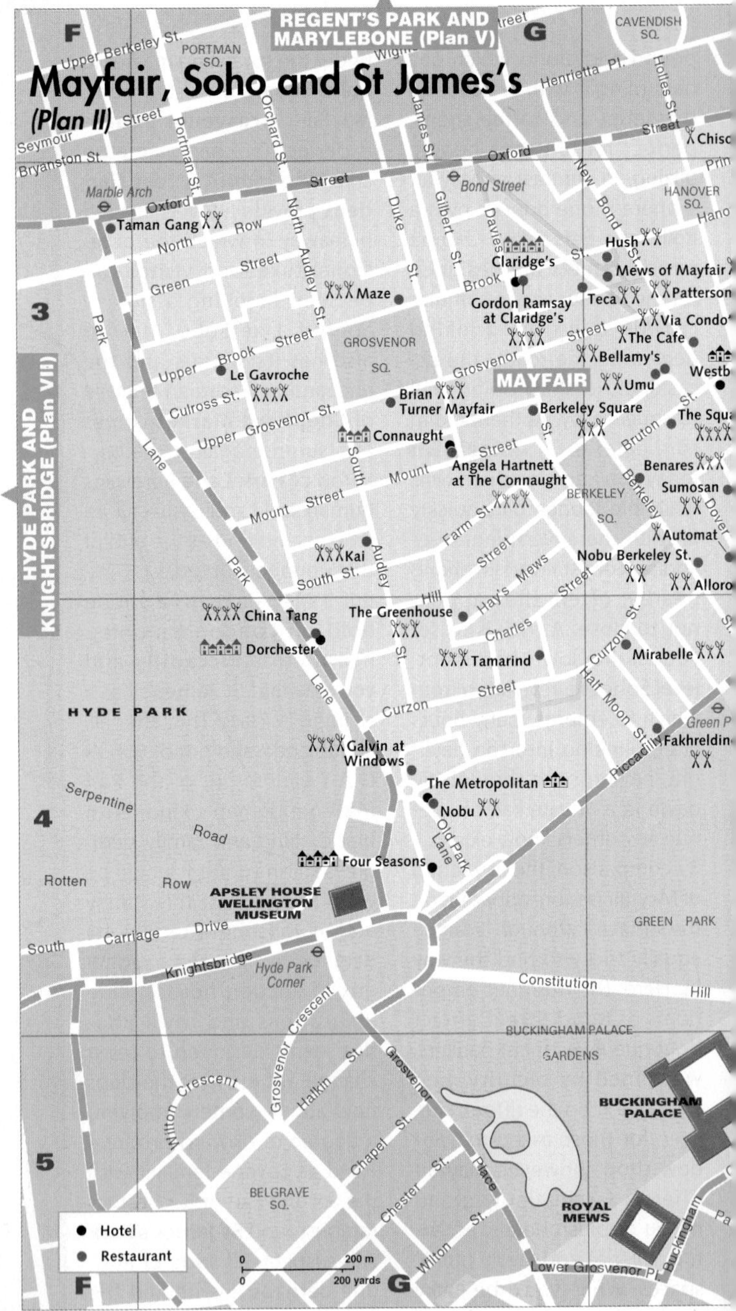

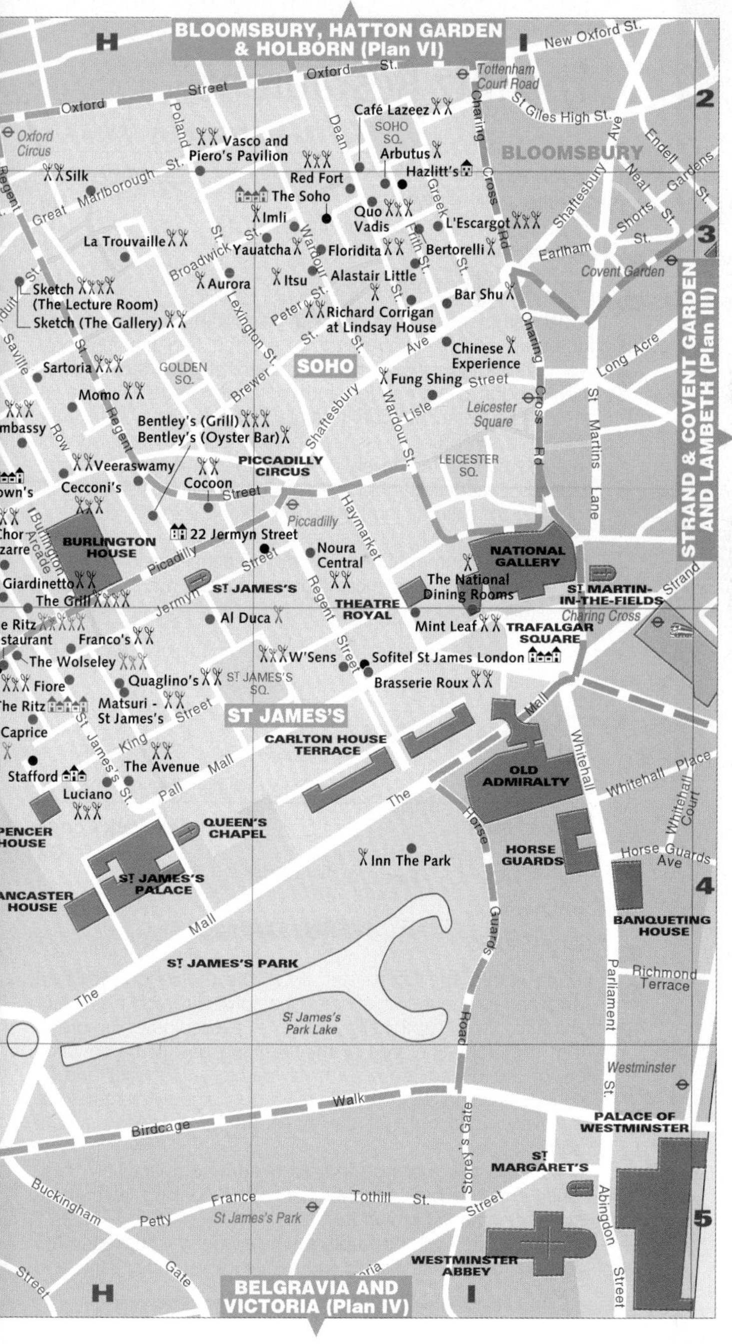
BLOOMSBURY, HATTON GARDEN & HOLBORN (Plan VI)
BELGRAVIA AND VICTORIA (Plan IV)
STRAND & COVENT GARDEN AND LAMBETH (Plan III)
SOHO
ST JAMES'S
BLOOMSBURY
Café Lazeez
Vasco and Piero's Pavilion
Silk
Red Fort
Arbutus
Hazlitt's
The Soho
Imli
Quo Vadis
L'Escargot
La Trouvaille
Yauatcha
Floridita
Bertorelli
Aurora
Itsu
Alastair Little
Bar Shu
Sketch (The Lecture Room)
Sketch (The Gallery)
Richard Corrigan at Lindsay House
Chinese Experience
Sartoria
Fung Shing
Momo
Bentley's (Grill)
Bentley's (Oyster Bar)
Veeraswamy
Cecconi's
Cocoon
22 Jermyn Street
Noura Central
Giardinetto
The Grill
Al Duca
The National Dining Rooms
Mint Leaf
Franco's
The Wolseley
W'Sens
Sofitel St James London
Fiore
Quaglino's
Brasserie Roux
Matsuri - St James's
Caprice
The Avenue
Stafford
Luciano
Inn The Park
PICCADILLY CIRCUS
BURLINGTON HOUSE
NATIONAL GALLERY
ST MARTIN-IN-THE-FIELDS
THEATRE ROYAL
TRAFALGAR SQUARE
CARLTON HOUSE TERRACE
OLD ADMIRALTY
QUEEN'S CHAPEL
HORSE GUARDS
ST JAMES'S PALACE
BANQUETING HOUSE
ST JAMES'S PARK
St James's Park Lake
PALACE OF WESTMINSTER
ST MARGARET'S
WESTMINSTER ABBEY
Oxford Circus
Tottenham Court Road
Covent Garden
Leicester Square
Piccadilly
Charing Cross
Westminster
St James's Park

The Ritz Restaurant

Traditional XXXXX

at The Ritz H., ⊖ Green Park
150 Piccadilly ✉ W1V 9DG **H4**
✆ (020) 74938181 – **Fax** (020) 74932687
Web www.theritzlondon.com

A/C · VISA · MC · AE · D · ♀

Menu £37/80 – Carte £48/80

Social commentators are constantly sounding the death knell for pomp and pageantry and we're often told that the only worthwhile dining experience is a shared refectory table. Thankfully, London is big enough and confident enough to offer us all types of restaurant. The Restaurant at The Ritz is a strikingly lavish and sumptuously elegant room, decorated in the style of Louis XVI, and offers levels of unmatched luxury. Gilt bronze garlands, chandeliers, gold leaf and immaculately set tables all combine to make dining here a memorable experience.
The menu is equally classical, served by an army of waiters all loyal to the common cause. The dinner dances held on Friday and Saturday evenings make fitting use of such a magnificent and dazzling setting.

China Tang

Chinese XXXX

A/C · VISA · MC · AE · D

at Dorchester H., ⊖ Hyde Park Corner
Park Lane ✉ W1A 2HJ **G4**
✆ (020) 76299988 – **Fax** (020) 76299595

Closed 25 December

Carte £40/75

Found within The Dorchester Hotel, the titular Tang is David Tang, entrepreneur and jet-setter extraordinaire, and his restaurant suits him exceptionally well. It's all exceedingly glamorous, from the cruise-line style of the stunning bar to the art deco feel of the dining room, with its marble and murals and its etched glass and cushions. You really don't know where to look, especially when most of the diners are as decorative as the room.
By contrast, the cooking tends to tread a comparatively traditional, if pricey, path through Cantonese cooking, with some modern elements thrown in.
How could you not love a place where poetry is recited in the loo and the private dining rooms are called Ping, Pang and Pong?

Le Gavroche

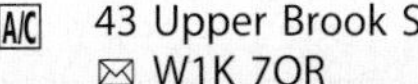

French

A/C
VISA
MC
AE
D

43 Upper Brook St
W1K 7QR
(020) 74080881 – **Fax** (020) 74914387
e-mail bookings@le-gavroche.com **Web** www.le-gavroche.co.uk

Marble Arch
G3

Closed Christmas-New Year, Sunday, Saturday lunch and Bank Holidays – booking essential

Menu £48 (lunch) – Carte £59/130

Le Gavroche

British gastronomy owes a huge debt to the Roux brothers because without Le Gavroche there would certainly be fewer good restaurants in London today and even fewer good chefs. However, Le Gavroche should not just be celebrated as a de facto training school for chefs, for this was London's first great restaurant, was responsible for introducing Londoners to the best of French cuisine and still shines today.

It opened in 1967 in Chelsea before moving to its current premises in the early 1980's where it continues to flourish under the seasoned guidance of Silvano Giraldin. The lower ground floor room retains a clubby and masculine feel but care is taken to ensure that the atmosphere is never daunting or intimidating. Now with Michel Junior at the helm, the restaurant continues to hold its own against the new wave of modern restaurants. The cooking is still classically French but with every generation comes new influences and one can now detect a lighter aspect to some of the dishes. However, those who still prefer their cooking to be luxuriant in its richness will not be disappointed.

A LA CARTE

FIRST COURSE

- Hot foie gras and crispy duck pancake flavoured with cinnamon.
- Asparagus tips with smoked salmon and brioche, egg and caviar sauce.

MAIN COURSE

- Roast saddle of rabbit with crispy potatoes and parmesan.
- Grilled turbot with cauliflower gratin, lemon and herb sauce.

DESSERT

- Pear and puff pastry layers with salted butter caramel sauce and pistachios.
- Cheesecake with strawberries and praline ribbon.

Angela Hartnett at The Connaught ✿

Modern European XXXX

16 Carlos Pl
W1K 2AL
(020) 75921222 – **Fax** (020) 75921223
Web www.angelahartnett.com
Booking essential

Menu £30/70

Bond Street
G3

Gordon Ramsay Holdings

The Connaught has always been one of London's more traditional hotels, harking back to a time when things were as they seemed and "social mobility" meant riding in the Daimler with friends. However, in 2002, a mere 105 years after opening, the sound of soup spluttering could be heard across London as Angela Hartnett became the first woman to be made Head Chef.

Cleverly, the style and feel of the room were updated but still managed to remain utterly respectful of the history of the hotel. The mahogany panelling lends grandeur to the room but it's lightened by the artwork and the engaging service. The softer green hue of the Grill Room is also available, where the same menu is served.

The base of the highly skilled and accomplished cooking is classical with a modern overlay of Mediterranean influence and more than a passing nod to Italy. To accompany the accomplished cooking is a well chosen Italianate wine list.

The restaurant will be closing, along with the hotel, for an extended period in 2007 when a major refurbishment will be undertaken.

A LA CARTE

FIRST COURSE	MAIN COURSE	DESSERT
• Farfalle with roasted ceps and langoustine, new season truffle shavings.	• Veal fillet, parmesan cream, new season peas, leeks and veal jus.	• Coconut parfait, exotic fruit salsa and pineapple chausson.
• Scottish scallops with pea emulsion, mint and potato cress.	• Roast John Dory with semolina gnocchi and cauliflower.	• Roast yellow peaches with puff pastry and salted almond ice cream.

Gordon Ramsay at Claridge's ✿

Modern European 

Brook St
W1K 4HR
(020) 74990099 – **Fax** (020) 74993099
Web www.gordonramsay.com
Booking essential

Bond Street
G3

Menu £30/75

A/C · VISA · MC · AE

Gordon Ramsay Holdings

They've pulled off quite a design feat here. By mixing strikingly elegant surroundings with a hint of modernity, while also respecting the traditions of the world famous Claridge's Hotel in which it's located, they've created a dining room that's as grand as it is fashionable. Gordon Ramsay opened this "branch" of his empire in 2001 and, judging by the challenging process of getting a table, it's proving to be quite a hit. It's on the ground floor with its own street entrance but it's far more glamorous to walk through from the hotel. The dramatic three-tiered light shades, the rich colours and the original 1930's features also make it the group's most conspicuously lavish environment.
As expected, the kitchen produces delicate and detailed cooking supported by a classical base. Those who cannot decide from the choice available on the *à la carte* should head for the schooled elegance of the dishes found on the *Menu Prestige*. Those more interested in cooking-watching than people-watching can reserve the table in the kitchen.

A LA CARTE

FIRST COURSE	MAIN COURSE	DESSERT
• Roast foie gras with cherries, pickled ginger, cauliflower and almond cream.	• Braised turbot with caviar, lettuce, root vegetables and coriander sauce.	• Citrus and passion fruit jelly with banana ice cream and warm orange Madeleine.
• Braised pork belly with langoustines and white bean purée.	• Best end of lamb with confit of shoulder, asparagus and tarragon.	• Pear and amaretti cheeesecake, almond and Fleur de Sel sorbet.

The Square ✿✿

French XXXX

6-10 Bruton St ⊖ Green Park
W1J 6PU **H3**
(020) 74957100 – **Fax** (020) 74957150
e-mail info@squarerestaurant.com
Web www.squarerestaurant.com

Closed 25-26 December, 1 January and lunch Saturday, Sunday and Bank Holidays

Menu £30/65

The Square

The Square may aptly describe the shape of the room but it is so called because the restaurant began life just off St James's Square. It then moved to its current, more glamorous, address which was fortunate to also have a square nearby, in this case Berkeley Square.
Ask a gaggle of chefs to name their favourite restaurant and The Square will probably be near the top. There's no doubt that this relatively large restaurant is well run and elegantly dressed but what appeals to so many is that here is a place where diners gaze admiringly at their food, not around at their fellow diners.
Philip Howard's cooking is finely judged and sophisticated with assured, confident flavours. It also manages to be technically skilled without ever being overwrought. The wine list is particularly meritorious for its range and depth.
That is not to say this is an over-formal gastronomic temple. In fact, as the room is always full and the service unobtrusive, the atmosphere is never less than animated and comes with a pervading air of approval. It's probably all those chefs enjoying their night out.

A LA CARTE

FIRST COURSE
- Lasagna of crab with shellfish and basil cappuccino.
- Warm salad of skate and smoked eel with chard, red wine and anchovy dressing.

MAIN COURSE
- Herb-crusted saddle of lamb with shallot purée and rosemary.
- Steamed turbot with langoustine claws, poached oysters, lettuce and caviar.

DESSERT
- Bitter, milk and white chocolate served hot, warm and cold.
- Poached pineapple with tropical jellies and lime ice cream.

Sketch (The Lecture Room & Library) ✿

French XXXX

A/C VISA MC AE

First Floor, 9 Conduit St ⊖ Oxford Street
✉ W1S 2XG **H3**
✆ (0870) 7774488 – **Fax** (0870) 7774400
Web www.sketch.uk.com

Closed 23-30 December, 1 January, Sunday, Monday, Saturday lunch and Bank Holidays

Menu £35/65 – Carte £57/102

Sketch

"Anyone who lives within their means suffers from a lack of imagination" – Oscar Wilde would have loved Sketch. It's theatrical, decoratively over the top, exclusive but, above all, fun.

It opened in 2002, as a partnership between Mourad Mazouz (known to his friends as Momo) and celebrated chef Pierre Gagnaire, and it's housed within an 18th century townhouse. The Lecture Room and Library is the "fine dining" part of the operation, but don't let those words conjure up images of a sombre shrine to gastronomy. Sure, the room is grandiose but the colours and fabrics are rich and flamboyant and there's a joyful showiness to the place.

The menus come in a manner of guises, with individual dishes vertiginously priced. The Tasting menu represents not only the best value but also the most rounded experience and a chance to fully appreciate the skill of the kitchen. The cooking is highly elaborate, original and detailed, with the quality of produce beyond reproach, as you would expect at these prices.

A LA CARTE

FIRST COURSE

- Custard of foie gras, crab and eel, broccoli and cauliflower.
- Braised aubergine and rabbit rillette, beetroot juice with passion fruit sorbet.

MAIN COURSE

- Grilled sea bass with dried fruit marmalade and apple.
- Rump of milk-fed veal with asparagus velouté, almond and sorrel cream.

DESSERT

- Coffee and dried plum macaroon.
- Roasted pineapple with almond biscuit.

The Grill

British XXXX

A/C VISA MC AE D

at Brown's H.,
Albemarle St ✉ W1S 4BP
✆ (020) 75184004 – **Fax** (020) 75184064
Web www.brownshotel.com

⊖ Green Park
H3_4

Menu £25 (lunch) – Carte £38/51

In 1880 Brown's was the first hotel in London to offer its guests their own dining room. In December 2005 the hotel and restaurant re-opened after an extensive refurbishment but they have managed to retain that aura of a bygone age which has always been its hallmark. It also kept the wood panelling which contributes to the clubby feel and the atmosphere that makes it one of the preferred dining options of the Establishment. They come for the reassuringly British menu with roasts, grills and a carving trolley, all precisely served by a regiment of well-drilled staff.
While there is no strict dress code any longer, if you are not going to wear your best suit and club tie then expect the odd sideways glance of disapproval.

Galvin at Windows

French XXXX

A/C VISA MC AE D

at London Hilton H.,
22 Park Lane ✉ W1K 1BE
✆ (020) 72084021
Web www.hilton.co.uk

⊖ Hyde Park Corner
G4

Closed Saturday lunch and Sunday dinner

Menu £28/65 – Carte £33/56

When you're 28 floors up the views alone will make a visit worthwhile. The restaurant atop the Hilton Hotel was re-launched in 2006 following an extensive makeover. Along with the adjacent cocktail bar, it's now a neat and elegant space with a centrally raised section, although the designer was clearly very tall because all his chairs are far too low. There are three sides of wonderful views but those looking south are probably the best.
The kitchen, under the control of Chris Galvin, is finding its feet with the menus, which offer up a selection of quite detailed and ambitious dishes, all using top-notch produce.
An international clientele have really taken to the place and shows that expensive restaurants can be spirited environments.

The Greenhouse ✿

French XXX

27a Hay's Mews
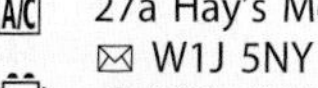
W1J 5NY

(020) 74993331 – **Fax** (020) 74995368
Web www.greenhouserestaurant.co.uk
Closed 25-26 and 31 December, 1 January, Saturday lunch and Sunday

Menu £32/60

⊖ Hyde Park Corner
G4

A/C VISA AE

The Greenhouse

The Greenhouse opened in the 1970's and has had a number of makeovers, as well as a number of talented chefs, over the years. It now belongs to the Marlon Abela collection and constant investment has ensured that it continues to be one of the smarter places around. The charming mews location is certainly hard to beat and the walkway through the little garden ensures that everyone arrives in a relaxed frame of mind.
Inside, it's all quite slick and contemporary, with subtle design references to the outside greenery. The room's shape makes it feel far more intimate that the number of tables would suggest. The kitchen has had a solid classical education in the culinary arts but is not afraid to add the odd twist which may be an Asian flavour or a challenging ingredient combination. Seasonality is taken seriously, the tasting menus often prove to be the popular option and the wine list is an impressively weighty tome with over 2000 bins. A large team provide detailed and attentive service and, for private parties, the glass enclosed private dining room is particularly attractive.

A LA CARTE

FIRST COURSE
- Scottish langoustines with apple jelly, celeriac purée and black sugar.
- Salad of quail with baby carrots, coriander and cumin dressing.

MAIN COURSE
- Anjou pigeon, pomegranate and baby daikon.
- Saddle of lamb with wild garlic and goat's curd.

DESSERT
- Warm chocolate tart with chestnut ice cream and orange marmalade.
- Banana millefeuille with rum and raisin ice cream.

Mirabelle

Modern European

56 Curzon St
W1J 8PA
(020) 74994636 – **Fax** (020) 74995449
e-mail sales@whitestarline.org.uk **Web** www.whitestarline.org.uk

Green Park
H4

Closed 26 December

Menu £21 (lunch) – Carte £33/55

Mirabelle

The Mirabelle is one of London's most recognisable restaurant names and this pre-war gem still shines brightly today. The huge mirror ball certainly helps.
After a nod from the doorman you descend the marble staircase, are greeted by a hostess and then shown through to the restaurant. Just make sure you stop at the bar because it's one of the more agreeable places in which to have a pre or post dinner drink. The dining room is elegant and discreet, with fewer tables than in previous years increasing the comfort and privacy. The terrace lets in plenty of light and is popular on summer days. Deep leather seating, huge displays of flowers and immaculate table settings complete the picture of graceful dining.
The hand, or certainly the influence, of Marco Pierre White is clearly evident in the menu. Classics of Anglo-French persuasion come thick and fast, from *duck à l'orange* to *omelette Arnold Bennett*. Dishes arrive smartly presented and well timed from the kitchen. The wine list merits much of your time and consideration.

A LA CARTE

FIRST COURSE

- Tarte Tatin of endive with scallops, beurre à l'orange.
- Terrine of foie gras with green peppercorns and Sauternes jelly.

MAIN COURSE

- Daube of Aberdeen Angus with celeriac and Provençale garnish.
- Caramelised wing of skate with winkles, beurre noisette, jus à la Parisienne.

DESSERT

- Lemon tart.
- Champagne poached strawberries with vanilla cream.

Maze

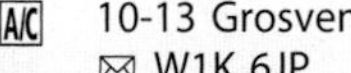

Innovative XXX

10-13 Grosvenor Sq — Bond Street
W1K 6JP — **G3**
(020) 71070000 – **Fax** (020) 71070001
e-mail maze@gordonramsay.com **Web** www.gordonramsay.com

Carte £33/50

A/C · VISA · MC · AE · ⊕ · Y

Gordon Ramsay Holdings

There won't be many times in your life when you can look the waiter in the eye and say you'll have the whole menu. Don't try this at Maze unless there are at least three of you at the table but, if you do, you won't be disappointed.

The raised entrance on Grosvenor Square is easy to miss so expect to see some diners arriving with the flustered look of the lost and tardy. The David Rockwell designed room is a very bright and stylish affair, with an attractive bar and a counter with extra settings for those just dropping by. The atmosphere always appears to be lively.

Service plays a large part in the success, with charming and helpful staff willing to offer sensible advice and explanation of the dishes. Those dishes are perfectly formed and artfully crafted little tasting plates. The detail is exquisite, the ingredients exemplary and the combinations original and balanced. Five or so dishes per person should suffice from the menu of about twenty choices. Alternatively, let the chef decide and go for the set menu.

A LA CARTE

FIRST COURSE	MAIN COURSE	DESSERT
• Bacon and onion cream, chilled lettuce velouté and tomato.	• Beef "tongue 'n cheek" with capers, raisins and ginger carrots.	• Peanut butter and cherry jam sandwich with salted nuts and cherry sorbet.
• Honey and soy roasted quail with foie gras, peach and saffron chutney.	• Roasted sea bass with candied aubergine, asparagus, tomato and caviar.	• Pineapple carpaccio with ginger lime syrup and coconut sorbet.

The Wolseley

Modern European XXX

A/C
VISA
MC
AE
⓪
🍷

160 Piccadilly ⊖ Green Park
✉ W1J 9EB **H4**
✆ (020) 74996996 – **Fax** (020) 74996888
Web www.thewolseley.com

Closed dinner 24-25 December, 1 January and August Bank Holiday – booking essential

Carte £28/48

When Chris Corbin and Jeremy King sold The Ivy, restaurant regulars were left lamenting the loss of two of the city's foremost restaurateurs. Fortunately, their lament did not last because, in 2003, the two opened The Wolseley. The name honours the ornate surroundings commissioned by Wolseley cars in the 1920's for what must have been a hugely impressive showroom. Fittingly, the restaurant runs on wheels and such has been the success that it feels as though it's been here for years. In the manner of a grand European brasserie, it is open all day for breakfast, pastries, lunch, tea and dinner and the choice is considerable, from *bouillabaisse* to bagel and caviar to *croque monsieur*. The clientele boasts a high percentage of celebrity members.

Embassy

Modern European 

A/C
VISA
MC
AE
🍷

29 Old Burlington St ⊖ Green Park
✉ W1S 3AN **H3**
✆ (020) 78510956 – **Fax** (020) 77343224
Web www.embassylondon.com

Closed Sunday, Monday and Bank Holidays

Menu £39.50 – Carte £27/58

A fashionable restaurant in the middle of Old Burlington Street may sound a little unlikely but Embassy sits there rather confidently. The buzzy nightclub downstairs is on the circuit for an assortment of celebrities on lists A to C but the restaurant, found on the ground floor, is no mere addendum to the club and has become a destination in its own right.

A large bar, with plenty of brown leather seating, leads up to the dining area which comes decorated in stylish creams with well-spaced tables. Floor to ceiling windows and a pavement terrace give it extra appeal in the summer. The menu is that of a classically trained kitchen and features a fair share of extravagant ingredients, used with flair and understanding.

Benares ✿

Indian XXX

12a Berkeley Square House, ⊖ Green Park
✉ W1J 6BS **H3**
✆ (020) 76298886 – **Fax** (020) 74992430
Web www.benaresrestaurant.com

Closed 25-26 December, 1 January, lunch Saturday and Bank Holidays

Menu £20 (lunch) – Carte £33/67

Benares

Named after the Holy northern city on the Ganges, Benares represents another chapter in the coming of age of Indian restaurants in the UK. It is not just the cooking but the chic surroundings on Berkeley Square that set it apart. From being led up the stairs from the entrance to a farewell from the doorman, all the staff are attentive, intuitive to your needs and, most importantly, clearly proud of the restaurant in which they work.

The sleek bar with its water pools filled with flowers, handmade furniture and moody lighting sets the tone for the restaurant, with its leather and suede and immaculately laid tables. Tables for two are set around the sides of the room and the atmosphere is relaxed and convivial.

A veritable army of staff deliver the dishes from chef Atul Kochhar's kitchen, proving an equal match for the style and sophistication of the surroundings. The first rate home-made chutneys and fresh breads set the tone. Flavours from across India are featured in specialities demonstrating an innovative touch by being light, delicately spiced and sweetly scented.

A LA CARTE

FIRST COURSE

- Soft shell crab in spiced batter with squid and potato salad, passion fruit dressing.
- Ground lamb kebabs with mint and tamarind chutney, mango salad.

MAIN COURSE

- Sea bass in coconut milk and tamarind sauce with coconut kedgeree.
- Braised chicken with ground chicken and liver on a red and black pepper sauce.

DESSERT

- Vanilla infused yoghurt cheesecake with peppermint and lime sorbet.
- Warm carrot pudding with reduced milk and pistachio.

L'Escargot ✿

French XXX

48 Greek St
✉ W1D 4EF
✆ (020) 74372679 – **Fax** (020) 74370790
Web www.lescargotrestaurant.co.uk

Tottenham Court Road
I3

Closed Sunday and Saturday lunch. Picasso Room also closed August and Monday

Menu £18 (lunch) – Carte £27/31

A/C · VISA · MC · AE

L'Escargot

In the 1920's George Gaudin opened L'Escargot and was the first to serve snails. That's him in the bust above the window, riding a snail with the words "slow and sure" above his head. Despite changing hands a few times over the years, it remains a celebrated landmark and is now equally famous for its collection of lithographs, ceramics and bronzes.
It's really two restaurants under one roof. The ground floor is more brasserie in style, with a long bar dividing it again in two. The warm yellow walls and mirrors compensate for a lack of natural light and the atmosphere is always energetic, making the piped music a fairly redundant feature.
Those who prefer to eat in more sedate surroundings need merely to head upstairs. The Picasso Room is half the size of downstairs and ideal for those wanting a little more privacy.
The cooking upstairs is no better than downstairs - it is merely different. Downstairs, you'll find more classic, robust French-inspired fare while up the stairs the cooking is just a little more detailed, elaborate (and expensive).

A LA CARTE

FIRST COURSE

- Open ravioli of snails and morels, creamed parsley and mushroom emulsion.
- Gravadlax of sea trout, tarragon and orange, fennel and citrus salad.

MAIN COURSE

- Braised shoulder of lamb with curly kale, garlic and thyme jus.
- Baked cod with cabbage, cockles and mussels and watercress sauce.

DESSERT

- Warm chocolate fondant with milk ice cream.
- Rhubarb cheesecake with candied orange and rhubarb ripple ice cream.

Tamarind ✿

Indian XXX

20 Queen St
W1J 5PR
(020) 76293561 – **Fax** (020) 74995034
Web www.tamarindrestaurant.com

⊖ Green Park
G4

Closed 25-26 December, 1 January and lunch Saturday and Bank Holidays

Menu £19 (lunch) – Carte £35/60

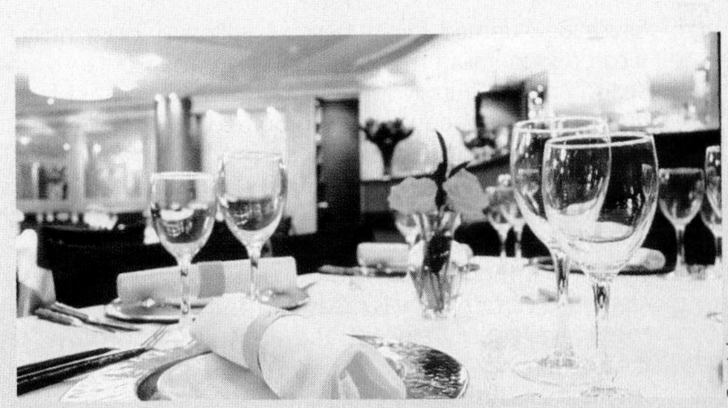

Tamarind

Much of the success of Tamarind can be put down to the fact that the menu appeals to traditionalists as well as offering plenty of interesting choices to those of more modern tastes. The starting point is the Moghul cooking of the North West and the tandoor oven. However, the cooking here continues to evolve and there are more recent additions to the menu which reflect a lighter style of eating. Common to all the dishes is careful preparation, enticing presentation, exciting flavours and contrasting textures. The subterranean space is far from tenebrous and has an elegance and sophistication to it. It is decidedly smart and comfortable but never wanders into the realms of the stuffy - the only starchiness is in the white cloths over the tables. The open window into the kitchen adds a little theatre.

The service is thoughtful and attentive enough to make the room feel smaller than it is and the suited managers doing the rounds clearly run a tight ship.

As with all the best restaurants, it is a decidedly busy operation but one where the standards remain consistently high.

A LA CARTE

FIRST COURSE

• Grilled scallops with green, pink and black peppercorns, roasted peppers and fenugreek.

• Potato cakes with lentils, ginger, cumin and spinach.

MAIN COURSE

• Leg of Spring lamb with cinnamon, rose petals and ground spices finished in the tandoor.

• Mixed seafood in coconut milk with curry leaves and ginger.

DESSERT

• White chocolate and cardamom mousse with a ginger semifreddo.

• Basmati rice pudding with cashew nuts and orange marmalade.

Sartoria

Italian XXX

20 Savile Row
W1S 3PR
(020) 75347000 – **Fax** (020) 75347070
Web www.conran.com

Green Park
H3

Closed 25-27 December, 1 January, Sunday, Saturday lunch and Bank Holidays

Menu £24.50 – Carte £29/39

Savile Row, famed for its bespoke tailoring, plays host to this well-dressed Italian restaurant, cut from the Conran cloth. It's a stylish and flatteringly lit room with a sophisticated feel which complements its equally well-groomed regulars.
The kitchen produces reliably consistent and easy-to-eat Italian food with the emphasis on freshness and it's clearly well suited to both the surroundings and the customers, whether they're in for a figure-conscious bite or something a little fuller. The set price lunch menu comes at a snip in comparison to the rather steep *à la carte*; service is measured and slick. The private dining rooms are equally elegant and are tailored to those after increased privacy.
Any more puns, on a postcard please.

Quo Vadis

Italian XXX

26-29 Dean St
W1D 3LL
(020) 74379585 – **Fax** (020) 77347593
e-mail sales@whitestarline@org.uk **Web** www.whitestarline.org.uk

Tottenham Court Road
I3

Closed 24-25 December, 1 January, Sunday and Saturday lunch

Menu £18 (lunch) – Carte £21/36

Where, indeed...
Quo Vadis, with its red neon sign, black exterior and stained glass windows, has long been a landmark in Soho. Karl Marx was reputed to have lived upstairs and the restaurant was founded by Peppino Leoni in the '30's. It's now a member of Marco Pierre White's collection of restaurants and the cooking is once again Italian. The *à la carte* menu is nicely balanced and the kitchen is unafraid of adding the occasional unexpected flavour. The lunch and early evening menus represent very good value.
The room retains a sturdy, masculine feel, but is softened by the artwork which pays homage to Damien Hirst. Service is well organised and correct. Where once there was an upstairs bar, there is now private dining.

W'Sens

French Mediterranean XXX

12 Waterloo Pl ⊖ Piccadilly Circus
✉ SW1Y 4AU **I4**
✆ (020) 74841355 – **Fax** (020) 74841366
e-mail reservations@wsens.co.uk **Web** www.wsens.co.uk

Closed lunch Saturday and Sunday

Menu £23.50 (lunch) – Carte £27/39

W'Sens, regional finalist in the Most Unpronounceable Name Category, is the London outpost of the Pourcel twins' celebrated Montpelier restaurant, Le Jardin des Sens.
The façade may be classic Grade II St James's but inside it's all very energetic in style and effervescent in design. The bar plays chill out music, serves tapas and is a destination all of its own, while the hugely eclectic surroundings of the dining room use a mix of leather, glass and wood to challenge your ideas and expectations.
The menu also steers away from the conventional and is divided into four sections: Vegetables, French, Mediterranean and World, where the French colonies and spice routes are celebrated.
There are rumours of changes in 2007.

Fiore

Italian XXX

33 St James's St ⊖ Green Park
✉ SW1A 1HD **H4**
✆ (020) 79307100 – **Fax** (020) 79304070
Web www.fiore-restaurant.co.uk

Closed Saturday lunch and Sunday

Carte £23/41

The handsome, broad expanse of St James's Street has always been famous for its purveyors of assorted accoutrements considered essential to a gentleman. However, among the hunting suppliers, cigar shops and wine merchants, you'll now find Fiore, a bright and pretty Italian restaurant. Whether or not you like the décor is largely dependent on whether you like the brightly lit artwork, which is changed regularly and available to buy. The high ceiling adds extra grandeur but the place does need to be busy to create an atmosphere.
With dishes priced individually, a traditional four courser can cause the bill to rack up quite quickly. Nevertheless, expect elaborately presented and delicate cooking, from across all parts of Italy.

Brian Turner Mayfair

British XXX

at Millennium Mayfair H., ⊖ Bond Street
44 Grosvenor Sq ✉ W1K 2HP **G3**
✆ (020) 75963444 – **Fax** (020) 75963443
Web www.brianturneronline.co.uk

Closed Christmas, Sunday, Saturday lunch and Bank Holidays

Menu £26.50 (lunch) – Carte £29/46

In the corner of the lobby of the Millennium Mayfair hotel, with its striking 18th century façade overlooking Grosvenor Square, you'll find the entrance to this spacious 80 seater restaurant, named in honour of the proud Yorkshireman who is known to many through his television appearances.
The menu showcases his love and respect for British food, especially in the decidedly homespun puddings, but he also offers his own interpretation of more contemporary cooking. The room has a fresh and luminous feel and tries to break up its capaciousness through raised sections which offer slightly more privacy. Service is obliging and professional and the place has enough of its own personality to stand out from its hotel surroundings.

Cecconi's

Italian XXX

5a Burlington Gdns ⊖ Green Park
✉ W1S 3EP **H3**
✆ (020) 74341500 – **Fax** (020) 72342020
e-mail giacomo@cecconis.co.uk **Web** www.cecconis.com

Closed 25 December

Carte £28/48

Those who longingly look back at those halcyon days of excess that were the 1980's will no doubt have fond memories of Cecconi's for it certainly captured the zeitgeist of the era. After a number of re-launches over the years, the restaurant appears to have finally found the right combination and in July 2005 it reopened under the ownership of Nick Jones, known for his Soho House clubs.
There remains an air of exclusivity about the place but now it comes with a little more playfulness and a little less brashness. The kitchen starts by offering breakfast then a cleverly balanced all-day menu to appeal to everyone, from those just wanting a *cichetti* or tapas-style lunch to those after a plate of pasta or something substantial.

Berkeley Square

Modern European XXX

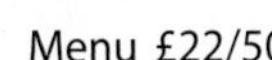

7 Davies St — Bond Street
W1K 3DD — **G3**
(020) 76296993 – **Fax** (020) 74919719
Web www.theberkeleysquare.com

Closed last 2 weeks August, Christmas, Saturday, Sunday and Bank Holidays

VISA · MC · AE · Diners

Menu £22/50

It may not actually be on Berkeley Square but, then again, Davies Street doesn't have the same ring to it. However, if you try hard enough, when the whole darn world seems upside down, you may just hear the nightingale sing.

The restaurant has a clean, relaxed feel and is attractively dressed in an understated way, with colours coming in muffled tones of chocolate, aubergine and lime. A retro styled bar and more tables are downstairs but the ground floor is where it all happens and the pavement terrace is quite an attraction in the summer.

A well priced menu at lunch pulls in the crowds but at dinner, when the restaurant becomes a little moodier and more romantic, the menu becomes more descriptive and the cooking more exploratory.

Kai

Chinese XXX

A/C

65 South Audley St — Hyde Park Corner
W1K 2QU — **G3**
(020) 74938988 – **Fax** (020) 74931456
e-mail kai@kaimayfair.com **Web** www.kaimayfair.com

Closed 25-26 December and 1 January – booking essential

VISA · MC · AE · Diners

Menu £22/75 – Carte £28/72

If you get any strange looks from fellow diners it'll be because you've got their favourite table and they've turned up without booking. Kai is a very 'Mayfair' Chinese restaurant: it's all marble and glass and very swish.

Spread over two floors, you'll find most of the action's on the ground floor, which includes the occasional harpist and a strangely hypnotic fish tank.

There's no faulting the enthusiasm of the staff who are supervised by the very charming manageress who knows all her regulars. All the dishes come exotically titled and you'll find a balanced blend of the classic and the more adventurous. You have to give five day's notice to the kitchen (and your bank manager) if you want the *Buddha jumps over the wall* soup.

Bentley's (Grill)

Traditional XXX

11-15 Swallow St. ⊖ Piccadilly Circus
W1B 4DG **H3**
(020) 77344756
Web www.bentleysoysterbarandgrill.co.uk

Closed 25-26 December

Carte £34/49

That veritable institution called Bentley's, secreted in this narrow little lane off Regent Street, is now enjoying a new lease of life following a top to bottom refurbishment in 2005. You now enter into a striking bar, to the rear of which is the elegant staircase leading up to this richly decorated dining room.
William Morris wallpaper, high backed chairs at smart, flawlessly laid tables create a clean, fresh feel while still evoking the clubby atmosphere of a more sedate age. Seafood still features strongly, with oysters and Dover Sole remaining specialities, but there is also now an equally pronounced meat presence on the menu, sourced with equal care, as well as some subtle Irish hints and modern twists to the crisp cooking.

Red Fort

Indian XXX

77 Dean St ⊖ Tottenham Court Road
W1D 3SH **I3**
(020) 74372525 – **Fax** (020) 74340721
e-mail info@redfort.co.uk **Web** www.redfort.co.uk

Closed Saturday lunch, Sunday and Bank Holidays

Carte £26/46

The Red Fort is now one of the more senior members of the Soho restaurant fraternity but it has never stood still nor rested on its laurels in either its decoration or its food. The restaurant's aspirations are revealed by the high standard of cooking, which follows the 300 year old traditions of the Mughal Court and the region of Lucknow. Dishes come subtly perfumed, are delicately spiced and display a high level of refinement.
The room is well-dressed, elegant without being showy, and uses sandstone, mosaics, Indian art and a water feature in its homage to Lal Quila, the Red Fort in Delhi. Service is particularly assiduous and considerate. Akbar, the basement bar, is popular with those wanting to mingle with media types.

Luciano

Italian XXX

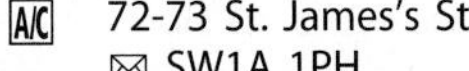

A/C · VISA · MC · AE

72-73 St. James's St. — Green Park
SW1A 1PH — **H4**
(020) 74081440
Web www.lucianorestaurant.co.uk

Closed 24-26 December, Sunday and Bank Holidays

Menu £22.50 (lunch) – Carte £34/46

Marco Pierre White goes back to his Italian roots in this restaurant, named after his son. The Man may not, sadly, be cooking any longer but he has put together a good team who deliver satisfyingly wholesome Italian classics, from a balanced and appealing menu.

The ubiquitous David Collins has designed a space which fits effortlessly into the gracious surroundings of St James's. The art deco bar is a favoured local spot for lunch, but descend a few steps and you'll find yourself in the elegant dining room, where the art comes courtesy of Marco's own collection.

Staff may bicker amongst themselves but are the embodiment of politeness at your table and the kitchen delivers the promise of the menu at the correct pace.

Le Caprice

Modern European XX

A/C · VISA · MC · AE

Arlington House, Arlington St — Green Park
SW1A 1RJ — **H4**
(020) 76292239 – **Fax** (020) 74939040
Web www.caprice-holdings.co.uk

Closed 24-26 December, 1 January and August Bank Holiday

Carte £31/49

Le Caprice has recently celebrated its twenty-fifth anniversary and this is one restaurant where you'll find you either belong or you don't. If you do fit in, then you'll join a select group who give the place such a clubby feel. That group comprises of St James's stalwarts, the artistic, the connected and those who have walked along the sunny side of Celebrity Street.

The menu has evolved over the years and is now a tad more modern in its European leanings. However, some things can never change and if they ever took off the Caesar salad or the salmon fishcake, there would be a riot, albeit a very orderly and well mannered one. The monochrome décor and live music make it a good place for a date, in this case about 1982.

Umu

Japanese

14-16 Bruton Pl
W1J 6LX
(020) 74998881 – **Fax** (020) 74995120
Web www.umurestaurant.com

Bond Street
H3

A/C VISA MC AE

Closed Christmas-New Year, Sunday, Saturday lunch and Bank Holidays

Menu £38 (lunch) – Carte £60/70

Umu

These days, the more exclusive the place, the more understated the façade. Finding Umu's entrance is only half the challenge - you then have to then figure out how to open the door. Having a touch-screen electronic door may sound clever but baffling diners before they're even inside is a curious form of welcome.
However, you'll find the mellow surroundings to be calming and comforting. The sculptured 'gathering table' sets the tone for the design, with walnut, glass, chocolate brown lacquer and handmade pottery. The large sushi bar is the striking centrepiece of the room.
Umu, meaning "born of nature", is London's first Kyoto-style *Kaiseki* restaurant. This means a series of the most delicate and intricate dishes, all finely and exquisitely balanced, through which one can attempt to understand the meaning of *unami,* the 'fifth' taste. These beautifully crafted dishes use ingredients of unparalleled quality: not only is the fish imported daily from Japan but so is the water as London's own is considered too harsh.
Umu isn't cheap but think Dr.Johnson: "it is better to live rich than to die rich".

A LA CARTE

FIRST COURSE

- Deep-fried fig with sea urchin, grated white radish and spring onion.
- Tsukuri of tuna back, avocado, olive oil and yuzu citrus.

MAIN COURSE

- Grilled salmon with soy sauce, hot soba noodles and mixed salad.
- Simmered Iberico pork with okra and Japanese mustard.

DESSERT

- Green tea ice cream.
- Chocolate fondant with black sugar sorbet.

Nobu ✿

Japanese XX

at The Metropolitan H.,
19 Old Park Lane ✉ W1Y 4LB
✆ (020) 74474747 – **Fax** (020) 74474749
Web www.noburestaurants.com

⊖ Hyde Park Corner
G4

Closed 25-26 December and 1 January – booking essential

Menu £50/70 – Carte £34/40

Nobu

Nobu burst onto the London restaurant scene in 1997, having already wowed them in New York. There are now branches around the world and the number of imitators bear testament to its hugely successful formula.

There are all sorts of hybrid cuisines out there but few as unusual in its origins. Nobu Matsuhisa, the founding chef and inspiration, found it difficult to find Japanese ingredients when working in Peru as a young man so substituted them with local produce. The result became this highly original mix of styles, with the delicacy and poise of Japanese food given a jolt by the more robust flavours of South America. It really is like nothing else.

Those on their first visit are usually surprised by the relative lack of glamour in the surroundings but this understated and minimalist design of blond wood sits perfectly in tune with the Metropolitan Hotel in which it's located. Anyway, enough glitz comes courtesy of all the celebrities and the dressed up, glamorous in-crowd who have thus far displayed a hitherto unknown capacity for loyalty.

A LA CARTE

FIRST COURSE
- Yellowtail tartar with caviar.
- Tomato rock shrimp ceviche.

MAIN COURSE
- Anti-cucho Peruvian style spicy chicken skewer.
- Black cod with miso.

DESSERT
- Apple jelly with pistachio ice cream and walnut crunch.
- Chocolate bento box, green tea ice cream.

Giardinetto

Italian XX

39-40 Albemarle St ⊖ Green Park
W1S 4TE **H3**
(020) 74937091 – **Fax** (020) 74937096
e-mail info@giardinetto.co.uk **Web** www.giardinetto.co.uk

Closed 25 December, Saturday lunch, Sunday and Bank Holidays

Menu £25 (lunch) – Carte £32/67

The chef owner hails from Genoa and his Ligurian roots are evident in the use of herbs and vegetables in some of the dishes that feature at this stylish Mayfair Italian restaurant. Rising from the basement kitchen, plates come very attractively presented and the large brigade of staff offer attentive levels of service that are never suffocating.
The glass front hints at the style of the interior - it's all very modern with chrome, glass and leather and fits into the stylish surroundings of Albemarle Street. Divided into three rooms, the front area is the largest with two smaller areas at the back, one of which is raised and semi-private and so perfect for larger parties, with racks of the exclusively Italian wines on display.

Patterson's

Modern European XX

4 Mill St ⊖ Oxford Street
W1S 2AX **H3**
(020) 74991308 – **Fax** (020) 74912122
Web www.pattersonsrestaurant.com

Closed 25-26 December, Saturday lunch and Saturday

Menu £25/40

Mayfair is not perhaps the most obvious place in which to find that most admirable, and sadly these days all too rare, of establishment: the family restaurant.
Patterson's is the most genuine of family affairs with parents, son and daughter all involved with the day-to-day running of this modern, comfortable eatery on this narrow little street. The décor is stylishly understated and the menu offers up a selection of precisely executed and decoratively presented dishes. Lunchtime sees a well-priced set menu alongside the *à la carte*, which features a choice of five dishes per course.
Service is swift and smooth for those on a time schedule but dinner on the whole is an altogether more languorous affair.

Teca

Italian XX

A/C VISA MC AE

54 Brooks Mews
W1Y 2NY
(020) 74954774 – **Fax** (020) 74913545
Web www.tecarestaurant.com

Bond Street
G_H3

Closed Christmas-New Year, Saturday lunch, Sunday and Bank Holidays

Menu £37.50 (dinner) – Carte £30/45

Approach Teca from Upper Brook Street and you'll walk past the staff entrance to Claridge's in Brooks Mews which resembles a theatre's stage door such is the plethora of colourful uniforms going in and out. Teca is a couple of doors down and dominates the corner of this mews, with its large windows, flower displays and its welcoming light and warmth.

The glass enclosed wine cellar is made a feature of this stylish Italian restaurant, as is the bar which comes into its own when the place is full. Popular with local business types at lunch, the pace is altogether more relaxed at dinner when the menu becomes a fixed priced affair and guests are more prone to lingering longer. The home-made pastas are particularly worthy of note.

Alloro

Italian XX

A/C VISA MC AE

19-20 Dover St
W1S 4LU
(020) 74954768 – **Fax** (020) 76295348
e-mail alloro@hotmail.co.uk

Green Park
H3

Closed 24 December-2 January, Saturday lunch, Sunday and Bank Holidays

Menu £29/33 – Carte £31/38

Alloro represents that new breed of fashionable Italian restaurant where style, good food and slick service blend successfully together. This certainly is not the place for the whisperers who haunt so many places. Thanks to the adjacent bar and the principle of osmosis, the atmosphere here is always pretty exuberant.

Lunchtimes are popular with dealers of both the art and wheeler variety while dinner draws a typically metropolitan mix of types, all attracted by both the warm styling of the room and the modernity of the menu. Cooking has a slight Northern Italian attitude and the pasta dishes will no doubt be one of the highlights of your meal. The waiting staff carry out their duties with a confident swagger.

Hush

Modern European XX

8 Lancashire Court, Brook St — ⊖ Bond Street **H3**
W1S 1EY
(020) 76591500 – **Fax** (020) 76591501
e-mail info@hush.co.uk **Web** www.hush.co.uk

Closed 24-26 December, 31 December-3 January, Saturday lunch and Sunday

Menu £26.50 (lunch) – Carte £33/48

The setting is delightful - in the courtyard of a charming mews – and the outside terrace must surely be one of the places to be on a summer's day. You'll easily forget you're in the heart of the city. Hush indeed.

The brasserie on the ground floor is the mainstay of this surprisingly large operation and is quite a perky little number. The vibe is cool with a hint of flirtatiousness in the air. The menu reads like a comprehensive guide to modern European brasserie dining. Those who prefer their dining to be a little more exclusive should head upstairs to Le Club: the more formal room where the menu is altogether more your classic French. You'll also find the rather swanky cocktail lounge on this floor.

Via Condotti

Italian XX

23 Conduit St — ⊖ Oxford Circus **H3**
W1S 2XS
(020) 74937050 – **Fax** (020) 74097985
e-mail info@viacondotti.co.uk **Web** www.viacondotti.co.uk

Closed Sunday and Bank Holidays

Menu £24.50

How refreshing to find a restaurant christened with some thought. They have borrowed the name of a famous Roman street, whose cafés were celebrated meeting places and where there are now even more designer boutiques than on Conduit Street.

Opened by restaurateur Claudio Pulze in the summer of 2006, the restaurant celebrates rustic Italian food, with the chef featuring specialities from his Neapolitan homeland. Olives and a wheel of parmesan greet you as you enter and guarantee that your taste buds are in the mood. The freshness and vitality of this kind of food explains why Sophia Loren still looks the way she does.

It's appealingly decorated with Italian themed prints but the upstairs is the nicer room with large picture windows.

Richard Corrigan at Lindsay House ✿

Modern European XX

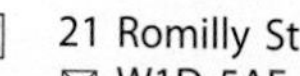

21 Romilly St
W1D 5AF
(020) 74390450 – **Fax** (020) 74377349
Web www.lindsayhouse.co.uk

⊖ Leicester Square
I3

Closed Saturday lunch and Sunday

Menu £27/52

Richard Corrigan at Lindsay House

Lindsay House is a handsome four storey 18th century building in the heart of Soho. To gain entry, you ring the doorbell and you'll then be ushered into one of the two dining rooms. Regulars may have their favourite but there's little to choose between them – they're both warm and welcoming, although the first floor room is slightly larger than the ground floor.
There is something about being cosseted in a characterful house that makes dining here such a pleasure and it provides the perfect antidote for those feeling bruised and buffeted by the bigger, more boisterous places.
The cooking is modern in its approach and presentation but flavours are far more vigorous and full bodied than one expects and the marriages of various ingredients bear testament to real talent. Evidence of Richard Corrigan's Irish roots pops up here and there, from the soda bread to the Irish cheeses and his homeland provides much of the produce. There are some interesting small producers featured on the wine list.

A LA CARTE

FIRST COURSE

- Roast scallops with pea gnocchi, wilted lettuce and crispy bacon.
- Pressed vine tomato with langoustine, courgette and gazpacho.

MAIN COURSE

- Roast rump of veal with sweetbreads, cauliflower purée and beignets.
- Loin of rabbit with langoustine, lasagna of crab and spiced carrot.

DESSERT

- Passion fruit and pistachio parfait with apricot sorbet.
- Irish apple tart with Single Malt cream.

Nobu Berkeley St ✿

Japanese XX

A/C VISA MC AE

15 Berkeley St
W1J 8DY
(020) 72909222 – **Fax** (020) 72909223
Web www.noburestaurants.com
Closed Saturday and Sunday lunch and Bank Holidays

Carte £43/79

⊖ Green Park
H3

Nobu

For those of us unburdened by celebrity, it is often easier to get a job than a reservation in many of London's glitzier restaurants. The opening of another Nobu showed not only how much London had taken to the first one but also made getting a table to experience this fashionable 'chain' a much more likely prospect. The glitterati have not been scared off by the possibility of being within gawping distance of 'ordinary people' and this branch of the ground-breaking Japanese restaurant group remains as chic and cool as the mother ship at the Metropolitan Hotel.
The large and energetic bar occupies the ground floor; upstairs, the restaurant seats about 400 and has the David Collins design stamp of neutral colours and clear lines.
The menu is the same blend of Japanese delicacies with South American influences and, if you're a regular, you'll find many of your favourites. However, alongside the *sushi*, *sashimi* and *tempura* comes more robust dishes courtesy of the wood oven section. Staff are all up to speed and more than willing to offer sound and sensible advice.

A LA CARTE

FIRST COURSE
- Seared toro with yuzu miso and jalapeño salsa.
- Lobster salad with spicy lemon dressing.

MAIN COURSE
- Crispy Gloucester Old Spot pork belly with spicy miso.
- Baby squid with ginger sake soy.

DESSERT
- Chestnut brûlée with tonka foam and dark chocolate sorbet.
- Seasonal exotic fruit selection.

Taman Gang

South-East Asian XX

A/C VISA MC AE Diners

141 Park Lane
W1K 7AA
(020) 75183160 – **Fax** (020) 75183161
e-mail info@tamangang.com **Web** www.tamangang.com

Marble Arch
F3

Closed Sunday – dinner only

Carte £23/45

As with many of today's fashionable hotspots, the casual passer-by will barely know it is there. The understated entrance to Taman Gang leads down to the moodily lit basement restaurant that's been added to the circuit of the bold and the beautiful. Split into various levels and decorated with silks, mahogany and stone, the place gets gradually busier and noisier as the night progresses. The cooking, though, is of a far better standard that one would expect from such a consciously fashionable place, although it does come at a price. The kitchen takes its cue from a number of South East Asian countries but adds its own original touches; the desserts are particularly modern.
The loos are a triumph of style over practicality.

Sketch (The Gallery)

International XX

A/C VISA MC AE Diners

9 Conduit St
W1S 2XG
(0870) 7774488 – **Fax** (0870) 7774400
e-mail info@sketch.uk.com **Web** www.sketch.uk.com

Oxford Street
H3

Closed 24-26 December, 1 January, Sunday and Bank Holidays – dinner only

Carte £33/53

Art and food have been linked since bison first appeared in Palaeolithic cave drawings. The Gallery at Sketch just connects the two in more of a 21st century sort of way.
During the day it's an art gallery, with regularly changing exhibitions featuring mostly video art thanks to the projectors and the huge white space. In the evening it transforms itself into a lively brasserie, with the videos still dancing around the walls.
France provides the starting point for the cooking but along the way it picks up influences from Italy to Japan which seems to suit the international crowd. It doesn't come cheap but that's the price for exclusivity.
For a more languorous, less frenzied affair, head upstairs to The Lecture Room & Library.

Momo

Moroccan XX

25 Heddon St ⊖ Oxford Circus
W1B 4BH **H3**
(020) 74344040 – **Fax** (020) 72870404
e-mail info@momoresto.com **Web** www.momoresto.com

Closed 25-26 and 31 December, 1 January, Sunday lunch and Bank Holidays

Menu £16 (lunch) – Carte £29/40

Momo is one of those places that are perennially busy and it's easy to see why. Tucked away on a little side street, it's kitted out like a souk, with window screens and hanging lanterns, but it also comes with a soundtrack.
The candlelight and the low slung tables add to the exotic romance of the room, although adoring couples may find intimacy curtailed by the close proximity of the neighbouring table. It's much more fun to come in a group and spend some time in the hip surroundings and the hopping bar, glancing adoringly at all the beautiful people who fill the place on a nightly basis. The food is predominantly Moroccan, with *pastilla, couscous* and *tagines* all there, although there are other more contemporary Maghrebian choices available.

Floridita

Latin American XX

100 Wardour St ⊖ Tottenham Court Road
W1F 0TN **I3**
(020) 73144000 – **Fax** (020) 73144040
Web www.floriditalondon.com

Dinner only and lunch mid November - December

Carte £32/61

Not so much a meal out, more your full Cuban Spectacular - just head downstairs for vibrant cocktails, fiery food and a little salsa. The name and concept pay homage to Havana's legendary bar of the same name, the birthplace of the daiquiri and favoured haunt of Ernest Hemingway.
An impressive cocktail list, live music and dancing prove to be a contagious combination and, thanks to the swivel chairs, even those eating will find the rhythm hard to resist.
The food lends a predictably modern edge to some rustic dishes but keeps flavours authentic and crosses the wider Latin America countries in search of inspiration. But, this is all about the buzz and the great atmosphere and, as such, means coming here for partying and general merrymaking.

Brasserie Roux

French XX

8 Pall Mall
SW1Y 5NG
(020) 79682900 – **Fax** (020) 77472251
Web www.sofitelstjames.com

Piccadilly Circus
I4

Menu £24.50 – Carte £34

It's part of the Sofitel Hotel but Brasserie Roux benefits from having its own entrance on Pall Mall, allowing it to feel more like a stand-alone restaurant. The room once formed part of a banking hall, hence the impressive height of the ceiling, while the comfort levels are also considerably higher than one would expect from a place with 'brasserie' in its title. The leather armchairs, large tables and rich colours all add stature to the room – think St James's, not the Left Bank.
When it comes to the food, 'brasserie' does makes more sense, with the kitchen delivering French regional specialities, from *boudin noir* to *cassoulet, bouillabaisse* to *andouillette,* with a decently priced set menu on the side that includes wine, water and coffee.

Quaglino's

Modern European XX

16 Bury St
SW1Y 6AL
(020) 79306767 – **Fax** (020) 78392866
Web www.conran.com

Green Park
H4

Closed 26 December and 1 January – booking essential

Menu £17.50 (lunch) – Carte £25/46

Sir Terence Conran's twin careers as design guru and innovative restaurateur reached its apotheosis in 1993 with the opening of Quaglino's. He immediately captured the zeitgeist by recreating and reinterpreting the most legendary restaurant of the 1950's and giving us glamour without the exclusivity. Busby Berkeley would have loved it.
It's all great theatre, from the views of the vast, bright restaurant from the bar, the sweeping central staircase and the scurrying waiters carrying shoulder-high trays from the on-view kitchen. In the intervening years the make-up may have slipped a little but Quaglino's still represents the best of times when London restaurants finally cast off their dour image and emerged full of poise and bursting with confidence.

Mint Leaf

Indian XX

Suffolk Pl ⊖ Piccadilly Circus
✉ SW1Y 4HX **I4**
✆ (020) 79309020 – **Fax** (020) 79306205
Web www.mintleafrestaurant.com
Closed lunch Saturday and Sunday and Bank Holidays

Carte £27/41

Being surrounded by playhouses has clearly rubbed off because Mintleaf provides a thoroughly theatrical experience. Just watch your entrance as the stairs down are cloaked in darkness.
You'll firstly encounter a long, tenebrous and highly fashionable bar. The dining room beyond splits into five areas, all equal in their moodiness and energised by the constant pulse of lounge music. Don't be alarmed when the staff leave what looks like a catwalk and crouch down at your table – it's their way of offering reassuring service.
In such surroundings one would expect decidedly eclectic Indian food but instead they keep things traditional and grounded, except for the very European desserts. Try the specially created Indian salads at lunch.

Noura Central

Lebanese XX

22 Lower Regent St ⊖ Piccadilly Circus
✉ SW1Y 4UJ **I3**
✆ (020) 78392020 – **Fax** (020) 78397700
Web www.noura.co.uk

Menu £15/34 – Carte £15/35

The nearer one got to Piccadilly Circus, the fewer choices of restaurant one usually had. However, Noura Central changed all that when it opened in 2004.
This capacious Lebanese restaurant, together with its equally roomy bar, offers a wide selection of Levantine dishes, in richly colourful surroundings. Assorted *mezes*, charcoal grilled meats, various fish platters and rich, sweet pastries all feature on the extensive menus and provide sufficiently varied choice for all tastes.
The decoration is exuberant and lavish, matched by an atmosphere that's never less than animated, thanks in part to the extensive cocktail list and the decent prices found on the wine list.
The occasional DJ also ensures that the noise levels don't fall below party mode.

Bellamy's

Traditional XX

A/C VISA MC AE

18 Bruton Pl. ⊖ Bond Street
✉ W1J 6LY **H3**
✆ (020) 74912727 – **Fax** (020) 74919990
Web www.bellamysrestaurant.co.uk
Closed Saturday lunch, Sunday and Bank Holidays

Menu £28.50 – Carte £35/57

First find the little mews of Bruton Place, snake through the appetising deli out front, glide through the double doors and you'll find yourself in Bellamy's restaurant.

This is a decidedly clubby little place with a hint of the brasserie about it. It's also perennially full of Mayfair regulars, some of whom are a little more 'Horse and Hounds' and a little less 'Hello'.

Prices here are hard to quantify: there is a very reasonable set menu for under £30 but this comes juxtaposed with £340 for Beluga Caviar. The menu covers an equally broad field with everything from whitebait to *foie gras*, mixing the English with the French. The scrambled eggs with truffles are ideal for the louche late riser. Puds are more your classic French.

The Avenue

Modern European XX

A/C VISA MC AE

7-9 St James's St ⊖ Green Park
✉ SW1A 1EE **H4**
✆ (020) 73212111 – **Fax** (020) 73212500
e-mail avenue@egami.co.uk **Web** www.egami.co.uk
Closed 25-26 December, 1 January, Saturday lunch and Sunday

Menu £22 – Carte £28/37

This bold, brash restaurant opened in 1995, mischievously at odds with the rather buttoned-up, old fashioned reputation that St James's likes to show the world. It occupies a huge space and comes with an appropriately minimalist décor which manages to distribute plenty of light to all corners. Large paintings provide whatever colour there is in the room and noise levels can reach exhilarating levels. Diners must first navigate their way through the long bar which appears as popular now as when the place first opened.

The menu is very much *de nos jours*: no frills, just decent ingredients, simply prepared, with modern European influences. Come at lunchtimes to benefit from the keenly priced set menu and witness a restaurant in full flow.

Matsuri - St James's

Japanese XX

15 Bury St — Green Park
SW1Y 6AL — **H4**
(020) 78391101 – **Fax** (020) 79307010
Web www.matsuri-restaurant.com

Closed 25 December and 1 January

Carte £23/34

The façade of this Japanese restaurant may be a little drab but the location - in among the art galleries of Bury Street - explains why lunch is such a busy affair. It is also much nicer all round once you're inside, where you're greeted by a very charming hostess who escorts you downstairs to one of the teppan-yaki tables or, if you're quick, you can grab one of the few seats at the neighbouring sushi bar.
The managers have a tendency to stand around looking important while the service is undertaken by very helpful and earnest waitresses, traditionally kitted out.
Once you have chosen from one of the many different menus available, watch the chef at your table slice and dice and your appetite will get going immediately.

Vasco and Piero's Pavilion

Italian XX

15 Poland St — Tottenham Court Road
W1F 8QE — **H2_3**
(020) 74378774 – **Fax** (020) 74370467
e-mail eat@vascosfood.com **Web** www.vascosfood.com

Closed Sunday, Saturday lunch and Bank Holidays

Menu £27 (dinner) – Carte £25/34

Vasco and Piero's firmly established Pavilion proves that it is the atmosphere which makes a restaurant, not the design, and that it comes directly from the owners.
Their pride in their Umbrian roots is clearly evident, particularly in the homemade pasta dishes which are a must here, as are the hams, salamis and anything with truffles. The emphasis is on freshness, enabling the quality of the ingredients to shine through.
The restaurant is a decidedly family affair and this is reflected in the homely style of the decoration, providing a worthy contrast for those jaded by the plethora of 'concept' restaurants. The pay-off is a fiercely loyal clientele, clearly appreciative of the considerate and amiable service.

Silk

International XX

A/C VISA MC AE

at Courthouse Kempinski H., ⊖ Oxford Circus
19-21 Great Marlborough St ✉ W1F 7HL **H3**
✆ (020) 72975555 – **Fax** (020) 72975566
Web www.courthouse-hotel.com

Closed Sunday and Monday

Carte £18/35

The Courthouse Kempinski Hotel, so named because it was converted from a former magistrate's court, offers a number of dining options, the most notable being Silk, which is housed in the handsome, oak panelled surroundings of what was once Court Number One. The benches are still there to prove it.

The name not only refers to the QC's who once paced this room but it also, perhaps more tortuously, outlines the culinary identity of the place. The menu follows the 'silk route', taking in Italy, India and Asia. This somewhat bewilderingly varied cooking actually works perfectly satisfactorily, due mostly to the decent ingredients. It's also the perfect menu for friends who can't agree on which nationality of restaurant they fancy.

Fakhreldine

Lebanese XX

A/C VISA MC AE

85 Piccadilly ⊖ Green Park
✉ W1J 7NB **H4**
✆ (020) 74933424 – **Fax** (020) 74951977
e-mail info@fakhreldine.co.uk **Web** www.fakhreldine.co.uk

Carte £29/46

Ascend the marble staircase and you enter into this stylish and urbane Lebanese restaurant which comes with its own smart lounge bar where large sofas provide the perfect spot for pre-dinner cocktails. The restaurant, reinvented by a refurbishment and named after an 18th century Lebanese Prince, benefits from its large picture windows which let in plenty of light, as well as providing great views of Green Park for those with window tables. The stone, oak and muted palate all lend a sensual contemporary edge to the decoration.

It's not just the meze which blend the traditional with the modern: the Lebanese home cooking is equally fragrant and no less accomplished, with daily changing specials and tasting plates available.

Sumosan

Japanese XX

A/C VISA MC AE

26 Albemarle St — ⊖ Green Park
✉ W1S 4HY — **H3**
✆ (020) 7495 5999 – **Fax** (020) 7355 1247
e-mail info@sumosan.co.uk **Web** www.sumosan.com

Closed 25,26 and 31 December, 1 January and Saturday lunch

Menu £22.50 (lunch) – Carte £29/51

Any restaurant which posts bad reviews as well as good ones on its website can't take itself too seriously. One of Sumosan's great strengths has been its lack of attitude and its welcoming atmosphere, despite its undeniably fashionable reputation.
It came to London in 2002, courtesy of its Russian owners who have since opened branches in Moscow and Kiev. Whilst it may be a member of the post-Nobu school of modern Japanese restaurants, it clearly attracts its very own loyal punters as well as those who feature regularly in the shinier pages of the chat-rags. The club downstairs certainly plays its part.
The menu is fairly extensive and, along with some ubiquitous modern Japanese classics, includes some original creations.

Mews of Mayfair

British XX

VISA MC AE

10-11 Lancashire Court, New Bond St. — ⊖ Bond Street
✉ W1S 1EY — **H3**
✆ (020) 75189388 – **Fax** (020) 75189389
Web www.mewsofmayfair.com

Menu £19.50/40 – Carte £28/42

Look out for the narrow little lane opposite D&G because down there you'll find Mews of Mayfair. This is a bright and pretty first floor restaurant, on a site dating from 1902 which was once used as storage rooms for Savile Row. A cocktail bar occupies the ground floor, with a lounge bar in the basement, but upstairs you'll find the relative serenity of the restaurant. It's nicely decorated with very comfortable cream leather seating and attractive silk embroidered wallpaper.
The atmosphere is far more relaxed than the size suggests, thanks largely to the delightfully enthusiastic service. The kitchen makes good use of produce from across the British Isles but does so in a contemporary, yet restrained, style.

Chor Bizarre

Indian XX

A/C

VISA

16 Albemarle St ⊖ Green Park
✉ W1S 4HW **H3**
✆ (020) 76299802 – **Fax** (020) 74937756
Web www.chorbizarre.com

Closed 25-26 December, 1 January, Sunday lunch and Bank Holidays

AE

Menu £16.50 (lunch) – Carte £17/27

Mark Twain described India as "the most extraordinary country that the sun visits" where "nothing seems to have been forgotten, nothing overlooked". His words seem particularly apt when describing Chor Bizarre, which translates as "thieves market", for it's decorated in such an exuberant and playful way that one cannot fail to be charmed. Every chair, every table is different and this imaginative jumble of furniture and trinkets perfectly captures that spirit of a bazaar.
Specialities feature from across India from *chaat* or street food to *tak-a-tak* platters as well as vegetarian selections from the Kashmiri ceremonial feast called the *Wazwan*. A well chosen wine list shows that, with a little thought, wine can do justice to Indian cooking.

Cocoon

South-East Asian XX

A/C

65 Regent St ⊖ Piccadilly Circus
✉ W1B 4EA **H3**
✆ (020) 74947600 – **Fax** (020) 74947607
Web www.cocoon-restaurants.com

VISA

Closed Saturday lunch and Sunday

Carte £35/70

AE

Stanley Kubrick meets Buck Rogers. One's initial impression of this first floor restaurant is of an ultra modern, space-age landing craft looking down on the more prosaic sights of Regent Street below.
A long narrow room is divided into smaller spaces by the judicious use of curtains and silk nets. The chairs are swivelling pods beloved of 1960's films; the tables have glass-enclosed silk petals and the staff are unnervingly good-looking and self assured.
Modernity continues in the menu which sweeps aside national borders by offering a range of Pan-Asian dishes. *Sushi* comes courtesy of the central counter and many of the Chinese specialities are designed for sharing.
The customers are as smooth and luminous as the place itself.

Veeraswamy

Indian XX

Victory House, 99 Regent St (entrance on Swallow St) ⊖ Piccadilly Circus
✉ W1B 4RS **H3**
✆ (020) 77341401 – **Fax** (020) 74398434
Web www.realindianfood.com

Menu £16 (lunch) – Carte £29/54

Not many Indian restaurants can boast Nehru and Gandhi as former customers but then not many Indian restaurants began life in 1926.
Such longevity may lead you to imagine it has something of an old fashioned feel but Veeraswamy was re-launched in late 2005 as a sleek and contemporary restaurant, while still managing to respect the restaurant's own glorious past. Colour and light are everywhere, from the hanging display of turbans to the coloured glass, silver screens, chandeliers and large picture windows.
Visually enticing choices from across India are showcased, from recipes garnered from palaces and royal courts to humble homes, with many designed for sharing. Veeraswamy looks set to be around for another 80 years.

La Trouvaille

French XX

12A Newburgh St ⊖ Piccadilly Circus
✉ W1F 7RR **H3**
✆ (020) 72878488 – **Fax** (020) 74344170
Web www.latrouvaille.co.uk

Closed 25 December, Sunday and Bank Holidays

Menu £18/33

It may be just yards from Carnaby Street but its corner location on a narrow cobbled street seems a world away. This really is a very sweet little restaurant which can't fail to charm you. It's a great place for a date.
On the ground floor sits the delightful little wine bar, a perfect place to order a plate of cheese or charcuterie to accompany a bottle from France's southwest. But upstairs is where you'll find the restaurant which is all very fresh and clean, but with a simple, effortless intimacy.
The menus, like the staff, are French, with lunch and pre-theatre representing good value. The fixed price main menu offers plenty of interest but keeps you on your toes with occasional moments of playfulness - much like a good date.

Franco's

Italian XX

61 Jermyn St ⊖ Green Park
SW1Y 6LX **H4**
(020) 74992211 – **Fax** (020) 74951375
Web www.francoslondon.com

Closed 24-30 December, Sunday and Bank Holidays – booking essential

A/C VISA MC AE

Carte £30/35

Franco's first opened in the 1940's and, understandably, was beginning to show his age until gracefully withdrawing from the scene for a while, before bursting back at the end of 2005 with a new, fresh image. He then managed the difficult trick of both attracting new admirers and hanging onto the loyalty of existing fans.

The dining room is spread over two floors, with the ground floor the most popular, and the new decoration pays homage to the era of its original opening. The sartorially immaculate regulars have been highly receptive to the new image so booking, especially at lunch, is recommended. The seasonally-biased Italian menu is constantly evolving and the cooking is both bold and generous but refined where it should be.

Café Lazeez

Indian XX

21 Dean St ⊖ Tottenham Court Road
W1D 3TN **I2**
(020) 74349393 – **Fax** (020) 74340022
e-mail Soho@cafelazeez.com **Web** www.cafelazeez.com

Closed Sunday

A/C VISA MC AE

Menu £20/35 – Carte £27/35

Attached to the Soho Theatre, the busy bar occupies the ground floor and offers a selection of light snacks but head downstairs to the more formal main dining room if you're after a tad more privacy. It's a little haven of tranquillity in the heart of Soho. The rich red walls and on-view kitchen lend the room a little bit of theatre of its own. If there are numbers in your party, try to get one of the golden coloured alcove tables. The service is never less than conscientious and considerate.

For those pushed for time, the lunchtime buffet is a popular choice. Otherwise, the *à la carte* menus offer a mix of recognisable Indian favourites in its 'traditional' section and more ambitious, modern creations in the 'evolved' section.

Arbutus ✿

Modern European

63-64 Frith St. ⊖ Tottenham Court Rd.
W1D 3 JW I3
(020) 77344545 – **Fax** (020) 72878624
Web www.arbutusrestaurant.co.uk
Closed 24-26 December and 1 January

Menu £15.50 (lunch) – Carte £27/34

Arbutus

Anthony Demetre, the chef owner, has come full circle: his new restaurant, Arbutus, opened in May 2006 on the site of what was once Bistrot Bruno, in whose kitchen he worked over a decade ago. Those who remember Bistrot Bruno will find it's now a much bigger place – it's been knocked through into next door – but the new incarnation shares the same informality and relaxed vibe. It's U shaped, with counter seating by the bar on one side and most of the action around the corner in the main room. The simple styling and clean, bright lines ensures that the focus remains on the quality of the food.
At first glance the menu reads as bistro food but in reality it is so much more than that. The chef takes his modernist approach and gives some classic dishes a tweak here and a little refinement there. The result is an original selection of dishes bursting with flavour which belies their somewhat delicate presentation. By using less expensive or unusual cuts the prices are also kept low. Full marks for the wine list. All the bottles are on offer as 250 ml carafes. Now there's an original idea.

A LA CARTE

FIRST COURSE
- Chicken oysters with macaroni, lemon thyme and hazelnuts.
- Squid and mackerel "burger" with barbecue sauce.

MAIN COURSE
- Saddle of rabbit, cottage pie of shoulder, cabbage and mustard sauce.
- Poached and roasted chicken with gnocchi and pea velouté.

DESSERT
- Floating Island with pink pralines.
- Vanilla cheesecake with English strawberries.

Yauatcha ✿

Chinese (Dim Sum)

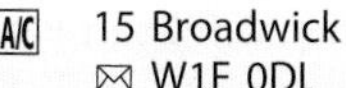

A/C 15 Broadwick St — ⊖ Tottenham Court Road
✉ W1F 0DL — **I3**
VISA ✆ (020) 74948888 – **Fax** (020) 74948889
MC **e-mail** mail@yauatcha.com
Closed 24-25 December
AE Carte £25/38

Yauatcha

Having wowed Londoners with Hakkasan, the owner Alan Yau turned his attention to reinventing dim sum. Yauatcha was the result and proved to be another instant success. Tradition was broken by not only serving *dim sum* at dinner as well as lunch but the meandering trolley is nowhere to be seen.
Located beneath the Richard Rogers' Ingeni building, it's divided into two with a brighter and lighter ground floor and the shadowy but strikingly decorated basement. Twinkling lights, a colourful fish tank the length of the cocktail bar, cherry blossom and glass screens all set the mood.
The menu features a dazzling amount of choice. The best bet is to order something from each of the different sections: stir-fry, steamed, fried, baked, grilled and cheung fun; some are traditional Chinese treats, most are in a more modern idiom. Plates usually contain three pieces so the more people in your party the more you can experience the array of delicate and precise specialities.
You'll understand why dim sum translates literally as "heart's delight".

A LA CARTE

FIRST COURSE	MAIN COURSE	DESSERT
• Scallop shumai; prawn and enoki mushroom dumpling; crispy duck roll.	• Sweet and sour seabass with pine kernel; jasmine tea smoked organic ribs.	• Ginger lemon soufflé with milk chocolate and ginger ice cream.
• Prawn cheung fun; baked venison puff; salt and pepper quail.	• Roast silver cod with red date and rice wine; stir-fry Mongolian rib-eye beef.	• Green tea crème brûlée with raspberry sorbet and coconut tuile.

Alastair Little

Modern European

A/C · VISA · MC · AE · D

49 Frith St — Tottenham Court Road
W1D 5SG — **I3**
(020) 77345183 – **Fax** (020) 77345206

Closed Sunday, Saturday lunch and Bank Holidays – booking essential

Carte £35/38

It may seem an age ago but there was a time when Soho was a place one avoided after dark, unless searching for entertainment altogether more corporeal. The eponymous former owner of this Soho stalwart was not only at the vanguard of the new wave of British chefs in the 1980's, but was also one of those responsible for turning Soho into the diners' delight that we enjoy today.
Alastair Little may no longer be involved in the restaurant but his philosophy - of letting the quality of the ingredients shine through - lives on. The sparseness of the restaurant itself was also ground-breaking in its time and matched the cooking in its rustic simplicity. Twenty years after opening, the place remains as popular as ever.

Al Duca

Italian

A/C · VISA · MC · AE

4-5 Duke of York St — Piccadilly Circus
SW1Y 6LA — **H4**
(020) 78393090 – **Fax** (020) 78394050
Web www.alduca-restaurant.co.uk

Closed 25 December-2 January, Sunday and Bank Holidays

Menu £22.50/24.50

It is value for money, rather than the naked cost, which should be considered when judging a restaurant bill. This value comprises a number of elements: the ingredients used, the skill of the kitchen, the service, the comfort and even the location.
Al Duca represents good value for money because the Italian cooking is tasty, fresh and flavoursome; there is sufficient choice on the set menu; the ingredients are top drawer; the service is prompt and efficient and the decoration clean and bright. It is also not easy finding affordable restaurants in this neck of the woods.
Sound levels can get a little high but that's what comes with places that are busy and popular. Al Duca is one of those reliable places to always fall back on.

Bentley's (Oyster Bar)

Seafood X

11-15 Swallow St. — ⊖ Piccadilly Circus

✉ W1B 4DG — **H3**

✆ (020) 77344756

Web www.bentleysoysterbarandgrill.co.uk

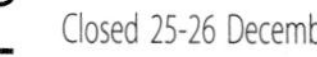

Closed 25-26 December

Carte £27/39

Once the place where sons took their ageing fathers or bewildered tourists took themselves, but now, following its full makeover, it's attracting an altogether sprightlier group of pescatarians.

The elements remain largely the same: white jacketed staff open native or rock oysters by the bucket load while others serve smoked salmon, fish pie, Dover sole and assorted seafood dishes. The difference is that the cooking is undertaken with a little more care these days.

The panelled walls, marble topped tables and leather banquettes are also a great improvement and provide highly civilised surroundings in which to indulge.

Reservations are not taken for the rather smart place settings up at the bar so get in early if you want one of these.

Inn The Park

British 

St James's Park — ⊖ Charing Cross

✉ SW1A 2BJ — **I4**

✆ (020) 74519999 – **Fax** (020) 74519998

e-mail info@innthepark.co.uk **Web** www.innthepark.co.uk

Closed 25 December

Menu £27.50 – Carte £27/40

In the north east corner of St James's Park, the oldest Royal Park in London, you'll find architect Michael Hopkins' striking eco-friendly pavilion which blends effortlessly into its surroundings - even the roof is covered with grass. Through the sliding glass walls or from the large terrace you can enjoy views across lakes, woodland and even the Mall. It is a wonderful addition to a park already steeped in royal, political and literary history.

Open for breakfast, lunch, afternoon tea and dinner, Inn the Park offers just the sort of food you want if you've been strolling around the park. It's fresh, healthy and wholesome and, most appropriately, comes with pride in its Britishness.

The other parks have got some catching up to do.

The Café (at Sotheby's)

Modern European

34-35 New Bond St — Bond Street
W1A 2AA — **H3**
(020) 72935077 – **Fax** (020) 72936993
e-mail ken.hall@sothebys.com **Web** www.sothebys.com

Closed 2 weeks August, 22 December-3 January, Saturday and Sunday – lunch only

Carte £22/32

The world famous auctioneers may not seem the obvious location for lunch but whether you're buying, selling or merely hungry, you'll find the Café at Sotheby's to be just the ticket. It sits adjacent to the main reception from where it's separated by a velvet rope, and is prettily decorated with black and white photographs, mirrors and some wood panelling.
The atmosphere is nicely relaxed, helped along by the polite and very well informed service.
It's only open during the day with breakfast and afternoon tea popular with those in the know so it's certainly worth making reservations for lunch. The menu may be relatively short, with three choices per course, but the food is crisp, fresh and balanced and leaves you ready for the hammer.

Fung Shing

Chinese

15 Lisle St — Leicester Square
WC2H 7BE — **I3**
(020) 74371539 – **Fax** (020) 77340284
Web www.fung.shing.co.uk

Closed 24-26 December and lunch Bank Holidays

Menu £17/35 – Carte £15/29

Chinatown offers a colourful, varied and, to the new visitor, a rather bewildering selection of Chinese restaurants. Fung Shing was one of the first to open and remains one of the best.
For a start, it offers bright and well-looked-after surroundings and, by dividing itself into two, manages to create a more personable feel. It also rises above the norm in the service - many of the staff have been around for years and make the effort to know and recognise their regulars.
The main menu features an extensive selection of the tried and tested but those who wish to delve deeper into the mysteries of Cantonese cooking, and to experience some of Fung Shing's more ambitious creations, should head straight for the 'specials' selection.

Chisou

Japanese

4 Princes St — ⊖ Oxford Circus
W1B 2LE — **H2**
(020) 76293931

Closed 21-31 August, 23 December-4 January, Sunday and Bank Holidays

Menu £17 (lunch) – Carte £20/38

Hanover Square and the surrounding streets are becoming something of a Japanese quarter and Chisou stands out from the crowd with its decidedly smart façade.
Inside, it's equally plush, with its clean and fresh theme of slate, glass and polished wood. The high ceiling brightens what is actually quite a small room.
Lunchtimes sees some good value set menus but the kitchen's creativity is more evident in the evening when dishes such as monkfish liver with *ponzu* merit exploration. Evenings are certainly busier so reservations are advisable. Traditionalists, though, are far from ignored and the sushi bar at the back of the room offers top notch *sashimi* and *sushi*. The waitresses provide engaging and very capable service.

Automat

American 

33 Dover St — ⊖ Green Park
W1S 4NF — **H3**
(020) 74993033 – **Fax** (020) 74992682
e-mail info@automatlondon.com **Web** www.automat-london.com

Closed Sunday dinner

Carte £23/39

Whether it is to ease the homesick blues of all these Hollywood types who have made London their home, or for just recreating that whirlwind weekend you had in New York, Automat offers up a darn fine impression of an American brasserie.
Those looking for authentic American tastes will find them all here, from chowder, crab cakes and burgers to Rib Eye steaks and cheesecake, and it's all done in relaxed and suitably lively surroundings.
The place is divided into three: the front is used to serve the all-day menu, the middle section is the best for small groups and conversations as it's decked out like a railway dining car with individual booths but the back room, with its tiled walls and open kitchen, is where the action lies.
You say tomato...

Chinese Experience

Chinese

118 Shaftesbury Ave. ⊖ Leicester Square
✉ W1D 5EP **I3**
✆ (020) 74370377
Web www.chineseexperience.com

Menu £23 (dinner) – Carte £17

Those strangely hypnotic and curiously warming neon lights may compete for your attention along the length of Shaftesbury Avenue but Chinese Experience more than holds its own with its shimmering façade of silver and glass. Step into its equally bright and airy interior and you'll find that the distinctly friendly and obliging nature of the staff belies its touristy location.
It's divided into two rooms: the first with bench tables for those communally inclined and the second with individual tables and a simple, crisp décor of white or red walls and calligraphy. The *dim sum* is worthy of note and the menu offers an extensive choice of classics and other dishes of a more individual nature, all served in a fun and buzzy atmosphere.

Aurora

Mediterranean 

49 Lexington St ⊖ Piccadilly Circus
✉ W1F 9AP **H3**
✆ (020) 74940514

Closed 23 December-3 January, Sunday and Bank Holidays – booking essential

Carte £19/27

Not to be confused with the Conran restaurant of the same name, this Aurora is a charming and intimate little Soho favourite in one of the mid terrace 18th century houses and whose sense of bohemian independence perfectly reflects the general feel of Lexington Street.
The limited space, closely set tables lit by candles and the pretty little walled garden all conspire to lend an air of secrecy to the place, somewhere the regulars would rather not share with outsiders.
The cooking also takes an uncomplicated and unfussy approach, with the main emphasis being on Mediterranean colours and flavours, although a little Asian influence occasionally slips in. The service is, as you would expect, friendly and well meaning.

Bar Shu

Chinese (Szechuan)

28 Frith St
W1D 5LF
(020) 72878822 – **Fax** (020) 72878858
Closed 25-26 December

Leicester Square
I3

Menu £19.50/24.50

Bar Shu opened in May 2006 and is detached, both geographically and qualitatively, from the restaurants in Chinatown. Not only is this serious Szechuan cooking but it is also unapologetically authentic.
Those who like their food hot and spicy may have to reset their thermometers. The dishes here pack a ferocious punch and when some are described as "hot and numbing" you know they're serious. Fantastically named choices such as "pock marked old woman's beancurd", "smacked cucumbers" or "man and wife offal slices" also prove this is no ordinary Chinese restaurant, despite the retro glossy menus with (undeniably helpful) photographs of the dishes.
The restaurant is spread over three floors - avoid the rather dull basement level.

National Dining Rooms

British

Sainsbury Wing,
The National Gallery, Trafalgar Sq
WC2N 5DN
(020) 77472525
Web www.thenationaldiningrooms.co.uk
Closed Christmas – lunch only and dinner Wednesday

Charing Cross
I3_4

Menu £19.95 – Carte £23/38

The UK's dismal culinary reputation abroad may be hopelessly outdated but will remain so until overseas visitors see evidence to the contrary. Credit then to Oliver Peyton for opening a restaurant in one of our great popular landmarks - The National Gallery. This Peyton place is on the first floor of the Sainsbury Wing, looking down over Trafalgar Square.
The menu is a decidedly British affair, with carefully sourced ingredients from across our sceptred isle. So, Dorset crab can be followed by Scottish beef and the cheese selection shows off our great repertoire.
Adjacent to the David Collins designed restaurant is a 'bakery', serving up evocative treats like jammy dodgers and fig rolls for those who haven't been to a gallery since that school trip.

Portrait

Modern European

3rd Floor, National Portrait Gallery, St Martin's Pl
WC2H 0HE
(020) 73122490 – **Fax** (020) 79250244
e-mail portrait.restaurant@searcys.co.uk **Web** www.searcys.co.uk

Charing Cross
PLAN III **I3**

closed 25 December,1 January and Sunday – lunch only and dinner Thursday-Friday

Carte £25/39

Thankfully, there are fewer museums and galleries around who assume that visitors seek nothing more than intellectual nourishment and will therefore be happy enough with a stale, overpriced cheese sandwich. Not only is the National Portrait Gallery as splendidly varied and fascinating as ever but it also provides a agreeably bright and modern restaurant, on the top floor of the Ondaatje wing.
The menu features reliable and modern dishes which do far more than merely sustain you through another tour. Wisely the room does not try to compete with the galleries; its minimalist décor soothes the senses and the large curved windows provide great views across the roof tops towards Nelson and the Eye.

Imli

Indian

167-169 Wardour St
W1F 8WR
(020) 72874243 – **Fax** (020) 72874245
e-mail info@imli.co.uk **Web** www.imli.co.uk

Tottenham Court Road
I3

Carte £14/18

Imli comes courtesy of the people behind Tamarind and provides Soho regulars with an easy and accessible Indian restaurant, but one where the food is still prepared with care and attention.
The place may look simple, with paper mats and napkins, but they've clearly had the designers in and there is a certain slickness and sleekness to the room. But you don't come here to while away a whole evening - the atmosphere is pretty hectic and turnover can be swift, which in turn helps keep the prices down.
The menu is divided into three main sections: 'light and refreshing', 'new traditions' and 'signature dishes', with the emphasis firmly on sharing. Those who cannot decide for themselves can ask the kitchen to choose.

Bertorelli

Italian

11-13 Frith St ⊖ Tottenham Court Road
✉ W1D 4RB **I3**
✆ (020) 74943491 – **Fax** (020) 74399431
Web www.santeonline.co.uk

Closed 25-26 December

Carte £25/40

Bertorelli restaurants have been around for a while and they offer decent value for their unchallenging Italian food. This Frith Street outlet sits in the heart of Soho and usually has its doors thrown open and its narrow terrace fully occupied.
There's live music from Thursday to Saturday and the room is never less than lively, with the young staff getting more points for artistic impression than technical merit. Tables are quite small, unless you can grab one of the four booths. There's a separate bar upstairs.
They may be owned now by a chain but the word *mama* still appears on the menu to describe the provenance of some dishes. All points are covered, from pizza to pasta, and the cooking is perfectly sound and sensibly priced.

Itsu

Japanese 

103 Wardour St ⊖ Piccadilly Circus
✉ W1F 0UG **I3**
✆ (020) 74794790 – **Fax** (020) 74794795
Web www.itsu.com

Closed 25 December

Carte £20

Where to eat when you don't fancy a sandwich and haven't got time to do the whole menu-ordering-waiting thing? Itsu really comes into its own for those on a schedule or merely looking to fill a whole.
The concept is simple. You sit, mostly in rows, and in front of you pass Japanese specialities on a conveyor belt going at the average speed of traffic around Soho. Train set enthusiasts will love it.
Dishes are colour coded and priced accordingly - white dishes are the cheapest and gold, where there's the greatest choice, the most expensive. You'll find yourself accumulating plates quite quickly. Other dishes, such as grills and hand rolls, can also be ordered.
There are other branches dotted around the city.

Strand & Covent Garden

C. Eymenier/MICHELIN

Bang in the middle of theatreland, it's fair to say that **Covent Garden** has always had a flair for the dramatic. The **Royal Opera House** and the **Coliseum** both offer a huge range of opera and ballet, while the numerous theatres play everything from Greek tragedy to the latest musical. If that all sounds a bit too much like hard work then stroll down to **Leicester Square** to catch the latest blockbuster: the red carpets are rolled out for the big film openings most weekends if you fancy a bit of star spotting. If crowds aren't your thing then why not meander down to **Trafalgar Square** – you can take in a bit of art at the **National Gallery**, soak up the splendid vistas down **Whitehall** or simply cross the **Strand** to lean on the banks of the Thames and watch life go by.

The range of entertainment is matched by the dining options. You can large it up at one of the über-fashionable restaurants such as The Ivy on West Street, which has paparazzi permanently stationed outside to snap the latest starlet. Otherwise the streets are lined with eateries to suit every budget – it's worth looking out for special pre and post-theatre deals, specially designed for those in town to catch a show.

A LITTLE HISTORY...

Covent Garden started life as the kitchen garden to **Westminster Abbey**, pre-shadowing its development as London's most famous market, selling fruit and vegetables, as well as fresh flowers from all over the country. The Italianate piazza was developed in the early 17C by the Earl of Bedford. Given the area's theatrical bent it's little surprise that the designer Inigo Jones was not only a brilliant architect, instrumental in introducing the classical Palladian style to London, but also a talented painter and set builder who collaborated with Shakespeare and Ben Jonson on several court masques.

Although the market moved out to Battersea in the 1970s there are still plenty of reminders of Covent Garden's mercantile past. The covered market, right in the heart of the piazza, is a tempting warren of shops and stalls: in particular the **Apple Market** is devoted entirely to stalls selling everything from designer jewellery to hand-carved toys.

If you're interested in Covent Garden's showbiz past, then check out the often overlooked **St Paul's Church** on **Bedford Street**, better known as the actor's church because of its long association with the theatrical community. The inner walls and garden are lined with memorial plaques to famous personalities – from English lions such as the satirist Samuel Butler to Hollywood greats such as Vivien Leigh. But the drama of Covent Garden isn't confined to the past, nor always contained in the theatres – street performers are a common sight in the piazza, often drawing large crowds for an impromptu show.

The Strand was originally the main artery of London connecting the City and Westminster and is still a busy thoroughfare today. In medieval and Renaissance times it was also one of the most desirable addresses in London, lined with royal palaces whose grounds stretched right down to the river. Although most of these have now disappeared, the Palace of the Savoy lives on as the **Savoy Hotel**, home to many a celebrated visitor, including Oscar Wilde who took up residence at the hotel at the height of his career. **Somerset House**, formerly the registry for births, deaths and marriages, is another grand house that's well worth a visit: today it is home to collections from the Courtauld Institute of Art, acts as a popular venue for live music and in winter the fountain court is transformed into a stunning outdoor ice-rink.

While there are some extremely fine dining options on the Strand itself, if you're on a budget then you might find it worthwhile stepping off the beaten track and exploring some of the quieter streets leading down to the river. And there's no need to stop once you reach the water: boats moored off **Victoria Embankment** provide popular drinking spots and an excellent way to enjoy this vibrant area.

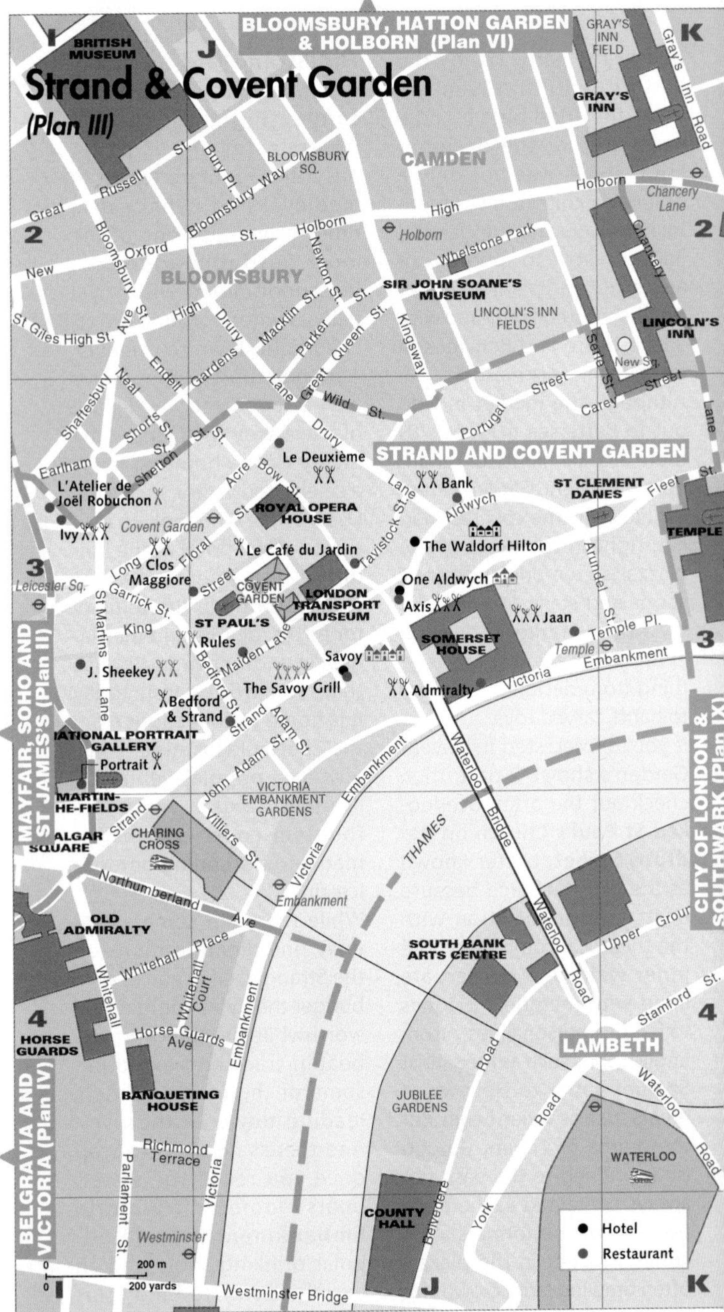
Strand & Covent Garden
(Plan III)
BLOOMSBURY, HATTON GARDEN & HOLBORN (Plan VI)
STRAND AND COVENT GARDEN
MAYFAIR, SOHO AND ST JAMES'S (Plan II)
CITY OF LONDON & SOUTHWARK (Plan IX)
BELGRAVIA AND VICTORIA (Plan IV)
BRITISH MUSEUM
BLOOMSBURY
CAMDEN
LAMBETH
SIR JOHN SOANE'S MUSEUM
LINCOLN'S INN FIELDS
LINCOLN'S INN
GRAY'S INN
ROYAL OPERA HOUSE
LONDON TRANSPORT MUSEUM
ST PAUL'S
SOMERSET HOUSE
ST CLEMENT DANES
TEMPLE
NATIONAL PORTRAIT GALLERY
OLD ADMIRALTY
HORSE GUARDS
BANQUETING HOUSE
SOUTH BANK ARTS CENTRE
COUNTY HALL
WATERLOO
JUBILEE GARDENS
VICTORIA EMBANKMENT GARDENS
CHARING CROSS
THAMES
Le Deuxième
L'Atelier de Joël Robuchon
Ivy
Clos Maggiore
Le Café du Jardin
Bank
The Waldorf Hilton
One Aldwych
Axis
Jaan
Rules
J. Sheekey
Savoy
The Savoy Grill
Admiralty
Bedford & Strand
Portrait
Hotel
Restaurant
200 m
200 yards

The Savoy Grill 

Modern European

at Savoy H., Strand ✉ WC2R 0EU
⊖ Charing Cross
J3

(020) 75921600 – **Fax** (020) 75921601
Web www.marcuswareing.com

Menu £30/65

A/C · VISA · MC · AE

Gordon Ramsay Holdings

Throughout the 20th century this was the Establishment's establishment and the piles of Melba toast on each table said it all. Now in the 21st century it has been re-invented. The trolleys of broiled roasts have gone and the cooking has reached levels of excellence its old incarnation never came close to achieving. Cleverly, the designers have managed to both respect and update the art deco origins by using wood panelling, a shimmering ceiling, large circular lamps and striped booth seating. The kitchen has also found that satisfying balance between tradition and modernity; a trolley of smoked salmon is there for those who believe it's the only way to start a meal. For those pushing out the proverbial boat there is much to savour and all the menus successfully blend the French and the British in a very appealing way.
Service comes courtesy of a battalion of highly organised staff with an exemplary knowledge of the menu and those curious about the pointy end of the operation can book the chef's table in the kitchen.

A LA CARTE

FIRST COURSE	MAIN COURSE	DESSERT
• Omelette Arnold Bennett with Scottish lobster and hollandaise.	• Pan-fried fillet of Scottish beef with potato galette and truffle sauce.	• Earl Grey tea cream with Garibaldi biscuits.
• Baked pithivier of quail and forest mushrooms, walnuts and Madeira sauce.	• Steamed fillet of sea bass with braised leeks and smoked eel.	• Hot chocolate fondant with lemon thyme ice cream and praline tuiles.

Strand & Covent Garden

Jaan

Innovative XXX

at Swissôtel The Howard, ⊖ Temple
Temple Pl ✉ WC2R 2PR **J3**
✆ (020) 73001700 – **Fax** (020) 72407816
e-mail jaan.london@swissotel.com
Web www.swissotel-london.com

Closed Saturday lunch and Sunday

Menu £22/38

'Swissotel The Howard' may not have the most recognisable name amongst the capital's hotels but it certainly boasts one of the best locations, overlooking the river. Unfortunately the hotel's restaurant, Jaan, isn't able to match these river views as it is tucked away behind the lobby, but what is does provide is a calm and serene spot whose most striking feature is the floor to ceiling windows which open out onto a pleasant courtyard, where meals are served in summer.
The room is elegant without being overformal and the service efficient without being over solicitous.
The kitchen displays a deft touch and an understanding of Asian flavours and spices, as it adds them to ingredients of more European provenance.

Axis

Modern European XXX

at One Aldwych H., ⊖ Covent Garden
1 Aldwych ✉ WC2B 4RH **J3**
✆ (020) 73000300 – **Fax** (020) 73000301
e-mail axis@onealdwych.com **Web** www.onealdwych.co.uk

Closed 24 December-4 January, Easter, Sunday, Saturday lunch and Bank Holidays

Menu £21 (lunch) – Carte £28/37

Axis belongs to One Aldwych Hotel but is marketed as a separate entity and is helped considerably in this by having its own street entrance. You descend spirally from the reception and bar area and come out into a double height space with a vast futuristic mural on one wall and lots of curves and pillars.
Noise levels can be a little full-on, especially if there's a large table of business types in from the hotel, but there are quieter sections. The menu offers an unthreatening selection of assorted European-influenced food, with a grill section for those who prefer to keep things simple.
Its proximity to a number of theatres and the popularity of its pre-theatre menus means that the restaurant is already jumping by early evening.

Ivy

International XXX

A/C
VISA
MC
AE
D

1 West St — ⊖ Leicester Square
✉ WC2H 9NQ — **I3**
✆ (020) 78364751 – **Fax** (020) 72409333
Web www.the-ivy.co.uk

Closed 25-26 December, 1 January and August Bank Holiday

Carte £26/57

If celebrity is indeed the currency of our age, then this is the Bank of England. On any given day it will have more than its share of those whose business is show, while the snappers will be outside hoping to catch someone with someone else.
However, it would be unfair to class it as merely a glitterati hang-out, for it remains one of the best run restaurants around, with that reassuring hum one finds when the service is choreographed with precision and élan. The menu too has a satisfying balance to appeal to all tastes and appetites with everything from eggs Benedict to foie gras. An actor once said "fame means nothing except a good table in a restaurant"; we mere mortals may find getting in a rather more challenging experience.

J. Sheekey

Seafood XX

A/C
VISA
MC
AE
D

28-32 St Martin's Court — ⊖ Leicester Square
✉ WC2N 4AL — **I3**
✆ (020) 72402565 – **Fax** (020) 72408114
Web www.caprice-holdings.co.uk

Closed 25-26 December, 1 January and August Bank Holiday – booking essential

Carte £22/49

'Fashionably traditional' may sound like an oxymoron but J.Sheekey effortlessly combines a tangible sense of London history with the sensibilities and expectations of modern life. For over one hundred years, its very essence of Englishness and theatricality have been at the heart of the operation; the wood panelled walls are adorned with photographs of the greats who have trod the local boards, regulars mix with assorted celebrities and everyone seems to have their favourite spot.
The good and the great come also for the quality of the seafood, which the kitchen handles with skill and understanding. The classics merit attention, as do the carefully prepared desserts, while service is as assured and reliable as a David Niven anecdote.

Rules

British XX

35 Maiden Lane ⊖ Leicester Square
✉ WC2E 7LB **J3**
✆ (020) 78365314 – **Fax** (020) 74971081
e-mail info@rules.co.uk **Web** www.rules.co.uk

Closed 4 days Christmas – booking essential

Carte £30/41

Such is the transient nature of restaurants that anywhere over 15 years old is referred to as 'well-established'. Rules opened its doors in 1798 and, as London's oldest restaurant, is fully entitled to look down on all those johnny-come-lately's.
It is simply bursting with character and history and its quintessential Englishness is something to behold. Every inch of wall is covered with paintings, cartoons and drawings and its customers, from Charles Dickens to Charlie Chaplin, have always been drawn from the literary and theatrical worlds.
The cooking too celebrates the best of British by specialising in game, often from its own estate on the Pennines, so this is the place for grouse, partridge and pheasant or a great steak and kidney pie.

Clos Maggiore

French XX

33 King St ⊖ Leicester Square
✉ WC2 8JD **I_J3**
✆ (020) 73799696 – **Fax** (020) 73796767
e-mail enquiries@maggiores.uk.com **Web** www.maggiores.uk.com

Closed Saturday lunch, Sunday and Bank Holidays

Menu £19.50/24.50 – Carte £27/41

Those wanting something more than a stale slice of overpriced pizza have always found Covent Garden to be a little challenging in the restaurant stakes. Fortunately, Clos Maggiore proves that good food and tourist attractions are not always mutually exclusive.
The place certainly has charm and the blossom hanging everywhere adds a romantic touch. The glowing fire warms the winter evenings, while in summer ask for a table in the back room where the glass roof opens.
The menu reads like a Frenchman who lives in the countryside but still likes to travel. The cooking is grounded in sound culinary techniques but occasionally slips in a contemporary twist. Wine here is clearly taken seriously and the list certainly merits careful exploration.

Admiralty

French XX

VISA Somerset House, The Strand ⊖ Temple
✉ WC2R 1LA **J3**
✆ (020) 78454646 – **Fax** (020) 78454658
Web www.somerset-house.org.uk

Closed 24-27 December and dinner Sunday and Bank Holiday Mondays

Menu £19.50 (lunch) – Carte £40

Stride across the striking fountain courtyard, wonder how it could have been just a car park for so many years, and enter the South building to find Admiralty restaurant, named in honour of the Royal Navy's long connection with Somerset House. The restaurant is divided into two rooms, along with a cocktail bar. The high ceilings and large arched windows allow in plenty of light, with the added bonus of a striking galleon shaped chandelier.

Some of that naval history has rubbed off on the staff, who have an upright bearing and go about their task without fanfare. What Lord Nelson would think of a restaurant serving French inspired cooking is anyone's guess but there's certainly some serious dining going on here.

Bank

Modern European XX

1 Kingsway, Aldwych ⊖ Covent Garden
✉ WC2B 6XF **J3**
✆ (020) 73799012 – **Fax** (020) 73799014
Web www.bankrestaurants.com

Closed Sunday dinner

Menu £16 (lunch) – Carte £26/42

This was the first of the three Bank restaurants to open, in 1996, and was, unsurprisingly, converted from a bank which may explain the number of suited businessmen doing deals at lunchtimes and celebrating in the evenings. The bar certainly gets a good hammering with the after-work crowd and its proximity to many of the city's theatres ensures the large take-up of the pre-theatre menus.

This is perhaps not the place for that romantic first date -it can get noisy here – and only those with exaggerated enunciation will find communication easy.

The restaurant has a modern, industrial feel with lots of light and glass, offset by a beach-themed mural. The menu offers a selection of traditional and updated brasserie dishes.

Le Deuxième

International XX

65a Long Acre
WC2E 9JH
(020) 73790033 – **Fax** (020) 73790066
Web www.ledeuxieme.com

Covent Garden
J3

A/C VISA MC AE

Closed 24-25 December

Menu £15.50 (lunch) – Carte £25/29

Le Deuxième is the sister restaurant to Le Café du Jardin but, like most sisters, is more demure and less excitable than her elder brother. It's also less geared towards passing business and instead has established itself as something of a destination, which may explain the more sedate pace.

Despite its location, in the heart of Covent Garden, the atmosphere is quite intimate, helped by the privacy afforded by the smoked glass façade. Decoratively, it's unthreateningly modern, with a quietly neutral colour scheme.

The same chef oversees both the cooking and menus here and at Le Café du Jardin. Along with weekly changing set menus, expect an extensive *à la carte* that's fairly global in its reach.

A PINT OF THE HARD STUFF

At over 300 years old, the Lamb & Flag on Rose Street is the oldest pub in Covent Garden and a great, if busy, place to sup a pint. However, former names hint at a more violent past. The pub used to be known as the Bucket of Blood because of the bare-knuckled fights held there; while the upstairs Dryden room commemorates the poet laureate who, in 1679, was beaten up outside for writing a satire on the king's mistress.

L'Atelier de Joël Robuchon ✿

Innovative 

A/C
VISA

13-15 West St
✉ WC2H 9NE
✆ (020) 70108600 – **Fax** (020) 70108601

⊖ Leicester Square
I3

Menu £30/80 – Carte £33/82

L'Atelier de Joël Robuchon

Joël Robuchon, one of France's greatest chefs, came out of retirement with a bang when he launched L'Atelier in Tokyo and introduced the concept of counter eating, no bookings and small tasting plates. Branches have opened across the world and now London has its turn to be dazzled.

There are two dining rooms: on the ground floor sits L'Atelier itself where reservations are only taken up to 7pm. The counter seating, the clever lighting and the slick and seductive red and black backdrop are like nowhere else. Upstairs you'll find La Cuisine, a slightly more structured restaurant in a monochrome theme, appropriate for a kitchen, and this is the better choice for larger parties when a counter won't do. There's a cool bar on the top floor.

The menus are largely the same, with a choice of the tasting sized plates or the more traditional *à la carte*, with the chefs in full view in hushed concentration. Dishes are highly original and creative in their design and construction. The contrasting textures and clean, clear and defined flavours make this a memorable experience.

A LA CARTE

FIRST COURSE

- Fresh mackerel tart with parmesan shavings and olives.
- Soft poached egg with crispy rice batter and Oscietra caviar.

MAIN COURSE

- Free range quail stuffed with foie gras, truffled mashed potatoes.
- Pan-fried sea bass with lemongrass foam and stewed leeks.

DESSERT

- Coffee ice cream with chicory jelly.
- Lychee and grapefruit smoothie.

Le Café du Jardin

French

28 Wellington St — ⊖ Covent Garden
✉ WC2E 7BD — **J3**
✆ (020) 78368769 – **Fax** (020) 78364123
Web www.lecafedujardin.com

Closed 24-25 December

Menu £15.50 (lunch) – Carte £25/29

At around 7.15pm there'll be a flurry of activity, as theatre-goers check the time and all ask for their bills simultaneously. To the outsider this may look like your classic tourist trap found in all theatre districts, with tables being forever pushed together or pulled apart and a 15% service charge added to bills. However, those who have more time and are tempted by the *à la carte* menu will find the cooking undertaken with more skill and care than they expect, accompanied by a thoughtful and considered wine list.
The basement level is the more spacious but the glass framed ground floor is where you'll find most of the action and is clearly the more popular. The staff all work hard to justify that added service charge.

Bedford & Strand

Traditional

1a Bedford St — ⊖ Charing Cross
✉ WC2E 9HH — **J3**
✆ (020) 78363033
Web www.bedford-strand.com

Closed 25-26 December, 1 January, Saturday lunch and Sunday – booking essential

Menu £15.50 – Carte £17/27

They call themselves a 'wine room and bistro' which neatly sums up both the philosophy and the style of the place - interesting wines, reassuringly familiar food and relaxed surroundings.
It's named, American-style, after the cross streets so it's easy to find and the basement location shouldn't be off-putting. The after-work crowd have largely dispersed by 8ish in the evening but it all remains fairly energetic, helped along by a bright and sprightly team. British and Mediterranean comfort food is the feature of the menu, with a choice ranging from fish soup and risotto to cottage pie, with classic deli food served at the bar. The wine list has been thoughtfully put together and comes accompanied by some sensible pricing.

C. Barrely/MICHELIN

Belgravia and Victoria

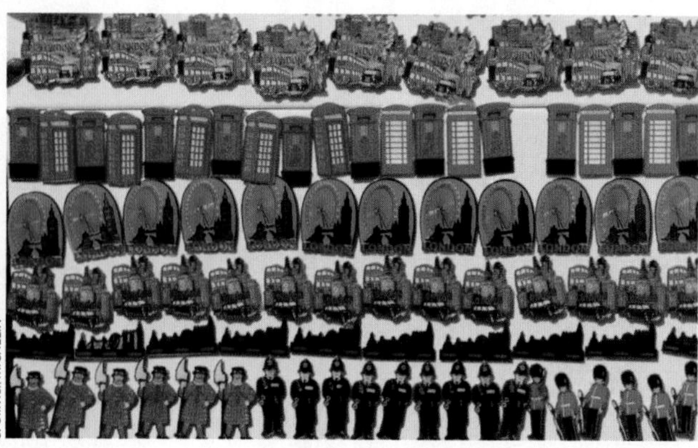

S. Ollivier/MICHELIN

'Central' is a good word to describe this area. The gentle stucco and harmonious greys of **Belgravia** belie its status as the diplomatic heart of London, with embassies from all over the world lining the streets and squares. While if you follow **Victoria Street** down to **Parliament Square** you're right in the centre of political life in London, and indeed the whole country.

The transport hubs of **Victoria Station** and **Coach Station** provide easy access from airports and mean that Victoria is often the first port of call for visitors to London. **Buckingham Palace**, the queen's official residence, and the "royal peculiar" **Westminster Abbey** are obvious draws for the crowd. Unsurprisingly there are plenty of serviceable eateries and an embarrassment of hotels to cater for the tourists, but step off the well-worn trails and you can enjoy a touch of old world gentility among the cobbled mews and gracious townhouses of Belgravia. As you might expect from such an upmarket area there are a number of excellent restaurants modestly located on the quiet streets. If that's a little tame for your tastes you can always venture down to Westminster, take in the views that Turner and Monet painted, and indulge in gossip with the politicians and hacks at any of the surrounding pubs – all within hearing of the **House of Common's** division bell.

A LITTLE HISTORY...

The area of Belgravia takes its name from Belgrave Square, which was laid out in the 19C by Thomas Cubitt, at the time London's most prolific builder and developer, and a man with a keen eye for a bargain. A little misleadingly the square is actually named after a village in Cheshire, which forms one of the secondary titles of the landlord, the Duke of Westminster.

Belgravia has been at the cutting edge of fashionable London since it was developed by Cubitt and there's no sign of it slipping off the radar yet. The lavishly porticoed townhouses that now account for some of the most expensive real estate anywhere in the world were originally designed to be the London bases for moneyed families coming to town for "the season". Today the area is relatively quiet but still gently reeking of money. Famous residents include Baroness Thatcher, the actress Joan Collins and Ian Fleming – the creator of James Bond. In many ways the area can be said to perfectly represent the suave secret agent – urbane, impeccably turned out and with an eye for the finer things in life. As you might expect, the shops here are aimed at the high end of the market with exclusive designer boutiques nuzzling up to wallet-busting antiques and interior shops. However, it's not all objets d'art – even the rich have to eat, and **Elizabeth Street** in particular offers a mouth-watering series of treats for the dedicated gourmet. Stand out shops include the wine and cheese merchants **Jereboams**, bakers **Poilane** and **Baker & Spicer** will cater for all your carbs, greengrocer extraordinaire **Mash** boasts of being a specialist in fruit baskets, while the **Chocolate Society** offers its customers something a little more indulgent.

If Belgravia is notable for its harmonious lines and muted, neutral palate, the same cannot be said of Victoria. The best way to describe the bustling hub of **Victoria Street** is chaotic – both for the volume of traffic and people, and for the jumble of architectural styles. The Victorian mass of the station gives way to the neo-Byzantine façade of **Westminster Cathedral** – then further down to the medieval **Westminster Abbey**, and Pugin's neo-gothic **Houses of Parliament**. However, despite this mish-mash, its proximity to the so-called Westminster Village gives Victoria an undeniable buzz.

If politics is not your thing then take a stroll down the river to Pimlico and **Tate Britain,** which houses the greatest collection of British art in the world. From there you can hop onto the popular ferry service, which uses a specially decorated Damien Hirst boat and goes between the Tate and its younger sister, the **Tate Modern** on **Bankside**.

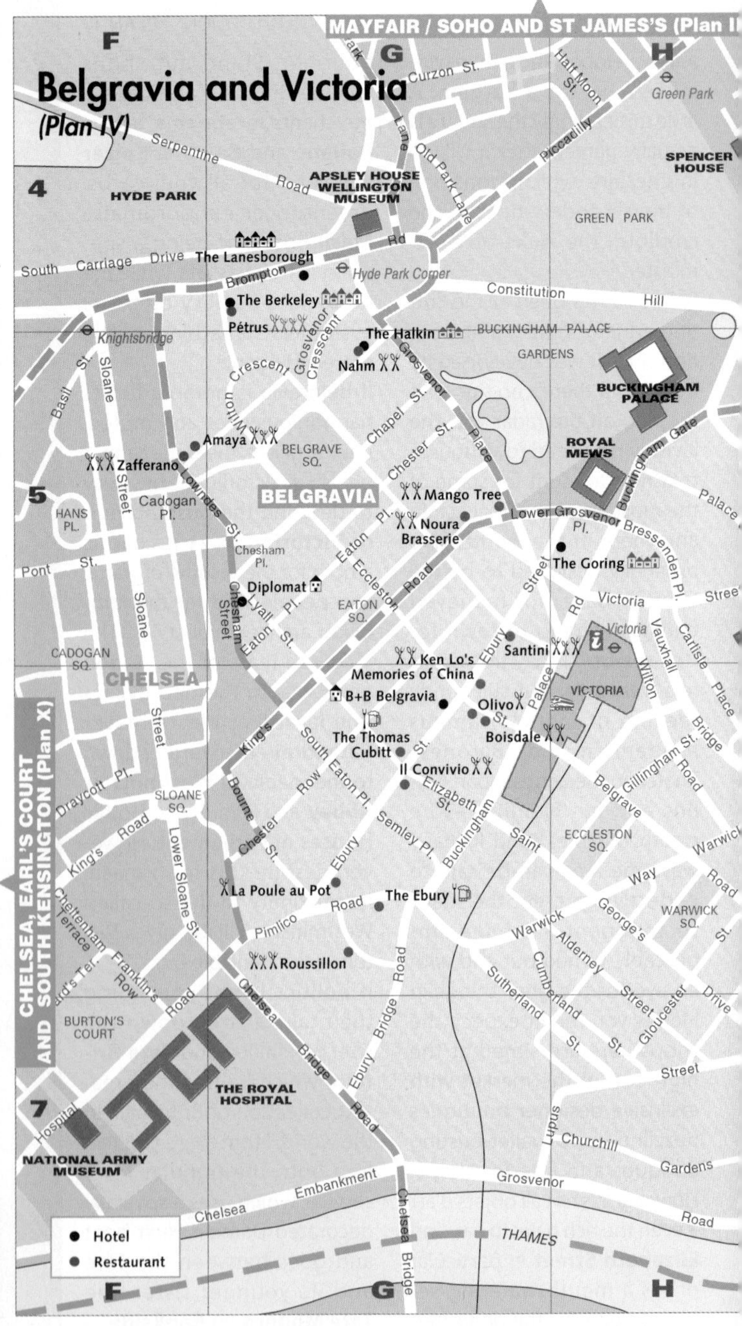
Belgravia and Victoria
(Plan IV)
MAYFAIR / SOHO AND ST JAMES'S (Plan II
CHELSEA, EARL'S COURT AND SOUTH KENSINGTON (Plan X)
HYDE PARK
APSLEY HOUSE WELLINGTON MUSEUM
GREEN PARK
SPENCER HOUSE
BUCKINGHAM PALACE GARDENS
BUCKINGHAM PALACE
ROYAL MEWS
BELGRAVIA
BELGRAVE SQ.
EATON SQ.
CHELSEA
CADOGAN SQ.
HANS PL.
SLOANE SQ.
VICTORIA
ECCLESTON SQ.
WARWICK SQ.
BURTON'S COURT
THE ROYAL HOSPITAL
NATIONAL ARMY MUSEUM
THAMES
The Lanesborough
The Berkeley
Pétrus
The Halkin
Nahm
Amaya
Zafferano
Mango Tree
Noura Brasserie
The Goring
Diplomat
Santini
Ken Lo's Memories of China
B+B Belgravia
Olivo
The Thomas Cubitt
Boisdale
Il Convivio
La Poule au Pot
The Ebury
Roussillon
Hyde Park Corner
Knightsbridge
Green Park
Victoria
Hotel
Restaurant

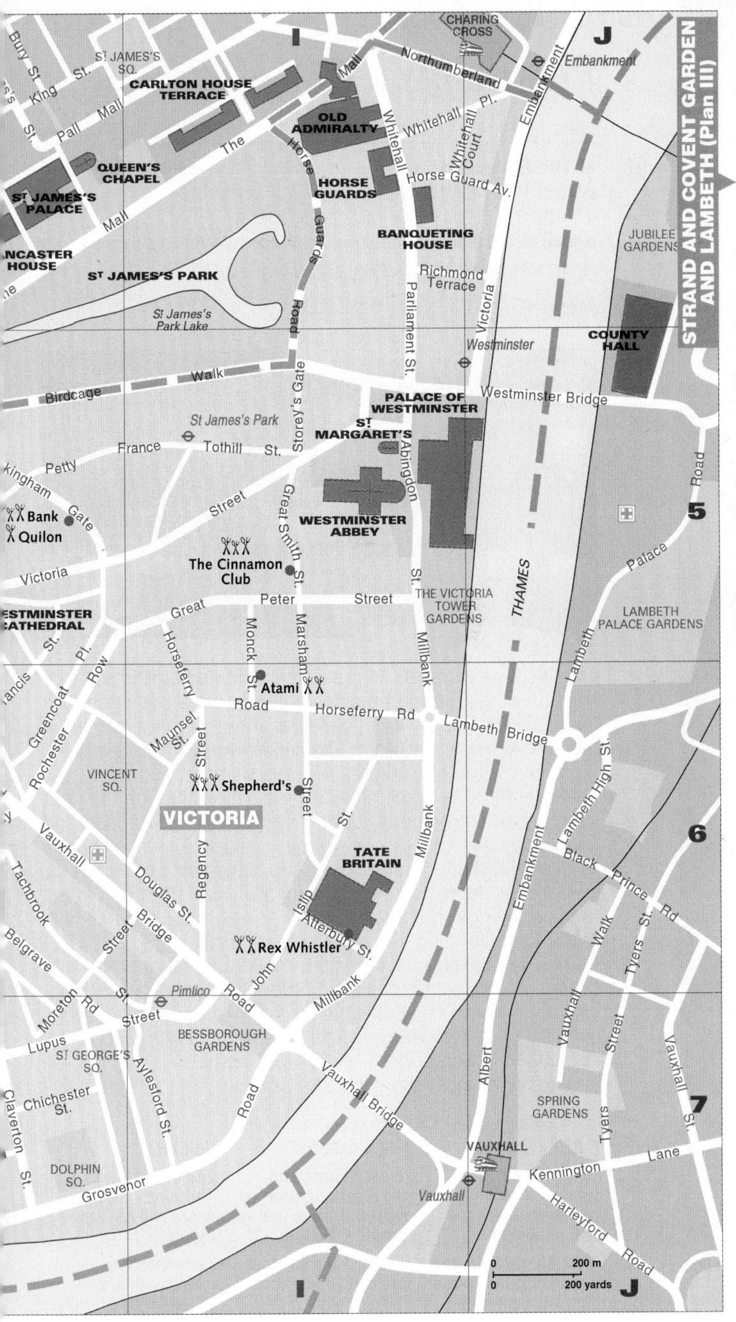
STRAND AND COVENT GARDEN AND LAMBETH (Plan III)
The Cinnamon Club
Bank
Quilon
Atami
Shepherd's
Rex Whistler
WESTMINSTER ABBEY
PALACE OF WESTMINSTER
TATE BRITAIN
VICTORIA
ST JAMES'S PARK
COUNTY HALL
BANQUETING HOUSE
HORSE GUARDS
OLD ADMIRALTY
CARLTON HOUSE TERRACE
QUEEN'S CHAPEL
ST JAMES'S PALACE
THAMES

Pétrus ✿✿

French XXXX

at The Berkeley H., ⊖ Knightsbridge
Wilton Pl ✉ SW1X 7RL **G4**
✆ (020) 72351200 – **Fax** (020) 72351266
e-mail petrus@marcuswareing.com **Web** www.marcuswareing.com

Closed 1 week Christmas, Saturday lunch, Sunday and Bank Holidays

Menu £30/80

A/C · VISA · MC · AE · D

Gordon Ramsay Holdings

The famous Chateau of Pétrus is found in Pomerol, one of the smallest wine producing regions of Bordeaux, and is celebrated for the velvety richness of its Merlots. The restaurant, named in the wine's honour, moved to The Berkeley Hotel in 2003 and the lavishness of the dining room provides a fitting tribute.
Entrance is via the hotel but as soon as you're through the glass doors you'll find yourself looked after by an experienced and knowledgeable team who have the confidence and personality to ensure that the atmosphere never becomes too sombre or serious. The room is certainly luxurious, with the claret motif running through the decoration and some original touches such as the large abacus with coloured glass beads.
However, the main attraction is the impeccably executed cooking of Marcus Wareing, a protégé of Gordon Ramsay. His own personality now informs his cooking which has a poise and confidence about it. Dishes are elegantly crafted and expertly balanced.
Those whose wallets don't stretch to a bottle of Pétrus will still find plenty of more affordable alternatives.

A LA CARTE

FIRST COURSE	MAIN COURSE	DESSERT
• Roasted veal sweetbread with garden peas, black olives and veal vinaigrette.	• Braised turbot with wild asparagus, poached quail eggs, caviar and nasturtium flowers.	• Peanut parfait with rice crisp crunch, chocolate mousse and candied peanuts.
• Scottish scallops with boudin noir, fried shallot rings and baby capers.	• Poached and pan-fried pigeon on a liver and truffle crouton.	• Warm chocolate moelleux with fudge cube and nougatine tuile.

Zafferano ✿

Italian XXX

15 Lowndes St — ⊖ Knightsbridge

✉ SW1X 9EY — **F5**

(020) 72355800 – **Fax** (020) 72351971

Web www.zafferanorestaurant.com

Closed Christmas-New Year

Menu £34.50/49.50

Zafferano

Zafferano still manages to retain a genuine neighbourhood feel, although that feel comes neatly coiffured and elegantly attired-we're talking Belgravia here.

In 2005 the restaurant bought the antique shop next door and bashed through to generate more space, which has been used to create a very agreeable bar that seems to have opened up and brightened the whole restaurant. The main dining room has also been given a nip here and a tuck there and has a modern, fresher look. Those who prefer their dining surroundings to be a little more rustic need not panic as they still have their adjoining room with the exposed brick walls and closer-set tables.

The standard of the Italian cooking remains a reliable and accomplished constant. The menu comes fixed priced and the produce is never less than exemplary; flavours are exact and bold while the balance of the menu makes taking four courses the easy option. Service is personable and positive and the regulars, who appear to make up the majority of the customers, are treated with familiar ease.

A LA CARTE

FIRST COURSE

- Stuffed peppers with pan-fried scallop and baby squid.
- Flat spaghetti with lobster and fresh tomato.

MAIN COURSE

- Pan-fried veal cutlet with semolina, tomato and oregano.
- Chargrilled monkfish with courgettes and sweet chilli.

DESSERT

- Pear and almond tart with mascarpone ice cream.
- Hazelnut parfait with fresh mango.

Amaya ✿

Indian XXX

A/C

Halkin Arcade, 19 Motcomb St ⊖ Knightsbridge
✉ SW1X 8JT **F5**
✆ (020) 78231166 – **Fax** (020) 72596464
e-mail info@realindianfood.com **Web** www.realindianfood.com

Menu £27 (lunch) – Carte £30/50

VISA AE

Amaya

Amaya calls itself a 'bar and grill', a clue that this is unlike other Indian restaurants. Specialising in refined and delicate grills and kebabs, it does it all with a sense of theatre.
Come with friends because the idea is to order a selection of small dishes to share and then finish off with a biryani or curry. The subtly spiced and aromatic kebabs and grills arrive in no particularly order - to ensure they're piping hot - and you'll quickly get into the rhythm. Novices should consider one of the set menus, which show off the chef's expertise.
It's like the UN when it comes to staff: there are over 14 nationalities represented but they are all well versed in the menu and offer helpful advice and contagious enthusiasm.
The room is an unusual shape – this was once three boutiques in an otherwise non-descript 'arcade' – with splashes of colour. The best place to sit is in the raised section under the conservatory roof where you can watch the chefs at their griddle, grill and tandoor stations. Alongside the rich, red bar there's a large table to accommodate those without reservations.

A LA CARTE

FIRST COURSE
- Punjabi chicken wing "lollipops", chargrilled with chilli, lime and cinnamon.
- Flash grilled rock oysters with coconut and ginger sauce.

MAIN COURSE
- Leg of baby lamb, slow roasted with cumin and garam masala.
- Tandoori black pepper chicken tikka with rich pepper marinade.

DESSERT
- Chocolate tart with cinnamon, flourless mousse and cardamom.
- Bread and butter pudding with ginger, banana and chocolate.

Quilon

Indian XXX

at Crowne Plaza London St James H., ⊖ Victoria
45 Buckingham Gate ✉ SW1E 6AF **H5**
✆ (020) 78211899 – **Fax** (020) 72339597
Web www.thequilonrestaurant.com

Closed Saturday lunch

Menu £15.95 (lunch) – Carte £27/36

Quilon is named after the seaport on the south west coast of India, and it is from here that many of the recipes at this stylish restaurant originate. The kitchen prepares seafood specialities with particular aplomb but is also unafraid of using more contemporary techniques and combinations and vegetarians will also find they have plenty of choice.
The restaurant itself is smoothly and professional run and is discreet and comfortable but with a brightness and vitality to its decoration. This is certainly one of a band of Indian restaurants responsible for weaning us off the tired old dishes served in so many restaurants which it does by showcasing the huge diversity and possibilities that exist.

Santini

Italian XXX

29 Ebury St ⊖ Victoria
✉ SW1W 0NZ **G5**
✆ (020) 77304094 – **Fax** (020) 77300544
Web www.santini-restaurant.com

Closed 25 December, 1 January, lunch Saturday and Sunday

Carte £36/56

Whether it is the relatively discreet location, the long-standing family ownership or the classic Italian cooking, but what is certain is that over the years Santini have attracted its fair share of the high profile celebrity market, from Presidents to actors and all points in between.
The décor is sleek and understated and the service formal and deliberate. A pretty foliage-fringed terrace provides a pleasant spot for alfresco dining for those unafraid or unlikely to be troubled by passing admirers.
The menu keeps it classic with a subtle Venetian accent and the focus rightly falls on the quality of the ingredients. Those whose ambition outweighs their wallet should try the more reasonably priced pre-theatre menu.

The Cinnamon Club

Indian XXX

A/C Great Smith St ⊖ St James's Park
✉ SW1P 3BU **I5**
(020) 72222555 – **Fax** (020) 72221333
e-mail info@cinnamonclub.com **Web** www.cinnamonclub.com
Closed Sunday and Bank Holidays

Menu £22 (lunch) – Carte £27/52

Housed within the century old Grade II listed former Westminster Library one finds this stylish and very comfortable Indian restaurant. The main dining room has many of the original features, including the mezzanine floor and parquet flooring, while the bars are certainly worthy of exploration – one is quieter as it's the former reference room of the library and the other screens scenes from Bollywood films. The place has a lively and convivial ambience and provides perfect revenge for anyone who has been shushed in a library. Appropriately, it really does feel clubby.
The kitchen imports many of its ingredients from India but uses modern European techniques to create original and colourful specialities with more than a hint of personality

Shepherd's

British XXX

A/C Marsham Court, Marsham St ⊖ Pimlico
✉ SW1P 4LA **I6**
(020) 78349552 – **Fax** (020) 72336047
Web www.langansrestaurants.co.uk
Closed 25-26 December, Saturday, Sunday and Bank Holidays – booking essential

Menu £33

A good lunch at Shepherd's may explain the apparent somnolent poses of some of our politicians in afternoon debates. This is very much a favoured dining room of the Westminster crowd, who are no doubt attracted by its clubby feel, the degree of privacy offered and the type of cooking that'll gladden the heart of your average Eurosceptic. The set menu lists a veritable who's who of popular British classics, from potted shrimps and Dover sole to rib of beef and calves liver and bacon, supplemented by some brasserie favourites. The service is effortlessly smooth from the well-versed team.
Those seeking a definition of Britishness in all its glory, from food to customer, need look no further.

Roussillon ✿

French XXX

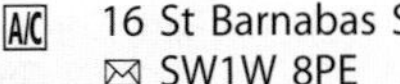

16 St Barnabas St — ⊖ Sloane Square
SW1W 8PE — **G6**
(020) 77305550 – **Fax** (020) 78248617
e-mail alexis@roussillon.co.uk **Web** www.roussillon.co.uk

Closed 1 week August, 25 December, Saturday lunch, Sunday and Bank Holidays

Menu £35/48

Roussillon

How many ingredients these days taste truly of themselves? The sign of a good chef is to take a familiar ingredient - something as simple as a pea - and re-introduce us to its true flavour. This is done through an absolute insistence on prime quality and seasonality and this is the great strength of Roussillon.

Chef Alex Gauthier has been doing his thing here for ten years, without fanfare and without recourse to daytime TV. His intelligent and considered cooking draws a deeply loyal following, many of whom are further attracted by the restaurant's ability to fly below the radar of the fashionistas.

As well as the main menu come 'vegetable' and 'tasting' menus. Dishes come with an inherent French bias but with many ingredients sourced from the British Isles. The wine list focuses on the South West of France and praise should be heaped for the introduction of the twice-monthly Mini-Gastronome Menu which introduces young diners to good food through visual and sensory means.

The dining room is comfortable, unthreatening and nicely laid out and with dollops of colour from the artwork.

A LA CARTE

FIRST COURSE

- Wild purple asparagus with poached quail eggs and lemon zest.
- Grilled scallop salad, tomato and sage tempura and crustacean jelly.

MAIN COURSE

- Highland venison with poached pear, caramelised pumpkin and celeriac.
- Wild sea bass with yellow and green courgettes, marrow and beef jus.

DESSERT

- Apricot soufflé with dark chocolate sauce.
- Raspberry millefeuille with raspberry sorbet.

Nahm ✿

Thai XX

at The Halkin H., ⊖ Hyde Park Corner
5 Halkin St ✉ SW1X 7DJ **G5**
✆ (020) 73331234 – **Fax** (020) 73331100
Web www.halkin.co.uk

Closed lunch Saturday, Sunday and Bank Holidays – booking essential

Menu £26/49.50 – Carte £37/43

Nahm

On the ground floor of one of the original boutique hotels, The Halkin, you'll find Nahm, a restaurant to blow away any preconceptions you may have about Thai cooking.
The kitchen is overseen by David Thompson, who became Sydneysiders' favourite chef with his Darley Street Thai restaurant in the 1990's. In 2001 he was persuaded to cross the world and with him came his considerable knowledge and appreciation of all things Thai, including his vast collection of traditional Thai recipes. Nahm (Thai for 'water') comes with plenty of marble, gold and teak. This lends a feeling of undisputed Eastern opulence but also means it needs plenty of customers in to create an atmosphere. The cooking is guaranteed to re-awaken tired taste buds as it showcases the variety of Thai cuisine, with the differing flavours and textures, all countered and balanced. Divided into various sections, the menu can appear a little confusing at first but wait for an explanation from your server and be prepared to share. Alternatively, place yourself entirely in their hands by ordering the *nahm arharn* banquet.

A LA CARTE

FIRST COURSE
- Hot and sour soup of mussels with tomatoes, chillies and coriander.
- Lemongrass salad with prawns, squid and shredded chicken with peanuts and mint.

MAIN COURSE
- Stir-fried "middle-white" pork with dried prawns, ginger, peanuts and tamarind.
- Minced quail curry with ginger and kaffir leaves.

DESSERT
- Custard apple with sweetened coconut cream, sticky rice and sugar bananas.
- Lychees, mangosteens and rambutans in perfumed syrup.

Atami

Japanese XX

A/C
VISA
MC
AE

37 Monck St (entrance on Great Peter St)
✉ SW1P 2BL **I6**
✆ (020) 72222218 – **Fax** (020) 72222788
e-mail mail@atami-restaurant.com **Web** www.atami-restaurant.com

Closed Sunday

Carte £19/41

Named after one of Japan's best known hot spring resorts, Atami is the latest in a line of stylishly decorated Japanese restaurants that have proved very popular over the last few years by mixing the traditional with the decidedly contemporary. The difference is that here prices are a little more down to earth.
The serving team offer the novice expert guidance around the menu and, alongside the *sushi* and *sashimi*, expect to find ingredients of a more European provenance, paired in some unexpected yet delicate combinations.
Bamboo, leather, mirrors, glass and natural woods combine to create a sensual and striking space, illuminated by four large ceiling orbs. The bar is tucked away discreetly but is equally appealing and strangely calming.

Il Convivio

Italian XX

A/C
VISA
MC
AE

143 Ebury St ⊖ Sloane Square
✉ SW1W 9QN **G6**
✆ (020) 77304099 – **Fax** (020) 77304103
Web www.etruscarestaurants.com

Closed 25 December and Sunday

Menu £26.50/38.50 (lunch) – Carte £30

Il Convivio is a decidedly grown-up kind of Italian restaurant and so fits rather snugly into the fabric of everyday Belgravia life. It's also a place with plenty of regulars, many of whom have their favourite spots. There are three different dining areas to choose from, as well as a comfortable bar area, but there can be fewer more charming spots on a sunny day than the rear space with the retractable roof. The style is bright, smart and elegant - as you would expect from somewhere that has the poetry of Dante embossed on the walls.
The fixed price menus offer up a balanced and appetising selection of Italian dishes, where the quality of produce shines through. The smartly uniformed staff provide formal and structured service.

Rex Whistler

British XX

Tate Britain, Millbank
✉ SW1P 4RG
✆ (020) 78878825 – **Fax** (020) 78878902
e-mail tate.restaurant@tate.org.uk **Web** www.tate.org.uk

⊖ Pimlico
I6

Closed 25 December – booking essential - lunch only

Carte £28/32

The restaurant may be in the basement of Tate Britain but the views are better than most thanks to the specially commissioned mural by Rex Whistler, "The Expedition in Pursuit of Rare Meats", painted in 1927. It is also a highly civilised haven of tranquillity, in comparison to the more frantic pace found in the neighbouring café.
Just as upstairs celebrates English artists, downstairs does its bit by using mostly home-grown ingredients and offers a choice of both modern British as well as European specialities. The wine list is hugely impressive thanks to the restaurant's history of cellaring wine for over thirty years. Commendably, it also offers over sixty half bottles for those wishing to make use of the afternoon.

Ken Lo's Memories of China

Chinese XX

65-69 Ebury St
✉ SW1W 0NZ
✆ (020) 77307734 – **Fax** (020) 77302992
Web www.memories-of-china.co.uk

⊖ Victoria
G6

Carte £28

The restaurant may have changed hands over the years but the late Ken Lo was responsible for putting the place on the map all those years ago and so it's appropriate to find his name still in the title.
The restaurant belies its age in its looks. It is bright, modern and quite minimalist in its design but also manages to be warm and welcoming. Chinese script, lattice panels and well dressed tables ensure a sense of comfort and style.
The length of the menu can appear a little bewildering, as can the seemingly eccentric numbering system, but the dishes come carefully prepared. The set menus are often the easier option and take you on a gastronomic tour of China.
Service is positive, well marshalled and clued-up.

Boisdale

British XX

15 Eccleston St — ⊖ Victoria
✉ SW1W 9LX — **G6**
✆ (020) 77306922 – **Fax** (020) 77300548
e-mail info@boisdale.co.uk **Web** www.boisdal o.uk

Closed Christmas and Sunday

Carte £29/48

Those waiting for the day when a Scottish Em ssy opens in London can more than make do with Boisdale, fo they will be unlikely to find anywhere, outside of Scotland, m Scottish than this. The owner is a proud Macdonald and the cdonald tartan is everywhere, along with a plethora of prints d paintings. The menu showcases the best of Scotland's fine oduce from salmon to game and matured beef.
There is a choice of dining room within this charming R ency town house, from the clubby atmosphere of the Macdona Bar to the more formal and demure surroundings of the restaurant. In summer the retractable roof makes the Courty Garden a popular choice.
The one element to break from all things Scottish is the nightl jazz band.

Mango Tree

Thai XX

46 Grosvenor Place — ⊖ Victoria
✉ SW1 7EQ — **G5**
✆ (020) 78231888 – **Fax** (020) 78389275
e-mail info@mangotree.org.uk **Web** www.mangotree.org.uk

Closed 25 December, 1 January and Saturday lunch

Carte £25/40

The mango may be one of the best known of tropical fruits common to South East Asia but those expecting a laid-back beach-hut style Thai restaurant will be in for something of a surprise. This Mango Tree is a decidedly Belgravian affair.
For one thing it's a big, shiny room with contemporary styling that's usually always busy. This can yank up the decibel levels and, as such, makes it a favourite after-work spot, helped in turn by an interesting selection of cocktails. This may not be the place for romantic dinners for two but it is the place to come with a group of friends and the menu is helpfully divided into soups, curries, stir-fries and grills.
Vegetarians and vegans are offered plenty of choice with their own dedicated menus.

Bank

Modern European XX

45 Buckingham Gate
SW1E 6BS
(020) 73799797 - **Fax** (020) 73795070
e-mail westres@bankrestaurants.com
Web www.bankrestaurants.com

⊖ St James's
H5

Closed Saturday lunch and Sunday

Menu £17.95 (lunch) - Carte £27/40

Adjoined to the Crowne Plaze Hotel but with its own street entrance, this branch of Bank is a little less frenzied than the one in Aldwych but can, nonetheless, still provide a fun night out.
You first have to get past the Zander Bar which purports to be the longest bar in the country. Those not wishing to proceed further will find the bar also has a food menu.
The restaurant itself is a large conservatory affair and looks out onto an attractive Victorian courtyard. The lunchtime clientele can be a little more business orientated but is less so in the evenings.
You'll find classic, familiar choices alongside more contemporary influences on the extensive à la carte, which is supplemented by a fixed priced option.

Noura Brasserie

Lebanese XX

16 Hobart Pl
SW1W 0HH
(020) 72359444 - **Fax** (020) 72359244
e-mail noura@noura.co.uk **Web** www.noura.co.uk

⊖ Victoria
G5

Menu £17/38 - Carte £23/33

Having made their name in Paris, the owners set their sights across the Channel and opened their first London restaurant here in Belgravia in 2000.
It undoubtedly challenged any preconceptions by being a big, bold and brash room which was both decidedly contemporary and reflective of the zeitgeist. Today, it's as busy as ever, especially with larger tables and parties for whom the surroundings are ideal. Nonetheless, the staff remain stoically immune to the enthusiasm of their customers.
A slightly less formal approach is adopted at lunch, with a keenly priced lunch menu on offer. The main menu is a dazzlingly long affair, with authentic Lebanese delicacies designed for sharing. Those new to it all should try the set menus or selected platters.

Olivo

Italian X

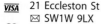

21 Eccleston St — ⊖ Victoria
SW1W 9LX — **G6**
(020) 77302505 – **Fax** (020) 78235377
e-mail maurosanna@oliveto.fsnet.co.uk

Closed lunch Saturday, Sunday and Bank Holidays

Menu £19.50 (lunch) – Carte £28/35

All restaurants work best when the owner is present. At Olivo, Mauro not only keeps a steady hand on the tiller but he also ensures that the atmosphere remains bright and welcoming - that's what makes Olivo such an attraction. It still feels like a local restaurant, although some diners are prepared to travel some distance to get here. Its approaching anniversary of twenty years of operation bear testament to its continued popularity. The rustic décor and the closely set tables within this relatively small space also ensure a highly convivial feel, helped by a keen team of servers.
The menu and the wine list are both Italian, with subtle hints of Sardinia. The char-grill is a house speciality and the produce used is top notch.

La Poule au Pot

French traditional 

231 Ebury St — ⊖ Sloane Square
SW1W 8UT — **G6**
(020) 77307763 – **Fax** (020) 72599651

Closed 25 December

Menu £16.50 (lunch) – Carte £26/41

Trends may come, styles may go, but the one constant will always be La Poule au Pot. As Gallic as a Gauloise and as French as a frog's leg, this long-standing favourite, with its exuberant decoration of hanging baskets of dried flowers and assorted horticultural knick-knacks, has been entertaining everyone, from the romantically inclined to groups of friends out for fun, for many years. Somehow all the disparate elements just seem to gel wonderfully well and it's reassuring to know that not everything is fashion led.
It's not just the atmosphere: the classic country cooking is also responsible for drawing the crowds. Expect a selection of rustic favourites from *coq au vin* to *crème brûlée*, supplemented by daily specials.

The Thomas Cubitt

Gastropub 

VISA MC AE

First Floor, 44 Elizabeth St. — ⊖ Sloane Square
SW1W 9PA — **G6**
(020) 77306060 – **Fax** (020) 77306055
Web www.thethomascubitt.co.uk

Closed 4 days Easter, 25 December and 1 January – booking essential

Menu £21.50 (lunch) – Carte £27/47

Welcome the world of the pub, Belgravia style. Thomas Cubitt was the master builder responsible for landmark local squares, Eaton and Belgrave, and he would surely have approved of this decidedly handsome establishment.

Regency and Georgian styles have been put to good effect, with oak flooring, panelling and fireplaces, to create a warm and welcoming feel, from the delightful ground floor bar in which to enjoy more casual dining to the charming and more formal upstairs room where the period feel really comes into its own. Here the menu is more structured and features seasonal produce, carefully sourced from across the British Isles, in unfussy and flavoursome dishes. Service also hits the right note in its unobtrusiveness and warmth.

The Ebury

Gastropub 

A/C VISA MC AE

11 Pimlico Rd, — ⊖ Sloane Square
SW1W 8NA — **G6**
(020) 77306784 – **Fax** (020) 77306149
e-mail info@theebury.co.uk **Web** www.theebury.co.uk

Closed 25-26 December

Carte £23/29

The Ebury has become an established feature in this part of town and has done so by successfully offering both satisfyingly hearty food and by providing its customers with the choice of two different dining options. On the ground floor one finds the busy and lively brasserie/pub with floor to ceiling windows and a thrusting young crowd, with a bar that is equally adept at satisfying their demands. Ascend the oak staircase and you come upon altogether more tranquil and restful surroundings, where the added formality and pretty decorative touches help create a very soothing ambience.

The menu is the same throughout so it is merely a case of deciding which floor best suits the occasion or the repartee of your dining companions.

C. Barrely/MICHELIN

CENTRAL LONDON - **PLAN V**

Regent's Park & Marylebone

C. Eymenier/MICHELIN

Regent's Park is one of those rare places in London where it is hard to suggest ways in which it could be improved. This lush green expanse, with secret corners that are accessible to all, is imbued with both graceful grandeur and pastoral never-may-care, so that promenading and picnicking go hand in hand. It is much loved and well used - but stroll through the Italianate gardens on a weekday evening and you could almost believe you're in the grounds of your own Tuscan villa, taking a quiet moment to admire the topiary or recline in one of the sequestered pavilions.

Round the outside

Though much pleasure is to be had in a simple sojourn in the rose gardens of the **Inner Circle** or sharing a punnet of strawberries in the northern meadows, more involved activities are also possible. Boating lakes and sports pitches are available for the energetic, while Shakespeare in the **Open Air Theatre** is a reliable inducement to midsummer dreaming. **London Zoo** is also here and in recent years has worked hard to improve enclosures so that the animals are as happy as the visitors. Not to be missed is the view of Lord Snowdon's netted tetrahedral aviary from the **Regent's Canal**, the latter cutting the zoo in two, with horned residents of the **Into Africa** zone gazing curiously at iPod joggers whizzing by on the tow path below.

More than a moated impasse, the fringe-skirting canal is an indication of how the park's surrounds flow out of this urban oasis. To the west, the park's handsome mansions evolve into St John's Wood, an apparent bastion of Englishness but one where the village cricket pitch happens to be **Lords** and local place of worship the **London Central Mosque**. To the east, the white Regency terraces, provide a natural home for estimable institutions, before blending into the street-smart chaos of Camden Town. And, most subtly of all, to the north the park stretches into Primrose Hill, a high-class bohemian enclave with a view of the London skyline that many rate as the capital's best.

A LITTLE HISTORY...

Perhaps it's no surprise that an area as harmonious and elegant as this did not evolve haphazardly but was meticulously planned. The lease of Marylebone Park, an unprepossessing piece of land that had been used for farming, reverted to the Crown in 1811. The architect John Nash, backed by his patron the Prince Regent, jumped at the chance to design the park and surrounding houses in order to lure the moneyed classes north away from the centre of London. Today **Marylebone Road** is a busy thoroughfare, the skyline punctuated by the verdigrised dome of the **Planetarium**, the Grecian cupola of **St Marylebone Parish Church** and the spiky sputnik of the **BT tower**. It may appear a trifle bleak after the verdant greenery of the park, however, the road is also home to the **Royal Academy of Music**

C. Eymenier/MICHELIN

– an excellent place to find cheap or even free concerts of classical favourites and brand new compositions.

MARYLEBONE VILLAGE

Turn south off the road and you come to the self-consciously styled Marylebone village; the narrow, winding streets are in contrast to the geometric Georgian layout of Regent's Park and in many places still follow the course of the underground Tyburn river, which gives the area its name. Cafés spill out onto the pavement and in summer it has an almost Mediterranean feel: it's certainly a challenge to imagine you're a shout away from the bustle of Oxford Street.

BAKER AND BREAD

As ever in London, these moneyed nooks are excellent places to find a bite to eat. There are several good specialist shops, including **La Fromagerie**, which of-

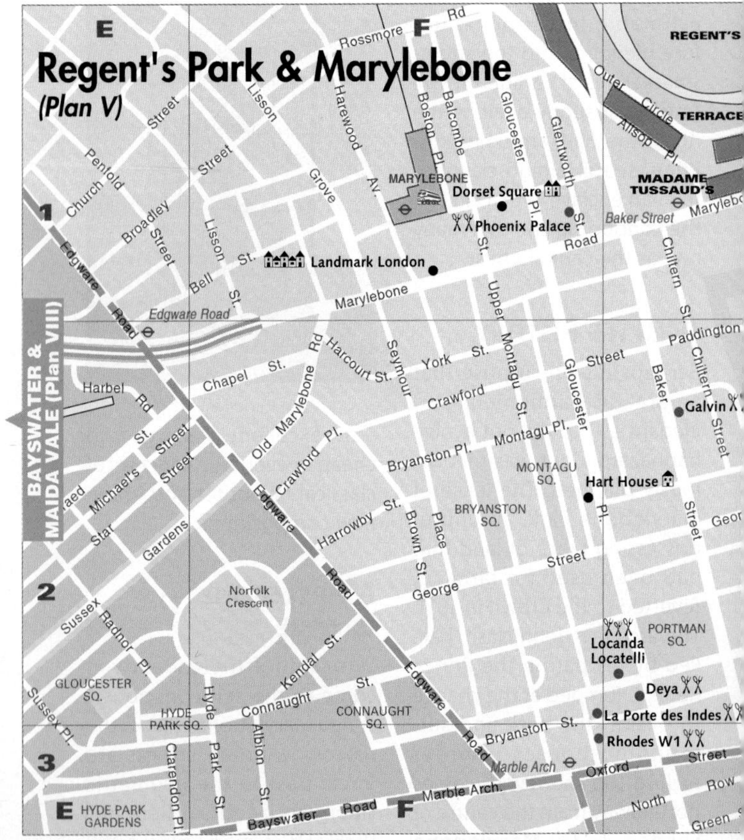

fers an eye-opening and mouth-watering array of cheeses. There's also a farmers' market in the **Moxton Street car park,** which takes place on Sundays the whole year round.

If you fancy delving into the area's literary past, head east and onto **Baker Street**, whose most famous resident, Sherlock Holmes, still dominates the area: there's a museum sited aptly enough at 221b Baker Street – although, ironically, the address was as fictional as Holmes until the museum was built there.

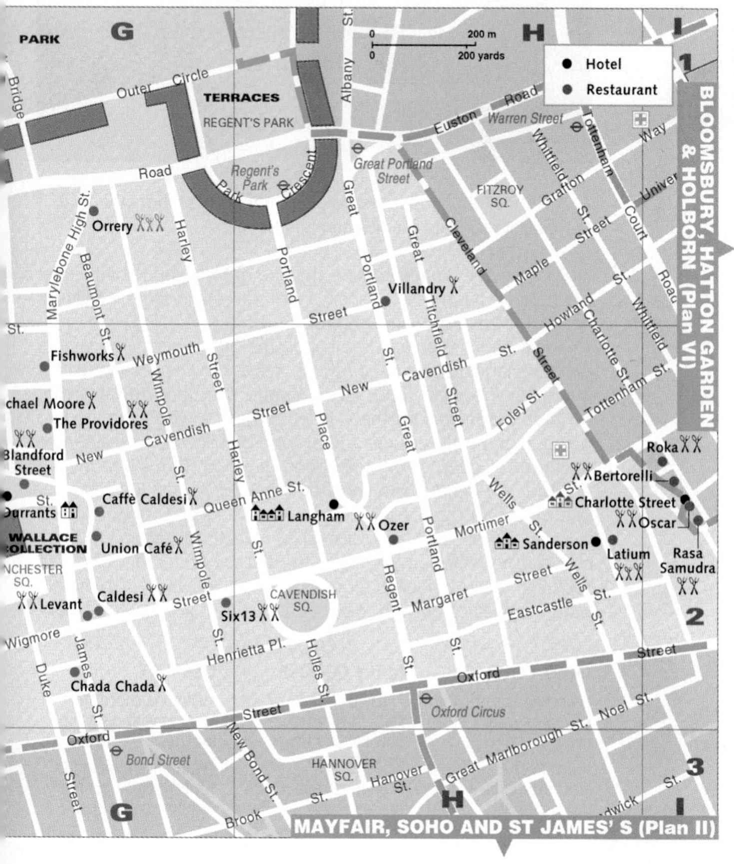

Orrery ✿

French XXX

55 Marylebone High St
W1U 5RB
(020) 76168000 – **Fax** (020) 76168080
Web www.conran-restaurants.co.uk

⊖ Regent's Park
G1

VISA MC AE

Closed Christmas and New Year – booking essential

Menu £23.50 (lunch) – Carte £31/50

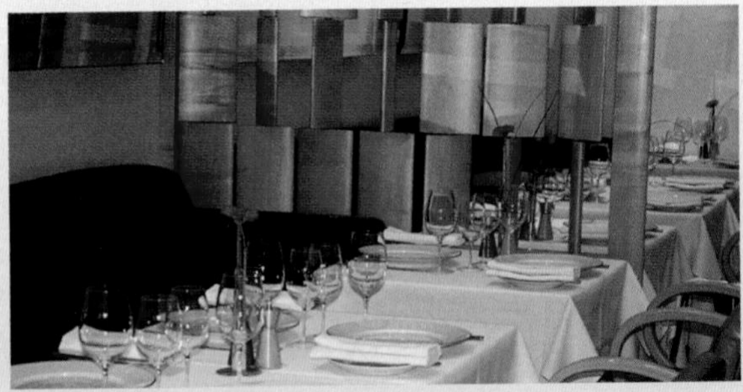
Orrery

As Orrery is the undoubted star in the Conran firmament, it is perhaps appropriate that it's named after a clockwork model of the solar system.

Sir Terence does appear to have this end of Marylebone High Street sown up. He has his design shop, a well stocked épicerie, and Orrery, occupying what was once a stable block.

This first floor restaurant is a handsome affair, with large arched windows letting in plenty of light as well as providing views over St Marylebone Church. Those facing inward need not miss anything as the tilted mirrors on the wall let you catch who's coming and going. That mostly includes a loyal band of followers who are more interested in good eating than good gawping. This is a restaurant of choice for people who know their onions.

The kitchen displays a lightness of touch and a real awareness of the seasons. There are no alarming combinations, just an emphasis on clean, fresh flavours. Alongside the *à la carte* comes a well priced set lunch menu, as well as six course tasting and vegetarian menus, both of which come with the option of wine pairings by the glass.

A LA CARTE

FIRST COURSE
- Poached scallops with Vermouth cream, broad beans and girolles.
- Ham hock and globe artichoke terrine, quince purée.

MAIN COURSE
- Poached breast of chicken with truffle bouillon and thyme gnocchi.
- Pan-fried halibut with braised Puy lentils, Pinot Noir jus.

DESSERT
- Valrhona chocolate fondant with pistachio ice cream.
- Warm rice pudding, spiced Victoria plum compote and sorbet.

Locanda Locatelli 

Italian XXX

8 Seymour St
W1H 7JZ
(020) 79359088 – **Fax** (020) 79351149
e-mail info@locandalocatelli.com **Web** www.locandalocatelli.com

⊖ Marble Arch
G2

Closed Bank Holidays

Carte £31/60

VISA · MC · AE

Locanda Locatelli

When Giorgio Locatelli opened his eponymous Italian restaurant in 2002 he inadvertently caused a journalistic feeding frenzy, of the literal kind. The wonderful reviews he garnered ensured that the restaurant attracted quite a following, particularly from the ranks of the glitterati. Today it remains as popular as ever, giving the restaurant that enviably buzz of busyness and glamour.
The David Collins decoration manages to be both modern and redolent of the '50's, with the cherry wood room dividers, glass panels, convex mirrors and very soothing cream leather banquettes. The room just feels right, pitched at perfect levels of comfort and formality and still feels fresh and original.
Meanwhile, the cooking manages to be refined, precise, restrained yet, at the same time, robust and earthy. There are no extraneous elements and the seasonally pertinent ingredients shine through. Not to have all four courses, including pasta, would seem a wasted opportunity.
Getting a table can still be tortuous but at least you know that everyone comes to this Italian to be fed not photographed.

A LA CARTE

FIRST COURSE
- Salad of baby spinach with smoked ricotta, red onions, walnuts and red wine dressing.
- Home made tagliatelle with kid goat ragout.

MAIN COURSE
- Fillet of wild sea bass with artichoke purée and Vernaccia wine sauce.
- Pan-fried veal with sage and ham, aubergine cake and girolles.

DESSERT
- Strawberry and rhubarb compote with passion fruit jelly and mascarpone ice cream.
- Chocolate and coffee tart with amaretto ice cream.

Latium

Italian XXX

21 Berners St
✉ W1T 3LP
✆ (020) 73239123 – **Fax** (020) 73233205
e-mail info@latiumrestaurant.com **Web** www.latiumrestaurant.com

⊖ Oxford Circus
H2

Closed Saturday lunch, Sunday and Bank Holidays

Menu £32.50

In contrast to the über trendy Sanderson Hotel opposite, Latium has steadily built up a loyal following by providing surroundings which are less challenging and altogether more down to earth. That is not to say the restaurant is without personality for it has a certain well-groomed, understated chic, but comfort and relaxation are clearly the priorities.
The strength also lies in the service which is executed with a confidence which comes from having pride and belief in your establishment - names and faces of returning customers are remembered. The chef-owner hails from Lazio and his set-price menu offers a balanced selection of specialities which all come with a certain degree of elaboration and top-notch ingredients.

Rhodes W1

British XX

at The Cumberland H.,
Great Cumberland Pl ✉ W1A 4RF
✆ (020) 74793838 – **Fax** (020) 74793888
e-mail rhodesw1@thecumberland.co.uk
Web www.garyrhodes.com

⊖ Marble Arch
F3

Menu £20 (lunch) – Carte £23/37

The Cumberland Hotel was re-launched in 2006 after enormous sums of money had been spent on doing it up and, within it, came a sizeable restaurant from the stable of Gary Rhodes.
Those who remember the Simply Rhodes chain will have some sort of idea about the food served here, although there are few chefs whose repertoire is as instantly recognisable as Gary Rhodes'. Here he brings his carefully tuned, crisp yet simpler style of modern British cooking to the restaurant.
That restaurant is all very open, with a split level and separate bar area. The atmosphere can be a little 'hotel dining room' on occasions but this great position within yards of Marble Arch should surely attract plenty of punters from outside the hotel.

Oscar

Modern European XX

at Charlotte Street H.,
15 Charlotte St ✉ W1T 1RJ
✆ (020) 79074005 – **Fax** (020) 78062002
e-mail charlotte@firmdale.com
Web www.charlottestreethotel.co.uk

⊖ Goodge Street
I2

Closed Sunday lunch – booking essential

Carte £33/49

Charlotte Street always appears to be full of life and the sheer range of restaurants, snack bars and cafes may be the cause or the effect. The unimaginatively, but undeniably accurately, named Charlotte Street Hotel offers up another popular option with their Oscar restaurant. It's located at street level in this fashionable hotel, while its bar fills the front and often spills out onto the pavement.

The place is a wonderfully colourful affair, with murals, stained glass lanterns and striped seating. The pace can be quite frenetic and reminds us all that restaurants are there as places of enjoyment, not worship. Cooking is decidedly modern and dishes come neatly presented. They offer a commendable number of wines by the glass.

Deya

Indian XX

34 Portman Sq
✉ W1H 7BY
✆ (020) 72240028 – **Fax** (020) 72240411
Web www.deya-restaurant.co.uk

⊖ Marble Arch
G2

Closed 2 weeks August, 26 and 31 December, Saturday lunch and Sunday

Menu £32.50 – Carte £24/33

Deya opened in the summer of 2004, when much was made of it being the restaurant that enticed Sir Michael Caine back into the business. It's quite easy to miss but, then again, so are most things on Portman Square. The steps up to the restaurant certainly contribute to the discreet feel and there aren't many Indian restaurants housed in Grade II listed 18th century houses. To compete with such spacious surroundings and moulded high ceilings, the restaurant has added vast splashes of colour, including a huge mural and it's all quite stylish, as is the bar.
Trend bucking continues in the kitchen. For starters, the cooking is a shade lighter and its approach is decidedly more modern. The set menus certainly merit exploration.

Galvin

French XX

66 Baker St — ⊖ Baker Street
W1U 7DN — **G2**
(020) 79354007 – **Fax** (020) 74861735
Web www.galvinbistrotdeluxe.co.uk

Closed 25-26 December and 1 January

Menu £15.50 (lunch) – Carte £23/37

Some said a restaurant would never succeed on this site, the 'wrong end' of Baker Street. Well, Galvin opened in September 2005 and there has hardly been a spare table since.
The Galvin brothers proved the doomsayers wrong by pooling their considerable culinary experience and expertise in creating what they describe as a *bistrot de luxe*. They took as their model the new wave of bistrots modernes and their cooking is a refreshingly uncomplicated celebration of French cuisine and one executed with care and understanding.
The L shaped room also has the character of a Parisian bistro, with wood panelling, slate flooring and large globe lights hanging from the ceiling. You feel that everyone is dining in their favourite restaurant.

Six13

Kosher XX

19 Wigmore St — ⊖ Bond Street
W1H 9LA — **G2**
(020) 76296133 – **Fax** (020) 76296135
e-mail inquiries@six13.com **Web** www.six13.com

Closed Jewish Holidays, Friday and Saturday

Menu £24.50 (lunch) – Carte £28/45

'Kosher fusion' may sound like one of the more unlikely culinary images but that is exactly what is found at Six13. Named after the 613 mitzvoth or commandments, Six13 produces elaborately presented cooking using influences from around the world, but all strictly within the laws of kashrut. The kitchen needs to be both inventive and imaginative in the creation and conception of the dishes and in this it mostly succeeds.
The room is a high-ceilinged, rather smart affair with two large lampshades providing the only real decorative features of any note. Otherwise it's all rather understated, with a bar at one end and tables laid out in long rows. Private functions can be held on the lower ground floor.

La Porte des Indes

Indian XX

A/C

32 Bryanston St — ⊖ Marble Arch
✉ W1H 7EG — **F2**
✆ (020) 72240055 – **Fax** (020) 72241144
Web www.laportedesindes.com

Closed 25-28 December and Saturday lunch

Carte £22/40

The façade gives little away but step in and you'll be instantly transported to what looks like the set from the latest Bollywood movie. Spread over two floors, La Porte des Indes really is vast and it's decorated in a spectacularly unrestrained display of palms trees, murals and waterfalls. The equally exuberant Jungle Bar is a popular place to kick off the evening.
The menu offers something for everyone, including specialities from Pondicherry and others influenced by French India. Vegetarians are particularly well catered for and cookery demonstrations are held regularly for those wishing to learn more about Indian food. For those after a memento of their meal here, there is a little shop in the entrance lobby.

The Providores

Innovative XX

A/C

109 Marylebone High St — ⊖ Bond Street
✉ W1U 4RX — **G2**
✆ (020) 79356175 – **Fax** (020) 79356877
e-mail anyone@theprovidores.co.uk **Web** www.theprovidores.co.uk

Closed 25-26 and 31 December and 1 January

Carte £23/47

'Fusion cooking' too often means 'confusion cooking' as chefs wrestle with unfamiliar ingredients they recently encountered on an exotic holiday. However, New Zealander Peter Gordon was one of the first to showcase what could be achieved with a sound appreciation and understanding of other cuisines. His first floor restaurant, The Providores, displays his original and complex dishes, in a room of decorative simplicity which is reached by fighting through the ever-popular ground floor Tapa Room where globally inspired tapas is served.
The menu may seem full of unusual and unfamiliar sounding ingredients but the keen young staff are more than happy to answer questions. The wine list has some interesting Kiwi selections.

Roka

Japanese XX

A/C VISA MC AE D

37 Charlotte St
W1T 1RR
(020) 75806464 – **Fax** (020) 75800220
e-mail info@rokarestaurant.com **Web** www.rokarestaurant.com

Goodge Street
I2

Closed 25-26 December and 1 January

Menu £25/50 – Carte £28/39

When a restaurant has been designed by a company called 'Super Potato' you can be pretty sure it's going to be all shiny and modern, and Roka doesn't disappoint. The walls are made of glass so expect passers-by to gaze covetously at your lunch and they open up fully in summer (the walls, not the passers-by). There's also a lot of wood, from the tables to the large counter wrapped around the robata grill where the chefs all do their thing in full view. The menus can appear a little bewildering at first so don't be afraid to ask for help. The grill is the main event but it's certainly worth ordering from a variety of sections and the dishes have a robustness that belies their delicate presentation.
There's a great bar downstairs.

Ozer

Turkish XX

A/C VISA MC AE

4-5 Langham Pl, Regent St
W1B 3DG
(020) 73230505 – **Fax** (020) 73230111
e-mail info@sofra.co.uk **Web** www.sofra.co.uk

Oxford Circus
H2

Carte £15/28

The front section, for cocktails, can take a good pounding in the evenings, especially in the summer when the large windows at the front are thrown open onto Regent Street, and the place is seemingly packed with BBC staff discussing DJ's salaries.
If you fight your way through, you'll find yourself in a spacious yet equally frenetic restaurant. It's decorated in very bold colours of red and gold and framed by an ornately modern chandelier. Noise levels remain high, especially when the music is pumped up.
Service makes up in efficiency what it may lack in personality, while the menu offers a full range of fresh and revitalising Turkish food. Fish lovers and vegetarians are particularly well catered for.

Rosmarino

Italian XX

1 Blenheim Terrace
NW8 0EH
(020) 73285014 – **Fax** (020) 76252779
e-mail rosmarinouk@yahoo.co.uk

⊖ St John's Wood
PLAN page 257 G2

A/C VISA MC AE

Closed 25 December, 1 January and lunch Friday-Sunday

Carte £25/32

Residents of St John's Wood may enjoy easy access to Lord's but they are not exactly overwhelmed by places to eat in their neighbourhood. At least they have Rosmarino, an Italian restaurant which combines the looks one usually finds in the West End with the more convivial atmosphere of a local.
The place really comes into its own in the summer with its large raised terrace at the front. Inside, you'll find the chairs are comfortable, the colours bright and the tables set just close enough to one another to create a mood of togetherness. Service may not always have the slickness but has the heart and the menu mixes the traditional specialities one recognises with others displaying some unexpected touches.

Rasa Samudra

Indian seafood and vegetarian XX

5 Charlotte St
W1T 1RE
(020) 76370222 – **Fax** (020) 76370224
Web www.rasarestaurants.com

⊖ Goodge St
I2

MC AE

Closed 24-30 December, 1 January and Sunday lunch

Menu £22.50/30 – Carte £13/24

So how best to draw attention to yourself when you're competing for business in a street filled with an abundance of restaurants and cafés? Full marks go to Rasa Samudra for painting their façade a shocking shade of pink, which certainly makes them stand out, although intriguingly they have also decided to paint the interior in the same hue.
The front room fills up first but go through to the rooms at the back which are far inviting.
The restaurant is also decorated with silks, carvings and assorted Indian ornaments but the food's the main attraction here with the menu divided into two main parts: rich and creamy seafood specialities from Kerala and fragrant vegetarian dishes. Begin your meal by trying typical Keralan tea shop snacks.

Levant

Lebanese XX

Jason Court, 76 Wigmore St — ⊖ Bond Street
W1U 2SJ — **G2**
(020) 72241111 – **Fax** (020) 74861216
e-mail info@levant.co.uk **Web** www.levant.co.uk

Closed 25 December

Menu £15 (lunch) – Carte £24/45

This atmospheric basement restaurant is ideal for entertaining groups of friends - not only are the cocktails as exotic as the low slung, laid-back bar but watching the nightly belly dancing is an activity best appreciated from behind the security of a large table.
The restaurant has turned its basement location into a positive, by decorating the room in a colourful and vibrant manner, with wood carvings, lanterns and the aromatic scent one associates with the mysteries of the Levant.
The Lebanon provides most, but not all, of the inspiration behind the cooking, with the assorted *mezes* and salads providing the best opportunities for sharing with your fellow diners and, as such, another reason for coming in a group.

Caldesi

Italian XX

15-17 Marylebone Lane — ⊖ Bond Street
W1U 2NE — **G2**
(020) 79359226 – **Fax** (020) 79359228
e-mail tuscan@caldesi.com **Web** www.caldesi.com

Closed Sunday, Saturday lunch and Bank Holidays

Carte £34/40

There's something reassuring about a restaurant bearing the owner's name, in this case Giancarlo's, who has been here since 1994. The abundance of mirrored panelling makes the room feel larger than it actually is, while the candlelight adds to the general atmosphere of intimacy and warmth. Chairs can be a little uncomfortable for those who have insufficient padding of their own.
Signor Caldesi hails from Tuscany and it is to this region of Italy that the kitchen seeks inspiration, with the appropriately muscular wines to match. The waiters come dressed in black, know what they're doing and deliver chosen dishes promptly. The striking upstairs room used for private parties comes colourfully painted and has its own bar.

Blandford Street

Modern European XX

5-7 Blandford St — ⊖ Bond Street
✉ W1U 3DB — **G2**
✆ (020) 74869696 – **Fax** (020) 74865067
e-mail Info@blandford-street.co.uk
Web www.blandford-street.co.uk
Closed Sunday, Saturday lunch and Bank Holidays

Menu £23 (lunch) – Carte £27/37

Its frosted glass front and shiny bright interior match perfectly the increasingly sophisticated nature of Marylebone High Street and the surrounding streets. In this age of corporate ownership, bourgeoning franchises and chains, it is becoming increasingly rare to find the restaurant's owner on duty but the genuinely welcoming local atmosphere created here is due in no small part to the presence of the enthusiastic proprietor, Nick Lambert, and he knows all his regulars well.
Hand painted wallpaper and red leather seating add to the slick and contemporary feel while the kitchen makes good use of seasonal ingredients, well sourced from all corners of the British Isles. Dishes are robust in flavour and generous in size.

L'Aventure

French traditional XX

3 Blenheim Terrace — ⊖ St John's Wood
✉ NW8 0EH — **PLAN page 257 G2**
✆ (020) 76246232 – **Fax** (020) 76255548
Closed Easter, Sunday, Saturday lunch and Bank Holidays

Menu £18.50/32.50

You can just about make out the small neon sign through the foliage which twinkles with fairy lights and frames the delightful little terrace. L'Aventure is as French a restaurant as you can get and has been satisfying St John's Wood regulars since 1979. It is also a very romantic and intimate little restaurant although, if you want to impress your date, you may want to brush up on your linguistic skills as the handwritten menu is all in French.
That menu contains all the classics for which our Gallic chums are celebrated, along with others displaying the kitchen's own personality. There are daily specials and all courses are satisfyingly robust.
Booted and suited staff ensure it all runs smoothly, with accents as rich as the *pot au chocolat.*

Bertorelli

Italian XX

19-23 Charlotte St — ⊖ Goodge Street
W1T 1RL — **I2**
(020) 76364174 – **Fax** (020) 74678902
Web www.santeonline.co.uk

Closed 24-27 December, 1 January and Sunday

Menu £18.50 (lunch) – Carte £20/45

There are a bewildering number of dining options available in Charlotte Street these days. On the west side of the street is a branch of the Bertorelli chain, which offers a couple more choices to the undecided, as it comes divided into two. The ground floor is the relaxed, café style operation with pizzas and simpler fare on the menu. Upstairs is where you'll find a generally more grown-up affair with more comfortable surroundings.
The tables are nicely dressed and the service more orderly. Sensibly, there's no reinventing of any wheels going on with the cooking. The menu is well balanced and comes with recognisable and reassuringly familiar Italian food. Bills can mount up quickly, though, if you push the proverbial boat out.

Phoenix Palace

Chinese XX

3-5 Glentworth St. — ⊖ Baker Street
NW1 5PG — **F1**
(020) 74863515 – **Fax** (020) 74863401
e-mail phoenixpalace@btconnect.com

Closed 25 December

Menu £16/27 – Carte £20/55

The unassuming entrance gives few hints as to the enormity of what lies within. Firstly, you walk through a small bar, where the photo wall of fame includes Jackie Chan, Gordon Ramsay and Ken Livingstone (which sounds like an interesting table). This leads you into the absolutely vast dining room which has a galleried level and seating for well over 200.
It's nicely decorated, though, with black lacquer, elaborate Oriental artwork and smartly dressed tables. Service is smooth and personable although, perhaps understandably, it can get a little stretched at times.
The menu can appear a little daunting at first, as dishes are numbered and the count doesn't stop until 218. But it is sensibly subdivided and comes with a mix of the recognisable and the more unusual.

Michael Moore

International 

19 Blandford St — ⊖ Baker Street **G2**
✉ W1U 3DH
✆ (020) 72241898 – **Fax** (020) 72240970
Web www.michaelmoorerestaurant.com

Closed Christmas-New Year, Saturday lunch, Sunday and Bank Holidays

Menu £20 (lunch) – Carte £25/40

No, it's not that Michael Moore - although the portly American polemicist clearly enjoys his food - but the name of the chef-owner who runs this sweet little neighbourhood restaurant.
It seats just 32 so booking is imperative to avoid disappointment. The locals clearly know this as most evenings a procession of interlopers try their luck but find themselves welcomed by smug and contented looks from the regulars at their tables.
The chef has worked in kitchens across the continents and his influences are widespread, hence his description of his cooking as 'global cuisine'. However, all his dishes arrive underpinned by a solidly classical base thanks, no doubt, to his time spent in the kitchens of The Savoy and Dorchester Hotels.

Villandry

French 

170 Great Portland St — ⊖ Regent's Park **H1**
✉ W1W 5QB
✆ (020) 76313131 – **Fax** (020) 76313030
e-mail bookatable@villandry.com **Web** www.villandry.com

Closed Sunday dinner and Bank Holidays

Carte £23/35

It describes itself as a 'foodstore, restaurant and bar' but it could also include 'takeaway, bakery, outside caterer and great place to get a picnic'. To the right, as you enter, is the bar which is usually bursting with locals and serves light meals and snacks throughout the day; to the left is a terrific deli, full of very fresh and very appealing seasonal produce. Behind the charcuterie bar is the restaurant which takes its cue from the deli by offering rustic dishes from a well balanced menu, with daily changing *plats de jour*, and an emphasis again on freshness and seasonality.
A pile of daily newspapers and food based magazines make it a perfect place for the single diner or those taking a conversational break.

Union Café

International

96 Marylebone Lane — ⊖ Bond Street **G2**

✉ W1U 2QA

✆ (020) 74864860 – **Fax** (020) 74351537

e-mail unioncafe@brinkleys.com **Web** www.brinkleys.com

Closed 25-26 December, 1 January and Sunday dinner

Carte £22/35

This corner restaurant, with its arched windows and welcoming clamour of contentment, fits seamlessly into the surroundings of this rapidly smartening neighbourhood. Inside, it's all open-plan, with the chefs on view at one end of the room and exposed air conditioning vents overhead. Comforts are all very classless and egalitarian, with uncovered tables and chairs from Van Gogh's bedroom.

The menu represents that section of the culinary zeitgeist where influences range from Thailand to the Med, and those coming in for a post work bowl of pasta are as welcome as those going high on the hog. The young staff come dressed in black T-shirts and make up for any efficiency deficiencies thanks to their sunny dispositions.

Caffè Caldesi

Italian 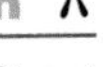

Ist Floor,118 Marylebone Lane — ⊖ Bond Street **G2**

✉ W1U 2QF

✆ (020) 79351144 – **Fax** (020) 79358832

e-mail people@caldesi.com **Web** www.caldesi.com

Closed Christmas and Bank Holidays

Carte £28/34

This is more than merely a younger sibling to the owner's other restaurant, Caldesi, for this is the sort of place every neighbourhood would love to have on its doorstep. You can pop into the ground floor of this bright converted pub for coffee, snacks or a bottle of wine or go upstairs to the simply furnished restaurant where the cooking is as vibrant as the atmosphere, while service comes with a certain vim. Caldesi may focus more on Tuscany, but here at Caffe Caldesi the influences derive from all parts of Italy but also include some lesser-known recipes and undiscovered treasures.

Those feeling particularly inspired by the experience merely have to go next door to enrol in the cookery school.

Chada Chada

Thai

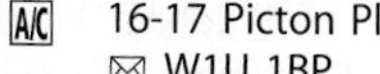

16-17 Picton Pl — ⊖ Bond Street
✉ W1U 1BP — **G2**
✆ (020) 79358212 – **Fax** (020) 79242178
e-mail enquiry@chadathai.com **Web** www.chadathai.com

Closed Sunday and Bank Holidays

Menu £12.50 (lunch) – Carte £16/37

In Picton Place, just slightly removed from the melee of populist eateries in James Street, sits Chada Chada, a Thai restaurant and offspring of the Battersea original. Its comforts may be modest but it has an appealingly sweet atmosphere, thanks largely to the staff who always appear to have just been told a good joke. The first half of the restaurant allows you views of the open kitchen and there is a nicely decorated downstairs room which is used more as an overflow. The seats are not overly upholstered but fortunately delivery from the kitchen is fairly swift. The dishes on the menu are numbered and go all the way up to 112 but are clearly divided. They come authentically prepared, generously proportioned and appropriately priced.

Fishworks

Seafood 

89 Marylebone High St — ⊖ Baker Street
✉ W1U 4QW — **G2**
✆ (020) 79359796 – **Fax** (020) 79358796
e-mail Marylebone@fishworks.co.uk **Web** www.fishworks.co.uk

Closed Monday – booking essential

Carte £25/49

Following the success of the first outlet in Chiswick, there followed Fishworks Number Two which slotted effortlessly into Marylebone High Street which is positively awash with restaurants and cafés these days.
The principle remains the same: the front section is your local fishmonger - for when you're knocking up that little Rick Stein number at home – which in turn leads into a bright and simple restaurant where seafood is the catch of the day.
The menu is really quite substantial and your choice of fish can arrive at your table by means of frying or grilling. Along with lobsters, prawns and assorted shellfish, there are platters and oysters and even a separate menu for the kids.
Perhaps we're finally realising we live on an island.

The Salt House

Gastropub 

63 Abbey Rd
NW8 0AE
(020) 73286626 – **Fax** (020) 76044804

St John's Wood
PLAN page 257 G2

VISA

Closed 25 December

Carte £18/30

Despite changing their name from The Salt House to The Abbey Road, then back again to The Salt House, this remains a reliable and inviting neighbourhood pub, with cooking that has a sunny, country feel and comes in man-size portions.

The dining room's a few steps down from the bar at the back, where the large picture windows overlook the pleasant semi-enclosed outside terrace and its style is of the relaxed, higgledy-piggledy school, with posters and lamps; some tables are dressed with tablecloths, others are nude. There's an upstairs for the weekend overflow and a snackier menu available in the bar.

If approaching by car, allow for the extra time spent at a certain zebra crossing, as Beatles fans remove their shoes and have their photos taken.

THE WINTER'S TALE

Conspiracy theorists still like to claim that 17C man of letters Sir Francis Bacon wrote Shakespeare's plays, but more startling (and true) is the fact that Bacon lost his life in the furtherance of culinary science. The Highgate resident tried to prove that meat could be preserved by freezing. Unfortunately, while putting this to the test by stuffing a dead chicken with snow he caught a chill, which eventually killed him.

Bloomsbury, Hatton Garden & Holborn

C. Eymenier/MICHELIN

From the highs of Senate House and the Centre Point Tower to the lows of the Fleet Valley, this is an area steeped in history. With its gracious streets and tree-lined squares, Bloomsbury is famed for its intellect, and houses such august institutions as the British Museum, RADA and University College. Not to be outdone by its bluestocking neighbour, Holborn is the city's legal district and home to the **Royal Courts of Justice**: pin-striped lawyers, gowned barristers and even the odd be-wigged judge can all be seen on the narrow streets, many of which feature in Dickens' novels – he lived in the area and there is a museum devoted to his life on **Doughty Street**. Tucked into the north-east corner of Holborn, Hatton Garden may not have as many academic credentials to its name, but as London's jewellery quarter and home to over 300 businesses devoted to the trade, it has more than enough bling to keep up with its bigger neighbours.

The area has a superb array of traditional pubs, some descended from 17C coffee houses, as well as a good selection of bars. It also hosts a wide range of restaurants with something to suit every taste and budget – from student eateries where poets and artists can debate long into the night, to more upmarket establishments suitable for celebrating a big day in court.

A LITTLE HISTORY...

The land on which Bloomsbury stands was sold in the 13C to William of Blemund: his name, together with 'bury' or manor, survives as the district's name. **Bloomsbury Square** was originally laid out in the 1650s as part of the push to expand London – such squares were designed to function as "little towns" according to the diarist John Evelyn, and Bloomsbury retains that sense of identity today. It's particularly famous for the eponymous 1920s group of artists and writers – the most famous of whom was Virginia Woolf – who were known as much for their tangled love lives as for their fierce intellect and avant-garde ideas.

The British Museum – with art and antiques from around the world and the dazzling space of the Great Court, recently redesigned by Sir Normal Foster – is well worth a visit. You might then wander down to **Russell Square**, overlooked by the art deco Senate House – these days it houses the University of London Library but during the Second World War it acted as the Ministry of Information and was the inspiration for the Ministry of Truth in George Orwell's *1984*.

Meander west down Southampton Row and perhaps linger at **Lincoln's Inn**, one of the four Inns of Court established as centres for learning in the 14thC. Lincoln's Inn Field, once a popular venue for duels, is now a calm, green space amid the bustle of busy Holborn. From there you might stroll down to **Gough Square** where the house of another famous resident, Dr Johnson, survives and has been restored to its original 18C condition. While the main streets of Holborn are lined with chi chi bars

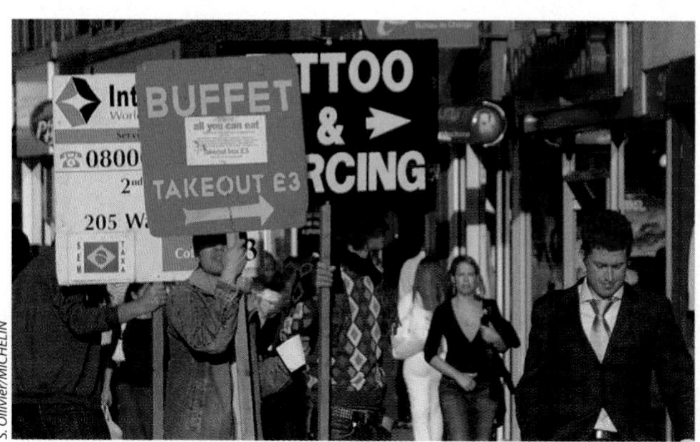

S. Ollivier/MICHELIN

and some of the best tailors outside Savile Row – lawyers have to look the part – the winding backstreets, a legacy of medieval civic planning or lack thereof, are stuffed with sandwich shops, old pubs and eclectic eateries.

Hatton Garden was named after Sir Christopher Hatton, a favourite of Elizabeth I. The story goes that he took a fancy to the gardens of the Bishops of Ely; at first the bishop was reluctant to give up the land but changed his mind after the Queen made him an offer he couldn't refuse. He was paid £10, ten loads of hay and a red rose each year. The rents in Hatton Garden are considerably steeper these days but there are other reminders of the district's past. Strawberries from the gardens are mentioned in Shakespeare's *Richard III,* and a Strawberry Fayre is held every June. Newly-engaged couples wandering dewy-eyed as they shop for engagement rings are a common sight; luckily some of Holborn's finest pubs, many of which offer excellent food as well, are on hand to provide Dutch courage for those parting with their money.

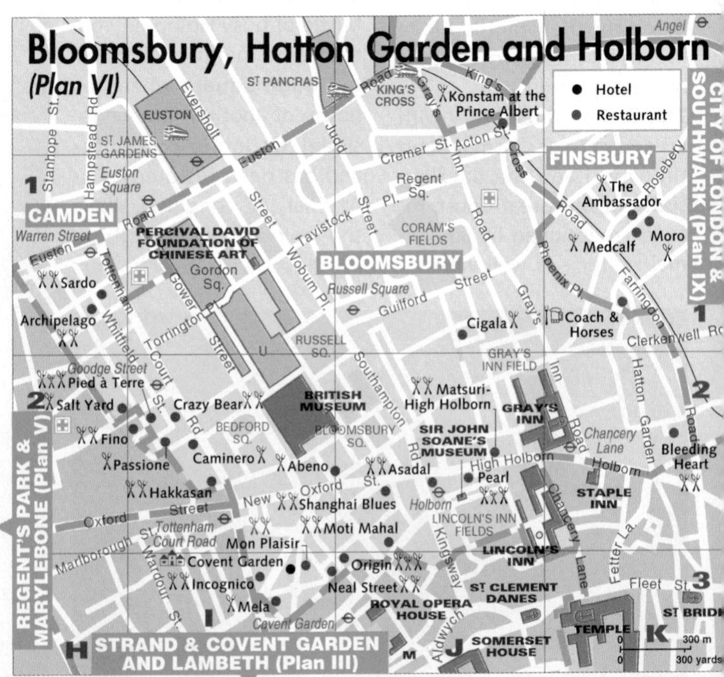

Pied à Terre ✿✿

Innovative XXX

34 Charlotte St — Goodge Street
W1T 2NH — I2
(020) 76361178 – **Fax** (020) 79161171
Web www.pied-a-terre.co.uk

Closed last week December-first week January, Saturday lunch and Sunday

Menu £30/60

A/C · VISA · MC · AE

Pied à Terre

Pied à Terre opened in 1991 and proved that Charlotte Street could offer so much more than plate-smashing Greek restaurants. Its success has allowed others to try their luck in this busy street but, in cooking terms, it remains head and shoulders above them all. This hard earned reputation was put at risk in 2004 when the restaurant was gutted by a fire. It took nearly a year to re-open but was rewarded by its loyal clientele who came flocking back. Founder David Moore and his co-owner, Australian head chef Shane Osborn, have redesigned the restaurant. It now comes divided into two, with four tables in the front section and ten in the main one. Here, a skylight brightens a room decorated with brown suede on one wall and smoked glass on the other. There's now a bar upstairs and a private dining room.
The service is as polished as the glasses and ensures one's journey through the set price menu is an effortlessly enjoyable experience. That menu showcases the kitchen's deep understanding of classical techniques and whose delicate touch produces dishes full of originality and poise.

A LA CARTE

FIRST COURSE

- Scallop ceviche with avocado and crème fraiche purée, basil oil and sesame filo.
- Pan-fried foie gras with carrots and cumin purée and caramel foam.

MAIN COURSE

- Best End of Salt Marsh lamb, courgette and basil cream, pine nut and lemon emulsion.
- Slow poached wild sea bass with crushed peas and shellfish bisque.

DESSERT

- Bitter chocolate tart with stout ice cream and macadamia nut mousse.
- Damson jelly with buffalo ricotta, orange salad and fromage frais sorbet.

Origin

Modern European XXX

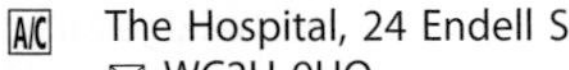

The Hospital, 24 Endell St ⊖ Covent Garden
✉ WC2H 9HQ **J3**
✆ (020) 71709200 – **Fax** (020) 71709221
Web www.origin-restaurant.com

Closed Saturday lunch, Sunday and Bank Holidays

Carte £33/49

The Hospital is another in the list of private members clubs which are springing up everywhere - this one is aimed at those in the 'creative industries', which presumably includes anyone who have ever filled in their own expenses claim. Origin is the restaurant on the first floor and is open, along with its accompanying bar, to non members. Softly lit and stylishly decked out with a certain retro ebullience, it features an impressive collection of artwork, including pieces by David Hockney.

The menu is appealingly laid out, with all main courses also available to have as starters. The style and presentation of the cooking is as contemporary as the surroundings in which it is served. Lighter, more tapas sized dishes are on offer in the bar.

Pearl

Innovative XXX

at Renaissance Chancery Court H., ⊖ Holborn
252 High Holborn ✉ WC1V 7EN **J2**
✆ (020) 78297000 – **Fax** (020) 78299889

Closed Saturday lunch and Sunday

Menu £26.50/45 – Carte £30/45

If we'd known how grand all these banking halls were, we'd have asked more questions about where our money was. This one belonged to Pearl Assurance, before becoming part of the multi-syllabled Renaissance Chancery Court Hotel and their appropriately named restaurant, Pearl.

It must have been a daunting space for the designers to fill, but they pull it off successfully courtesy of a stylish, and impressively stocked bar, with its striking design of hanging threads of pearl, lighting that is both subtle and clever, and the addition in the middle of the room of a vast cave holding an impressive 1400 wine bottles.

Expect cooking that adds touches of originality and elaboration to dishes with a mostly classical base.

Mon Plaisir

French traditional XX

VISA 21 Monmouth St ⊖ Covent Garden
✉ WC2H 9DD **I3**
✆ (020) 78367243 – **Fax** (020) 72404774
e-mail eatafrog@mail.com **Web** www.monplaisir.co.uk
Closed Saturday lunch, Sunday and Bank Holidays

Menu £15.95 (lunch) – Carte £26/42

London's oldest French restaurant is also one of its most gloriously unpretentious and individual. If you think the Eurostar transports you to France in an instant, try walking into Mon Plaisir, family run for over fifty years, where cries of *'Bonjour!'* greet every arrival.
The walls are decorated with a plethora of posters, pictures and paraphernalia and the bar is from a Lyonnais brothel. Regulars all have their favourite of the numerous interconnecting rooms, all of which ooze unmistakeable Gallic charm.
But this is no themed restaurant. This is as real as the *coq au vin* or *cassolette d'escargots*. The fixed price lunch and pre-theatre menus represent excellent value and periodically held evenings featuring a particular region of France are popular events.

Incognico

French XX

A/C 117 Shaftesbury Ave ⊖ Tottenham Court Road
✉ WC2H 8AD **I3**
VISA ✆ (020) 78368866 – **Fax** (020) 72409525
Web www.incognico.com
Closed Christmas, Sunday and Bank Holidays

AE Carte £21/32

The name is not down to a faulty spell-check but is a none-too-subtle reference to the founder, Nico Ladenis, who reached majestic heights with his own cooking before retiring from the kitchen. His legacy in London not only includes a number of talented chefs who learnt from him, but also this authentic brasserie, designed by the ubiquitous David Collins.
The wood panelling, red leather chairs and slick way it is run gives the impression that it's been part of the London scene far longer than it actually has. The brasserie theme is very evident in the menu which is a successful mix of French and Mediterranean influences. Its location and set menus also mean it fits the bill perfectly for those looking for a pre or post theatre restaurant.

Neal Street

Italian XX

26 Neal St ⊖ Covent Garden
WC2H 9QW **I3**
(020) 78368368 – **Fax** (020) 72403964
Web www.carluccios.co.uk

Closed Christmas, Easter, Sunday and Bank Holidays

Menu £25 – Carte £31/48

Lovers of funghi and all things Italian have been coming to Antonio Carluccio's flagship restaurant for over thirty years. Those who share the great man's passion for the mushroom in its many forms will always find it on the menu in one dish or another and all the real enthusiasts are in during truffle season. Lunchtimes are particularly busy here, with a mix of couples, friends and those fortunate enough to be expense account beneficiaries, all generating satisfied murmurs of enjoyment. The room is bright and light and the service is efficient, with many getting that extra attention which comes from being a regular. Those wishing to take a bit of Carluccio home can pop next door where sumptuous bounty is on offer at the Neal Street Food Shop.

Sardo

Italian XX

45 Grafton Way ⊖ Warren Street
W1T 5DQ **H1**
(020) 73872521 – **Fax** (020) 73872559
Web www.sardo-restaurant.com

Closed Saturday lunch and Sunday

Carte £25/34

Some restaurants are full because there are no local alternatives and some are always full because they do everything well - Sardo fits into this latter category. Its sunny and light interior will warm you on a winter's night and entice you in on a summer's evening. It occupies a narrow room where the tables are smartly dressed and are set quite closely together which adds to the atmosphere. This is a central London restaurant which still manages to feel like a local. They also make a real effort with the service which is rarely less than warm and enthusiastic.
Sardinia provides the influences on the menu and indeed many of the ingredients come directly from the area, producing robust and satisfying dishes. There is a sister branch in Primrose Hill.

Hakkasan ✿

Chinese XX

A/C VISA MC AE

8 Hanway Pl
✉ W1T 1HD
(020) 79277000 – **Fax** (020) 79071889
e-mail mail@hakkasan.com

⊖ Tottenham Court Road
I2

Closed 24-25 December

Carte £34/101

Hakkasan

Don't let the shabbiness of Hanway Place and the muscle on the door scare you off: once you're inside, you'll find yourself in one of the most glamorous, original and seductive restaurants around. Alan Yau made his name through the communal inclusiveness of Wagamama but his Hakkasan restaurant is, ironically, all about exclusivity. Stepping down into the cavernous basement will get the pulse going of the most experienced restaurant-goer and the orchid filled reception heightens expectations.
The darkly mysterious and large dining room comes with black lattice oriental screens to separate it from the bar, with light coming from the hazy blue glass and the spot-lit tables.
Hakkasan not only brought a new, nightclub-style chic to restaurants but it also introduced London to a modern interpretation of Chinese cooking. Those who believe authenticity is everything need to relax and open up. Tantalising dim sum is served at lunch, with the dinner menu showcasing delicately crafted, innovative Chinese dishes, some with unexpected or unusual ingredients and added Western sensibilities.

A LA CARTE

FIRST COURSE
- Jasmine tea smoked organic pork ribs.
- Stir-fry wild mushroom and water chestnut lettuce wrap.

MAIN COURSE
- Steamed crab claw in chilli yellow bean sauce.
- Braised belly pork claypot with salted fish, baby leek and dried chilli.

DESSERT
- Mint and fruit salad with vanilla mint syrup.
- Chocolate lemon mousse with coconut jelly.

Matsuri - High Holborn

Japanese XX

VISA Mid City Pl, 71 High Holborn ⊖ Holborn
✉ WC1V 6EA **J2**
✆ (020) 74301970 – **Fax** (020) 74301971
e-mail eat@matsuri-restaurant.com
Web www.matsuri-restaurant.com

Closed 25 December, Sunday and Bank Holidays

Menu £15/70 – Carte £25/43

Not unlike the original branch in St James's, this newer member of the group offers you the choice of three restaurants in one: a large, bright main dining room, a stylish *sushi* bar and, downstairs, an authentic *teppan-yaki* room. Unlike the more traditional looking St James's, this branch is modern and contemporary in its decoration with a mix of slatted screens, glass and clean, crisp lines.
The clued up team are also on the ball, offering helpful advice to any novices and generally being unerringly courteous.
With such a broad range of dishes and styles of cooking, the menus vary enormously in scope. However, what they all share is the use of exemplary ingredients, skilled craftsmanship and precise presentation.

Shanghai Blues

Chinese XX

A/C 193-197 High Holborn ⊖ Holborn
✉ WC1V 7BD **J2**
✆ (020) 74041668 – **Fax** (020) 74041448
e-mail info@shanghaiblues.co.uk **Web** www.shanghaiblues.co.uk

Closed 25 December

Carte £30/50

Another stylish Chinese restaurant arrived in 2005 in the form of Shanghai Blues, housed in the Grade II listed former St Giles library. With seating for 180, the sleek design divides the room into differing spaces, along with a cool bar and mezzanine lounge, and uses hand painted silks, colourful lampshades and Chinese antiques to create a highly original, moody and atmospheric restaurant. The kitchen sticks with the traditional by offering *dim sum* at lunchtime while in the evening the extensive *à la carte* menu offers an array of dishes, including regional specialities from Shanghai.
The wine list features a number of floral wines to accompany the food but the list of Chinese teas, including some unusual blends, is well worth considering.

Fino

Spanish XX

VISA 33 Charlotte St, ⊖ Goodge Street
(entrance on Rathbone St)
MC ✉ W1T 1RR **I2**
AE ✆ (020) 78138010 – **Fax** (020) 78138011
e-mail info@finorestaurant.com **Web** www.finorestaurant.com
Closed 25 December and Bank Holidays

Carte £21/33

They don't make it easy on themselves by giving their address as Charlotte Street when, in fact, the discreet entrance to this basement restaurant is actually on Rathbone Street. Perhaps that's the reason why, once you've descended the staircase, you'll find that it has something of a secretive and local vibe.
Tapas is the order of the day, although it's all structured slightly more formally than you'd find in Spain and the room itself is decidedly more stylish than you'd expect. Five or six dishes per couple to share should suffice, although set menus are available for the undecided. Try a Sherry or something from the exclusively Spanish wine list. Helpful waitresses are more than willing to offer advice as well as a translation of unfamiliar words.

Crazy Bear

South-East Asian XX

A/C 26-28 Whitfield St ⊖ Goodge Street
✉ W1T 2RG **I2**
VISA ✆ (020) 76310088 – **Fax** (020) 76311188
Web www.crazybeargroup.co.uk
MC Closed Saturday lunch, Sunday and Bank Holidays
AE

Carte £23/34

This bear's not just crazy, he's exotic and somewhat mysterious. Even the sign is just a discreet floor mosaic by the door. The dining room on the ground floor is an effervescent fusion of art deco, Asian ornament and cosmopolitan gloss. Downstairs, the idiosyncratic design is given full rein in the ultra trendy bar and is well worth a trip in itself, provided you pass muster on the personal presentation stakes. A hostess is there at the door to greet arrivals and deliver them safely; service is well organised and pleasantly informal.
More sensory challenges come courtesy of the extensive menus which take their influence and inspiration from a number of Asian countries but do so with due respect for the ingredients.

Archipelago

Innovative XX

110 Whitfield St — ⊖ Goodge Street
✉ W1T 5ED — **H1**
✆ (020) 73833346 – **Fax** (020) 73837181
Web www.archipelago-restaurant.co.uk
Closed Christmas, Saturday lunch and Sunday

VISA, MC, AE, Diners

Carte £32/37

Archipelago's strikingly original and exotic menu means that you don't have to be a C-list celebrity in the jungle if you fancy facing your very own 'bush-tucker-trial'. Peacock, locusts, wildebeest and crocodile have all featured at some time, as has a dessert of chocolate covered scorpion. This is food designed for those living by the maxim that you should try everything once, although there are more familiar sounding dishes for those of a more delicate disposition.
The décor is as quirky as the food, with every nook and cranny stuffed with trinkets, artefacts and ornaments, adding to the atmosphere of mystery and intrigue.
Despite its laborious reservation system, this is worth trying as it's a genuine one-off.

Bleeding Heart

French XX

Bleeding Heart Yard (off Greville St) — ⊖ Farringdon
✉ EC1N 8SJ — **K2**
✆ (020) 72428238 – **Fax** (020) 7831 1402
Web www.bleedingheart.co.uk
Closed Christmas, Saturday, Sunday and Bank Holidays

VISA, MC, AE, Diners

Carte £24/40

The restaurant is named after the cobbled courtyard in which it is found - Bleeding Heart Yard certainly has its own dramatic history, involving grisly murders and crimes of passion in the 17th Century and is mentioned by Charles Dickens in *Little Dorrit*.
The basement restaurant in this notable location is a popular choice for business lunches due to its proximity to The City but at dinner it becomes an altogether more romantic spot, with its wood panelling, candlelight and authentic sense of history.
The menu has a strong French accent and the wine list is one of the best and includes wines from the owners' own vineyard in New Zealand.
With a more informal bistro, tavern and crypt also available, all dining options appear to be covered.

Moti Mahal

Indian XX

A/C 45 Great Queen St ⊖ Covent Garden
✉ WC2B 5AA **J2**
✆ (020) 72409329 – **Fax** (020) 78360790
VISA **e-mail** reservations@motimahal-uk.com
Web www.motimahal-uk.com
MC Closed 25-26 December, 1 January and Sunday
AE **Menu £14.95 (lunch) – Carte £28/36**

Moti Mahal continues the trend for Indian restaurants to be big, confident and stylish. Tandoor is the speciality of the house here, in deference to the owners' original restaurants in Delhi. The kitchen exhibits a skilled, classically trained base but they work within a more contemporary idiom and presentation is skilled and attractive.
The ground floor is where the action is, including the cooking action in the open-plan kitchen, and the general atmosphere is one of noisy contentment with a feeling of spaciousness. Those who prefer a little more in the way of seduction and discretion should head to the moodier and gentler surroundings of the basement restaurant.
Bar lovers will find an impressive choice, from champagne to whisky.

Asadal

Korean XX

A/C 227 High Holborn ⊖ Holborn
✉ WC1V 7DA **J2**
VISA ✆ (020) 74309006
e-mail info@asadal.co.uk **Web** www.asadal.co.uk
MC Closed 25 December, 1 January and Sunday lunch
AE **Menu £17.50 – Carte £9/25**

Every nationality of cuisine has enjoyed its moment in the spotlight and now Asadal, a basement restaurant adjacent to Holborn tube, successfully argues the case for Korean cooking to be given a higher profile.
There may be a barbecue in the centre of most of the tables but there is so much more to Korean cooking. The philosophy is built upon harmony of taste, it's all made for sharing and there's even a health dividend to most of the specialities.
Novices will find that the menu is helpfully descriptive but don't be shy about using the call buttons under the table to summon help.
The room is a perfectly comfortable, with lots of wood and plenty of partitions; there are quieter corners for those wishing to escape the general clamour.

Passione

Italian

10 Charlotte St — ⊖ Tottenham Court Road
✉ W1T 2LT — **I2**
✆ (020) 76362833 – **Fax** (020) 76362889
e-mail liz@passione.co.uk **Web** www.passione.co.uk

VISA · MC · AE · Diners

Closed Christmas, Saturday lunch and Sunday – booking essential

Carte £40/49

Chef owner Gennaro Contaldo, Jamie Oliver's great mentor, hails originally from Amalfi and it is from the sun-drenched Southern Italian coast that he seeks inspiration for his cooking. The menu offers a wide selection of dishes using the very best fresh and seasonal produce and dishes such as rabbit with rosemary and wild sorrel risotto remain perennial favourites. The restaurant, like the cooking, comes refreshingly free of unnecessary adornment. It is warm, simply decorated and brightly coloured.
In a street offering a plethora of dining options, Passione stands out not just for the quality of the cooking but also for its intimate and relaxed atmosphere. Many clearly agree as it is always busy so reservations are essential.

Cigala

Spanish

54 Lamb's Conduit St — ⊖ Holborn
✉ WC1N 3LW — **J1**
✆ (020) 74051717 – **Fax** (020) 72429949
e-mail tasty@cigala.co.uk **Web** www.cigala.co.uk

VISA · MC · AE · Diners

Closed 24-26 December, 1 January, Easter Sunday and Monday

Menu £18 (lunch) – Carte £230/35

The young chef-owner proves at Cigala that he has genuine passion and understanding of Spanish cooking in all its vibrant colours and sunny flavours. The restaurant itself is simply furnished in a clean, bright style with the large picture windows overlooking the part-pedestrianised street outside. The atmosphere is never less than convivial, especially in the more intimate evenings.
The staff all display a keen willingness to help and advise and the menu is complemented by an exclusively Spanish wine list with some very reasonably priced bottles, as well an impressive selection of Sherries. Lunchtimes represent particularly good value; a tapas menu is served in the basement bar.

Salt Yard

Mediterranean

54 Goodge St ⊖ Goodge Street
✉ W1T 4NA **H2**
(020) 76370657 – **Fax** (020) 75807435
e-mail info@saltyard.co.uk **Web** www.saltyard.co.uk

Closed Christmas-New Year, Sunday, Saturday lunch and Bank Holidays

Carte £20/40

These days we live and work in more flexible, less structured times and restaurants have had to learn how to adapt. Salt Yard shows how flexibility can be translated into a menu: it has adopted Spanish tapas, added an extra Italian flavour and allows customers to pop in either for a quick bite or something more substantial. The ground floor is given over to the bar where there can be fewer greater pleasures that pairing with your wine or sherry some sliced cured ham, which here they serve on little wooden boards.
Downstairs is more a restaurant, with comfortable leather chairs but always a lively atmosphere. The well sourced and well priced tapas come full of colour and flavour and are best enjoyed when shared. Vegetarians will also find they've got plenty of choice.

Camerino

Italian

16 Percy St ⊖ Tottenham Court Road
✉ W1T 1DT **I2**
(020) 76379900 – **Fax** (020) 76379696
Web www.camerinorestaurant.com

Closed 25 December, 1 January, Saturday lunch and Sunday

Menu £23.50 – Carte £28/37

Italian for 'theatre dressing room' Camerino occupies a useful position close to, but sufficiently removed from, the frantic activity of Charlotte Street and Tottenham Court Road. The sense of the theatrical comes courtesy of the large red curtains which bring vibrancy and a sense of oomph to the room, with skylights adding more light. It's comfortable without being formal, relaxed without being too casual.
The kitchen successfully adopts the first rule of cooking - use good quality and very fresh produce. The end result is Italian dishes which are full of flavour and easy to eat.
If you see any bewildered looking diners outside, explain that this restaurant was indeed once called Paolo, but remains under the same ownership.

Mela

Indian

A/C VISA MC AE D

152-156 Shaftesbury Ave ⊖ Leicester Square
⊠ WC2H 8HL **I3**
(020) 78368635 – **Fax** (020) 73790527
e-mail info@melarestaurant.co.uk **Web** www.melarestaurant.co.uk

Closed 25-26 December

Menu £10.95/34.95 – Carte £14/33

Decoratively it's light years away from your traditional Indian restaurant. In place of fading flock wallpaper and a sticky carpet comes brightly coloured walls, twinkling lights, wood flooring and a general air of freshness and vitality. The resplendently attired staff are also demonstratively proud of their restaurant and display a superior understanding of customer care.
The kitchen takes Indian country cooking as its starting point and, alongside the variety of keenly priced lunch menus, comes a comprehensive *à la carte* menu helpfully divided into "traditional", featuring favourites from across India, to "exotic" which allows the chefs to show off their creativity. Its Shaftesbury Avenue location makes it a popular with theatre-goers.

Abeno

Japanese (Okonomi-Yaki)

A/C VISA MC AE D

47 Museum St ⊖ Tottenham Court Road
⊠ WC1A 1LY **I2**
(020) 74053211 – **Fax** (020) 74053212
e-mail okonomi@abeno.co.uk **Web** www.abeno.co.uk

Closed 25-26 and 31 December and 1 January

Menu £7.50 (lunch)/19.80 – Carte £14/34

In among the antiquarian bookshops and art galleries and, conveniently, just yards from the British Museum, sits this modest little restaurant which offers something altogether different, particularly to those who think they know Japanese food.
The speciality here is *Okonomi-yaki*, a dish which originated in Osaka and which represents their equivalent of fast food. It's a cross between a pancake and a pizza - the latter bearing a similarity in that it is the choice of accompanying filling that gives it the individual flavour. They are prepared at your table which doubles as a hotplate or *teppan* and are satisfyingly filling, although you can choose the size as well as the accompaniments. Novices should not be afraid to ask for advice.

Bayswater & Maida Vale

S. Ollivier/MICHELIN

As hinterlands to London stations go, the area behind **Paddington** used to be one of the worst. While the railway terminus was fondly regarded for its graceful Brunel spans and association with a certain bear who liked marmalade sandwiches, the surrounding bedsits, derelict goods yards and worse were somewhat less salubrious.

Today, the situation is all change, led by the reclamation of the old canal basin, which has been turned into a mini-Canary Wharf of blue chip HQs set against a modern waterscape. Uncannily convincing human sculptures substitute for a lack of pedestrians outside of business hours - but residential complexes are going up fast and it won't be long till the transformation from seedy to "chi chi" is complete.

The canals

Heading up the basin, the narrow-boat moorings and foliage thicken out as you approach the more established area of Warwick Avenue, popularly known as **Little Venice**. The appellation is a tad fanciful, referring to the intersection of the Regent's and Grand Union Canals, but Londoners have a habit of making the most of such features. Indeed, absent the intrusion of crooning gondoliers, lovely waterside cafes and pubs have a pleasant peacefulness that is all but miraculous considering that, beyond the tree line, the Westway roars past.

Further on and the grand esplanades and chic corners of **Maida Vale** may not claim a Venetian connection, but they do evoke the flavour of a Parisian arrondissement - ironic, considering the area is named after a British victory in the Napoleonic Wars. The ubiquity of purpose-built Edwardian flats makes for a highly distinctive street scene and one of the capital's most well-to-do addresses. Behind the mansion blocks, sequestered communal gardens lie almost entirely hidden from view. Meanwhile, the Institute of Psychoanalysis - one of a scattering of curious facilities that eccentrically

S. Ollivier/MICHELIN

S. Ollivier/MICHELIN

colour the suburban character - attempts to probe the secret spaces of the mind.

Ducking and shopping

Duck back under the Westway and you're on **Westbourne Grove**, a perennially hip shopping street claimed by both **Bayswater** and neighbouring **Notting Hill**. But while familiar chain stores begin to outnumber the darling little boutiques as you head towards the eastern district, Bayswater itself has enjoyed something of a resurgence in cool in recent years.

Whose side are you on ?

Though it has long been known for its cosmopolitan nature and convenient location within striking distance of the capital's glamour hotspots, Bayswater used to suffer from its reputation - in estate-agent speak - of being 'the wrong side of the park'. Those who could afford to bought in

Knightsbridge and **Kensington** to the south, resulting in an odd hodgepodge ghetto north of Hyde Park, a combination of diaspora communities, transient hotel populations and stifling middle classness (this, after all, was where Charles Ryder ached to escape from in *Brideshead Revisited*).

ON THE UP

The bed and breakfasts are still here and the turnover of residents remains relatively high - but those choosing to make Bayswater their home are adding some real jazz. The area first knew it had arrived when Madonna bought a £7 million townhouse at its edge, with her erstwhile pro-

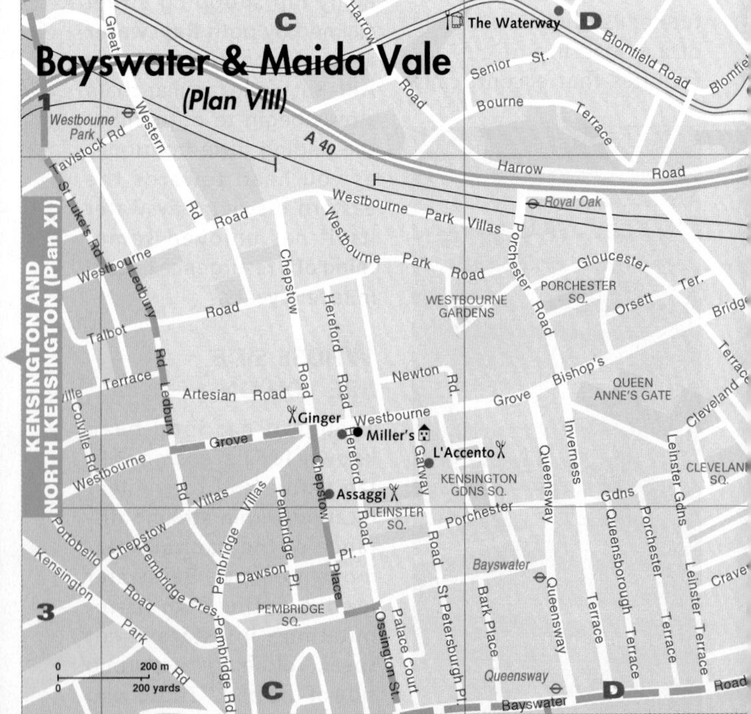

ducer wunderkind William Orbit close by. Yet it was the revelation that one Mr and Mrs Blair had purchased a post-prime ministerial pile in **Connaught Square** that really put the district on the map.

Their instinct may well be right - Bayswater is a handsome, diverse but neglected corner of London that seems to be on the up. Walking down **Queensway** has always exposed the eavesdropper to a barrage of languages, from Greek to Portuguese to Arabic. Now it is the area itself which is finding its voice.

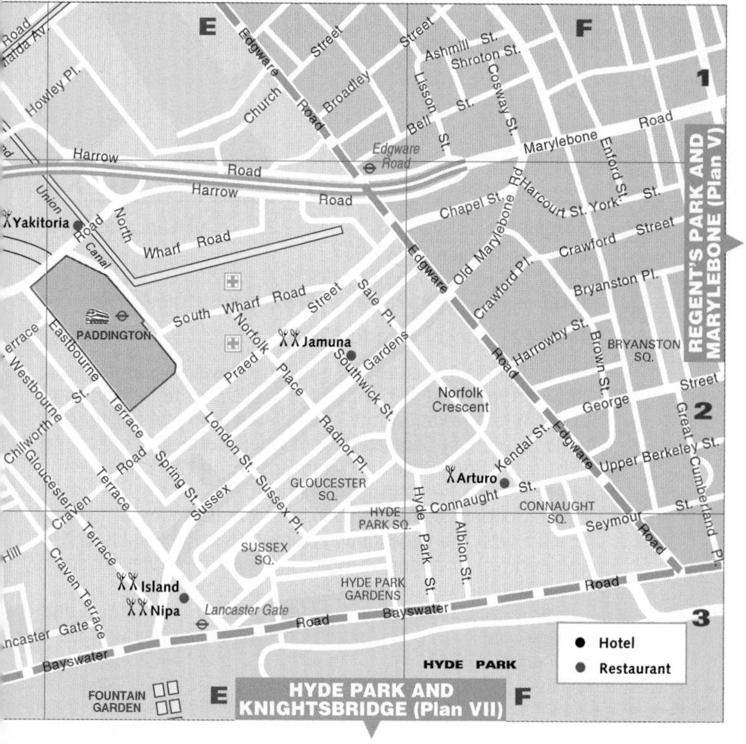

Jamuna

Indian XX

A/C VISA MC AE

38A Southwick St ⊖ Edgware Road
✉ W2 1JQ **E2**
✆ (020) 77235056 – **Fax** (020) 77061870
e-mail info@jamuna.co.uk **Web** www.jamuna.co.uk

Closed 25-26 December, 1 January and Sunday

Carte £24/43

Its largely transient population means that Bayswater has never been an area particularly noted for the quality of its restaurants. Jamuna is the latest to try its luck and its distinctly smart looking façade tells you that this is no ordinary Indian restaurant. It's similarly well turned-out inside, with neatly laid tables and modern artwork for sale on the walls, although, curiously, there are no clues in the décor with regard to the nationality of the cooking.
Locals seem hesitant in sampling the restaurant and a busy ambience remains elusive. That is a shame because the cooking is good. It has a broad regional base but with few predictable offerings. Dishes are well presented, display a certain refinement and are full of flavour.

Island

Modern European XX

A/C VISA MC AE

at Royal Lancaster H., ⊖ Lancaster Gate
Lancaster Terrace ✉ W2 2TY **E3**
✆ (020) 75516070 – **Fax** (020) 75516071
e-mail eat@islandrestaurant.co.uk **Web** www.islandrestaurant.co.uk

Menu £21 (lunch) – Carte £24/36

This restaurant is actually part of the Royal Lancaster Hotel, although you wouldn't know it if you enter from Bayswater Road. Far removed from the hotel dining rooms of old, this is a modern, tastefully decorated room where subtle use of lighting adds to the general calming atmosphere, in contrast with the never less than frenzied traffic outside.
The semi-open kitchen prides itself on its modern style of cooking, with the occasional adventurous combination, and is executed with considerably more skill than the indifferent spelling on the menu would suggest.
Service is well meaning and a keenly priced set menu is also available until 7pm. The raised cocktail bar appears to be a destination in itself.

Yakitoria

Japanese XX

25 Sheldon Sq
W2 6EY
(020) 32143000
Web www.yakitoria.co.uk

Paddington
E2

Closed Christmas, Saturday lunch and Sunday

Carte £26/36

'Paddington Central' is the imaginative name for this new development next to the station and after all the office blocks now come the restaurants. Yakitoria's owners have several places in Moscow but here they turn more to the US for their take on Japanese food, for it includes *aburi sushi* and assorted rolls alongside the Tokyo and Osaki specialities. The *Kushi-yaki* or skewers are something of a house speciality. Bento boxes are available for the local businesses.
The place is big in size, funky in design and lively in atmosphere. The service is enthusiastic and the chefs, in their natty little kimonos, go about their business with vim and vigour. There's direct access from Platform 8 for any sushi-loving commuters.

Nipa

Thai XX

at Royal Lancaster H.,
Lancaster Terrace W2 2TY
(020) 72626737 – **Fax** (020) 77243191
Web www.niparestaurant.co.uk

Lancaster Gate
E3

Closed Saturday lunch, Sunday and Bank Holidays

Menu £14.90/32 – Carte £22/28

The style and concept are based on the restaurant of the same name in the Landmark Hotel in Bangkok. This little Nipa is concealed on the first floor of the Royal Lancaster Hotel in the altogether less exotic surroundings of Bayswater, but the charming service from the traditionally dressed staff will at least stir memories of the Sukhumvit Road for some.
Its rich teak interior, with traditional Thai furnishings, urns and orchids, makes the room an enchanting setting in which to enjoy the fragrant Thai cooking, prepared by the all-female brigade of chefs. Dishes come helpfully scored as to their relative heat and reveal a harmonious and aromatic blend of flavours. At lunch and early evening the *khantoke* or 'all in one' menu is available.

Assaggi ✿

Italian

39 Chepstow Pl
(above Chepstow pub)
W2 4TS
(020) 77925501
e-mail nipi@assaggi.demon.co.uk **Web** www.assaggi.com
Closed 2 weeks Christmas, Sunday and Bank Holidays – booking essential
Carte £37

Bayswater
C2

Assaggi

Those in any doubt about the fact that Michelin Stars are awarded for the quality of the food on the plate and not for the style or decoration of a place should come to Assaggi. This is, in essence, just a sparsely decorated room above a pub, but the cooking is great. The welcome is still never less than fulsome and the atmosphere's wonderfully clubby – you feel everyone's found their own secret restaurant. The menu is written proudly in Italian - those who can't bluff their way through should wait for the verbal English translation which arrives proudly and loudly. There is, however, no great secret to the cooking, which is a lesson for all chefs: the ingredients are gloriously fresh and taste of themselves.

The crisp Sardinian bread *carta di musica* is a terrific way to start any meal and the balance and vitality of the dishes leave one feeling decidedly pleased with the world.

It would be nice to just scoot along to places like Assaggi when the mood takes you. Sadly, it is so popular that spontaneity has to be replaced by forward planning as bookings are essential.

A LA CARTE

FIRST COURSE	MAIN COURSE	DESSERT
• Pecorino con carpegna & rucola.	• Nodino di vitello al rosmarino.	• Flourless chocolate cake.
• Tagliolini alle erbe.	• Branzino alla griglia.	• Lemon tart.

L'Accento

Italian

VISA MC AE

16 Garway Rd
W2 4NH
(020) 72432201 – **Fax** (020) 72432201
e-mail laccentorest@aol.com

Bayswater
C2

Closed Sunday

Menu £19.50 – Carte £26/30

Garway Road may not be Bayswater's most iridescent boulevard but L'Accento makes a trip to these parts well worth it.
Italian food is oft the favoured cooking of the seen-it-all international gourmand and the reason is obvious: it lets the ingredients come to the fore, eschews the tendency to over-elaborate and respects the seasons.
This certainly applies here, where the food comes with a robust confidence and straightforwardness. What's more, the set price menu – which runs alongside the *à la carte* - represents exceptionally good value.
The décor is relatively modest but relaxing and the restaurant comes divided into two rooms. There's a palpable sense of neighbourhood and an atmosphere of convivial contentment.

Ginger

Bangladeshi

A/C VISA MC AE

115 Westbourne Grove
W2 4UP
(020) 79081990 – **Fax** (020) 79081991
e-mail info@gingerrestaurant.co.uk

Bayswater
C2

Closed 25 December – dinner only and lunch Saturday-Sunday

Carte £15/30

Many of London's Indian restaurants are actually Bangladeshi owned and run but, ironically, it has always been fairly difficult finding authentic Bangladeshi cooking. This all changed when Ginger opened. Home cooking and seafood specialities from the sea and rivers of West Bengal are from where the kitchen seeks inspiration. Specialities come with a decidedly healthy aspect, thanks to the natural qualities of the ingredients, and there is a lightness of touch in both spicing and presentation. Its vivid aquamarine façade is reflected in the shiny and contemporary interior, where the service is sweet natured, and the clientele agreeably mixed. The downstairs room used as an overflow on busy nights lacks the charm of the main room.

Arturo

Italian

A/C VISA MC AE

23 Connaught St
W2 2AY
(020) 77063388 – **Fax** (020) 74029195
Web www.arturorestaurant.co.uk
Closed Christmas, Easter and lunch Bank Holidays

Marble Arch
F2

Menu £16 (lunch) – Carte £16/27

Connaught Street stands in stark contrast to the rather drab surroundings of nearby Edgware Road and Arturo is a good example of the type of stylish establishment that is starting to crop up in this street. The large glass façade and moody lighting set the tone for the elegant informality within, with its sleek and modern design. The chef looks to two regions of Italy for inspiration, Tuscany and Sicily, and offers classic dishes from these areas alongside those with more original elements. The exclusively Italian wine list has some interesting little gems and the service is slick and attentive.
It retains the intimacy of a friendly, local Italian and may be just the place to appeal to anyone who owns property in Connaught Square.

The Waterway

Gastropub 

A/C VISA MC AE

54 Formosa St
W9 2JU
(020) 72663557
e-mail info@thewaterway.co.uk **Web** www.thewaterway.co.uk
Closed 25-26 December

Warwick Avenue
D1

Carte £20/28

Check ahead for the forecast because if it's a nice day and you fancy sitting on the terrace, then chances are that it's probably already booked up. You can understand why - it's a great spot, by the Grand Union Canal, to watch the boats go by and a hugely popular choice for a summer barbecue or weekend brunch.
Inside, it's more gastro-bar than pub, with blond wood and leather and a general air of slickness and sophistication. Staff, though, are on hand to prevent it becoming too self-satisfied and service is relaxed and down to earth.
The regularly changing menu offers up a wide selection of pleasingly robust dishes. So, whether you're a burger person or more the belly of pork type there'll be something for you.

Prince Alfred & Formosa Dining Room

Gastropub 

at Prince Alfred,
5A Formosa St ✉ W9 1EE
✆ (020) 72863287
e-mail princealfred@youngs.co.uk

⊖ Warwick Avenue
PLAN page 257 G3

VISA

AE

Carte £19/31

It is possible, if you're approaching from Warrington Crescent, to find yourself seated in the Formosa Dining Room and be virtually unaware of the pub to which it is attached. This would be a crying shame as the Prince Alfred is a magnificent Grade II listed pub which dates back to 1863. Its most striking feature, along with the etched glass, is the partitions creating individual private booths. Heritage enthusiasts may shudder at the more contemporary, almost semi-industrial, dining room which has been attached but local diners seemingly have little regard for such sensibilities and just enjoy the space.

The very open open-kitchen produces robust gastropub staples and the wine lists commendably features over thirty choices by the glass.

ROLL OUT THE BARREL

Horatio Nelson is celebrated by one of London's best-known landmarks; however he was not always treated with such respect. When he fell at the Battle of Trafalgar in 1805, his body was transported back to England preserved in rum or brandy. The story goes that when the ship arrived home the crew had drunk half the spirits from the barrel: although of dubious truth, the tale has given rise to the slang 'tapping the Admiral', for illicit drinking.

City of London, Clerkenwell, Finsbury & Southwark

C. Eymenier/MICHELIN

If you're looking for the real London, then this is where it all began. The original square mile was first settled by the Romans nearly 2,000 years ago and today is one of the financial capitals of the world. From the City you can head north to Finsbury to see remnants of the wall that once marked the boundaries of London, and then west to Clerkenwell where a magpie attitude to the past makes this one of the trendiest places to work and play. Alternatively you can cross the river at London Bridge and head over to Southwark. Once the City's poor relative, full of prisons, brothels and gambling dens, today it's enjoying a spectacular resurgence and fast becoming one of the most exciting and vibrant areas of London.

A LITTLE HISTORY...

The City of London has always been a trading centre. Today it's devoted to the business of money but you can still read signs of a different mercantile past in the street names – **Cheapside** (from the old English for market), **Poultry** and **Pudding Lane**, where the Great Fire of 1666 first started. **Leadenhall Market** offers retail therapy at a less frantic pace: the beautiful covered market stands on the site of a lead-roofed manor house, hence the name, which was owned in the 15C by one Richard Whittington, Lord Mayor of London. Today the cobbled market is full of shops, pubs and even a shoe-shining stand for the city gent or lady in a hurry.

If all this talk of money and shopping seems a little mercenary, then you can always seek sanctuary at the cultural oasis that is the **Barbican Centre**. The brutalist architecture is not to everyone's taste, but with a wide-ranging programme of theatre and music as well as its own cinema there's something to suit everyone. Just down the road is **Smithfield Market**, which has been London's main meat market for over 800 years. It still does a roaring trade in meat and poultry, as well as other foodstuffs. Unsurprisingly this has attracted a fair number of restaurants, which take advantage of the wealth of excellent ingredients right on their doorstep.

The City trend for building ever higher glass skyscrapers has yet to reach Clerkenwell, formerly full of artisans and factories and now occupying an interesting hinterland of decaying 60s tower blocks and reclaimed factory space. Although there's no shortage of offices, workers here are more likely to be sporting the latest designer jeans and trainers than wearing a suit. Graffiti is an overground art form and the labyrinthine streets are stuffed to the gills with gorgeous places to eat and drink, each more self-consciously hip than the last. Although the vibe is anything goes, there's a definite trend for reclaiming the past with flock wallpaper and rescued objects frequently displayed with a touch of knowing irony.

Southwark too is reclaiming its workaday past with **Tate Bankside**, the power station turned art gallery, and the recreated **Globe Theatre** leading the way. While Southwark has a rich tradition of fine pubs and inns – Chaucer's pilgrims set off from the Tabard Inn in Southwark – these days the bars and restaurants are likely to be converted from warehouses or dry docks. The **Borough Market** perfectly encapsulates the Southwark resurgence. There has been a market on this site for nearly 1,000 years; however, in the last few years it has made the jump from a respected wholesale market to a popular destination for weekend shoppers. Alongside excellent, often organic, produce there are also more unusual treats on offer: go to **Scandelicious** for Swedish delicacies, partake of a refreshing drink at **East Teas**, or visit **Dark Sugars** for some dangerously addictive chocolates. The market is open on Fridays and Saturdays but you'll need to get there early to beat the rush and spot top chefs buying in supplies. During the rest of the week **Bedale Street** and **Stoney Street** host a cluster of foody shops offering everything from organic poultry at **Wyndham House** to superb cakes at **Konditor & Cook.**

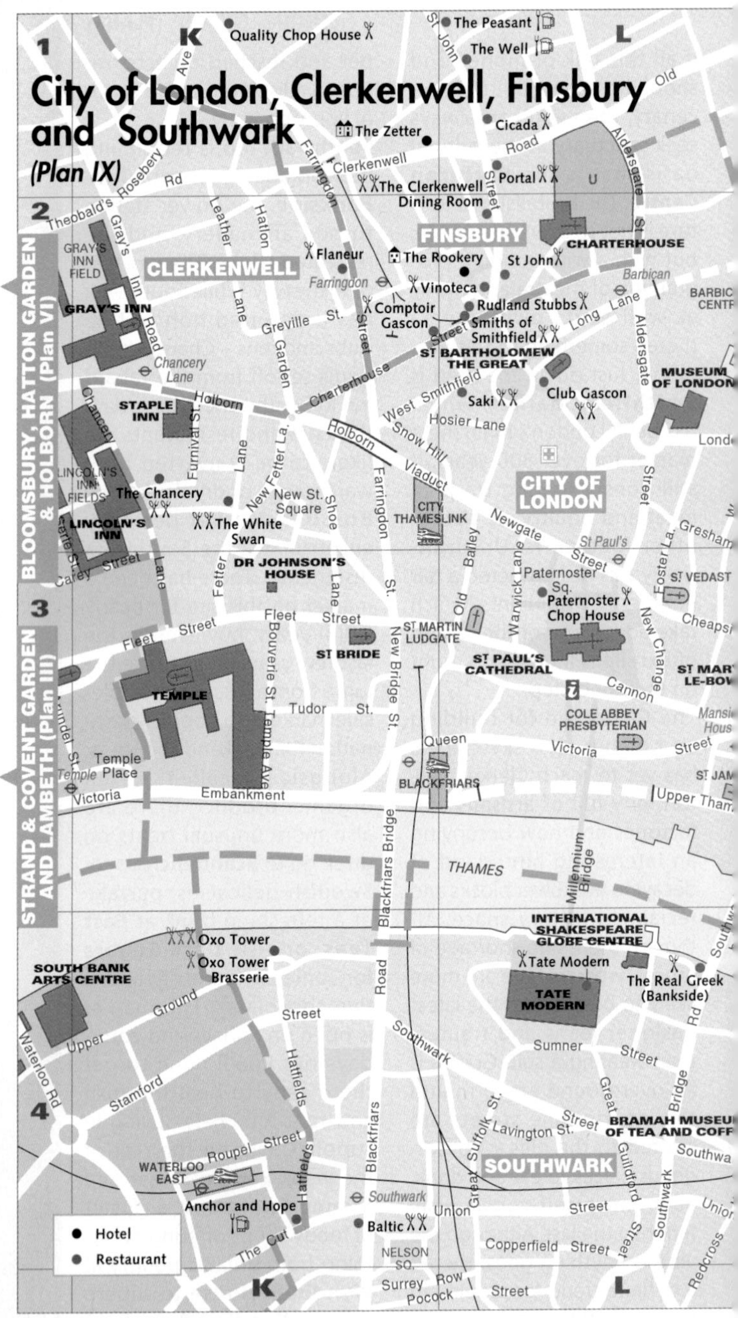

City of London, Clerkenwell, Finsbury and Southwark
(Plan IX)
Quality Chop House
The Peasant
The Well
The Zetter
Cicada
Portal
The Clerkenwell Dining Room
FINSBURY
CHARTERHOUSE
CLERKENWELL
Flaneur
The Rookery
St John
Vinoteca
Comptoir Gascon
Rudland Stubbs
Smiths of Smithfield
ST BARTHOLOMEW THE GREAT
Saki
Club Gascon
MUSEUM OF LONDON
GRAY'S INN
STAPLE INN
LINCOLN'S INN
The Chancery
The White Swan
CITY OF LONDON
CITY THAMESLINK
DR JOHNSON'S HOUSE
Paternoster Chop House
ST MARTIN LUDGATE
ST BRIDE
ST PAUL'S CATHEDRAL
COLE ABBEY PRESBYTERIAN
TEMPLE
BLACKFRIARS
THAMES
INTERNATIONAL SHAKESPEARE GLOBE CENTRE
Tate Modern
TATE MODERN
The Real Greek (Bankside)
Oxo Tower
Oxo Tower Brasserie
SOUTH BANK ARTS CENTRE
BRAMAH MUSEUM OF TEA AND COFF
SOUTHWARK
WATERLOO EAST
Anchor and Hope
Baltic
BLOOMSBURY, HATTON GARDEN & HOLBORN (Plan VI)
STRAND & COVENT GARDEN AND LAMBETH (Plan III)
Hotel
Restaurant

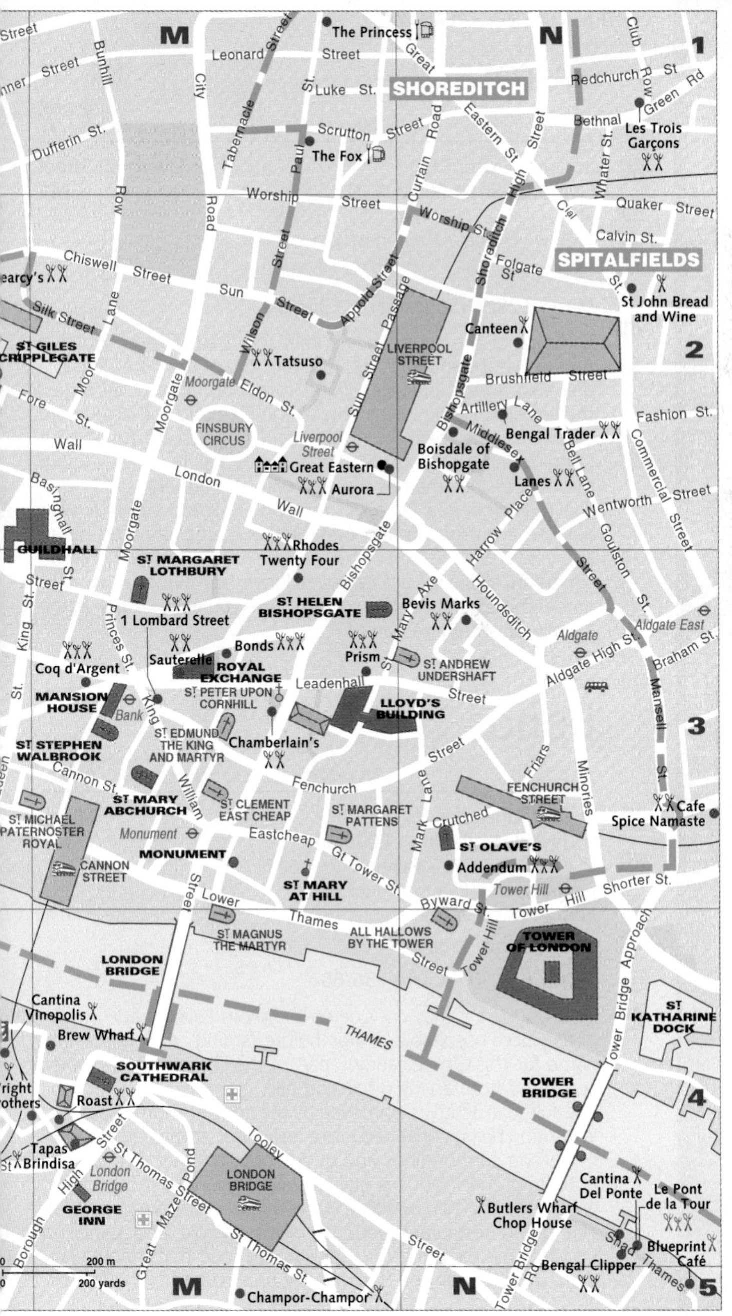

M
N
1
2
3
4
5
SHOREDITCH
SPITALFIELDS
The Princess
The Fox
Les Trois Garçons
St John Bread and Wine
Canteen
Tatsuso
Searcy's
Bengal Trader
Boisdale of Bishopgate
Great Eastern
Aurora
Lanes
Rhodes Twenty Four
1 Lombard Street
Bonds
Coq d'Argent
Sauterelle
Prism
Bevis Marks
Chamberlain's
Cafe Spice Namaste
Addendum
Cantina Vinopolis
Brew Wharf
Wright Brothers
Roast
Tapas Brindisa
Cantina Del Ponte
Le Pont de la Tour
Butlers Wharf Chop House
Blueprint Café
Bengal Clipper
Champor-Champor
LIVERPOOL STREET
Liverpool Street
FINSBURY CIRCUS
ST GILES CRIPPLEGATE
GUILDHALL
ST MARGARET LOTHBURY
ST HELEN BISHOPSGATE
ROYAL EXCHANGE
ST PETER UPON CORNHILL
ST ANDREW UNDERSHAFT
MANSION HOUSE
Bank
LLOYD'S BUILDING
ST EDMUND THE KING AND MARTYR
ST STEPHEN WALBROOK
ST MARY ABCHURCH
ST CLEMENT EAST CHEAP
ST MARGARET PATTENS
FENCHURCH STREET
ST MICHAEL PATERNOSTER ROYAL
Monument
MONUMENT
CANNON STREET
ST OLAVE'S
ST MARY AT HILL
Tower Hill
ST MAGNUS THE MARTYR
ALL HALLOWS BY THE TOWER
TOWER OF LONDON
LONDON BRIDGE
THAMES
ST KATHARINE DOCK
SOUTHWARK CATHEDRAL
TOWER BRIDGE
London Bridge
LONDON BRIDGE
GEORGE INN
Aldgate
Aldgate East
Moorgate
Leonard Street
Luke St.
Scrutton Street
Great Eastern St
Curtain Road
Worship Street
Tabernacle Street
Paul Street
City Road
Bunhill Row
Dufferin St.
Chiswell Street
Sun Street
Silk Street
Wilson Street
Appold Street
Sun Street Passage
Shoreditch High Street
Folgate St
Redchurch St
Club Row
Bethnal Green Rd
Whater St.
Quaker Street
Calvin St.
Commercial Street
Brushfield Street
Artillery Lane
Fashion St.
Middlesex Street
Bell Lane
Wentworth Street
Goulston St.
Moor Lane
Fore St.
Wall
London Wall
Moorgate
Eldon St.
Basinghall St.
Bishopsgate
Harrow Place
Houndsditch
St Mary Axe
Aldgate High St.
Braham St.
Mansell St.
Leadenhall Street
Princes St.
King St.
King William Street
Gresham Street
Cannon St.
Fenchurch Street
Mark Lane
Crutched Friars
Minories
Eastchcheap
Gt Tower St.
Byward St.
Tower Hill
Shorter St.
Lower Thames Street
Tower Bridge Approach
Tooley Street
St Thomas Street
Borough High Street
Great Maze Pond
Shad Thames
Tower Bridge Rd
200 m
200 yards

Aurora

Modern European XXX

at Great Eastern H.,
Liverpool St ✉ EC2M 7QN

⊖ Liverpool Street
M2

A/C VISA MC AE

✆ (020) 76187000 – **Fax** (020) 76185035
Web www.great-eastern-hotel.co.uk

closed Saturday- Sunday

Menu £28.50/500 – Carte £35/45

The pick of the restaurants within the Great Eastern Hotel is Aurora, whose entrance was formerly that of the hotel. This is a dramatic and impressive dining room, dominated by a vast stained glass dome which refracts the light into the large room below. Original panelling, pillars and mosaics are fused with Conran's more contemporary design touches to create a room that successfully merges the past with the present.
The menu offers a lesson in modern European cooking, with detailed construction and presentation, complemented by an impressive wine list.
Time and efficiency are issues at lunch but dinner is an altogether more languid affair so make sure you have a drink in the equally plush Aurora bar.

Bonds

Modern European XXX

at Threadneedles H.,
5 Threadneedle St ✉ EC2R 8AY

⊖ Bank
M3

A/C VISA MC AE

✆ (020) 76578088 – **Fax** (020) 76578089
e-mail bonds@theetongroup.com
Web www.theetoncollection.com

Closed Saturday and Sunday

Menu £24.50 – Carte £36/60

One wonders if they considered the more culinary apt 'Stocks' or the more hospitable 'Shares' before settling on 'Bonds' as the name for this City restaurant, part of the Threadneedles Hotel, converted from an 1856 banking hall.
The suited executives, unmoved by the irony of another financial institution being converted into a restaurant, come here to enjoy its striking surroundings and good cooking. Enter through the hotel and check out the stained glass cupola in reception, as well as the cocktails available in the bar, which also serves tapas. The grand restaurant, with its pillars, marble and panelling provides the backdrop for sophisticated food that's more elaborate in style than the descriptively understated menu lets on.

Rhodes Twenty Four ✿

British XXX

24th floor, Tower 42,
25 Old Broad St
✉ EC2N 1HQ

⊖ Liverpool Street

M3

✆ (020) 78777703 – **Fax** (020) 78777788
e-mail reservations@rhodes24.co.uk **Web** www.rhodes24.co.uk

Closed Christmas-New Year, Saturday, Sunday and Bank Holidays

Carte £234/50

Rhodes Twenty Four

One thing this restaurant won't ever get is passing trade. It's on the 24th floor of Tower 42, the unimaginative new name for the old Natwest Tower, and to reach it you have to pass through the airport style security on the ground floor. Once you've done that, it's onto the express lift to make your ears pop. Persevere, because it's worth it.
The adjoining bar has the better views but there's no doubting that the vista across east London is impressive, with the 'gherkin' dominating one side in an intimidating manner.
Sensibly, the restaurant doesn't try to compete and keeps the decorative touches to a minimum. The result, though, is that you feel as though you're still at the airport, albeit in a first class lounge.
No airline, however, is serving this sort of food. Gary Rhodes's signature is writ large across the menu. Alongside contemporary creations, expect inherently British words like 'pudding' to appear regularly, in the suet form with oxtail and kidney or following words like 'bread and butter'. If driving in for dinner, when it's considerably less 'corporate', park in Finsbury Circus.

A LA CARTE

FIRST COURSE

- Seared scallops with mashed potato and shallot mustard sauce.
- Broad bean and mint soup, buttered potato and poached egg.

MAIN COURSE

- Steamed oxtail suet pudding, buttered carrots and oxtail jus.
- Roast loin of veal, truffle macaroni cheese and tomato veal gravy.

DESSERT

- Iced summer pudding with mixed berries and cream.
- Glazed passion fruit tart with mango salad and sorbet.

1 Lombard Street ✿

French XXX

1 Lombard St
⊠ EC3V 9AA
(020) 79296611 – **Fax** (020) 79296622
e-mail hb@1lombardstreet.com **Web** www.1lombardstreet.com

⊖ Bank
M3

Closed 24 December-3 January, Saturday and Sunday – booking essential at lunch

Menu £39/45 – Carte £53/62

VISA · MC · AE · ① · 🍷

1 Lombard Street

It's easy to miss as there are no clear signs outside this former bank (what else?) in the middle of The City. However, finding it is just the start because you then have to get through the assault course.

To reach the restaurant you have to fight through the throngs of booted, looted and suited city workers in their favourite after-work habitat: the raucous, ear-wobblingly noisy bar/brasserie. When you reach the sanctuary of the restaurant, the scattered briefcases mean that you're unlikely to escape the feeling of being in The City but the room is perfectly pleasant, with a high ceiling and comfortable seating.

Austrian Herbert Berger is your man in charge of kitchen operations and his skilled and elaborately presented cooking comes courtesy of two menus: an *à la carte* or the full nine course Tasting Menu. The menu descriptions tell you all you need to know and, if your tastes are compatible, consider sharing one of the very appealing 'specialities for two'.

If you want to stand out from the crowd, don't wear a tie.

A LA CARTE

FIRST COURSE	MAIN COURSE	DESSERT
• Carpaccio of tuna with Oriental spices, ginger and lime vinaigrette.	• Beef tournedos with wild mushrooms, parsley purée and oxtail sauce.	• Feuillantine of apple, Guinness ice cream and glazed hazelnuts.
• Grilled scallops with Sauternes, lime and lobster emulsion.	• Roast turbot on the bone with mushrooms and lobster essence.	• Figs poached in mulled wine with spiced orange sorbet.

Coq d'Argent

French XXX

No 1 Poultry ⊖ Bank
✉ EC2R 8EJ **M3**
✆ (020) 73955000 – **Fax** (020) 73955050
e-mail coqdargent@conran-restaurants.co.uk
Web www.conran.com

Closed Saturday lunch, Sunday dinner, Christmas, Easter and Bank Holidays – booking essential

Menu £27 (lunch) – Carte £30/44

Take the lift up to the top of this modern office building and you come out in the middle of a terrace, around which is wrapped the restaurant. Al fresco summer dining really comes into its own here. The bar is very much a local destination in itself and is a popular choice for light meals and snacks. This being a Conran restaurant means the dining room is slick, stylish and polished, the urbane staff are used to being busy and the atmosphere is one of cool sophistication. By contrast, the French cooking is fairly classical, with the seafood and oyster bar a speciality. Ask for a table by the large picture window for the best views.
Jazz lunches on Sunday provide a more relaxed mood than the midweek power lunches.

Prism

Modern European XXX

147 Leadenhall ⊖ Aldgate
✉ EC3V 4QT **M3**
✆ (020) 72563885 – **Fax** (0870) 1916025
Web www.harveynichols.com

Closed Saturday and Sunday

Carte £22/40

This was once the Bank of New York and, with such strikingly grand surroundings, one wonders whether they considered naming it twice.
You'll find just as many bankers inside today, attracted by Prism's impressive use of the backdrop of its ornate, high ceilings and classic columns. All this potentially overbearing grandeur is neatly offset by the modern art on display. A bar runs down the full length of one side of the room, with another bar set among the vaults beneath and a large team of waist-coated staff provide polite and organised attention.
The decidedly current cooking comes carefully crafted and artfully arranged, as you would expect from a restaurant belonging to the Harvey Nichols stable.

Le Pont de la Tour

French XXX

36d Shad Thames, Butlers Wharf — London Bridge
SE1 2YE — **N4**
(020) 74038403 – **Fax** (020) 79401835
Web www.conran.com

Closed 25 December and 1 January

VISA MC AE

Menu £30 (lunch) – Carte £42/65

The regeneration of the River and Butlers Wharf were there for all to see in 1991 when Sir Terence Conran opened Le Pont de la Tour and its glamorous reputation was done no harm when Tony Blair entertained Bill Clinton here in 1997. The elegant room provides diners with terrific views of Tower Bridge and the activity on the river, especially from the delightful terrace, while the menu offers a comprehensive selection of dishes that borrow heavily from France, all served by a well-drilled team. For those after less formal surroundings then head for the Bar & Grill which specialises in crustaceans and *fruits de mer* while those wanting something to take home are catered for by an impressive array of produce in the adjacent food store.

Oxo Tower (Restaurant)

Modern European XXX

VISA MC AE

(8th Floor), Oxo Tower Wharf, Barge House — Southwark
SE1 9PH — **K4**
(020) 78033888 – **Fax** (020) 78033838
Web www.harveynichols.com

Closed 24-26 December

Menu £29.50 (lunch) – Carte £42/57

Sitting majestically on the top floor of the converted Oxo factory, which has gradually become one of the more recognisable Thames-side landmarks, the Oxo Tower Restaurant is one of the surprisingly few London restaurants able to offer diners a room with a view - in this case a terrific one of the river and beyond. Fortunately, the elegant surroundings of the interior mean than 'within' is as agreeable as 'without' and the stylish and very comfortable room is complemented by silky smooth and perfectly pitched service. Lunch is a fixed price affair, dinner *à la carte*, and the modern cooking displays a certain sophistication and creativity, using superior ingredients that are reflected in the price.

Addendum

Modern European XXX

A/C
VISA
MC
AE
D

No. 1 Seething Lane ⊖ Fenchurch Street
✉ EC3N 4AX **N3**
✆ (020) 79779500
Web www.addendumrestaurant.co.uk

Closed 23 December-3 January, Saturday, Sunday and Bank Holidays

Carte £39/55

The Apex Hotel opened at the end of 2005 and with it came the decidedly smart Addendum restaurant which is located, appropriately enough, at the back.
Having its own street entrance certainly helped establish its separate identity from the hotel while the chocolate leather seating, fresh flowers and mirrors contribute to the general atmosphere of style and comfort. As with most places in the city, lunchtimes are for animated deal making while dinners are far quieter affairs.
The cooking is undertaken with precision and élan but is far more robust and earthy than one would expect from such a glossy looking restaurant. The chef also clearly likes his offal and those who share his passion will find the *assiette* particularly appealing.

Sauterelle

French XX

A/C
VISA
MC
AE
D

The Royal Exchange ⊖ Bank
✉ EC3V 3LR **M3**
✆ (020) 76182483
Web www.conran-restaurants.co.uk

Closed Christmas-New Year, Saturday and Sunday

Carte £28/41

Opened originally in 1565, The Royal Exchange may have been rebuilt twice, most recently in 1842, but today it is one of the great rousing landmarks in The City. Within the Exchange and to complement the Grand Bar and Café one finds, on its mezzanine level, Sauterelle which opened in late 2005 and is yet another in the Conran kingdom of restaurants.
From its lofty position looking down at the bustle of the courtyard, Sauterelle (meaning "grasshopper" in French) provides slick and comfortable surroundings and the well drilled staff make light of the busy lunchtimes.
In contrast to such very British surroundings, the main feature of the menu is classic bourgeois French cooking, with *rillettes, marmites* and *saucissons* to the fore.

Club Gascon ✿

French XX

57 West Smithfield
EC1A 9DS
(020) 77960600 – **Fax** (020) 77960601

Barbican
L2

Closed 24 December-6 January, Saturday lunch, Sunday and Bank Holidays – booking essential

Menu £35 (lunch) – Carte £29/49

Club Gascon

For the few Brits left who haven't yet bought property in France, Club Gascon will provide an opportunity to experience, for an hour or two, the delights of Gascony and the gastronomy for which this part of south west France is famed.
Pascal Aussignac's homage to his homeland found its ideal outlet in this comfortable and clubby restaurant, which incidentally overlooks a site once used for public hangings.
The menu is neatly divided into differing themes and diners are advised to choose four or five plates and to share them to experience the full range of richly intense flavours. Naturally, there is a large section devoted to foie gras which comes both hot and cold and in some unusual combinations but all dishes are beautifully crafted with a delicacy all of their own. The tasting menu showcases the talents of the kitchen and can be paired with complementary wines, to take decision-making wholly out of the equation.
The room is elegant and prettily dressed without being overly formal; tables are set relatively close together which adds to the mood of shared appreciation.

A LA CARTE

FIRST COURSE

- Roasted black pudding with Jerusalem artichoke emulsion, mint and pine kernels.
- Pressed duck foie gras with king crab and hot tomato.

MAIN COURSE

- Charolais beef fillet with pickled chanterelles, oyster and coco beans.
- Grilled wild salmon with smoked voilet tea and aubergine.

DESSERT

- Sweet foie gras with crystallised roses and champagne jelly.
- Dark chocolate and coffee ice cream with light aniseed tapioca.

Bengal Clipper

Indian XX

Cardamom Building, ⊖ London Bridge
Shad Thames, Butlers Wharf
✉ SE1 2YR **N4**
✆ (020) 73579001 – **Fax** (020) 73579002
e-mail mail@bengalclipper.co.uk **Web** www.bengalclipper.co.uk

A/C VISA MC AE

Menu £27 (dinner) – Carte £13/27

Set among the converted wharves and warehouses by the part of the Thames where cargoes of Indian teas and spices were once traded, you'll find, fittingly enough, Bengal Clipper, a firmly established Indian restaurant whose reputation has been based on reliable cooking and big, bustling surroundings.
The size means that the restaurant is often the chosen venue of larger parties and tables so the atmosphere, particularly in the evenings, is usually fairly hectic, although the smartly kitted out staff are an unflappable lot.
Specialities from all parts of India are showcased, along with several originally conceived dishes which includes, in honour of the building in which the restaurant sits, a chicken curry flavoured with cardamom.

The Chancery

Modern European XX

9 Cursitor St ⊖ Chancery Lane
✉ EC4A 1LL **K2**
✆ (020) 78314000 – **Fax** (020) 78314002
e-mail reservations@thechancery.co.uk
Web www.thechancery.co.uk

Closed 22 December-8 January, Saturday and Sunday

A/C VISA MC AE

Menu £32

Surrounded by the law courts, The Chancery, open only during the week, provides the perfect spot for that last meal of freedom or the post-trial celebratory acquittal.
It is the sister restaurant to The Clerkenwell Dining Room and the bright main room benefits from the large picture windows and understated decoration. This is room in which to reserve your table, rather than the basement which can lack something in atmosphere.
Service is sufficiently fleet of foot and efficient to reassure those with an eye on the adjournment. The cooking also comes suitably well-judged and is modern in style but underpinned by a solid understanding of the ingredients. The wine list has some well-chosen bottles under £25.

Roast

British XX

The Floral Hall, Borough Market ⊖ London Bridge
SE1 1TL **M4**
(020) 79401300 – **Fax** (020) 79401301
e-mail info@roast-restaurant.com **Web** www.roast-restaurant.com

Closed Sunday dinner and Bank Holidays

Menu £21 (lunch) – Carte £32/47

The mouth-watering array of gastronomic delights on display in Borough Market cannot fail to entice the senses of the thousands who pass through it. For those who cannot wait to return home with their fresh produce there is now a restaurant at hand that shares the philosophy of the market by using high quality produce with verifiable provenance.
The best of British is celebrated here and that includes hitherto forgotten meats like mutton, which appears to be making something of a comeback. The daily specials are particularly classic, from Beef Wellington to Toad in the Hole.
Located atop Floral Hall, this contemporary restaurant comes with a split level so ask for the brighter higher one as the lower floor can get somewhat overawed by the bar.

Boisdale of Bishopgate

British XX

Swedeland Court, ⊖ Liverpool Street
202 Bishopgate
EC2M 4NR **N2**
(020) 72831763 – **Fax** (020) 72831664
Web www.boisdale.co.uk

Closed 25 December, 1 January, Saturday, Sunday and Bank Holidays

Carte £23/36

"My heart's in the highlands, wherever I go" said the Scottish Bard. Homesick Scots longing for a taste of home will find succour at this charming Scottish restaurant which specialises in dishes to gladden the heart, such as haggis, smoked salmon and beef, which is matured for 28 days.
The ground floor is given over to a pleasant Champagne and Oyster Bar but descend to the restaurant and you'll find a cosy and very characterful room, warmly decorated in rich reds with a subtle tartan motif and antique prints.
The atmosphere is distinctly clubby and indeed membership is available for their regularly held themed evenings, many of which seemingly appear drink-based. There is also a huge selection of Whiskies available.

Bevis Marks

Kosher XX

Bevis Marks ⊖ Aldgate
✉ EC3 5DQ **N3**
✆ (020) 72832220 – **Fax** (020) 72832221
Web www.bevismarkstherestaurant.com

Closed Saturday, Sunday, Friday dinner and Jewish Holidays

VISA · MC · AE

Carte £27/33

The restaurant is, in essence, a recent extension to the Bevis Marks synagogue which opened in 1701 and is the oldest Jewish place of worship in the UK. The glass enclosed space – with a retractable roof - was originally constructed for a festival, after which it was decided to turn it into a restaurant. Look out for the billboard and menu otherwise you'll never find it.
'Innovative kosher' describes the cooking and the choice is fairly extensive. The kitchen not only updates such classics as chicken soup with matzo balls but adds an Asian influence to some dishes like Sichuan duck and Cantonese chicken. Others have more of a European accent such as *cassoulet* and *fettuccine*. Wines are well chosen and several are Mevushal.

Lanes

Modern European XX

109-117 Middlesex St. ⊖ Liverpool Street
✉ E1 7JF **N2**
✆ (020) 72475050 – **Fax** (020) 72478071
Web www.lanesrestaurant.co.uk

Closed 25 December, Saturday lunch, Sunday and Bank Holidays

A/C · VISA · MC · AE

Menu £21.50 (dinner) – Carte £28/44

Claustrophobes need not fear its basement location for Lanes benefits from pavement-level windows and a general air of openness and space. The bar is a major attraction, especially at lunchtimes when it offers simpler food for stockbrokers on a deadline, but those after somewhere a little smarter and more comfortable should head through to the main restaurant. It's attractively kitted out, with art for sale on the walls, well-spaced tables with the full napery and enthusiastic service.
Expect colourful and modish European cooking, using good quality produce, much of which is British. Evenings are altogether more sedate affairs, highlighted by the good value supper set menu which runs alongside the *à la carte*.

Searcy's

Modern European XX

Barbican Centre, Level 2, Silk St ⊖ Barbican
✉ EC2Y 8DS **L2**
✆ (020) 75883008 – **Fax** (020) 73827247
e-mail searcys@barbican.org.uk **Web** www.searcys.co.uk

Closed 24-26 December, Sunday, Saturday lunch and Bank Holidays

Carte £36/40

In an area of the city where dining options remain rather limited, Searcy's is a more than useful restaurant for those looking for more than a quick snack before, or after, attending a performance or exhibition at the Barbican. It also offers the added bonus of letting you look out from, rather than at, this iconic architectural project. The picture windows offer views across the water features and city buildings, while the décor of the place is one of stylised utilitarianism.
The team of waiting staff are appreciative of the time considerations many have and so dishes are delivered swiftly and efficiently. The menu features a tried and tested formula of modern cooking, Eurocentric in its influences.

Chamberlain's

Seafood XX

23 - 25 Leadenhall Market ⊖ Bank
✉ EC3V 1LR **M3**
✆ (020) 76488690 – **Fax** (020) 76488691
e-mail info@chamberlains.org **Web** www.chamberlains.org

Closed 25-26 December, Saturday, Sunday and Bank Holidays

Menu £16.95 (dinner) – Carte £33/53

How heartening that the Victorian splendour of Leadenhall Market has not resulted in it becoming a twee little tourist arcade. It remains lively and atmospheric but also an integral part of the local scene thanks to places within it like Chamberlain's, built in 1880.
The restaurant is spread over three floors which become slightly more formal the higher you go; the vaulted basement has plenty of character and a simpler menu; the ground floor is the brightest with its mezzanine level and pavement tables while the top floor is often used for groups and private dining.
The theme here is predominantly seafood, delivered daily from Billingsgate market, although accompanying carnivores are not entirely forgotten.

Tatsuso

Japanese XX

32 Broadgate Circle
EC2M 2QS
(020) 76385863 – **Fax** (020) 76385864
e-mail info.tatsuso@btinternet.com

Liverpool Street
M2

Closed Saturday, Sunday and Bank Holidays

Carte £30/97

Tatsuso was among that pioneering wave of Japanese restaurants responsible for introducing Japanese food to inquisitive Londoners. Today it's one of The City's more mature restaurants and remains a favourite, although one that's beginning to slightly show its age.
There is a choice of dining room and, with them, two different dining experiences. On the ground floor it's *teppan-yaki*, where you sit round the counters and the chefs do their thing in front of you. Prices can rise to fairly lofty heights with some of the set menus, especially if you opt for the Kobe beef.
Downstairs is where you'll find more your traditional Japanese restaurant and prices here are a little more down-to-earth. Service is exceptionally polite and well meaning.

The White Swan

Modern European XX

1st Floor, 108 Fetter Lane
EC4A 1ES
(020) 72429696 – **Fax** (020) 74042250
Web www.thewhiteswanlondon.com

Temple
K2

Closed 24-26 and 31 December, 1 January, Monday dinner, Saturday, Sunday and Bank Holidays

Menu £25 (lunch) – Carte £20/30

It once went by the name of 'The Mucky Duck' but, in this age of the gastropub, such a name might not necessarily invoke images of culinary expertise. Far better to be thought of as an ugly duckling who was, in fact, a mighty swan.
Drinkers, though, should not despair because the ground floor is still very much a lively bar, with the restaurant found on the first floor. Upstairs it's all very designery and neat and is nicely juxtaposed with the more rustic charms and general clamour of the bar. A clean and bright feel to the room comes courtesy of large picture windows and a rather discombobulating mirrored ceiling.
The menu successfully blends the earthy with the adventurous to appeal to all tastes and degrees of customer adventure.

Saki

Japanese XX

4 West Smithfield ⊖ Barbican
EC1A 9JX **L2**
(020) 74897033 – **Fax** (020) 74891658
e-mail info@saki-food.com **Web** www.saki-food.com

Closed Christmas-New Year, Sunday and Bank Holidays

Menu £25/55 – Carte £22/60

Saki means "happiness" in Japanese, and, when you consider that the Japanese enjoy the longest life expectancy of any country in the world, you can understand the joy. That longevity must be due, in no small part, to a healthy diet. Now, thanks to places like Saki, we can all hopefully live a little longer, and a little better.

It's actually quite easy to miss, with a deli/foodshop on the ground floor, but head downstairs and you'll find yourself in a very sleek and contemporary space. Service is suitably slick.

The menu is a combination of the classic and the modern, focusing on seasonality through a mix of *kobachi* (small plates), *carbo* (rice or noodles based dishes) and *okazu* (protein based dishes), all prepared to exacting standards.

Smiths of Smithfield

Modern European XX

Top Floor, 67-77 Charterhouse St ⊖ Barbican
EC1M 6HJ **L2**
(020) 72517950 – **Fax** (020) 72365666
Web www.smithsofsmithfield.co.uk

Closed 25-26 December, 1 January, Saturday lunch and Sunday

Carte £28/46

If you ever arrange a get-together with a friend here just remember to be a little precise in your meeting spot. Smiths is housed in a vast building where all four of its floors are given over to eating, drinking and general merry making. As a rule of thumb, prices and levels of formality go up the higher up you go yourself.

The ground floor is a relaxed bar with an exposed brick warehouse feel and easy, snacky menu. Then it's the cocktail bar, followed by the large and lively 'dining room' which is actually more a brasserie and finally the 'top floor' which has a more corporate, groomed feel and boasts terrific views of the surrounding rooftops. Cooking is decidedly modern with well sourced meats something of a speciality.

The Clerkenwell Dining Room

French XX

69-73 St John St
✉ EC1M 4AN
✆ (020) 72539000 – **Fax** (020) 72533322
Web www.theclerkenwell.com

⊖ Farringdon
L2

Closed Christmas, Saturday lunch, Sunday dinner and Bank Holidays

Menu £19.50 – Carte £30/40

Its arched windows hark back to a time when this was a pub, but behind its bright red façade there sits a decidedly contemporary restaurant.
It's quite capacious inside but the owners, who also run The Chancery, have cleverly divided it up into different sections. The art is abstract and the tables smartly dressed.
Two menus, a *de jour* and an *à la carte*, are both offered. The former is competitively priced, no doubt in recognition of the growing number of restaurants available around these parts. The latter menu offers more choice and the kitchen is certainly not shy with flavours, which are predominantly modern French but with the occasional unexpected twist.

Portal

Mediterranean XX

88 St John St
✉ EC1M 4EH
✆ (020) 72536950

⊖ Farringdon
L1

Closed Christmas-New Year and Sunday

Carte £25/39

The sunny Southern Mediterranean is the featured attraction here. In the busy front bar plates of *petiscos* or Portuguese tapas, are the perfect accompaniment to a glass of Sherry, particularly at the end of a hard day, while in the main dining room the menu showcases dishes full of the colours and tastes of Southern France, Spain and Portugal.
Within this Grade II listed building the décor is one of industrial chic, with exposed brick and ventilation shafts and the best place to sit is in the glass walled extension at the back. Service is considerate and thoughtful, as you would expect in a restaurant run by the owner.
The small private dining room lined with wine bottles is a particularly attractive space.

Baltic

Eastern European XX

74 Blackfriars Rd ⊖ Southwark
✉ SE1 8HA **K4**
✆ (020) 79281111 – **Fax** (020) 79288487
e-mail info@balticrestaurant.co.uk **Web** www.balticrestaurant.co.uk

Closed 25 December and 1 January

VISA MC AE

Menu £13.50 (lunch) – Carte £25/30

The façade may be a little unprepossessing but persevere and you'll find yourself in a slick bar. If you can resist the tempting array of vodkas, including some appealingly original home-made flavours, then proceed further and you'll end up in the arresting space of the restaurant.
Alcoves around the edge and, above, a wooden trussed ceiling with vaulted glass combine with bright white walls to give this former industrial space a vividly modernist feel. At this point you'll probably expect some sort of pan-Asian fusion thing but fortunately Baltic enjoys the same ownership as Wódka, so the cooking here covers the altogether more muscular cuisines of Eastern Europe and the Baltic states. It is robust, full of flavour and requires an appetite.

Oxo Tower (Brasserie)

Modern European X

(8th Floor), Oxo Tower Wharf, ⊖ Southwark
Barge House St
✉ SE1 9PH **K4**
✆ (020) 78033888 – **Fax** (020) 78033838
Web www.harveynichols.com

Closed 24-26 December

A/C VISA AE

Menu £21.50 (lunch) – Carte £32/42

The brasserie provides an ideal alternative for those after a less formal and less expensive experience to the Oxo Tower Restaurant, but one that still offers the same commanding setting and impressive vistas. The glass enclosed restaurant, with its open plan kitchen and bustling atmosphere, provides the perfect place in which to entertain those new to the city; the changing light at dusk makes this an ideal period in which to time your arrival, especially if it's warm enough to sit outside on the terrace. 'Brasserie' may describe the room but the dishes on offer are far from what traditionalists would call brasserie classics: the extensive menu is made up of dishes with contemporary, and occasionally Asian, influences.

Blueprint Café

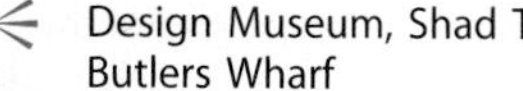

Modern European

Design Museum, Shad Thames, Butlers Wharf — ⊖ London Bridge

✉ SE1 2YD — **N5**

✆ (020) 73787031 – **Fax** (020) 73578810

Web www.conran.com

Closed 25-26 December, 1 January and Sunday dinner

Carte £24/39

The Design Museum opened in 1989 to international acclaim and celebrates both the history of design as well as what's best in contemporary design. Appropriately, the Blueprint Café is not merely an afterthought but an integral part of the experience, with its own sleek and understated décor.

However, the first thing one notices is the great views of Tower Bridge and The Thames and the room certainly makes the best use of the light and its raised position. Although the window tables are the first to be reserved, you'll find a pair of binoculars on all tables.

The daily changing menu, with understated dish descriptions, showcases a range of dishes, many of which share sunny European sensibilities.

St John

British

26 St John St — ⊖ Barbican

✉ EC1M 4AY — **L2**

✆ (020) 72510848 – **Fax** (020) 72514090

Web wwwstjohnrestaurant.co.uk

Closed Christmas, Easter, Saturday lunch and Sunday

Carte £34/46

A derelict 19c former smokehouse was converted in 1994 into St John, a restaurant which has introduced a new generation to old English recipes, forgotten treats and rediscovered favourites. 'Nose to tail eating' is how they describe themselves, celebrating the British traditional of 'waste not, want not' by using hitherto under-used parts of the animal to challenge our ever more timid palates. Dishes range from the more unusual, such as roast bone marrow, braised mutton or chitterlings with dandelion, to the more comforting, such as Arbroath Smokies or Eccles cake.

The starkly decorated white room provides surroundings that perfectly complement the apparent simplicity of the cooking and clued up staff willingly offer advice to the novice.

Tate Modern (Restaurant)

Modern European

7th Floor, Tate Modern, Bankside ⊖ Southwark
SE1 9LS **L4**
(020) 7401 5020
Web www.tate.org.uk/modern/information/eating.htm
Closed 25 December – lunch only and dinner Friday and Saturday

VISA

Carte £21/31

Tate Modern, opened in 2000 in the shell of the Bankside power station, has proved to be one of London's great attractions. The glass structure on top was the only addition to the original exterior and here on the 7th floor they opened a restaurant, making the very most of the stunning views of St Paul's, the river and the city's skyline. This was, therefore, the closest one could get to a sure thing.
Thankfully, they didn't disregard the cooking because the menu offers a varied and sensible choice, ranging from traditionally English to more colourful southern European specialities, as well as providing for those just wanting something light.
Another excuse, if indeed one was ever needed, to head over to Bankside.

Cantina Del Ponte

Italian

36c Shad Thames, Butlers Wharf ⊖ London Bridge
SE1 2YE **N4**
(020) 7403 5403 – **Fax** (020) 7940 1845
Web www.conran.com
Closed 25-26 December

VISA

AE

Menu £13.50 – Carte £24/32

This is one of those great-after-work sort of places, where you can grab a seat on the terrace under the huge canopy, order a pizza and a bottle of Chianti and admire the view. Even if you don't work in The City, it's still a pretty nice place to spend an evening.
As with most restaurants around these parts, it is one piece of the Conran empire but has a more down to earth, rustic feel to it than most of the others which are generally a little shinier. There's plenty of terracotta, a large mural on one wall and a general feeling of openness.
Apart from the pizzas, which are also available for takeaway, the menu offers a comprehensive selection of popular Italian dishes which are full of flavour and carefully prepared.

Moro

Mediterranean

34-36 Exmouth Market — ⊖ Farringdon
✉ EC1R 4QE — **PLAN page 138 K1**
✆ (020) 78338336 – **Fax** (020) 78339338
e-mail info@moro.co.uk **Web** www.moro.co.uk

Closed Christmas, New Year, Sunday and Bank Holidays – booking essential

Carte £24/31

The enduring popularity of Moro is easy to understand. The wholesome, vibrant Moorish food is certainly moreish, the atmosphere is never less than lively and the place just seems to complement the surroundings and atmosphere of Exmouth Market perfectly.

A zinc bar occupies one side, where tapas can be enjoyed, and the contagious bonhomie generated in the restaurant appears to be reflected in the open kitchen. They certainly make great use of their charcoal grill and wood-burning oven, particularly with the sourdough bread, and the menu changes fully every two weeks.

All budding cooks will learn here of the importance of using the freshest produce. If they want to learn any more they can buy the Moro cookbook.

Paternoster Chop House

British

Warwick Court, Paternoster Square — ⊖ St Paul's
✉ EC4N 7DX — **L3**
✆ (020) 70299400 – **Fax** (020) 70299409
Web www.conran.com

Closed 22 December-2 January, Saturday and Sunday dinner

Carte £32/46

Nestling behind St Paul's, in an area celebrated in pre-war days as the best place for ale and chop houses, one now aptly finds the Paternoster Chop House. Being part of the Conran group means the décor was clearly never going to be anything other than bright, light and modern. The menu, however, adopts a formula of back-to-basics of which John Major would have approved. Shellfish, grills and resolutely British classics such as jugged hare, potted shrimps and Dover sole are followed by treacle tart or spotted dick. Even better, all choices come in refreshingly generous portions and you'll leave dreaming wistfully of imaginary nannies.

City suits do have a tendency to dominate the room at lunch but the apron-wearing staff cope with aplomb.

Cantina Vinopolis

International

No.1 Bank End — ⊖ London Bridge
SE1 9BU — **L4**
(020) 79408333 – **Fax** (020) 70899339
e-mail cantina@vinopolis.co.uk **Web** www.vinopolis.co.uk
Closed 24 December-2 January and Sunday

Menu £29.95 (lunch) – Carte £22/37

Southwark is becoming something of a Utopia for today's gastronauts. Food supplies can be garnered at the wonderful Borough Market and oenologists will find relief and fulfilment at Vinopolis, the wine merchant and museum.
Cantina Vinopolis is the wine attraction's public restaurant and is housed under vast, magnificent Victorian arches that lend a palpable sense of history and atmospherics to the whole place. The exposed kitchen offers a menu that flits between continents and, as one would expect, the wine list offers an interesting and correspondingly diverse selection with many well priced bottles. The styling and comforts are simple and uncomplicated and the service is smoothly effective.

Village East

Modern European 

171 Bermondsey St — ⊖ London Bridge
SE1 3UW — **PLAN page 290 O1**
(020) 73576082 – **Fax** (020) 74033360
e-mail info@villageeast.co.uk **Web** www.villageeast.co.uk

Carte £24/36

Clever name - sounds a bit downtown Manhattan. But while Bermondsey may not be London's East Village, what Village East does is give this part of town a bit more 'neighbour' and a little less 'hood'.
It's tricky to find so look for the glass façade and you'll find yourself in one of the bars, still wondering if you've come to the right place. Once, though, you've seen the open kitchen you know the dining area's not far away. Wood, brick, vents and large circular lamps give it that warehouse aesthetic.
The menu is laid out a little confusingly but what you get is ample portions of familiar bistro style food, as well as some interesting combinations. The separately priced side dishes are not really needed and can push the bill up.

Butlers Wharf Chop House

British

36e Shad Thames, Butlers Wharf ⊖ London Bridge
SE1 2YE **N4**
(020) 74033403 – **Fax** (020) 79401855
Web www.conran.com

Closed 25-26 December, 1 January and Sunday dinner

Menu £26 (lunch) – Carte £30/46

The menu at Butlers Wharf Chophouse offers a comprehensive selection of British dishes that range from the classic to the reassuringly familiar. From oysters, dressed crab and prawn cocktails to fish and chips, sausages and roast beef, there are reminders of our own proud culinary heritage.
It is not, therefore, surprising that this roomy and bright chophouse on a converted wharf is always busy, especially at lunchtimes with swarms of suited city workers. The restaurant has the feel of a boathouse and affords terrific views of the river and Tower Bridge, particularly from the very agreeable terrace, while the bar offers a less expensive menu in more relaxed surroundings. The service throughout is diligent and attentive.

Champor-Champor

Malaysian 

62-64 Weston St. ⊖ London Bridge
SE1 3QJ **M5**
(020) 74034600
Web www.champor-champor.com

Closed Easter, Christmas and Monday – dinner only – booking essential

Carte £27/31

Spirits cannot fail to be lifted as soon as you find yourself in this beguiling restaurant with its exuberant and vibrant decoration; any Malay speakers out there will instantly appreciate the name, which roughly translates as "mix-and-match". That certainly applies to the two rooms into which it is divided and where no two tables are the same. The rooms are festooned with everything from Buddha statues to tribal artefacts, from masks to carvings and all with the added exoticism of incense fragrance in the air and flickering candle light.
The cooking also comes with a mix of influences and equal amounts of colour, panache and vitality, and is a fusion of Malaysian and assorted Asian cuisines.

Wright Brothers

Seafood

VISA MC AE

11 Stoney St, Borough Market — London Bridge
SE1 9AD — **L4**
(020) 74039554 – **Fax** (020) 74039558
Web www.wrightbros.eu.com

Closed 25-26 December and Sunday

Carte £23/43

This started life as an oyster wholesaler and then developed around the theme of an oyster and porter house – porter, or dark ale, being the traditional accompaniment to oysters.
The range of oysters is huge; they come from all over the world and are served either in their natural state or cooked in a variety of classic ways. Accompanying them is a range of prime shellfish, from winkles and crab to whelks and razor clams, as well as a handful of prepared dishes like fish pie. There's a shellfish barbecue on Saturdays.
Don't expect chips or any type of potato – the oyster is the main event and full marks for that. And there's no dessert, except for cheese and truffles.
Decoratively, it's equally no-nonsense and the atmosphere is all the better for it.

Tapas Brindisa

Spanish

VISA MC

18-20 Southwark St, Borough Market — London Bridge
SE1 1TJ — **M4**
(020) 73578880
Web www.brindisa.com

Closed Sunday and Bank Holidays – bookings not accepted

Carte £9/18

A converted potato warehouse on the fringe of Borough Market selling tapas - if that doesn't arouse interest, nothing will. The owners have spent years importing the best Spanish produce, so opening their own place was a logical step.
As in Spain, you have the option of standing or sitting for your tapas. The bar is a great place for a glass of Fino while you watch the acorn-fed Iberian charcuterie being sliced. The full length windows let the light stream in and the tightly packed tables add to the general conviviality.
The list of hot and cold tapas is extensive, from cured fish and speciality cheeses to grilled chorizo and sautéed chicken livers. No reservations are taken so get there early or be prepared to wait.

Vinoteca

Modern European

7 St John St ⊖ Farringdon
EC1M 4AA **L2**
(020) 72538786 – **Fax** (020) 74904282
e-mail enquiries@vinoteca.co.uk **Web** www.vinoteca.co.uk

Closed Christmas, Sunday and Bank Holidays – booking essential at lunch, not taken for dinner

Carte £19/25

'Think of a number, double it and add ten' seems to be how most wines are marked up these days. This makes it even more refreshing to find a place like Vinoteca, where the wine comes at realistic and reasonable prices and the choice is both varied and innovative. Vinoteca calls itself a 'Bar, Wine Shop and Kitchen' and it does all three things well.
At dinner you order at the bar from a subtly southern European influenced menu where each dish is paired with a recommended wine; table service is provided at lunch which is a far busier time. But the wine is the king here and those who haven't set foot in anything remotely resembling a 'wine bar' since its apotheosis or nadir (depending on your viewpoint) in the 1980's should think again.

Flâneur

Modern European 

41 Farringdon Rd ⊖ Farringdon
EC1M 3JB **K2**
(020) 74044422
e-mail mail@flaneur.com **Web** www.flaneur.com

Closed Sunday dinner and Bank Holidays

Menu £20 (dinner) – Carte £23/30

This veritable kingdom of foodie heaven shines ever brightly on the otherwise rather non-descript Farringdon Road. Part food-hall, packed to the gunnels with produce ranging from charcuterie and pasta to oils and sauces, and part-restaurant with outsized chairs lending a certain Alice in Wonderland quality, the aroma alone is enough to stimulate the most jaded of taste buds. Lunch can be a little 'on the hoof' but dinner is usually a slightly more relaxed affair as the store quietens.
The menu is tweaked daily to reflect the freshness of the produce and the style is modern European, refreshingly free from unnecessary frills. The wine list, slanted more towards France, reflects what's on the shelves.

Cicada

South-East Asian

132-136 St John St — Farringdon
EC1V 4JT — **L1**
(020) 76081550 – **Fax** (020) 76081551
Web www.cicada.nu

Closed 23 December-2 January, Saturday lunch and Sunday

VISA, MC, AE, DC

Menu £22.50/27 – Carte £17/30

Cicada was the first in Will Ricker's chain of excitable South East Asian restaurants to open and the bustle and buzz of St John Street, with all its bars, pubs and restaurants, now seems an inspired choice.
The principles of the other restaurants were clearly laid down here. Firstly, make the bar an integral part of the operation and add a tempting drinks list. Then make the restaurant equally lively and fun and, finally, ensure that the cooking is far better than anyone expects, with genuine respect for the ingredients and an appreciation of the featured Asian countries.
One of the best things is that you're made just as welcome if you're popping in after work for a quick beer and some noodles or if you're making it an occasion with friends.

Quality Chop House

British

A/C, VISA, MC, AE

94 Farringdon Rd — Farringdon
EC1R 3EA — **K1**
(020) 78375093 – **Fax** (020) 78338748
Web www.qualitychophouse.co.uk

Closed 25-26 December and Saturday lunch

Menu £9.95 (lunch) – Carte £26/30

This late 19th century chop house captures perfectly the no-nonsense Victorian approach to eating and the restaurant's stained glass window still proudly proclaims 'Progressive working class caterer'. This theme continues inside with the inimitable furnishings of oak benches, booths and black and white tiled flooring.
Oysters jostle with jellied eels on the starters and the main courses of Cumberland sausage or battered haddock underline the inherent Britishness of the operation, although other choices of a more Gallic persuasion vie for your attention. This culinary democracy comes complete with rows of sauce bottles on each table.
After work, pop in for a selection of 'chopas'- a mini version of some menu dishes.

Brew Wharf

Traditional

Brew Wharf Yard, Stoney St. — London Bridge
SE1 9AD — **M4**
(020) 73786601 – **Fax** (020) 79408336
Web www.vinopolis.co.uk

Closed Christmas-New Year

Carte £19/29

Underneath the arches, we can dream our dreams away. With the sound of trains rattling by overhead mixed with the clamour of contented diners, three large brick arches now form the carapace of a bar, an open-plan kitchen, a 90 seater restaurant and, behind a perspex wall, a micro brewery. Welcome to Brew Wharf.

These beers, along with an extensive range of imported bottles, prove to be the main draw for many of the young after-work crowd and the menu, which doubles as a place mat, provides just the right sort of no-nonsense food you'll fancy when you've got a beer in your hand. These include rotisserie dishes such as marinated whole or half chickens, rib-eye steak sandwiches, pints of prawns, *choucroute* and *cassoulet*.

Comptoir Gascon 

French

61-63 Charterhouse St — Barbican
EC1M 6HJ — **K2**
(020) 76080851 – **Fax** (020) 76080871

Closed Christmas-New Year, Sunday and Monday

Carte £20/26

It originally opened as a deli and bakery for their flagship restaurant Club Gascon (see restaurant listing), but happily the owners decided to turn it into this sweet little bistro, offering a wonderful range of specialities from Southwest France. It still retains elements of the deli, such as the dessert counter, and the rustic nature of the room complements the food perfectly - the enticing produce on display certainly has a Pavlovian effect on the customers. Blackboard specials supplement the menu where dishes are endearingly translated from the French and the service is obliging and relaxed.

There can be fewer dishes more warming on a winter night than *cassoulet* or duck *confit* and the prices charged are equally comforting.

Rudland Stubbs

Seafood

35-37 Green Hill Rents, Cowcross St — ⊖ Farringdon **L2**

EC1M 6BN

(020) 72530148

Web www.rudlandstubbs.co.uk

Closed Christmas, Saturday, Sunday and Bank Holidays

Carte £28/40

Messrs Rudland and Stubbs were two gentlemen who saw a gap in the market in the '70's. They thought that anyone working in an area dominated by the meat market of Smithfields would appreciate a bit of fish now and then and so converted an old sausage factory into a restaurant.

Re-launched in 2006, new owners have given the place a fresh lease of life, with just the marble top tables surviving the renovation. It still has a somewhat raffish charm and the plants, tiles and ceiling fans add a touch of the colonial.

The man-size menus list a comprehensive selection of assorted shellfish and seafood, prepared by a well travelled kitchen with more care and precision than you expect. The wine list on the back of the menu is equally global.

The Ambassador

Traditional

55 Exmouth Market — ⊖ Farringdon PLAN page 138 **K1**

EC1R 4QL

(020) 78370009

Web www.theambassadorcafe.co.uk

Closed Christmas and Sunday dinner

Menu £16 (lunch) – Carte £19/34

This Ambassador may raise a few eyebrows at the Court of St James's but his thoroughly egalitarian approach to dining sits very easily within the more urban setting of Exmouth Market. Whisper it quietly, but is that lino on the floor? The decorative simplicity to the room actually works well, adding to the generally languorous atmosphere. Staff do their bit by retaining a sense of cool detachment.

Commendably, it's an all day operation, with hangover cures in the morning, followed by satisfyingly continental lunches and seasonally honest and earthy cooking on offer during the more animated evenings. It's pretty evident that all produce has been diligently sourced, from the butter to the coffee, and the wine list pricing is honest and fair.

Medcalf

Modern European 

40 Exmouth Market — ⊖ Farringdon
✉ EC1R 4QE — **PLAN page 138 K1**
✆ (020) 78333533 – **Fax** (020) 78331321
e-mail mail@medcalfbar.co.uk **Web** www.medcalfbar.co.uk

VISA · MC

Closed 25 December-1 January – booking essential

Carte £25/32

As butchers' shops around the country fall prey to the supermarket behemoths, it is perhaps fitting that here is one former shop that firstly became a bar, but one where the quality of the food turned it from a mainly drinking establishment into a dining destination. Albert Medcalf, who established his original butchers shop here in 1912, would be proud and his original sign is emblazoned over the window.
The interior strikes the perfect balance between tradition and modern, between ragged and chic, while the staff remain charming and cool, even when under the pressure of large numbers. British and European influenced dishes come with a degree of rustic charm in their presentation, which belies the evident skill and care that goes into their preparation.

Konstam at the Prince Albert

Traditional 

2 Acton St — ⊖ King's Cross St Pancras
✉ WC1X 9NA — **PLAN page 138 J0**
✆ (020) 78335040 – **Fax** (020) 78335045
e-mail princealbert@konstam.co.uk **Web** www.konstam.co.uk

VISA · MC · AE

Closed Christmas and Sunday

Carte £23/32

Gentrification may remain elusive but at least King's Cross now offers somewhere to eat. Oliver Rowe has taken a shabby Victorian pub, named it after his great grandfather and has kept the décor functional, save for a striking ornamental lighting feature.
However, what makes this restaurant so unusual is that the produce is nearly all sourced from within the boundaries of the London transport network. Using local supplies is easy when you're in Devon but Central London throws up its own challenges and you'll spend most of the time wondering where exactly some of the ingredients on your plate came from. The open kitchen means that if curiosity gets the better of you, then the chefs are within questioning range.

The Real Greek (Bankside)

Greek

Units 1-2, Riverside House,
2A Southwark Bridge Rd
SE1 9HA
(020) 76200162 – **Fax** (020) 76200262
e-mail banksideàtherealgreek.com **Web** www.therealgreek.co.uk

Southwark
L4

A/C VISA

Carte £11/18

There are a number of Real Greeks around London but this one in Bankside, by the river, is one of the best located and is just moments from both the Globe Theatre and Tate Modern.
This chain began with the Real Greek in Hoxton, which put it on the culinary map a few years back, and the concept is both straightforward and appealing. Sharing is the key with the menu focusing on *meze*, small plates of flavoursome delicacies and *souvlaki*, grilled kebabs which are wrapped in flatbread and are the Greek version of fast food. Inside, it's all modern and shiny, with half the room given over to the bar. Although the Thames is no substitute for the Aegean, the outside terrace is a pleasant spot in summer.

Anchor and Hope

Gastropub

36 The Cut
SE1 8LP
(020) 79289898 – **Fax** (020) 79284595

Southwark
K4

Bookings not accepted

Carte £18/35

Its proximity to the Vic theatres, both Young and Old, combined with its growing culinary reputation, mean that the Anchor & Hope is always busy. As they don't take reservations it's worth getting here early - in fact very early - although if you're willing to share tables in this simply furnished dining room you'll find you'll be seated sooner.
The owners are of the sleeve-rolled-up school and take charge of the cooking, the delivery of the dishes and the serving of drinks. The general buzz creates a noisy but highly convivial atmosphere.
From the tiny kitchen they produce immensely satisfying dishes, in a rustic and robust style, drawing on influences from St John, but at prices which make the queuing worthwhile.

The Coach & Horses

Gastropub 

26-28 Ray St
✉ EC1R 3DJ
(020) 72788990 – **Fax** (020) 72781478
Web www.thecoachandhorses.com

⊖ Farringdon
PLAN page 138 K1

Closed Christmas, Saturday lunch and Sunday dinner

VISA · MC · AE

Carte £20/28

Those who feel the very fabric of society is being undermined by each pub modernisation will like the Coach and Horses, because it has managed the trick of subtly updating itself without losing its down to earth personality or local atmosphere.
The menu also eschews the gastropub standards of sausage and mash or lamb shank and instead has introduced more unusual meats, like pig's ear or ox tongue, as well as using ingredients which are not only fiercely seasonal but all vigorously sourced - traditional reared rare-breed meats are very much the house speciality.
A playful motif of fairy tales and nursery rhymes runs through the operation and there's a charming little terrace for summer's days.

The Hartley

Gastropub 

64 Tower Bridge Rd
✉ SE1 4TR
(020) 73947023
e-mail enquiries@thehartley.com **Web** www.thehartley.com

⊖ Borough
PLAN page 290 O2

Closed Christmas

VISA · MC · AE

Carte £16/30

There may not be too much local competition to fight off but The Hartley still makes an effort in flying the local gastro-pub flag. This red-bricked Victorian pub is also doing its bit to remember the diminishing local heritage by honouring, in name and decoration, the Hartley Jam Factory which once stood opposite and is now, predictably, a residential development.
There are original posters, black and white photos and even jars of jam scattered around the place. The open plan kitchen produces robust and appetite-satisfying food from the commendably concise menu, supplemented by daily-changing blackboard specials. Service is relaxed and cool headed.
The locals of this parish are clearly taken with The Hartley.

The Peasant

Gastropub

VISA

240 St John St ⊖ Farringdon
✉ EC1V 4PH **L1**
✆ (020) 73367726 – **Fax** (020) 74901089
booking essential

Carte £35/45

As a senior member of the London gastropub scene, The Peasant continues to set the standard for others to follow and one of its greatest strengths is that it is still very much a 'real' pub. The Victorian origins are there for all to see with its arched windows, high ceilings and mosaic floor, while the light bites and tapas served in the bar provide the perfect accompaniment to the range of beers on offer.
Those looking for a more structured dining experience and a less frenetic vibe should head for the upstairs restaurant, decorated with fairground-themed artwork. Here, the menu allows the kitchen to showcase its talent for producing robust and honest food with more than a degree of originality.

The Well

Gastropub

VISA

180 St John St ⊖ Farringdon
✉ EC1V 4JY **L1**
✆ (020) 72519363 – **Fax** (020) 74042250
e-mail drinks@downthewell.co.uk **Web** www.downthewell.co.uk
Closed Christmas

Carte £18/25

A fairly frenetic atmosphere is guaranteed at The Well as it's quite a small inside and the locals clearly rather like the place. It has built its reputation on giving the menu just the right balance and level of sophistication, so that you can order a pint of prawns or something a little more ambitious like saffron risotto or one of the daily specials.
The sliding screen windows let in the light and the wooden floorboards and exposed brick walls add to the atmosphere of a committed metropolitan pub. The benches outside are popular, particularly with those who don't mind a side order of CO_2 with their beer.
Downstairs you'll find an altogether sexier bar, complete with fish tank, which is available for private hire - the bar, not the tank.

C. Barrely/MICHELIN

Chelsea, Earl's Court, Hyde Park, Knightsbridge, South Kensington

S. Ollivier/MICHELIN

When London throws a party, the natural choice of summer venue is the city's most expansive central space: **Hyde Park**. The Rolling Stones, Pink Floyd and REM have all rocked out here, as did Live 8's pop Samaritans. But there's another side to this park - a slightly strange fringe element exemplified by the eccentric soapboxers of **Speaker's Corner** and the hardy souls dipping into the **Serpentine** on Christmas morning. Particularly intriguing is the gilded Gothicism of Queen Victoria's monument to love, the **Albert Memorial**. However, for true romance, the adjacent **Royal Albert Hall** offers a more seductive vision and a charismatic spirit that pokes fun at pomp and circumstance on the Last Night of the Proms.

The extent of the area's Victorian endowment becomes clear wandering south, with the museums of **Cromwell Road** preaching enlightenment today with as much conviction as after the Great Exhibition. Once again, frothier pursuits are close by, and in **Knightsbridge** the grand designs are replaced by glitzy designers, with two of the world's most renowned department stores vying for trade - **Harvey Nichols** attracting the pure fashionistas and **Harrods** those who also have a predilection for Egyptian mystique. The crowds here can indeed be madding (particularly during the sales season), but escape up a side street and you'll find lovely lanes of mews cottages, apparently of another place entirely - although no doubt their owners appreciate the glamorous corner shops at the end of the road.

The rest of **South Kensington** settles into a peaceful poshness until you get to the Sloane stomping ground of **Chelsea,** where suddenly the groove changes. It's true that this formerly bohemian enclave is less swinging than it used to be, but the original standard was fabulously high. When Kensington and Chelsea were brought under a single local authority in 1965, the 'Royal Borough' was rather sniffy about its new association with the heart of 'Swinging London', while those in Chelsea were too busy trying on miniskirts to notice, cruising down the **King's Road** straight into Mary Quant's Bazaar. Today, most of the avant-garde boutiques have been replaced by conventional high street chains and gentrified house prices leave little room for punks or hippies; indeed, the Sloane Ranger uniform of Alice band and pearls is much in evidence, worn by yummy mummies, teenage girls and shop mannequins alike. Yet the area's numerous art school students do assert a counter-cultural balance and the basement bar of the **Royal Court Theatre** - the original home of the angry young man - still provides a hang out for bright and engaged talents.

If Chelsea is now more comfortable playing host to its famous flower show than revolutionary flower power, the charm of its riverside streets makes a virtue of steadfastness. Rather than house numbers, **Cheyne Walk** could mark its abodes in the names of eminent ex-residents - Whistler, Rossetti, Brunel - and the historical roll call continues in the well-preserved lanes behind, once home to Thomas Carlyle and Oscar Wilde. By contrast, a skip along the Thames brings you to the unknown face of the future; plans to develop the disused **Lots Road** power station have generated controversy, though modern marina **Chelsea Harbour** perhaps lights the way, providing a pleasant and popular facility.

Of course, to many the name Chelsea begins and ends with foreign signings, friendly rou-

S. Ollivier/MICHELIN

Chelsea, Earl's Court, Hyde park, Knightsbridge, South Kensington

bles and championship trophies - but the district is far too genteel to house its own football stadium and by the time you arrive at **Stamford Bridge**, you're well on your way to the exhibition land of **Earl's Court**. Like Chelsea FC, money has poured into this once rather drab part of town;

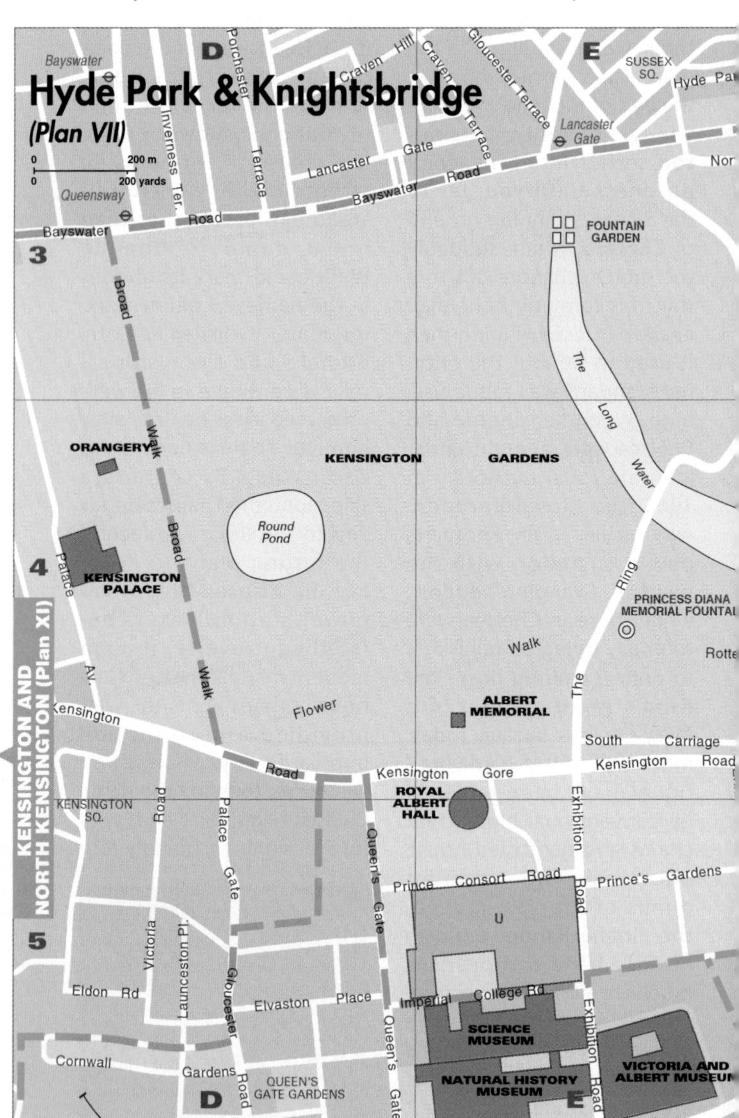

unlike the football club, many of its foreign players have been forced out. You still see the odd Kiwi or Aussie backpacker making their way to slumming it on a mate's floor - but with house prices almost as high as a star midfielder's transfer fee, the pearls and Alice bands are moving in.

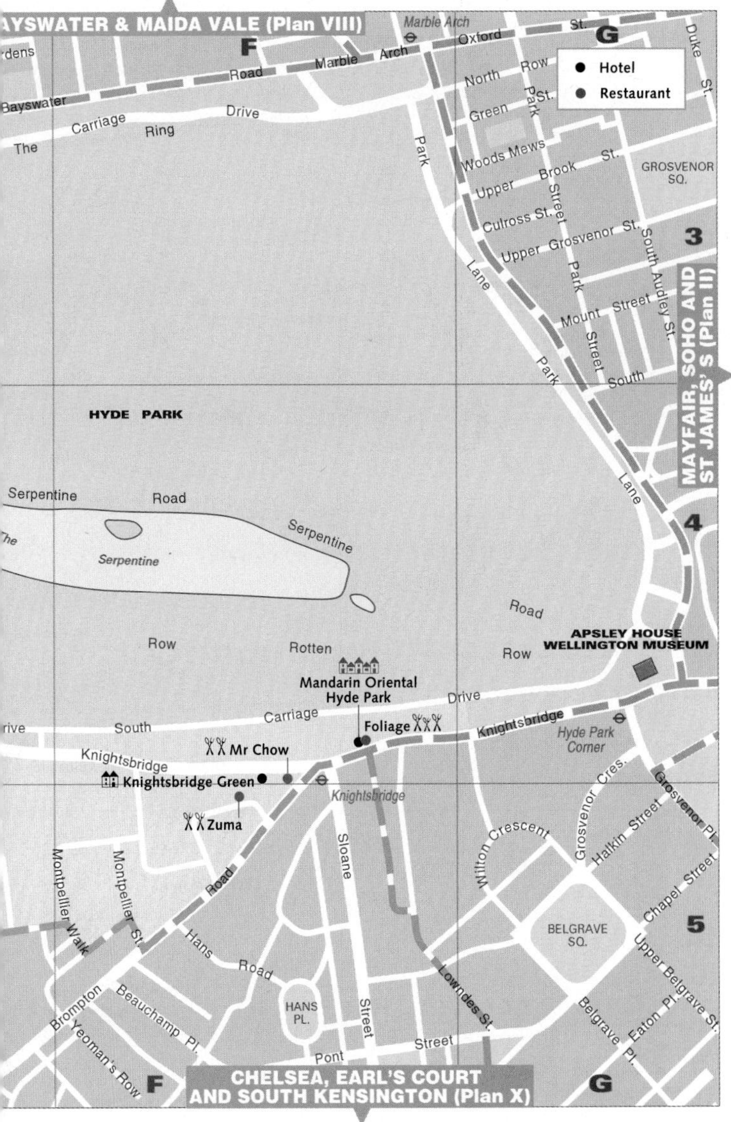

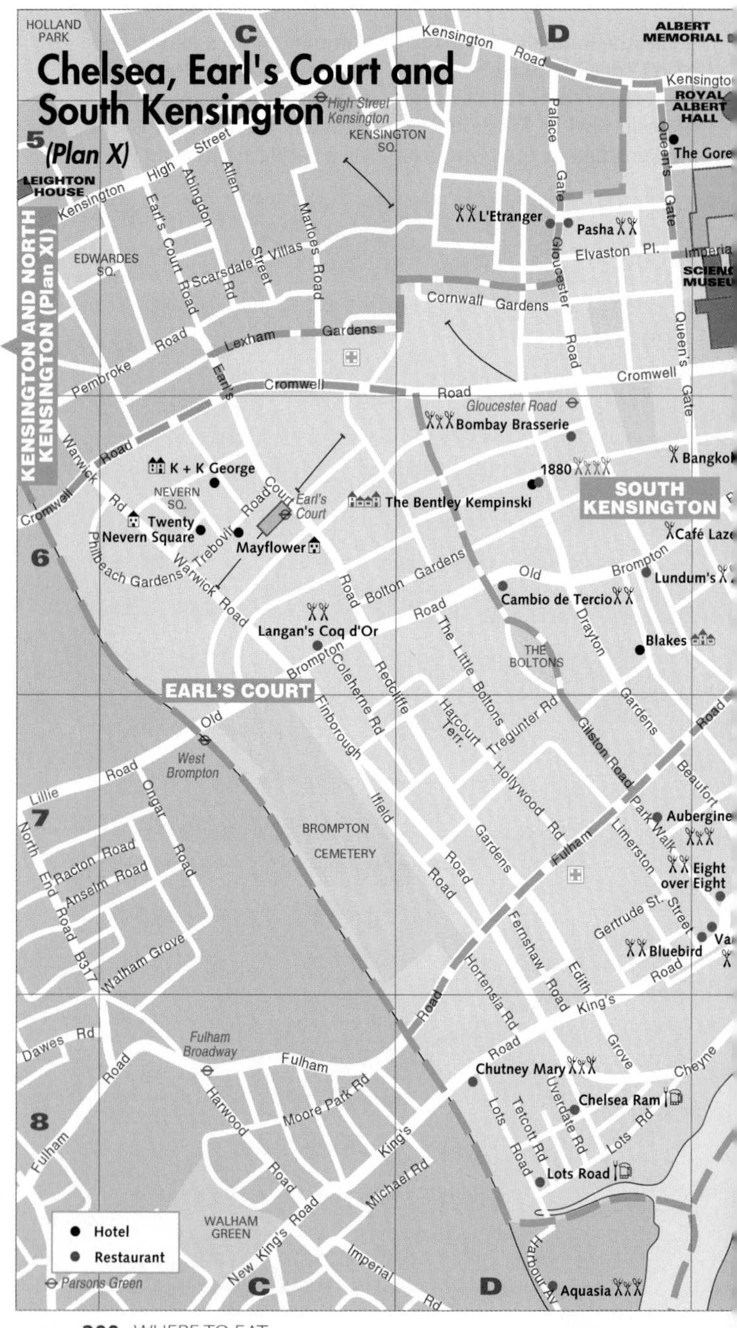

Chelsea, Earl's Court and South Kensington
(Plan X)
Hotel
Restaurant
L'Etranger
Pasha
Bombay Brasserie
1880
Bangkok
K + K George
The Bentley Kempinski
Twenty Nevern Square
Mayflower
Café Lazeez
Lundum's
Cambio de Tercio
Blakes
Langan's Coq d'Or
Aubergine
Eight over Eight
Bluebird
Chutney Mary
Chelsea Ram
Lots Road
Aquasia
SOUTH KENSINGTON
EARL'S COURT
KENSINGTON AND NORTH KENSINGTON (Plan XI)
HOLLAND PARK
LEIGHTON HOUSE
ROYAL ALBERT HALL
BROMPTON CEMETERY
WALHAM GREEN
THE BOLTONS

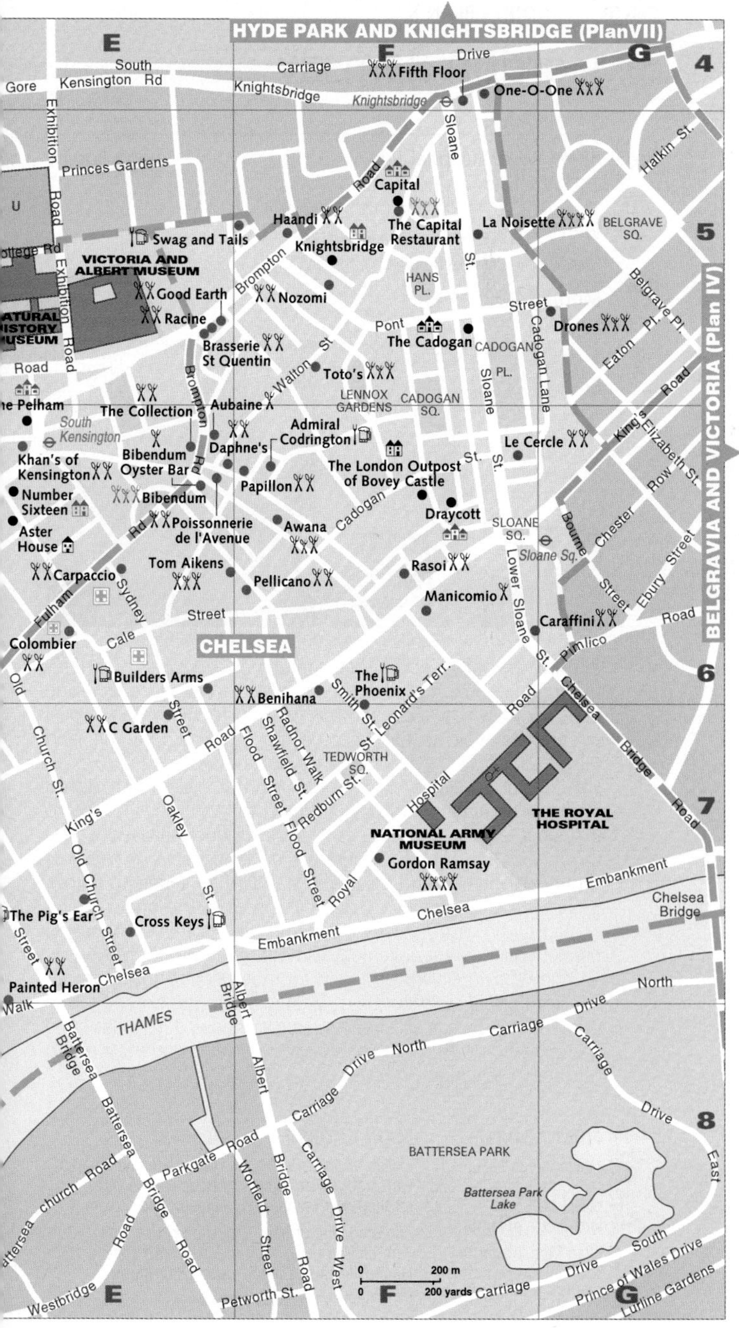
HYDE PARK AND KNIGHTSBRIDGE (PlanVII)
BELGRAVIA AND VICTORIA (Plan IV)
Fifth Floor
One-O-One
Capital
The Capital Restaurant
La Noisette
Haandi
Swag and Tails
Knightsbridge
VICTORIA AND ALBERT MUSEUM
Good Earth
Nozomi
Racine
Brasserie St Quentin
Drones
The Cadogan
Toto's
The Pelham
The Collection
Aubaine
Admiral Codrington
Daphne's
Le Cercle
Khan's of Kensington
Bibendum Oyster Bar
The London Outpost of Bovey Castle
Papillon
Number Sixteen
Bibendum
Draycott
Aster House
Poissonnerie de l'Avenue
Awana
Tom Aikens
Rasoi
Carpaccio
Pellicano
Manicomio
Caraffini
Colombier
CHELSEA
Builders Arms
The Phoenix
Benihana
C Garden
TEDWORTH SQ.
THE ROYAL HOSPITAL
NATIONAL ARMY MUSEUM
Gordon Ramsay
The Pig's Ear
Cross Keys
Painted Heron
THAMES
BATTERSEA PARK
Battersea Park Lake
0 200 m
0 200 yards

Gordon Ramsay ✿✿✿

French XXXX

68-69 Royal Hospital Rd
SW3 4HP
(020) 73524441 – **Fax** (020) 73523334
Web www.gordonramsay.com

⊖ Sloane Square
F7

A/C VISA MC AE

Closed 2 weeks Christmas-New Year, Saturday and Sunday – booking essential

Menu £40/85

Gordon Ramsay Holdings

In this world of 'celebrity', one sometimes struggles to remember the feats that garnered the fame in the first place. But dine at Gordon Ramsay's eponymous flagship restaurant and you'll understand why he has become the most recognisable and talked-about chef around. And it's not the swearing.

His cooking is simply of the very highest order, with dishes displaying hallmark intricacy and care; they are finely tuned to a degree where the textures provide distinct sensations and flavours exquisite clarity. There are no false notes or needless showy elaboration and it sets the standard for others to follow. Service is equally attentive to detail. Overseen by the long-standing manager who gently guides you through your meal, staff discreetly predict your every requirement without getting in the way.

The new David Collins designed room is elegant but understated, comfortable without being intimidating. With only 14 tables demand has always exceeded supply and now, due to the fame game, new fans keep on coming, so reservations are taken two months in advance.

A LA CARTE

FIRST COURSE
- Ballotine and sautéed foie gras with apple and cured beef and vinaigrette of lentils.
- Pan-fried lobster tail with aubergine gratin and black truffle.

MAIN COURSE
- Fillets of John Dory with crab, caviar and crushed new potatoes.
- Roasted fillet of pork with braised belly, baby langoustine and a light Madeira jus.

DESSERT
- Chocolate and amaretti biscuit soufflé with cinnamon ice cream.
- Lime parfait with honeycomb and chocolate sauce.

La Noisette

Innovative

164 Sloane St — Knightsbridge
SW1X 9QB — **F5**
(020) 77505000 – **Fax** (020) 77505001
e-mail lanoisette@gordonramsay.com
Web www.gordonramsay.com

Closed Saturday lunch and Sunday

Menu £21/50

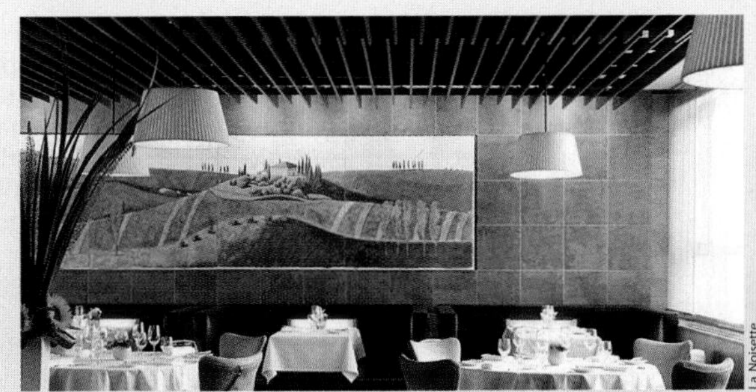

La Noisette

Much beard stroking greeted the news that Gordon Ramsay was going to try another restaurant on a site where the knell tolled for the two previous incumbents. Could it be third time lucky for this first floor restaurant?

Arrivals are greeted at a small reception desk then escorted up the art deco stairs to the restaurant, whose aesthetic is a tad more corporate than comely. Hazelnut colour blends with ligneous adornment to create a somewhat sober background which, in turn, is offset by the large painting of a Tuscan hillside, the relevance of which is not altogether clear.

Fortunately, the confident serving team keep everything moving along nicely and the staggered bookings ensure that there's a steady stream of arriving diners.

Bjorn Van der Horst is the man given free rein in the kitchen, having made his name and reputation at The Greenhouse. The menu layout needs some explanation from your server but expect the cooking to be a highly accomplished combination of inventive and detailed dishes alongside others of a more classical bent, but all displaying confidently bold flavours.

A LA CARTE

FIRST COURSE	MAIN COURSE	DESSERT
• Seared foie gras with coffee and amaretto.	• Slow cooked Atlantic cod with Jabugo ham and squid.	• Fromage blanc soufflé, apricots and toasted almond ice cream.
• Wild line-caught sea bass with samphire soubise and cockle ravioli.	• Roasted veal with rutabaga purée, radish and Bagna Cauda.	• Chocolate marquise with toasted brioche and praline shake.

1880

French XXXX

at The Bentley Kempinski H., 27-33 Harrington Gdns ✉ SW7 4JX — ⊖ Gloucester Road **D6**

A/C VISA MC AE D

✆ (020) 72445555 – **Fax** (020) 72445566
e-mail info@thebentley-hotel.com
Web www.thebentley-hotel.com

Closed Sunday-Monday – dinner only

Menu £54

The restaurant 1880, named after the date of the building, is found on the lower floor (basement sounds too grim) of the Bentley Kempinski Hotel and they have clearly decided that if your restaurant has no windows then use shock and awe tactics by blitzing the room with expensive materials: silk, gold and marble are used in quantities that would make the most flamboyant of designers blanch. Such largesse also extends to the comfort of the diner - tables are virtually a car drive away from one another and the deep armchairs will show no mercy to a dull dining companion.
The modern cooking comes presented by way of a number of 'grazing' menus. Ensure you have a pre or post dinner drink in the rather swish Malachite bar opposite.

JUST PEACHY

The famous opera singer Dame Nellie Melba may have spent much of her time in London having dishes named after her, but in fact neither Melba Toast nor Pêche Melba were so called at first. Auguste Escoffier, then maître chef at London's Savoy Hotel, named the former after Marie Ritz, wife of Cesar, before Dame Nellie came to stay. The dessert - delivered to the diva with an ice sculpture of a swan - was originally called Pêche au Cygne.

The Capital Restaurant

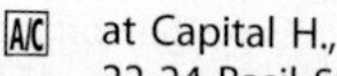

French

at Capital H.,
22-24 Basil St SW3 1AT
(020) 75895171 – **Fax** (020) 72250011
e-mail caprest@capitalhotel.co.uk **Web** www.capitalhotel.co.uk
Booking essential

Knightsbridge
F5

Menu £29.50/55

The Capital

Dining in a hotel restaurant can sometimes be a quite uninspiring practice, what with the anodyne décor and all those name tags. The Capital, however, never fails to provide a thoroughly enjoyable experience, due to the smooth choreography of the service and the understated style and elegance of the room. That the current chef is only the fourth in the position since The Capital opened in 1971 speaks volumes about the traditions of the hotel. But whereas tradition may weigh down some kitchens, here it positively energises and stimulates. Chef Eric Chavot creates dishes of grace and poise, undercut by French techniques and influences. The ingredients are of the highest order and the combinations of flavours are delicate and enticing. The wine list is noted for its enormous depth and breadth.
The latest redecoration is its most striking for many a year. The walls are panelled with sycamore; the powder blue chairs lend colour; the two sparkling chandeliers catch the eye while the silk drapes add softness to the room. It seats around thirty-four, ensuring it all stays very intimate.

A LA CARTE

FIRST COURSE

- Treacle salmon with deep-fried soft shell crab.
- Fricassée of frogs' legs, veal sweetbread and cep purée.

MAIN COURSE

- Honey roast slow cooked pork belly with horseradish and pommes mousseline.
- Saddle of rabbit with seared calamari and tomato risotto.

DESSERT

- Iced coffee parfait with chocolate fondant.
- Caramelised apple and toffee with caramel ice cream.

Foliage ✿

Innovative XXX

A/C VISA MC AE DC ⅄

at Mandarin Oriental Hyde Park H., 66 Knightsbridge ✉ SW1X 7LA

✆ (020) 72013723 – **Fax** (020) 72354552

⊖ Knightsbridge **F4**

Menu £25 (lunch) – Carte £48/50

Mandarin Oriental Hyde Park

The approach from the bar builds the levels of expectation and the glass walkway, with the displayed wine cellar, tells you this is no ordinary hotel dining room. Adam Tihany was the designer whose idea it was 'to bring the park into the restaurant'. Hyde Park certainly plays a leading role in this theatre: the floor is slightly raised to ensure that all tables have a view while the lighting behind the glass illuminates the leaves and changes with the seasons. The colours and textures have an earthy, natural feel.

Seating only forty-five, but with more than enough room to allow for generously sized tables, the restaurant is smart and elegant without feeling stuffy or too grand. Service is structured and well-organised, with a young yet confident team who are eager to please, which excuses the slight tendency to be over solicitous.

The kitchen demonstrates its skill and craftsmanship in a series of dishes that are as technically deft as they are full of flavour. There is a clear understanding of the ingredients used as well as the appeal of contrasting textures and tastes.

A LA CARTE

FIRST COURSE

- Slow-cooked belly of ham, date marmalade, black pudding and cauliflower cream.
- Roast scallop salad with caramelised cauliflower beignet.

MAIN COURSE

- Roast loin of venison with wild mushrooms and smoked artichoke purée.
- Pot roast saddle of rabbit with wild mushroom pithivier, asparagus and bacon.

DESSERT

- Pumpkin treacle tart with pecans, orange marmalade mousse, carrot and blood orange sorbet.
- Pistachio soufflé, milk chocolate mousse.

Tom Aikens ✿

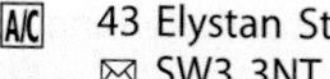

Innovative XXX

A/C
VISA
MC
AE

43 Elystan St
SW3 3NT
(020) 75842003 – **Fax** (020) 75842001
e-mail info@tomaikens.co.uk **Web** www.tomaikens.co.uk

South Kensington
E6

Closed last 2 weeks August, 10 days Christmas-New Year, Saturday, Sunday and Bank Holidays

Menu £29/60

Tom Aikens

The restaurant has an elegant simplicity, with its black leather chairs and black blinds contrasting with the white of the walls and some splashes of colour courtesy of a small collection of modern art. Tables are well spaced and impeccably laid.
Simplicity, though, is certainly not in the vocabulary of the eponymous chef when it comes to his modern take on cuisine which is definitely not for the faint-hearted. The kitchen certainly does not make it easy on itself as this type of labour intensive cooking requires an awful lot of chefs below stairs. Many dishes come in assorted parts on various vessels and with so many elements it is inevitable that some parts are greater than others. However, when considered overall, the craftsmanship and sheer ambition merit commendation.
The service is detailed and conscientious without being over-bearing and dishes are thankfully explained in detail on delivery. The wine list comes with a decent number of realistically priced bottles and a helpful sommelier.

A LA CARTE

FIRST COURSE

- Frogs' legs with chervil cassonade, white onion velouté and morels.
- Poached crayfish with artichoke, chicken and truffle jelly.

MAIN COURSE

- Roast pork cutlet with pork lasagna, pearl barley and caramelised onions.
- Seared and poached pigeon with choucroute and foie gras.

DESSERT

- Passion fruit jelly and mousse with vanilla anglaise and passion fruit syrup.
- Pineapple roasted with sesame, sesame sponge and tuile.

Aubergine ✿

French XXX

11 Park Walk
✉ SW10 0AJ
☎ (020) 73523449 – **Fax** (020) 73511770
Web www.auberginerestaurant.co.uk

⊖ South Kensington
D7

Closed Saturday lunch, Sunday and Bank Holidays – booking essential

Menu £34/60

Aubergine

Aubergine has been flying the flag for gastronomy in these parts for some years now – and the name has stayed the same since Gordon Ramsay made his reputation here.
William Drabble has been at the helm since 1998 and he has continued the theme of offering a comparatively classically French repertoire using much in the way of British ingredients. The descriptions of the dishes on the menu are refreshingly understated which belies the detail and care that has gone into their preparation. Dishes may look pretty but this isn't fancy-pants cooking – flavours are bold and earthy. A decently priced lunch menu comes with a half bottle, water and coffee included. The restaurant is divided in essence into two, with a further small seating area by the entrance. The dining room at the back is the lighter and brighter section. Comfy chairs provide sufficient comfort for those in for the long haul and the flawlessly laid tables are sufficiently separated to guarantee a certain privacy.
The experienced manager ensured that the service is formal and correct without being stiff.

A LA CARTE

FIRST COURSE
- Mousse of salmon and langoustine, basil and tomato emulsion.
- Fillet of red mullet with black olives, parsley and capers, courgette flower.

MAIN COURSE
- Roast monkfish with dill mash and truffle butter sauce.
- Veal sweetbreads wrapped in Bayonne ham with girolle purée, carrots and Sauternes.

DESSERT
- Dark chocolate chiboust with poached cherries.
- Queen of Puddings with pistachio and poached apricots.

Bibendum

French XXX

Michelin House, 81 Fulham Rd ⊖ South Kensington
✉ SW3 6RD **E6**
✆ (020) 75815817 – **Fax** (020) 78237925
Web www.bibendum.co.uk

Closed dinner 24-26 December and 1 January

Menu £28.50 (lunch) – Carte £37/60

Dine with the Editor of the Michelin Guide here and he'll go all misty eyed as he remembers when part of the restaurant was once his office.
This extraordinarily imaginative building, opened in 1911 and designed by a Michelin employee, anticipated the art deco movement of the 1920's, with its ceramic tiles and stained glass windows, and remained our UK HQ until the mid 1980's.
Named after the Michelin Man, Bibendum proved an instant hit as a restaurant by combining all the elements of style, design, service and carefully prepared food. Today, it remains a favourite by continuing to offer dependably good cooking that, appropriately enough, still retains that French connection, along with professional service and surroundings that never fail to impress.

One-O-One

Seafood XXX

at Sheraton Park Tower H., ⊖ Knightsbridge
William St ✉ SW1X 7RN **F4**
✆ (020) 72907101 – **Fax** (020) 72356196

Menu £25/48 – Carte £35/58

One-O-One sits at the base of the cylindrically shaped Sheraton Park, located at the starting grid for Knightsbridge shoppers. The restaurant has its own entrance on William Street in an attempt to give it an identity of its own and it certainly makes use of its shape, with a bank of windows letting in the light and letting out the views.
Nautical blues and aquamarines are the dominant colours of this rather smart room which is highly appropriate as this a seafood restaurant. The chef hails from Brittany which informs his culinary style - his whole sea bass baked in sea salt is something of a house speciality. The quality and freshness of the seafood is exemplary.
Tables are smartly dressed and service is polite and well organised.

Drones

Modern European XXX

1 Pont St ⊖ Knightsbridge
SW1X 9EJ **G5**
(020) 72359555 – **Fax** (020) 72359566
Web www.whitestarline.org.uk

Closed 26 December, 1 January, Saturday lunch and Sunday dinner

A/C · VISA · MC · AE · D

Menu £17.95 (lunch) – Carte £32/47

Drones is a grown-up restaurant for grown-up people. Having been in and out of the limelight since the 1970's, it was re-invigorated and re-opened in 2000 under the patronage of the Marco Pierre White Empire.
It's quite a long and narrow room where the gap between tables is slight but the tables themselves occupy decent acreage. The walls are lined with photographs of the good and the great of showbiz to remind you that this has always been something of a glamorous address. Service is correct and deliberate and the regulars don't go unrecognised.
This being a MPW outpost means that the menu is a mix of the best of French cuisine and British cooking. Choices range from Dover Sole and potted shrimps to *foie gras parfait* and *magret* of duck.

Fifth Floor

Modern European XXX

at Harvey Nichols, ⊖ Knightsbridge
Knightsbridge SW1X 7RJ **F4**
(020) 72355250
Web www.harveynichols.com

Closed Christmas and Sunday dinner

A/C · VISA · MC · AE · D

Menu £19.50/39.50 – Carte £28/44

The ladies who lunch have never had it so good.
Harvey Nichol's flagship Knightsbridge store boasts a top floor to satisfy the weariest of shoppers and the most jaded of palates. As well as a food store, sushi bar, café and cocktail bar one finds the strikingly stylish sanctuary of the main restaurant, decorated with a faux skylight and fibre-optic lit walls that change colour periodically. It sets the standards by which all department stores are judged by being so much more than merely an in-store restaurant for there is substance as well as style here.
The express lift from Sloane Street brings more customers up for the light, fresh and balanced dishes, service is polite and efficient and brunch is offered at weekends.

Chutney Mary

Indian XXX

A/C

535 King's Rd ⊖ Fulham Broadway
✉ SW10 0SZ **D8**
✆ (020) 73513113 – **Fax** (020) 73517694
Web www.realindianfood.com

Dinner only and lunch Saturday and Sunday

VISA MC AE

Carte £33/43

Chutney Mary is one of the senior members of the Indian restaurant fraternity but that doesn't mean it has rested on its laurels. In 2002 it was given a head-to-toe revamp which modernised what was already a very comfortable place.
The large conservatory is still there but now the room is fringed with storm-lamps and the mood is altogether more seductive and sophisticated. 1840's etchings of Indian life combine with mirrors to add a touch of glamour and the young team provide service that is both conscientious and attentive.
The menu is as interesting as it has always been, with good quality seasonal ingredients and strong presentation. The well chosen wine list challenges those who think only a Kingfisher beer can accompany an Indian meal.

Bombay Brasserie

Indian XXX

A/C VISA MC AE

Courtfield Rd ⊖ Gloucester Road
✉ SW7 4QH **D6**
✆ (020) 73704040 – **Fax** (020) 78351669
Web www.bombaybrasserielondon.com

Closed 25-26 December – buffet lunch

Menu £18.95/45 – Carte £29/39

Bombay Brasserie opened its doors in 1982 and its neon sign and doorman have become established local features. It was one of the first restaurants to prove to Londoners that Indian food merits glamorous surroundings just as much as any other cuisine and succeeds so well in its task that you'll never be able to look flock wallpaper in the eye again. The vast, perpetually busy, dining room is divided into two: the main room with its striking mural of Bombay life and the conservatory extension.
A whole army of staff all know exactly what to do and do so with aplomb. Influences from across India feature, from Kerala to Mughlai, and this includes seafood dishes from Goa and fragrant Parsi fare. The lunchtime buffet is a veritable institution.

Awana

Malaysian XXX

A/C VISA MC AE Diners

85 Sloane Ave — ⊖ South Kensington
✉ SW3 3DX — **F6**
✆ (020) 75848880 – **Fax** (020) 75846188
e-mail info@awana.co.uk **Web** www.awana.co.uk

Menu £15 (lunch) – Carte £23/32

Malaysia has been one of the few absentees as London embraces the cooking of the world but it is now proudly showcased at this very smart Chelsea restaurant, whose name translates as "in the clouds".
Start your meal with a *roti canai* and order *satay* from the deftly skilled chef behind the dedicated satay bar. The menu is divided into soups, curries, grills and stir-fry, with the "Malaysian Journey" tasting menu being a great introduction. The lunch menu is a virtual steal.
A smart bar provides a great spot for one of their original cocktails while the restaurant is designed using traditional elements such as teakwood and batik silk, with stylish glass screens and decorative panels. Very charming Malaysian servers offer sensible advice.

Toto's

Italian XXX

VISA MC AE Diners

Walton House, Walton St — ⊖ Knightsbridge
✉ SW3 2JH — **F5**
✆ (020) 75890075 – **Fax** (020) 75819668

Closed 3 days Christmas

Menu £23 (lunch) – Carte £35/50

This is a real Chelsea restaurant and one that's been part of local life for many a year. It comes from an era when people went to restaurants to eat rather than to gawp.
It's in an attractive period house in a secretive little spot and once you're seated you'll wonder why you don't live in Chelsea yourself (or be glad that you do).
Beyond the bar and small lounge by the entrance, you'll find a smart, marble-floored restaurant that's spread over two floors and is far larger than you're expecting. All the regulars have their own spots and there are various corners and tables for those after added privacy. Service is equally old school and the cooking is traditional and reliable, although it does come at a price. Well, this is Chelsea, after all.

Aquasia

International XXX

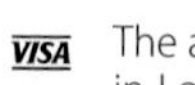

at Conrad London H., Chelsea Harbour ✉ SW10 0XG — ⊖ Fulham Broadway **D8**
✆ (020) 73008443

Carte £25/45

The all-suite Conrad Hotel may not be the most accessible place in London if you haven't got a limo, but have lunch on the sun deck of their restaurant Aquasia, overlooking the yachts of Chelsea Harbour, and you'll think you've landed in the Med.
The room is shaped like an ocean liner and is all very fresh and light in tone, with a wall of windows that open out on warm days. Most of the tables have a view, although some prefer to gaze inward in case any of the hotel's more famous guests wander in. As the name implies, the cooking blends Mediterranean ingredients with Asian aromatics and techniques to create appealingly refined dishes.
On Sundays the Champagne brunches have become very popular, helped no doubt by the offer of unlimited Champagne.

Daphne's

Italian XX

112 Draycott Ave ✉ SW3 3AE — ⊖ South Kensington **E6**
✆ (020) 75894257 – **Fax** (020) 72252766
e-mail office@daphnes-restaurant.co.uk **Web** www.daphnes.co.uk
Closed dinner 24 December and 25-26 December – booking essential

Menu £21.75 (lunch) – Carte £23/42

The interior design comes courtesy of Tuscany, the bronzed clientele from the pages of 'Hello Magazine'. With its tiled flooring, rough terracotta coloured plaster, exposed brickwork and greenery galore, one can easily feel one's lunching in a picturesque Italian hill town, especially if the sun's shining when you're in the appealing conservatory part of the restaurant. However, most diners spend more time eyeing, or avoiding the eye of, their fellow diners than their surroundings as Daphne's attracts more than its fair share of the beautiful people.
Expect equally attractively presented and decidedly wholesome Italian food, with influences stretching across the various regions and service that is as sharp as a tack.

Rasoi ✿

Indian XX

10 Lincoln St ⊖ Sloane Square
SW3 2TS **F6**
(020) 72251881 – **Fax** (020) 75810220
e-mail rasoi.vineet@btconnect.com **Web** www.vineetbhatia.com

Closed 25 December, Saturday lunch, Sunday and Bank Holidays

A/C VISA MC AE D

Carte £31/66

Rasoi

An end of terrace townhouse in a typically smart Chelsea street is not necessarily the place you'd expect to find an Indian restaurant but, then again, Rasoi (meaning 'kitchen') is no ordinary Indian restaurant.

The chef owner, Vineet Bhatia, made his name at Zaika but moved to open his own restaurant here in 2004 and his loyal band of customers have all since followed him. Ring the doorbell to enter and you'll find the interior still retains the feel of a family home. On the ground floor, the dining room is L shaped, with a small conservatory area at the back and is decorated with an assortment of ceramics, carvings, face masks and Indian trinkets. The upstairs rooms are often used for private parties and have an equally intimate feel.

To really appreciate the craft and creativity of the cooking one must first put aside one's preconceptions of traditional, everyday Indian restaurants. The cooking here is individual, inventive and innovative, spicing is subtle and controlled and the flavours have an impressive clarity.

A LA CARTE

FIRST COURSE
- Black pepper chicken tikka skewer with apple and raisin raita.
- Braised lime flavoured lamb seekh kebab with masala blue cheese naan.

MAIN COURSE
- Ginger and chilli lobster dusted with curry leaf and spiced cocoa powder.
- Banana wrapped sea bass with yellow lentils, cashew nut, lemon rice.

DESSERT
- Chocolate and roasted almond samosa, walnut and coffee mousse, masala tea ice cream.
- Fig, walnut and rice pudding with cardamom ice cream.

Racine

French XX

239 Brompton Rd
SW3 2EP
(020) 75844477 – **Fax** (020) 75844900

⊖ South Kensington
E5

Closed 25 December

Menu £18 (lunch) – Carte £26/36

A French brasserie so authentic that if it was on the Left Bank you'd have to listen to Parisians boasting. Except this restaurant is in the middle of Knightsbridge and the chef, who is also one of the two owners, is as English as the weather outside.

Once you've done your Eric Morecambe impression through the red curtain, you enter into a room decorated in warm chocolates with large mirrors and wood flooring. The French team of waiters, overseen by the other owner who *is* French, provide helpful and cordial service. The menu, priced very keenly considering the location, offers an enticing selection of bourgeois classics.

The whole experience will leave you with suggested memories of romantic Parisian adventures.

Nozomi

Japanese XX

15 Beauchamp Pl,
SW3 1NQ
(020) 78381500 – **Fax** (020) 78381001
Web www.nozomi.co.uk

⊖ Knightsbridge
F5

Closed Sunday

Carte £40/55

The fact that there's a liveried doorman standing outside should tell you that this is not your everyday Japanese restaurant, even for Knightsbridge. In fact, you may not even think you're in a restaurant at all because you'll find yourself in a glitzy bar, complete with loud music and a DJ, which sets the tone for the whole place with its dark styling and sleekness. It's up a few steps to the roomy dining area, beneath a large skylight, with a further sushi bar upstairs.

The kitchen attempts to match these fiercely fashionable surroundings with a selection of modern and original creations. A variation on the ubiquitous black cod with miso is there but then so is Genghis Khan Chicken, an altogether more threatening sounding dish.

Bluebird

Modern European XX

A/C 350 King's Rd ⊖ Sloane Square
✉ SW3 5UU **E7**
✆ (020) 75591000 – **Fax** (020) 75591115
e-mail enquires@bluebird-store.co.uk **Web** www.conran.co.uk

Closed 23-30 December, 12-27 August and Sunday – dinner only

VISA MC AE

Menu £30

Cars and girls, cars and rock n'roll, but cars and food? Bluebird is a giant brasserie housed in a former motor garage which was built in 1923 and was where Malcolm Campbell's famous Bluebird cars were built. The noise of revving engines has now been replaced by the sound of guffawing Chelsea locals but, with nearly 200 seats to fill, this place does need to be busy to get going.

Found at the end of King's Road at the point where you start wondering if you're still actually on the King's Road, the bar is something of a destination in itself while the menu sensibly offers considerable choice, with an English slant, as well as caring for those with less robust appetites. For quicker and simpler fare, try the ground floor café.

Poissonnerie de l'Avenue

Seafood XX

A/C 82 Sloane Ave ⊖ South Kensington
✉ SW3 3DZ **E6**
✆ (020) 75892457 – **Fax** (020) 75813360
Web www.poissonneriedel'avenue.co.uk

Closed 25-26 December and Sunday

VISA MC AE

Menu £28 (lunch) – Carte £27/39

This is one of those restaurants that's impossible to walk past without feeling drawn in. The smell of seafood and garlic is enough in itself to arouse your senses and if you peer, like a child, through the window it all looks so warm and inviting inside.

For over forty years this veritable institution has been satisfying the grown ups of Chelsea with its reliably classic seafood and its timeless and well-mannered atmosphere. The wood panelling, nautically themed paintings and the type of waiters they don't make anymore all contribute to the feeling that this is a restaurant that really belongs and one that has a soul. It also has *Sole Véronique,* to remind us that cooking wasn't invented in the 1990's.

Le Cercle

French XX

A/C VISA MC AE

1 Wilbraham Pl ⊖ Sloane Square
✉ SW1X 9AE **F6**
✆ (020) 79019999 – **Fax** (020) 79019111
e-mail info@lecercle.co.uk

Closed 23 December-8 January, Sunday and Monday

Menu £19.50 (lunch) – Carte £29/47

This offshoot of Club Gascon is housed within what was planned to be the swimming pool of the serviced apartments above so that explains the double height of the ceiling of this basement restaurant.
This is a very stylish room, with marble, leather, assorted little nooks and a long bar all divided up by billowing white drapes, lending an air of seduction and secrecy. Lovers should ask for table 24.
The menu comes divided into sections headed *vegetal, marin, fermier, terroirs* and *plaisirs*. Diners should choose three or four dishes – which are delicate little modern French creations - plus a dessert and, as they all come in 'tasting' sizes, now's your chance to order something unfamiliar. The exclusively French wines are thoughtfully paired.

Le Colombier

French traditional XX

VISA MC AE

145 Dovehouse St ⊖ South Kensington
✉ SW3 6LB **E6**
✆ (020) 73511155 – **Fax** (020) 73515124
Web www.lecolombier-sw3.co.uk

Menu £19 (lunch) – Carte £27/37

It's a French restaurant in Chelsea but could equally be a Chelsea restaurant in France. The loyalty and regularity of attendance shown by those in the neighbourhood ensures that there's always that cheery atmosphere of familiarity.
The restaurant, with a large covered terrace/conservatory at the front, has more than a little feel of a brasserie. It's also quite sizeable but manages to retain a certain intimacy, helped considerably by the presence of the experienced owner who will never knowingly let a face go unrecognised.
Classic French cooking is the order of the day and it's hearty, stout and generous in size. The munificence of the set price lunch menu is enough in itself to make regulars of us all.

Caraffini

Italian XX

61-63 Lower Sloane St ⊖ Sloane Square
SW1W 8DH **F6**
(020) 72590235 – **Fax** (020) 72590236
e-mail info@caraffini.co.uk **Web** www.caraffini.co.uk

Closed 25 December, Easter, Sunday and Bank Holidays – booking essential

Carte £25/33

One doesn't have to look far to see why Paolo Caraffini's restaurant is always so busy: it has a wonderfully genial host, smooth service, reliably good Italian food and a highly hospitable atmosphere. Just watching the number of regulars Paolo greets as friends, from Chelsea art dealers to King's Road shoppers, will make you want to become a part of the club. Warm and cosy in winter, bright and sunny in summer with pavement tables for alfresco dining, this really is a place for all seasons.
Daily specials supplement the already balanced menu that covers many regions of Italy and any requests to veer off-menu are satisfied without fuss or fanfare.
Caraffini is proof that good hospitality is very much alive and kicking.

Lundum's

Danish 

119 Old Brompton Rd ⊖ Gloucester Road
SW7 3RN **D6**
(020) 73737774 – **Fax** (020) 73734472
Web www.lundums.com

Closed 23 December-4 January and Sunday dinner

Menu £16.50/24.50 – Carte £28/56

Lundum's proves that there is a special kind of atmosphere in family-run restaurants, especially ones proudly showcasing the cooking of the owner's native country. Those unfamiliar with Danish cooking will soon find themselves converted when they experience the clean and natural flavours which are the hallmark of many Scandinavian cuisines.

Housed in a charming converted Edwardian former public library, the restaurant is surprisingly spacious yet, because of its thoughtful layout, always feels warm and intimate. The lunch menu offers more traditional Danish fare, with the assorted platters or open sandwiches well worth a try, while at dinner the cooking becomes altogether more ambitious and contemporary in style.

L'Etranger

Innovative XX

36 Gloucester Rd ⊖ Gloucester Road
✉ SW7 4QT **D5**
✆ (020) 75841118 – **Fax** (020) 75848886
e-mail sasha@etranger.co.uk **Web** www.etranger.co.uk

Closed lunch Saturday and Sunday – booking essential

Menu £16.50 (lunch) – Carte £34/78

The French are more protective of their culinary heritage than most so it's a little surprising to encounter what is, in essence, a thoroughly French restaurant serving fusion cuisine. L'Etranger indeed.

Lilacs, lavenders and greys all blend together with silk threads and recessed lighting to create a space that is both stylish and tasteful. The fashionable crowd and the large local French community are all followers.

The kitchen blends top notch ingredients such as lobster and foie gras with subtle Asian flavours but also exhibits a certain playfulness. So, alongside the ubiquitous black cod with miso, you'll find peppered steak with sumo chips. Vegetarians are well catered for and wine lovers will find much to admire in the selection and pricing.

Langan's Coq d'Or

Traditional XX

254-260 Old Brompton Rd ⊖ Earl's Court
✉ SW5 9HR **C6**
✆ (020) 72592599 – **Fax** (020) 73707735
Web www.langansrestaurants.co.uk

Closed 25-26 December

Menu £21.50 – Carte £26

The celebrated restaurateur Peter Langan may no longer be with us but Richard Shepherd has created a restaurant of which his friend would no doubt have approved. He has also named in honour of the original moniker of Langan's in Stratton Street. It is almost two restaurants in one: the glass enclosed front section goes by the name of the 'bar and grill', is more informal in style and opens out onto the street in summer while beyond is the main restaurant, whose walls are filled with a huge collection of artwork.

The menu is a no-nonsense celebration of the best of British combined with what Europe can offer. So, expect bangers and mash alongside rack of lamb. For the incurably louche, breakfast is served until early evening.

Zuma

Japanese

5 Raphael St
SW7 1DL
(020) 75841010 – **Fax** (020) 75845005
e-mail info@zumarestaurant.com **Web** www.zumarestaurant.com

Knightsbridge
PLAN VII F5

Carte £35/55

Japanese food meets Contemporary Japanese food at this stylish Knightsbridge restaurant, popular with the glittering and the glitterati and ideally located for those seeking a little respite from the strain of shopping or being photographed doing so. The place is certainly catching in its design, with a plethora of granite, stone, marble and wood creating a restaurant that successfully blends east with west.
Choose from a variety of seating options, from the bustle of the main dining area to the theatre afforded by the sushi counter. The menu offers up an intriguing mix of the traditional with the ultra modern, all expertly crafted and delicately presented. Lovers of sake will find over thirty varieties available.

Mr Chow

Chinese 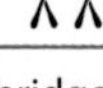

151 Knightsbridge
SW1X 7PA
(020) 75897347 – **Fax** (020) 75845780
e-mail mrchow@aol.com **Web** www.mrchow.com

Knightsbridge
PLAN VII F4

Closed 24-26 December, 1 January and Easter Monday

Menu £26 (lunch) – Carte £36/45

Mr Chow, the self styled Renaissance man, has branches of his Chinese restaurant in various American cities but London was his firstborn, opening its doors in 1968.
Over the years it has seen off assorted interlopers and has retained the affections of many. Newcomers should get something clear - this isn't the sort of Chinese restaurant where you plonk yourself down, order a *Tsingtao* and split your chopsticks in anticipation. Instead, a champagne chariot will be wheeled over to you as you peruse the menu, service is provided by a long standing team of Italian professionals while the room, and the clientele, enjoy a certain timeless elegance.
The Chinese food is reliably good and mixes the traditional with Mr Chow specialities.

Papillon

French XX

96 Draycott Ave. — South Kensington
SW3 3AD — **F6**
(020) 72252555 – **Fax** (020) 72252554
e-mail info@papillonchelsea.co.uk **Web** www.papillonchelsea.co.uk

Closed 24-26 December

Menu £16.50 (lunch) – Carte £27/36

Sometimes you just have to hand it to those designers. Papillon looks as though it has occupied this corner of Draycott Avenue for years but this little butterfly didn't flutter onto the scene until May 2006. From the wood and the mirrors, the lamps and the arched French windows thrown open in summer - everything seems new and old at the same time. It has the feel and the look of a timeless Parisian brasserie and the locals have been flocking in since the doors first opened.

The kitchen, too, does its bit for cross Channel relations by offering a comprehensive selection of Gallic classics, from the robust to the rustic, to appeal to all tastes. Salads from all corners of France remind you that this is also lunching-ladies land.

Pasha

Moroccan XX

1 Gloucester Rd — Gloucester Road
SW7 4PP — **D5**
(020) 75897969 – **Fax** (020) 75819996
Web www.pasha-restaurant.co.uk

Closed Sunday lunch

Carte £35/40

Now under the same ownership as Levant restaurant, Pasha has been recharged and refreshed and now represents a fun night out.

The ground floor is given over to the atmospheric cocktail lounge bar, with the exotic scent of hookah pipes and joss-sticks in the air. Downstairs, low tables are strewn with rose petals, light from lanterns and candles bounces off the mosaic floor while the cushions and rich colours add to the seductive feel. As does the belly-dancer.

Moroccan home-style cooking is the feature here, with sharing the key. Lunch is a simpler affair but in the evenings try one of the 'feast' menus. The main menu is divided into tagines, cous-cous or grills but don't forget Morocco offers good seafood as well as meats.

The Collection

International XX

A/C VISA MC AE

264 Brompton Rd ⊖ South Kensington
SW3 2AS **E6**
(020) 72251212 – **Fax** (020) 72251050
e-mail office@the-collection.co.uk **Web** www.the-collection.co.uk

Closed 25-26 December, 1 January and Sunday – dinner only

Menu £40 – Carte £29/41

Proving that a theme, in this case 'fashion', and a decent restaurant are not necessarily mutually exclusive, The Collection is still pulling in the crowds after more than ten years. Granted, the boys with clipboards are gone from outside but walking down the 'catwalk' entrance still feels like you've got a backstage pass to somewhere a little exclusive.
The cavernous warehouse, all girders and bricks, lends itself perfectly to an operation such as this, where the bar takes up all of the ground floor space and the restaurant sits up on the mezzanine level. Here noise levels are lower and, as one would expect, the menu is *à la mode*, with plenty of Asian influences sitting alongside others of more Southern European persuasion.

Cambio de Tercio

Spanish XX

A/C VISA MC AE

163 Old Brompton Rd. ⊖ Gloucester Road
SW5 0LJ **D6**
(020) 72448970 – **Fax** (020) 73738817
Web www.cambiodetercio.co.uk

Closed 20 December-3 January

Carte £26/32

The young and ambitious owners of this Spanish restaurant have settled comfortably into their surroundings and have been quietly building up a following over the last ten years. The restaurant is brightly coloured and full of life, particularly in summer when the tables spill out onto the pavement.
The cooking has soundly grounded roots but is not afraid to experiment or add innovative touches and presentation on the plate is intricate. Much of the produce is imported from Spain and along with a selection of Sherries comes an exclusively Spanish wine list with much to offer.
Tendido Cero is their very successful tapas bar on the other side of the street whose popularity means that table lingerers are given short shrift.

Khan's of Kensington

Indian XX

3 Harrington Rd — ⊖ South Kensington
SW7 3ES — **E6**
(020) 75844114 – **Fax** (020) 75812900
e-mail info@khansofkensington.co.uk
Closed 25 December and dinner 26 December

Menu £20/25 – Carte £20/27

Virtually opposite South Kensington tube, Khan's of Kensington has been a local feature for quite a few years now and the locals have been resolute in their loyalty.
It's really quite contemporary inside and the modern Warhol-esque pictures take you a little by surprise. The size is near perfect: big enough to generate an atmosphere but small enough to create a certain intimacy. The downstairs tables and chairs have been removed and the space has been turned into a comfortable lounge bar.
The menu provides a more modern and, consequently, more interesting selection of dishes, all of which are carefully prepared to a good standard with the emphasis on the North West frontier.
A takeaway service is also available.

Pellicano

Italian XX

19-21 Elystan St — ⊖ South Kensington
SW3 3NT — **F6**
(020) 75893718 – **Fax** (020) 75841789
e-mail pellicano@btconnect.com
Closed Christmas-New Year

Menu £18.50 (lunch) – Carte £25/40

This is another one of those neighbourhood Chelsea restaurants that makes you wonder why your street doesn't look like this. Unless, of course, this is your street.
The large blue canopy, with half a dozen tables nestled beneath, highlights the location of this popular local Italian. It has a fresh feel to the interior, with its warm yellows and blues, and the clever use of mirrors makes the place seem bigger than it is. The pelican motif is evident in some of the lively artwork.
It is from Sardinia that the kitchen takes its influence, which is evident as soon as the terrific basket of assorted breads arrives. From the pecorino cheese to the *culurgiones* (ravioli), the flavours are as bright and aromatic as the island itself.

Brasserie St Quentin

French traditional XX

243 Brompton Rd
✉ SW3 2EP
✆ (020) 75898005 – **Fax** (020) 75846064
Web www.brasseriestquentin.co.uk

⊖ Knightsbridge
E5

Closed Christmas

Menu £17.50 (lunch) – Carte £30

This was one of the first brasseries to open in the capital and, reassuringly for its clientele of loyal locals and weary shoppers, it is now back under private ownership where places like this really belong.

The success of Brasserie St Quentin is due in no small part to its authentic ambience and confident manner and it feels very much like the genuine article. Mirrors, red leather banquette seating and an ornate bar all fit the brasserie bill perfectly.

The menu is Gallic in essence but many of the ingredients, particularly the meats, come courtesy of some gloriously British estates. The lunchtime and early evening set menus represent excellent value of money, particularly in this neighbourhood.

Painted Heron

Indian XX

112 Cheyne Walk
✉ SW10 0DJ
✆ (020) 73515232 – **Fax** (020) 73515313
Web www.thepaintedheron.com

⊖ Gloucester Road
E7

Closed 25 December, 1 January and Saturday lunch

Carte £25/35

There is hardly a single house on Cheyne Walk without a blue plaque commemorating the literary and artistic talent of a past resident, but one wonders how many of the current occupiers realise they've also got a place like The Painted Heron on their doorstep.

The restaurant is immaculately laid out, with pillars dividing it in into cosier areas. The simple, fresh décor is enlivened by some contemporary paintings. Stylish leather chairs and neatly dressed tables complete the picture of an undeniably smart neighbourhood Indian restaurant.

The menu is printed daily according to what fresh produce is available and the cooking exhibits an understanding of those ingredients and a degree of originality in their preparation.

Vama

Indian XX

VISA MC AE ① 🍷

438 King's Rd ⊖ Sloane Square
✉ SW10 0LJ **E7**
✆ (020) 75658500 – **Fax** (020) 75658501
e-mail admin@vama.co.uk **Web** www.vama.co.uk

Closed 25-26 December and 1 January – dinner only and lunch Saturday-Sunday

Menu £15/45 – Carte £20/35

The Northwest Frontier and the Punjab provide inspiration for the cooking at Vama, so vegetarians will find that they have an equal number of dishes to choose from as the carnivores and that there will be an assortment of authentic breads to soak up the creamy sauces.
The brightly lit façade provides a welcoming beacon, particularly on a winter's evening, while inside the place is divided into three. The first section is where the action seems to be; the second area is a narrow tent-like space and this leads into the rear conservatory, ideal for those after a little more intimacy.
Teak carvings, oil paintings, Indian stone and pretty crockery all add to the Indian feel and help create very pleasant surroundings.

Carpaccio

Italian XX

A/C VISA MC AE ① 🍷

4 Sydney St ⊖ South Kensington
✉ SW3 6PP **E6**
✆ (020) 73523433 – **Fax** (020) 73523435
e-mail eat@carpaccio.uk.com **Web** www.carpaccio.uk.com

Closed Sunday

Carte £32/40

This long, narrow restaurant may be within a pretty Georgian house and fringed with chocolate coloured seating, but the decorative features are more from the testosterone school of interior design – walls come with stills from James Bond films and the owner has displayed his fondness for Formula 1 by hanging the full fibre glass cockpit of an Ayrton Senna racing car.
In this age when every chef is trying to do something different, it can sometimes be reassuring to find a kitchen sticking to the classics. As the name implies, *carpaccio* is the house speciality with beef, tuna and assorted fish given the treatment. Elsewhere on the menu you'll find familiar but nonetheless carefully prepared Italian classics.

Haandi

Indian XX

136 Brompton Rd
SW3 1HY
(020) 78237373 – **Fax** (020) 78239696
Web www.haandi-restaurants.com

⊖ Knightsbridge
F5

Carte £16/38

Brompton Road, with its glittering collection of chichi shops for the label conscious consumer, may not seem the obvious choice of location for an Indian restaurant but Haandi, named after the concaved-bottom cooking pot, provides a welcome alternative to the plethora of snack and coffee bars on this side of the street.
The entrance is a little dowdy but the basement restaurant works well, with the chefs on view in their little kitchen through a window. A laminate menu with photos of dishes again may not sound promising but the Punjabi-influenced dishes are always carefully prepared and deftly spiced.
The original branches are in East Africa but, closer to home, there is a second London branch in Edgware.

Eight over Eight

South-East Asian XX

392 King's Rd
SW3 5UZ
(020) 73499934 – **Fax** (020) 73515157
Web www.eightovereight-restaurants.com
Closed 25-26 December, 1 January and Sunday lunch

⊖ Gloucester Road
E7

Carte £22/40

What was once the Man in the Moon pub is now a fiercely fashionable pan-Asian restaurant, proving that the King's Road is not all high street chains and baby shops and can still cut it with the fashionistas.
The menu has a fairly wide remit to cover much of South East Asia with Chinese, Japanese, Malaysian, Korean and Thai influences all featuring and most dishes designed for sharing. Don't hesitate to ask for help from the charming, and alarmingly attractive, staff.
The room is all moody and cool, with a slick bar at the front and the restaurant at the back. Chocolate coloured leather seating and two shades of oak on the walls contrast with the delicate silk parasol styled lamps. Try not to covet the booths too openly.

C Garden

Italian XX

119 Sydney St ⊖ South Kensington
✉ SW3 6NR **E7**
✆ (020) 73522718
Web www.cgarden.co.uk
Closed Sunday dinner

VISA MC AE

Carte £28

'Dan's' occupied this site for nearly 25 years but in June 2006 Dan sold up and it became an Italian restaurant. The new owner, Guido Campigotto, not only provided the 'C'in the name but also had the contacts to ensure that business began briskly.
Before re-opening it also enjoyed a makeover. The new colour scheme of stone, fawn, light chocolate and cream suits the place well. At the back they've kept the tent-like conservatory and this leads onto the sheltered terrace which is surely one of Chelsea's finest.
Unthreatening, simply prepared and flavoursome Italian food is the order of the day here. However, the final bill can be higher than expected due to the separately priced side orders and the anachronistic cover charge.

Good Earth

Chinese XX

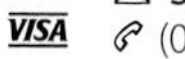

A/C VISA MC AE

233 Brompton Rd ⊖ Knightsbridge
✉ SW3 2EP **E5**
✆ (020) 75843658 – **Fax** (020) 78238769
e-mail goodearthgroup@aol.com **Web** www.goodearthgroup.co.uk
Closed 22-31 December

Menu £11.50/42 – Carte £22/31

Restaurants, boutiques, shops and salons have all come and gone on Brompton Road but good old Good Earth has outlasted them all, and just keeps on doing its thing.
This longevity can be put down to a number of factors: it has been impervious to fashion, its standards are reliable and it gives the punters what they want.
The welcome is guaranteed to be polite and the staff all know what they're doing and do it well. Spread over the ground floor and basement, it wouldn't necessarily win any designs awards but the atmosphere is never less than convivial.
The menu is large without being worryingly vast and performs a clever balancing trick of offering dishes of recognisable popularity alongside others of a more unusual bent.

Benihana

Japanese (Teppanyaki) XX

77 King's Rd — Sloane Square
SW3 4NX — **F6**
(020) 73767799 – **Fax** (020) 73767377
e-mail chelsea.benihana.co.uk **Web** www.benihana.co.uk

Closed 25 December

Menu £11.50/58

There are Benihana restaurants in a number of locations around the world, proving that they've latched onto a winning formula, understand their market and stick to their brief.
The Chelsea chapter is housed in a vast basement but is not without some appeal. Although this one's been around for over a decade it has also been well looked after.
As diners, you sit around a *hibachi* grill (be prepared to share with strangers as each one seats eight) and watch the chefs slice, chop, juggle and serve your food.
Various menus are available and most of the dishes come inclusive of appetisers, vegetables, rice and tea. Benihana is a fun place for larger groups and there are two other branches in Piccadilly Circus and Swiss Cottage.

Manicomio

Italian X

85 Duke of York Sq, King's Rd — Sloane Square
SW3 4LY — **F6**
(020) 77303366 – **Fax** (020) 77303377
Web www.manicomio.co.uk

Closed 25-26 December and 1 January

Carte £23/41

The literal translation is "madhouse", a less than politically correct reference to the building's post-war use as a military asylum. With a large terrace in front and a little deli and café next door, Manicomio dominates this part of the smart redevelopment of the former barracks. The room is divided into two, with a bar on one side. Exposed brick walls, oak flooring and an original fireplace contrast with the flame red seating and modern artwork and create a warm, sophisticated, yet suitably relaxed, atmosphere.
The waiting team are all confidently in control and very charming. The menu concentrates on bright, flavoursome and seasonal Italian cooking. All in all, ideal for those weary from the rigours of shopping.

Aubaine

French

260-262 Brompton Rd — South Kensington
SW3 2AS — **E6**
(020) 70520100 – **Fax** (020) 70520622
e-mail info@aubaine.co.uk **Web** www.aubaine.co.uk

Closed 25 December and 1 January

Menu £21 (dinner) – Carte £21/37

Whether it's a *croissant, croque monsieur* or *coq au vin*, Aubaine is among the increasing number of operations of a more fluid nature which recognise that we don't always want to eat three courses at 1pm.

Describing itself as a 'boulangerie, patisserie and restaurant', it opens early morning until late at night and offers a comprehensive choice of French specialities to satisfy all appetites at all times with the location making it especially busy during shopping hours. The breads are baked here and the 'shop' section does a roaring trade.

The dining area fuses country and city; dressers, flowers and distressed wooden tables are juxtaposed with the modernity of exposed air-con vents and it all opens out onto the pavement in summer.

Café Lazeez

Indian 

93-95 Old Brompton Rd. — South Kensington
SW7 3LD — **E6**
(020) 75816996 – **Fax** (020) 75818200
e-mail southkensington@cafelazeez.com
Web www.cafelazeez.com

Menu £25/30 – Carte £19/25

Those wanting just a drink and a quick bite to eat don't often find themselves in the same restaurant as those after a dining experience with a degree of refinement. Fortunately, by dividing itself in two, Café Lazeez can appeal to both parties.

The ground floor is where the action is, with a fairly lively vibe thanks to the loud music. Upstairs, it all becomes a little more formal, with crisp linen on the table and an altogether more sober ambience.

The same menu is served throughout and is also divided into two, with main courses split between 'traditional' and 'evolved'. Dishes are prepared with care, using decent ingredients and subtle spicing.

The bar stays open quite late but fortunately so does the restaurant

Bangkok

Thai X

A/C VISA MC

9 Bute St. ⊖ South Kensington
✉ SW7 3EY **E6**
✆ (020) 75848529

Closed Christmas-New Year and Sunday

Carte £19/31

Bangkok was the first Thai restaurant to open in London and is now not too far from celebrating its fortieth birthday. The same owner is still here and can often be seen at the stove.
Dishes may sound rather simple on the menu but the cooking is skilfully executed and the flavours are clear, fresh and nicely balanced.
Don't let the smart canopied façade raise your expectations too high: this is not the most comfortable restaurant around. Basic tables and chairs are close together and on the walls hang simple photographs of Thai life. But the open kitchen gives diners something to look at and there's always a sociable atmosphere.
Everyone appears to leave feeling sated and, more unusually these days, with wallets free of burn holes.

Bibendum Oyster Bar

Seafood X

VISA MC AE

Michelin House, 81 Fulham Rd ⊖ South Kensington
✉ SW3 6RD **E6**
✆ (020) 75891480 – **Fax** (020) 78237148
e-mail reservations@bibendum.co.uk **Web** www.bibendum.co.uk

Closed 25-26 December and 1 January – bookings not accepted

Carte £21/50

As an alternative to the more formal restaurant upstairs, Bibendum Oyster Bar provides relaxed surroundings in which to enjoy a variety of seafood. It is also just the sort of place we encounter on holiday in France and then ask why we don't have anything like it at home.
The speciality is, as the name suggests, oysters but the *plateau de fruits de mer* must come a close second. There are also salads, daily specials and plenty of other seafood from the extensive menu.
The tiled walls and mosaic floor add to the appeal and the atmosphere is generally relaxed. Service from the young team can be a little hit and miss.
If you haven't had your fill, you can stock up on more at Bibendum Crustacea, with its counter on the old garage forecourt.

Admiral Codrington

Gastropub 

17 Mossop St
SW3 2LY
(020) 75810005 – **Fax** (020) 75892452
Web www.theadmiralcodrington.co.uk

⊖ South Kensington
F6

Closed 24-26 December

Carte £23/31

'The Cod' was perhaps best known in the '80's when it became the unofficial common room of the 'Sloane Ranger'. Twenty years later the pearls and Barbours have long gone and the pub has reinvented itself as a stylish gastropub.
The bar is now a relaxed, easy-going spot for a drink with a short but well chosen menu. The separate long narrow dining room has been transformed into a comfortable and sophisticated space and comes with a clever retractable roof for summer days.
The menu is an appealing balance of erudite restaurant sophistication balanced with dishes of a more comforting and familiar nature. So whether it's *foie gras* with Muscat jelly or beer battered plaice, there's now something for everyone.

Chelsea Ram

Gastropub 

32 Burnaby St
SW10 0PL
(020) 73514008 – **Fax** (020) 73490885
e-mail bookings@chelsearam.com **Web** www.chelsearam.com

⊖ Fulham Broadway
D8

Carte £168/25

It's a local pub for local people, albeit Chelsea People. The Ram is a Young's pub, close to Chelsea Harbour, and has seemingly become something of a favourite in this part of the world. It is down to earth – insofar as anything is down to earth in Chelsea - and is one of those places where all the elements just seem to fit well together. It does the pub thing well and holds a weekly pub quiz but it also does proper food for all tastes and appetites, with a regularly changing menu supplemented by daily specials. The wine list isn't bad either.
Its welcoming staff and general atmosphere both play a big part in its success. Those put off by the self-congratulatory smugness of some gastropubs will find this place hard to dislike.

Swag and Tails

Gastropub

10-11 Fairholt St — ⊖ Knightsbridge
SW7 1EG — **E_F5**
(020) 75846926 – **Fax** (020) 75819935
e-mail theswag@swagandtails.com **Web** www.swagandtails.com

Closed 1 week Christmas-New Year, Saturday, Sunday and Bank Holidays

Carte £21/32

Found on an attractive, quiet mews a couple of minutes walk from Harrods is one of the prettier pubs around, with its charming display of hanging baskets and pots of flowers. It is also one that has that welcoming atmosphere which comes from being privately owned.

At the front part of the pub one finds the bar, with a log fire, original panelling and those swaged and tailed drapes, while the dining area is at the rear with a conservatory extension, although this is the sort of pub where you can eat where you want.

The kitchen clearly knows its customers and provides them with a balanced selection, combining modern, Mediterranean-influenced cooking with some classic pub favourites for those less adventurous.

Builders Arms

Gastropub

13 Britten St — ⊖ South Kensington
SW3 3TY — **E6**
(020) 73499040
Web www.geronimo-inns.co.uk

Closed 25 December and 1 January

Carte £22/40

The Builders Arms is a three storey Georgian pub, down your typically smart Chelsea street, and was given the full gastropub refurb treatment several years ago. Now, the only reminder of a time when the place was a little more boozer than blazer is in the name.

It certainly got all the elements of your thoroughly modern gastropub, with bookshelves and leather sofas, bright colours and a log fire. Expect from the daily menu a balanced assortment of pub favourites, mixed with others of a more ambitious nature. Its reputation for good food and tirelessly helpful service has spread throughout the Chelsea streets. Reservations are not taken so be prepared to wait your turn amid the boisterous cries of the young and the gilded.

The Pig's Ear

Gastropub

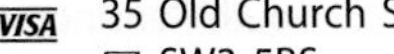

35 Old Church St — Sloane Square
SW3 5BS — **E7**
(020) 73522908 – **Fax** (020) 73529321
e-mail thepigsear@hotmail.co.uk **Web** www.thepigsear.co.uk

Closed 25-26 December and 1 January

Carte £22/36

Judging by the scrum of Chelsea's finest packed into the bar every night, some think it's actually a bit of a silk purse.
The pub certainly presses all the right buttons, from the chatty staff to the appetite-satisfying food. It has been updated without losing its personality – it's still a real pub - and the porcine-themed decorative touches have added a little quirkiness.
The downstairs bar can get a hammering of an evening so, if you want an altogether quieter dinner, merely head upstairs to the rather sweet wood panelled dining room.
The cooking is robust, keeps pace with the seasons by changing daily and is not afraid of offering punters something a little different, from the eponymous deep-fried pig's ears to roast bone marrow.

The Phoenix

Gastropub

23 Smith St — Sloane Square
SW3 4EE — **F6_7**
(020) 77309182
Web www.geronimo-inns.co.uk

Closed 25-26 December

Carte £15/25

More as a result of a comprehensive refurbishment of an existing pub rather than something raised from any ashes, The Phoenix provides the good burghers of Chelsea with another gastropub in which to enjoy modern, robust cooking with a side order of rusticity. It is also confident enough not to simply ape the menus of local restaurants and instead provides just the sort of food locals want to find in their pub.
The front bar, whose modernism is reigned in by the odd retro tweak, is ideal for all those louche local types, while the dining room at the rear provides a slightly more formalised setting, and more comfortable leather chairs.
Alfresco dining is such a rare treat in London that the small pavement terrace is hugely popular in summer.

Cross Keys

Gastropub 

A/C VISA MC AE

1 Lawrence St — ⊖ South Kensington
✉ SW3 5NB — **E7**
✆ (020) 73499111 – **Fax** (020) 73499333
e-mail cross.keys@fsmail.net **Web** www.thexkeys.co.uk

Closed 24-30 December and Bank Holidays

Menu £12.50 – Carte £21/28

Just look at the facade and you'll get the picture. This may be a pub with a history dating back well over 200 years, but the interior owes more to today's sense of irony and fun.
The bar offers plenty of elbow room and its own menu but, beyond, one finds the glass roofed dining room. This is the centre of things and comes complete with little statues, its own tree and an eye-catching frieze of garden implements.
The kitchen is more conventional, with food that is modern in style but robust in flavour. Blackboard specials supplement the set menus, with plenty of wines available by the glass.
The two private dining areas, in the gallery above the bar and on the top floor, come with their own eccentric touches.

Lots Road

Gastropub 

A/C VISA MC

114 Lots Rd — ⊖ Gloucester Road
✉ SW10 0RJ — **D8**
✆ (020) 73526645 – **Fax** (020) 73764975
e-mail lotsroad@thespiritgroup.com **Web** www.thespiritgroup.com

Carte £35/60

Unless you're fortunate enough to have something big and pointy moored in Chelsea Harbour, then this part of Chelsea is probably not somewhere that is too familiar. The aptly, and fully, named Lots Road Pub & Dining Room has turned this lack of passing-by business into a positive in that you feel everyone in the place is a local and that they would rather keep their place a secret.
As a gastropub it ticks all the boxes: the assorted old school chairs and mismatched tables, the quadrant shaped bar room and the open kitchen sending out robust, satisfying favourites. The lay out allows plenty of elbow room for those just wanting nourishment of a more liquid kind, while the laid-back atmosphere will have you pretending you're a local too.

Kensington, North Kensington & Notting Hill

S. Ollivier/MICHELIN

Kensington, the heart of the 'Royal Borough', has always had something of a regal air about it. When the asthmatic King William III grew tired of choking on 17th Century London's smog, he relocated to the village next door and got his friend Sir Christopher Wren to transform a handsome house at its edge into a royal residence. Today, **Kensington Palace** may be home to only minor royals but, as any proud Kensingtonian will tell you, the area's name itself perhaps derives from the Saxon for 'Kings Town' - with all the wealth, class and ease that implies.

At roughly £1,000 per square foot of property, this is a neighbourhood in which few can afford to live, but that many like to visit. The main thoroughfare, **Kensington High Street**, has a surprisingly down-to-earth array of shops, although the imposing Art Deco edifices of its once-famous department stores ensures it is not totally outdone in the style stakes by its more glamorous Chelsea rival, the King's Road. On top of one of these, high above the hoi polloi, sit the **Kensington Roof Gardens** - a pleasure-dome Kubla Khan would be proud of, appealing to today's urban sophisticates as Vauxhall once did to their Victorian counterparts. But street level has its own retreats and **Holland Park** - which extends a narrow green limb to the shops – is a refined, romantic hideaway of wooded walks, tranquil gardens and peacocks.

With the town hall tucked a few blocks behind the high street, however, the real character of Kensington lies in its residences. Victorian terraces, grand stucco villas and red-brick apartment blocks line streets which in spring are covered by a carpet of blossom. Blue plaques abound and window boxes keep up appearances while keeping out prying eyes – this, after all, is an area as discreet as it is resplendent. The old court buildings of **Kensington Square** evoke an earlier era and became home to such great men as John Stuart Mill and Joseph Addison. These days, London's most exclusive address is the nearby **Kensington Palace Gardens,** a spacious half-mile avenue of magnificent Victorian mansions, housing both embassies and the world's richest individuals.

Walk past security at the avenue's north entrance and things get more relaxed, if not a tad scruffy - **Notting Hill Gate** may not be the best introduction to the neighbourhood glamourised by Richard Curtis's film, but it is unmistakably part of it. In contrast to Kensington's establishment pedigree, this was a place where pigs used to outnumber humans three to one, and which by the 1960s had become known for little more than slums and race riots. Happily, the piggeries disappeared long ago, and the white stuccoed terraces, laid out in the 19th Century, have been restored to their former glory. Now, the area's ethnic diversity is a cause for celebration, with the ebullient **Notting Hill Carnival** calypsoing every August amid steel bands and the smells of jerk chicken.

Although carnival's energy can't be kept up all year, Notting Hill does sustain a hip laid-backness that draws a young(ish) and fashionable crowd. The restaurants and antiquarian art galleries of **Kensington Church Street** here mix with retro clothing stores and second-hand record shops. Former supermodels can be spotted picking the kids up from school, as yesterday's stars of Brit Pop browse designer boutiques. True, rejuvenation has given Notting Hill some middle-aged spread, but it keeps a finger on the pulse with bohemian cafes, period cine-

S. Ollivier/MICHELIN

mas, the avant-garde **Notting Hill Arts Club** and the daring **Gate Theatre**, while the pubs and market on **Portobello Road** remain as modish as ever. Should you tire of all this cooler-than-thou trendiness, however, a stroll among the pastel town houses and Victorian estates of **Ladbroke Grove** is the perfect antidote. It may not be advisable to do a 'Julia Roberts' and break into the residents-only gardens - but some of these private spaces are open to quite public sightlines, and it's a lovely place to dream.

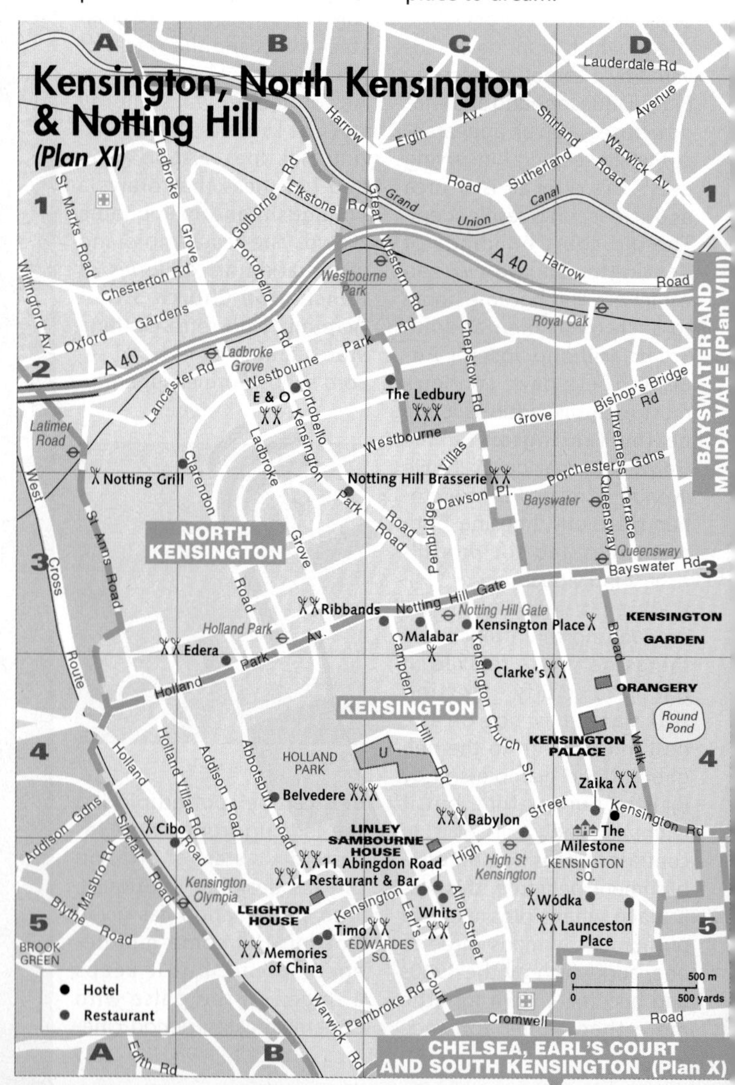

The Ledbury ✿

French XXX

127 Ledbury Rd
W11 2AQ
(020) 77929090 – **Fax** (020) 77929191
e-mail info@theledbury.com **Web** www.theledbury.com

Notting Hill Gate
C2

A/C
VISA
MC
AE

Closed 24-26 December and August Bank Holiday

Menu £29.50/45

The Ledbury

Opened in 2005 by the experienced team who brought you The Square, Chez Bruce and others, The Ledbury provides concrete evidence of the continued gentrification of Notting Hill. Locals may like the idea of gritty urban realism but they clearly also like the idea of having a stylish restaurant on their doorstep.
The Ledbury hits all the right buttons - it's smart without being stuffy and comfortable without being fussy. Large arched windows bring in plenty of light and stippled mirrors, relief-patterned dark chocolate drapes and cream leather chairs create a chic environment.
The serving staff all have specific roles which they undertake with consummate professionalism and the seriousness of the food never gets the better of the atmosphere, which is pleasingly mellow.
However, it is the cooking which is undoubtedly the attraction; it's quite elaborate in presentation but backed up by an expert understanding and an exact execution. The roots of the cooking, like its alma mater The Square, are classical but given a little modern tweak.
The tasting menu provides the ideal introduction.

A LA CARTE

FIRST COURSE	MAIN COURSE	DESSERT
• Scallops roasted in liquorice with fennel duxelle and white onion purée.	• Milk-fed lamb baked in hay with creamed potato, truffle and celery.	• Chicory crème brûlée with coffee ice cream and chocolate Madeleines.
• Loin of tuna wrapped in basil with a salad of radish and soy.	• Pan-fried halibut with white beans, chorizo, rosemary and squid.	• Rhubarb and vanilla tart with poached rhubarb and clementine sorbet.

Belvedere

French XXX

Holland House, off Abbotsbury Rd ⊖ Holland Park
✉ W8 6LU **B4**
✆ (020) 76021238 – **Fax** (020) 76104382
Web www.belvedererestaurant.co.uk

Closed 26 December, 1 January and Sunday dinner

Menu £18 (lunch) – Carte £30/43

If there was a prize for the most charming location for a London restaurant, this would undoubtedly be one of the favourites. The Belvedere, built in 17c and used as the summer ballroom to the Jacobean mansion that was Holland House, is in the delightful and tranquil surroundings of Holland Park. A summer's evening spent on the first floor balcony terrace overlooking the gardens makes it hard to believe you're in central London.
It's divided into three dining areas, decorated with gilt mirrors, mosaics, stained glass and fresh flowers and every regular has their favourite spot. The menu covers many bases but leans towards France, uses excellent ingredients and matches the surroundings in sophistication.

Babylon

International XXX

at the Roof Gardens ⊖ High Street Kensington
Kensington High St
(entrance on Derry St)
✉ W8 5SA **C4**
✆ (020) 73683993 – **Fax** (020) 73683995
Web www.roofgardens.com

Closed Christmas, New Year and Sunday dinner

Menu £21 (lunch) – Carte £30/59

Anyone searching for an acre and a half of landscaped garden in the Kensington area may not naturally think of it being atop a former department store but six floors up from Kensington High Street one finds the celebrated Roof Gardens, which opened in 1933. Babylon occupies the top floor, along with a nightclub, and takes advantage of its lofty position by offering majestic views of the London skyline and, from its wonderful terrace, views of the gardens. The décor inside is a contemporary reflection of this pastoral-setting-within-the-city.
With such a position it would have easy for them to neglect the cooking but they haven't and the kitchen adopts the modern approach of taking influences from across the globe.

Notting Hill Brasserie

French XX

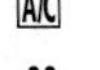

92 Kensington Park Rd ⊖ Notting Hill Gate
W11 2PN **B3**
(020) 72294481 – **Fax** (020) 72211246
Web www.nottinghillbrasserie.com

Closed Sunday dinner

VISA MC AE

Menu £19.50/30 – Carte £35/45

The name is really only half right. There is certainly no argument over it being in Notting Hill but the service, comforts, styling and cooking are all far beyond what one would expect from a brasserie. One enters into the very pleasant bar where live blues or jazz is played every night between 8pm and midnight. The restaurant is divided into assorted smaller rooms, all with their own character and atmosphere, and decorated with modern or African influenced artwork.
Multinational staff, all dressed in black, provide attentive, structured service. The cooking, too, is as sophisticated as the restaurant; some serious produce is used in fairly intricate dishes that come elaborately presented.

Zaika

Indian XX

1 Kensington High St ⊖ High Street Kensington
W8 5NP **D4**
(020) 77956533 – **Fax** (020) 79378854
e-mail info@zaika-restaurant.co.uk **Web** www.zaika-restaurant.co.uk

VISA MC

Closed 25-26 December and Saturday lunch

Menu £19 (lunch) – Carte £25/37

The ornate high ceilings, double height windows and handsome wood panelling mean than, once again, we find ourselves in another converted bank and for that we can all be grateful. There is, however, nothing staid about the surroundings because all the vibrant colours of India have been added to the mix, creating a room that is as bold as it is lively.
This twist of the refined yet creative is carried through to the accomplished cooking which nudges at the boundaries of what is considered traditional Indian cuisine. Those unable to choose between dishes such as spicy sea bass or coconut lamb on the *à la carte*, should consider trying the *Jugalbandi* menu - a five-course tasting menu which will give you the real Zaika experience.

Clarke's

Modern European XX

124 Kensington Church St ⊖ Notting Hill Gate
W8 4BH **C4**
(020) 72219225 – **Fax** (020) 72294564
e-mail restaurant@sallyclarke.com **Web** www.sallyclarke.com

Closed 10 days Christmas-New Year, Monday dinner, Sunday and Bank Holidays

Menu £39.75 (dinner) – Carte £27/32

For over twenty years Sally Clarke's eponymous restaurant offered a daily changing no-choice dinner menu until finally, in 2006, bowing to changing habits, she began offering a choice to her customers. The impressive longevity of the restaurant and the fact that she succeeded so long in her particular formula bear testament to her skill in the kitchen and her reputation. She succeeds through a combination of balanced dishes focusing on the seasonal freshness of ingredients and a lightness of touch in their preparation. It also helps when there's a welcoming atmosphere of intimacy and familiarity which in itself attracts so many loyal customers.
Those wishing to take a memento home will find the produce at her next-door deli and bakery hard to resist.

Launceston Place

British XX

1a Launceston Pl ⊖ Gloucester Road
W8 5RL **D5**
(020) 79376912 – **Fax** (020) 79382412
Web www.egami.co.uk

Closed 24-26 December, 1-2 January, Saturday lunch and some Bank Holidays

Menu £24.50 (lunch) – Carte £31/39

It's hard not to be drawn in by the warmth emanating from inside this former pub with its curved façade, located on a quiet residential area. Opened in 1986, it is divided into several adjoining rooms, some of which have glass roofs, and is decorated in a very English manner with Victorian oil paintings and mirrors. The menu, supplemented by weekly specials, takes its cue from the surroundings and this very Britishness is evident in dishes ranging from roast partridge to gooseberry fool while other dishes boast more Mediterranean influences in their make-up. The wine list has a pronounced French bias.
Launceston Place is one of those restaurants which just makes you pleased it exists.

Edera

Italian XX

148 Holland Park Ave ⊖ Holland Park
✉ W11 4UE **B4**
✆ (020) 72216090 – **Fax** (020) 73139700
Closed 25 December and 1 January

Carte £27/35

The bare wood floors, clean lines and muted coloured walls adorned with the odd mirror suggest a rather clinical West End restaurant which somehow landed in the leafier environs of Holland Park. Fortunately, the place is privately owned and the mood is rescued by the locals who need no help in creating their own atmosphere and have a laudable aversion to whispering.
Edera, meaning "ivy" in Italian, is bigger than you first think and the service, rather like any relationship, improves with time and familiarity. The cooking is earthy, satisfying and flavoursome and there are subtle hints of Sardinia in some of the dishes: the *bottarga* (grey mullet roe) is a speciality of the house, as is the suckling pig.

E & O

South-East Asian XX

14 Blenheim Crescent ⊖ Ladbroke Grove
✉ W11 1NN **B2**
✆ (020) 72295454 – **Fax** (020) 72295522
Web www.eando.nu
Closed Sunday, Monday and Bank Holidays

Carte £22/34

Once you've sidestepped the full-on bar of this Notting Hill favourite, a step from Portobello Road, you'll find yourself in a moodily sophisticated restaurant packed with the beautiful and the hopeful.
The room is understatedly urbane, with slatted walls, large circular lamps and leather banquettes, while noise levels are at the party end of the auditory index. Waiting staff are obliging, pleasant and often among the prettiest people in the room.
E&O stands for Eastern and Oriental and the menu journeys across numerous Asian countries, dividing itself into assorted headings which include dim sum, salads, tempura, curries and roasts. Individual dishes vary in size and price so sharing, as in life, is often the best option.

Whits

Modern European XX

A/C VISA MC AE

21 Abingdon Rd
W8 6AH
(020) 79381122 – **Fax** (020) 79376121
e-mail eva@whits.co.uk **Web** www.whits.co.uk

High Street Kensington
C5

Closed last 2 weeks August, 24 December-3 January, Sunday, Monday and Saturday lunch

Menu £17.50/22.50 – Carte £26/36

A shortened version of the chef owner's name explains the moniker of this enthusiastically run restaurant in a residential street, just off Kensington High Street. As homage to the restaurants other owner, subtle Hungarian influences can be found in the menu and in certain more robust dishes, but those unfamiliar with Magyar traditions or merely looking for something lighter are more than rewarded with a varied selection of elaborately executed dishes. It is also well worth leaving some trouser space for dessert, as soufflés are very much a house speciality.
The main dining room is in a raised section beyond the bar and is decorated in a fresh, clean style with modern artwork and smartly dressed tables.

11 Abingdon Road

Mediterranean XX

A/C VISA MC AE

11 Abingdon Rd
W8 6AH
(020) 79370120
e-mail eleven@abingdonroad.co.uk

High Street Kensington
C5

Closed Bank Holidays

Menu £17.50 – Carte £21/30

Opened late in 2005 and sister restaurant to Sonny's and The Phoenix, 11 Abingdon Road is already attracting quite a following who are helped along, no doubt, by not having to look up the street name and number first.
The stylish façade is reflected in the contemporary feel of the clean white lines and lighting of the interior which add to the general feeling of spaciousness. The owners' own art collection adorns the walls and the tables are set close together, adding to the atmosphere and general buzz.
The Mediterranean provides most of the influence in the kitchen, with bright, vibrant colours and fresh, clean flavours. There is a good value set menu available at lunchtimes and early evenings.

Timo

Italian XX

A/C VISA MC AE

343 Kensington High St. — High Street Kensington
W8 6NW — **B5**
(020) 76033888 – **Fax** (020) 76038111
e-mail timorestaurant@fsmail.net

Closed 25-26 December, Easter, Saturday lunch and Sunday dinner

Menu £16.50 – Carte £27/29

At the Olympia end of Kensington High Street sits this warm and inviting Italian restaurant. The colours of cream and beige, matched with summery paintings of garden landscapes, lend a sunny feel, whatever the season outside. The tables are as smartly dressed as the waiters, who provide conscientious service and the suited owner does the rounds and knows his regulars.
The set menu comes divided into the typically Italian four courses, although the impressive looking bread basket will test your powers of self-restraint. Daily specials to supplement the menu are temptingly described and the desserts merit particular investigation.
This is a solidly reliable neighbourhood restaurant which sensibly doesn't try to reinvent anything.

Ribbands

French XX

A/C VISA MC

147-149 Notting Hill Gate — Notting Hill Gate
W11 3LF — **C3**
(020) 70340301 – **Fax** (020) 72294259
Web www.ribbandsrestaurants.com

Closed Sunday, Monday and Bank Holidays

Menu £25/48 – Carte £40/56

For all of Notting Hill's cutting edge reputation, decent restaurants have always been a little thin on the ground. Ribbands is the latest to try its luck and opened on the corner of Campden Hill in June 2006.
The front area is given over to the bar, which doubles as a coffee shop in the mornings. A few steps down and you're in the restaurant proper, with a second, more discreet area at a lower level and another on a small balcony.
There are a confusing number of menus available and the service is over-formal but there is no denying that the eponymous chef-owner can cut the culinary mustard. Intricate and detailed creations, buttressed by sound techniques, are elaborately displayed on what must surely be the biggest plates in London.

Memories of China

Chinese XX

VISA MC AE

353 Kensington High St. ⊖ High Street Kensington
✉ W8 6NW **B5**
✆ (020) 76036951 – **Fax** (020) 76030848

Closed Easter and Christmas – booking essential

Menu £19.50/39.50 – Carte £22/35

Memories of China is a well established Chinese restaurant which pulls in both the locals, many of whom will never have a bad word said about the place, and those staying in one of the surrounding hotels. As such, it's always busy so it's well worth coming secure in the knowledge that you're made a reservation. The menu, rather like the room, is relatively compact and keeps things on the straight and narrow by focusing on classic Cantonese and Szechuan cooking. Set menus are available for groups or those who prefer others to make their decisions for them.
The glass façade of this corner restaurant chimes with the bright and modern décor of the interior with Chinese themed murals and calligraphy.

L Restaurant & Bar

Spanish XX

A/C VISA MC AE

2 Abingdon Rd ⊖ High Street Kensington
✉ W8 6AF **C5**
✆ (020) 77956969 – **Fax** (020) 77956699
e-mail info@l-restaurant.co.uk **Web** www.l-restaurant.co.uk

Closed 1 January, 25-26 December, Sunday dinner and Monday lunch

Carte £25/37

A relatively unremarkable façade gives little away but inside they've made great use of light and space to create a vivid and bright Iberian restaurant.
Past the bar - where you can join the locals in tapas and a glass of champagne - and suddenly it all opens out and you find yourself in a capacious dining room with a sloping glass roof and huge mirrors. It's been decked out in a thoroughly tasteful way, with top notch fixtures and fittings. Ask for a table on, rather than underneath, the mezzanine level.
The menu has an occasional tendency to veer off course into some unusual combinations so the best bet is to stick with the more traditional Spanish dishes and tapas.
The wine list is concise but balanced with the emphasis on affordability.

Kensington Place

Modern European

201 Kensington Church St — Notting Hill Gate
W8 7LX — **C3**
(020) 77273184 – **Fax** (020) 72292025
e-mail kpr@egami.co.uk **Web** www.egami.co.uk

Closed 25-26 December and 1 January – booking essential

Menu £19.50/39.50 – Carte £31/40

When the book is written about London's culinary history, Kensington Place will merit its own chapter and, of all the iconic restaurants of the late 1980's, it is hard to overestimate the impact this Place has had. This was one of the restaurants where Londoners were first introduced to the idea that good food could be enjoyed without the formality and stiffness that had gone before.
It also had a kitchen which gave legitimacy and authority to the concept of modern cooking, by focusing on seasonal ingredients, clear flavours and an avoidance of over-elaboration.
After all these years, the place is still permanently busy and the noise levels remain excitably high. Ask for a table furthest from the bar to better appreciate the theatre of it all.

Malabar

Indian

27 Uxbridge St — Notting Hill Gate
W8 7TQ — **C3**
(020) 77278800
Web www.malabar-restaurant.co.uk

Closed 1 week Christmas – buffet lunch Sunday – booking essential

Menu £15 – Carte £18/33

Malabar is tucked away in a residential side street in Notting Hill and is one of those restaurants which regulars like to keep as their own little secret. The restaurant has recently undergone a little nip and tuck, a procedure not entirely unfamiliar in this part of town, giving it a brighter complexion and ensuring it appears just as sprightly, and remains just as popular, as it has always been.
It's divided into three little rooms but it matters little where you sit. The staff all know their way around the menu and offer shrewd advice. The Indian cooking, which comes presented in metal *thalis*, is reassuringly authentic in flavour and comes at an affordable price, a combination that makes booking beforehand a must.

Kensington, North Kensington & Notting Hill

Cibo

Italian

3 Russell Gdns. ⊖ Kensington Olympia
W14 8EZ **A5**
(020) 73716271 – **Fax** (020) 76021371

Closed Easter, Christmas, Saturday lunch, Sunday dinner and Bank Holidays

Menu £22.50 (lunch) – Carte £23/36

Behind the rather elegant façade lies this personable and intimate Italian restaurant. Cibo has established itself over the years as something of a local landmark in this smart residential area, due to the mix of refreshingly unabashed and eclectic décor, reliably good Italian food and amiable service.
The menu leans towards seafood and the portion size is on the generous side. The wide variety of breads on offer merit full investigation as do the pasta specials.
The place is usually full of locals whose loyalty is such that they appear to exert an influence over the menu content. You're also likely to see one of two local celebrities on any given night. Cibo is one of the best reasons for moving to Holland Park.

Notting Grill

Beef specialities

123A Clarendon Rd ⊖ Holland Park
W11 4JG **B2**
(020) 72291500 – **Fax** (020) 72298889
e-mail nottinggrill@aol.com **Web** www.awtonline.co.uk

Closed 24 December-3 January and Monday lunch

Menu £17.50 (lunch) – Carte £28/42

From the outside it still looks like the pub it once was, but inside it's gone all soft and spongy. Cushions are everywhere and a mix of pictures, rich colours and exposed brick all give it a warm, rustic yet welcoming feel. It's certainly worth staying downstairs as the room upstairs can't compete on atmosphere and personality.
"Well Bred, Well Fed and Well Hung" proclaims the menu, referring not to the owner, Antony Worrall Thompson, but to the speciality of the house - their well sourced steaks and grilled meats, which explains the dubious pun in the name. Comfort food is very much the order of the day and lovers of the old classics will find much to stir nostalgic thoughts, although those more of the present are not forgotten.

Wódka

Polish 

 12 St Albans Grove
⊖ High Street Kensington
✉ W8 5PN
D5
 ✆ (020) 79376513 – **Fax** (020) 79378621
e-mail info@wodka.co.uk **Web** www.wodka.co.uk

Closed 25 December,1 January and lunch Saturday and Sunday

Menu £14.50 (lunch) - Carte £24/29

Come to Wódka to celebrate all things Eastern European. Housed in what was once the dairy to Kensington Palace, the décor inside is industrial-lite, where warmth and intimacy soften the sharper edges of the tough minimalism. The robust flavours and classic dishes of Polish and Eastern European cooking are all here, from *blinis* to *pierogi* and *golabki* (stuffed cabbage) to *Bigos* (Polish Hunters stew). Those who prefer dishes in a lighter, more modern style will find that they haven't been forgotten. The restaurant has been run by an exclusively Polish team, from a time when that was considered a novelty. With a variety of vodkas available, all served directly from the freezer, no one leaves without their heart a little warmer.
Na Zdrowie!

WHAT'S IN A NAME?

Victorian journalist Henry Mayhew, a keen reformer and surveyor of London life, noted that the city's 'Street-Sellers of Eatables and Drinkables' had the rather unfortunate habit of referring to themselves by the articles in which they dealt, leading one of them to enquire: "Is the man you're asking about a pickled whelk, sir?" With meat puddings, hot eels and lamb trotters also on offer, however, there were perhaps worse things to be called.

TIPS/PHOTONONSTOP

GREATER LONDON

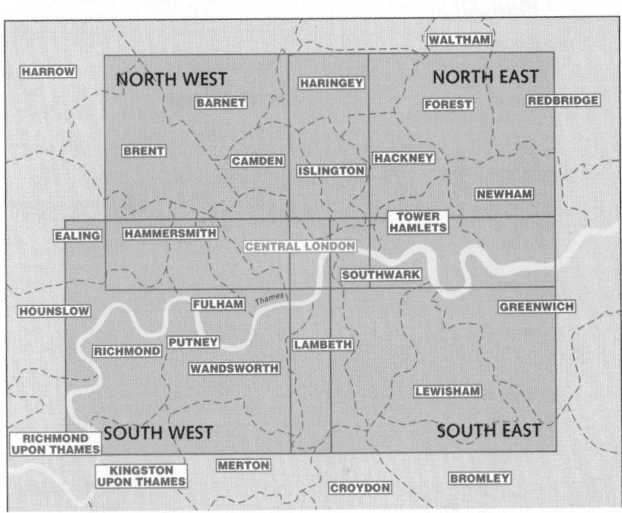

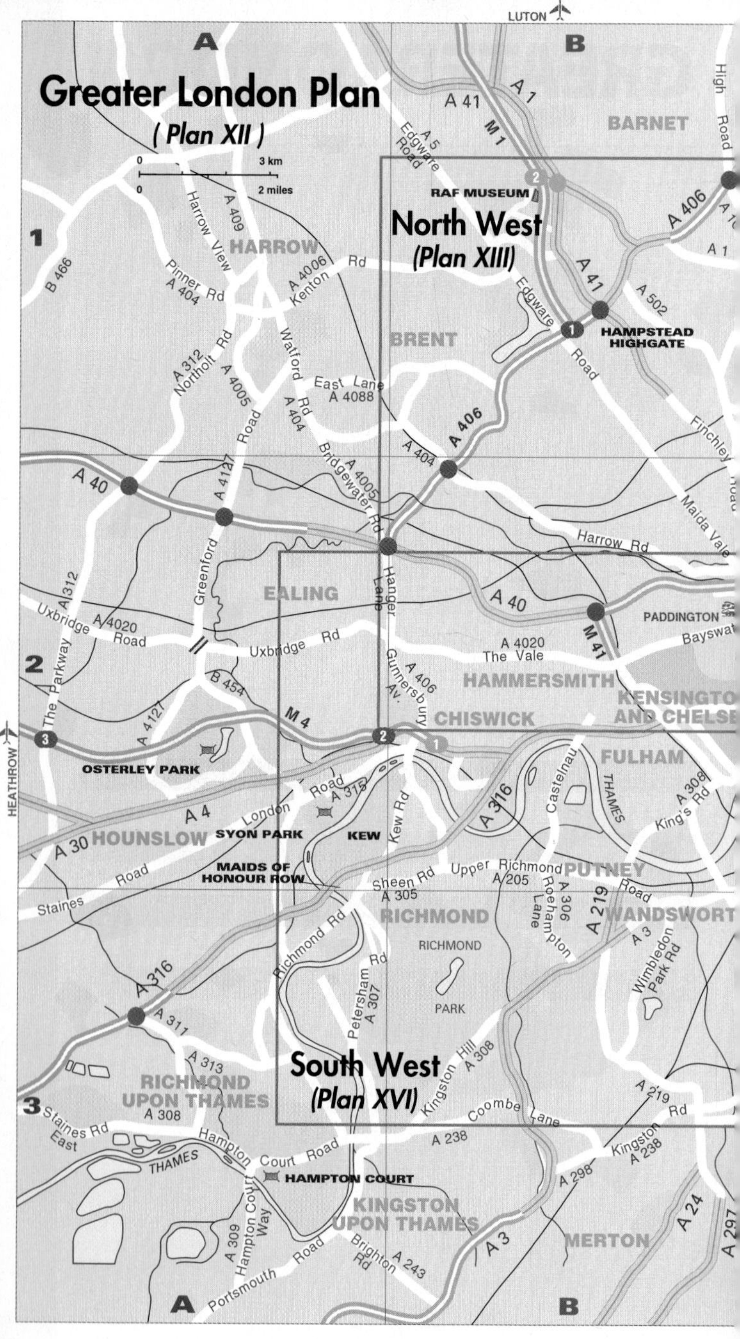
Greater London Plan
(Plan XII)
0 3 km
0 2 miles
North West
(Plan XIII)
South West
(Plan XVI)
LUTON
HEATHROW
BARNET
HARROW
BRENT
HAMPSTEAD
HIGHGATE
RAF MUSEUM
EALING
PADDINGTON
HAMMERSMITH
KENSINGTON AND CHELSEA
CHISWICK
FULHAM
OSTERLEY PARK
HOUNSLOW
SYON PARK
KEW
MAIDS OF HONOUR ROW
PUTNEY
WANDSWORTH
RICHMOND
RICHMOND PARK
RICHMOND UPON THAMES
HAMPTON COURT
KINGSTON UPON THAMES
MERTON
THAMES

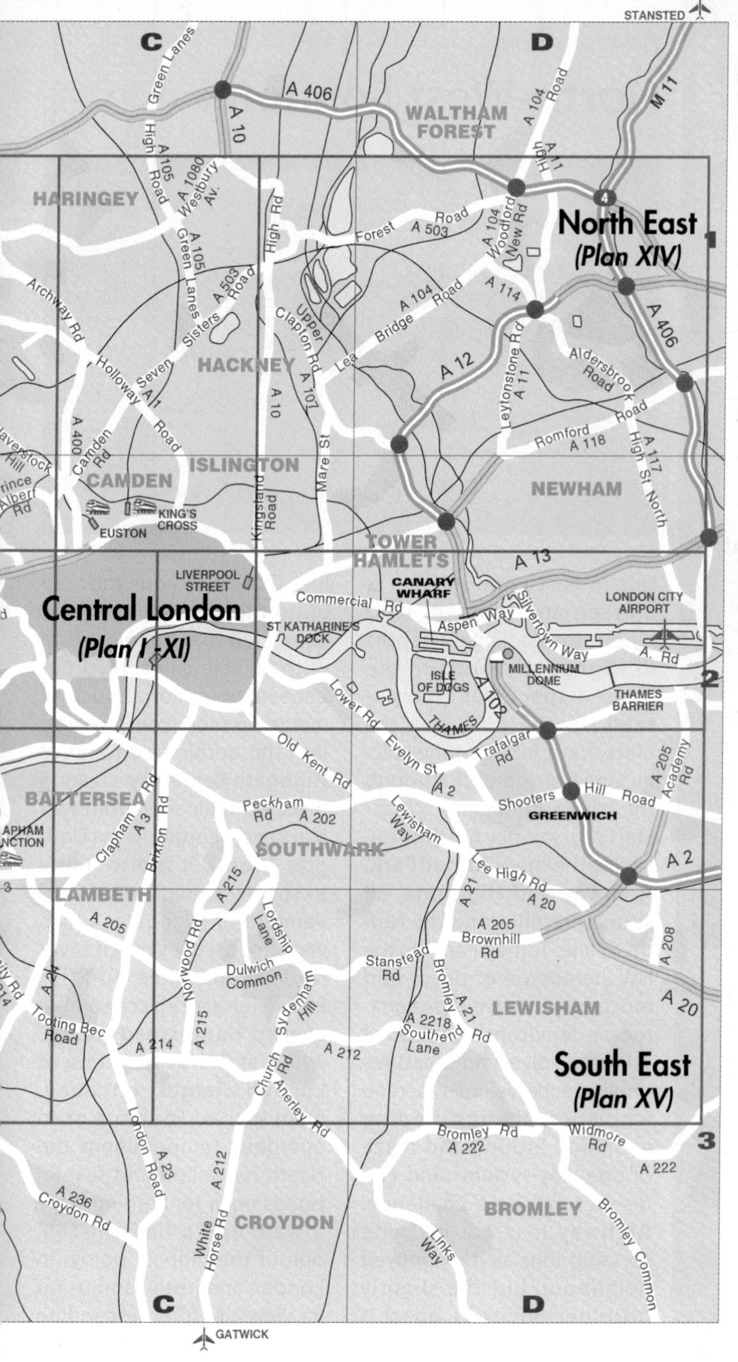
STANSTED
C
D
North East
(Plan XIV)
Central London
(Plan I -XI)
South East
(Plan XV)
HARINGEY
WALTHAM FOREST
HACKNEY
ISLINGTON
CAMDEN
NEWHAM
TOWER HAMLETS
CANARY WHARF
LONDON CITY AIRPORT
ISLE OF DOGS
MILLENNIUM DOME
THAMES BARRIER
ST KATHARINE'S DOCK
LIVERPOOL STREET
KING'S CROSS
EUSTON
BATTERSEA
SOUTHWARK
GREENWICH
LAMBETH
LEWISHAM
CROYDON
BROMLEY
GATWICK
1
2
3

North-West London

C. Eymenier/MICHELIN

North-west London truly is a green and pleasant land – from the cool, leafy depths of **Highgate Woods** to the rugged spaces of **Hampstead Heath**, NW is just the place for a lazy summer picnic or a bracing walk through the crisp autumn air.

Start your journey north by following the line of **Tufnell Park, Archway** and **Highgate**, all strung prettily along the Northern line. Tufnell Park fits the NW stereotype of peace and prosperity to a tee – designated an 'environmental area' the traffic diverting measures provide a marvellously serene ambience, though finding your way around the maze of one-way-systems and cul-de-sacs can be a challenge. **Archway** may not be quite so salubrious as its moneyed neighbour, but the slightly grubbier environs boast a varied and interesting nightlife. Continue your journey up to Highgate and you will be treated to a stunning vista of the whole city spread out beneath you. For a touch of memento mori, you can drop into the gothic splendour of **Highgate Cemetery** – resting place of luminaries from Karl Marx and George Eliot to Douglas Adams, it is also home to spooky stories such as the Vampire of Highgate, which was supposedly sighted several times during the 1970s.

From Highgate you can amble over to **Hampstead Heath,** which at 791 acres is one of London's largest untamed, open spaces. For those of an energetic temperament the Heath has a lido and several ponds open for bathing. Take a walk up Parliament Hill, one of the highest points in London and justly famous for its views, before descending to **Hampstead** village and succumbing to the temptations of its many fine pubs. If it's culture you're after then **Kenwood House** is the perfect destination. Set amid beautifully kept grounds on the edge of the heath, it is home to an impressive collection of paintings, including landscapes by Constable. It also hosts a series of concerts in summer – everything from pop hits to the classics – to which visitors are invited to bring a picnic and enjoy music and fireworks in the summer gloaming.

A little to the east of Highgate, **Crouch End** prides itself on its traditional village image and is lucky enough still to boast individual food shops, including an excellent butchers and fishmongers, while nearby **Alexandra Palace** is not just an impressive landmark, it also plays host to a thriving farmer's market on Sundays. If some of the locals look familiar then chances are you first saw that face on TV: Crouch End has a well-deserved reputation as a media enclave, beloved by bohemian and arty types. It gets starrier the further west you go, until by **Hampstead, Child's Hill** and **Primrose Hill** you could find yourselves rubbing shoulders with Hollywood A-listers or chart-topping musicians.

The attraction NW holds for artistic types might be explained by a thriving local scene as well as a wealth of historical associations. **Swiss Cottage** is right by **Abbey Road**, home to the legendary recording studio where The Beatles and Pink Floyd, among others, recorded seminal works. The literary cues range from cutting-edge hip – **Willesden Green** was immortalised by Zadie Smith in *White Teeth* – to the dearly departed – William Makepeace Thackery and Anthony Trollope are among those buried at Kensal Green Cemetery in **Kensal Rise**. No surprise that theatre is amply represented too – **Belsize Park** is close to the Roundhouse on **Chalk Farm Road**, while up on **Kilburn High Road** you'll find the Tricycle Theatre along with new music venue, the Luminaire.

S. Ollivier/MICHELIN

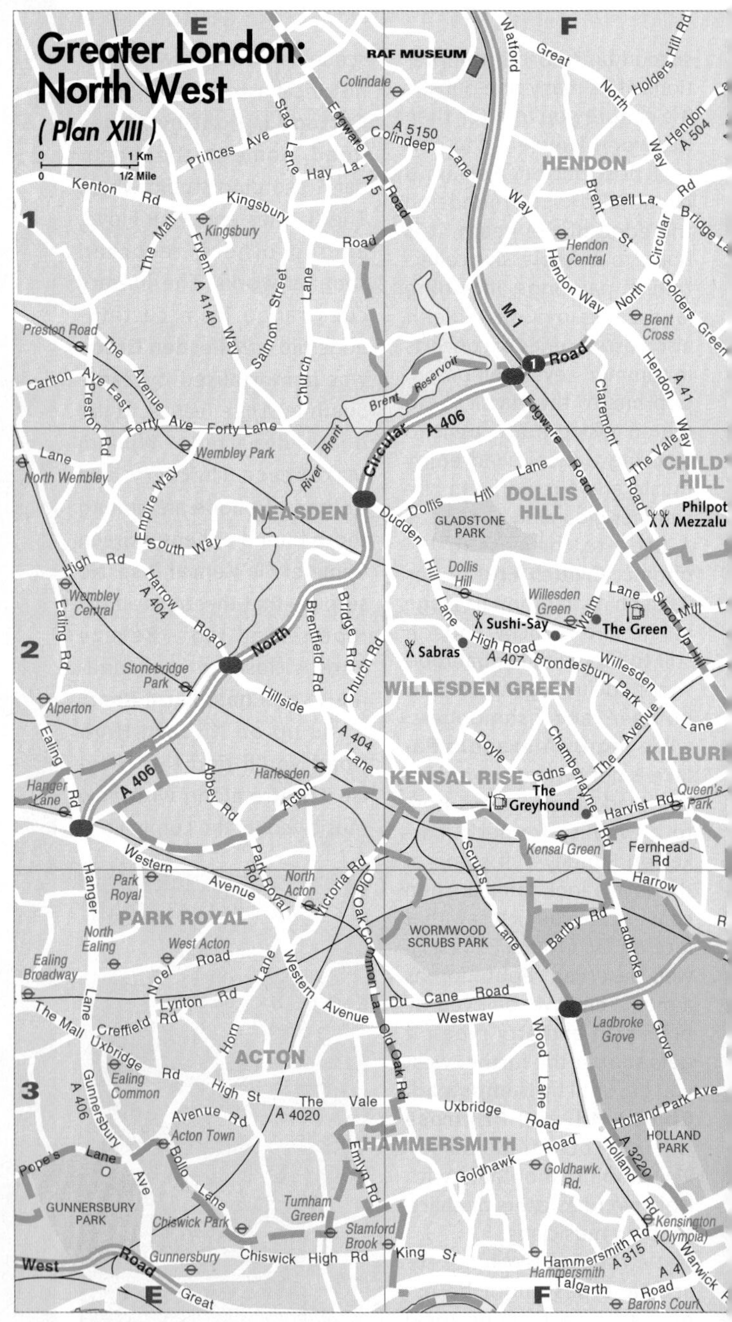
Greater London: North West
(Plan XIII)
0 1 Km
0 1/2 Mile
E
F
1
2
3
RAF MUSEUM
Colindale
Watford
Great
North
Way
Holders Hill Rd
Hendon
A 504
HENDON
Bell La.
Brent
St
Rd
Bridge La
Hendon Central
Hendon Way
North
Circular
Golders Green
Brent Cross
Hendon
A 41
Way
M 1
1 Road
Claremont
Road
The Vale
CHILD'S HILL
Philpot
Mezzalu
A 5150
Colindeep
Lane
Stag
Lane
Edgware
A 5
Road
Hay La.
Princes Ave
Kenton Rd
Kingsbury
Road
Kingsbury
The Mall
Fryent
A 4140
Way
Salmon
Street
Church
Lane
Preston Road
The
Avenue
Carlton Ave East
Preston Rd
Forty Ave
Forty Lane
Wembley Park
Lane
North Wembley
Empire Way
South Way
Brent Reservoir
River Brent
Circular
A 406
Edgware
Road
Lane
DOLLIS HILL
GLADSTONE PARK
Dollis
Hill
Dudden
Hill
Lane
Dollis Hill
NEASDEN
High Rd
Wembley Central
Ealing Rd
Harrow
A 404
Road
North
Brentfield Rd
Bridge Rd
Church Rd
Sabras
Sushi-Say
High Road
A 407
Willesden Green
Walm
Lane
The Green
Shoot Up Hill
Mill
Brondesbury Park
Willesden
Lane
The Avenue
WILLESDEN GREEN
Stonebridge Park
Alperton
Hillside
A 404
Lane
Doyle
Gdns
Chamberlayne
Rd
KILBURN
Ealing
Hanger Lane
Rd
A 406
Abbey Rd
Harlesden
Acton
KENSAL RISE
The Greyhound
Harvist Rd
Queen's Park
Kensal Green
Fernhead Rd
Harrow
Western
Avenue
Park Royal Rd
North Acton
Victoria Rd
Old Oak Common La
Scrubs
Lane
Hanger
Lane
Park Royal
PARK ROYAL
North Ealing
West Acton
Ealing Broadway
Noel
Road
Horn
Lane
Western
Avenue
WORMWOOD SCRUBS PARK
Barlby Rd
Ladbroke
Grove
Lynton Rd
Du Cane Road
Westway
Ladbroke Grove
The Mall
Creffield Rd
Uxbridge Rd
Ealing Common
ACTON
Wood Lane
Gunnersbury
A 406
High St
The Vale
A 4020
Uxbridge
Road
Holland Park Ave
HOLLAND PARK
Avenue Rd
Acton Town
HAMMERSMITH
Road
Holland
A 3220
Pope's Lane
Ave
Bollo
Lane
Emlyn Rd
Goldhawk
Goldhawk Rd.
GUNNERSBURY PARK
Chiswick Park
Turnham Green
Stamford Brook
Kensington (Olympia)
Warwick
West
Road
Great
Gunnersbury
Chiswick High Rd
King St
Hammersmith Rd
A 315
Hammersmith
Talgarth
Road
A 4
Barons Court
Old Oak Rd

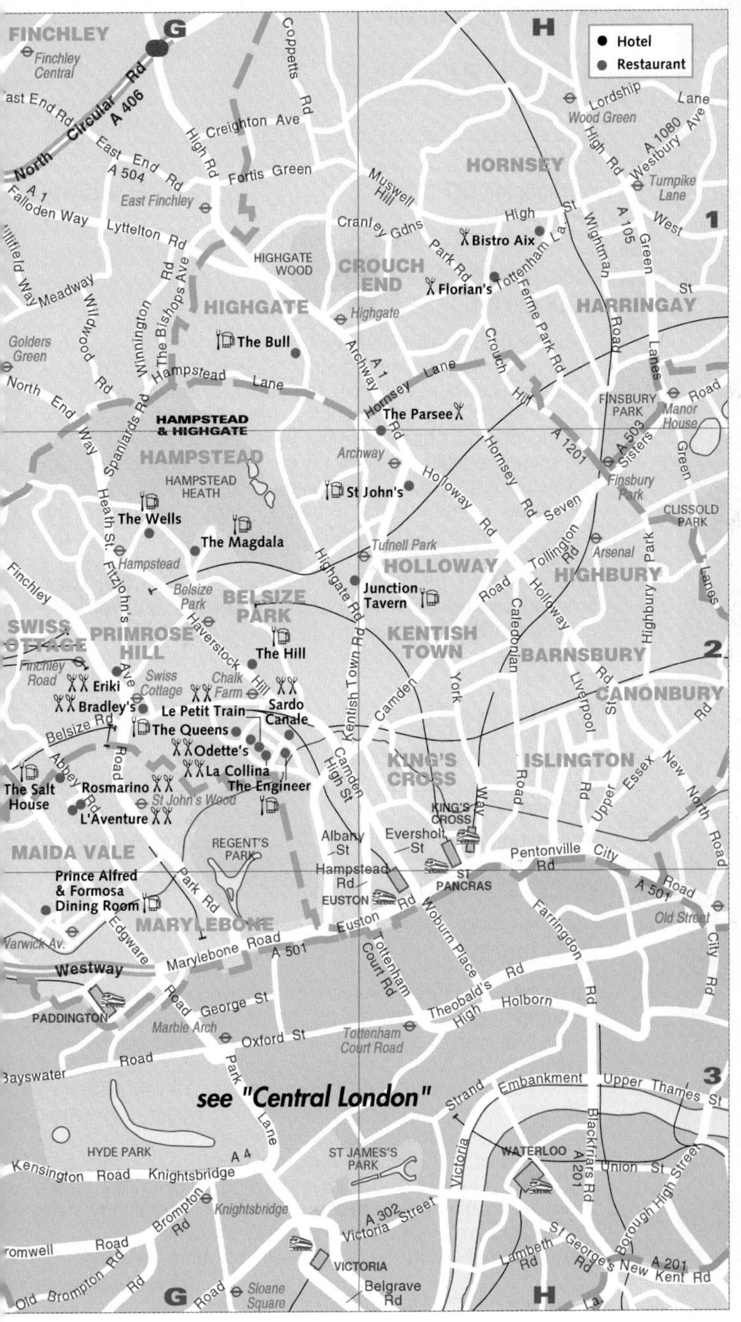

Hotel
Restaurant
G
H
1
2
3
FINCHLEY
Finchley Central
North Circular Rd
A 406
HORNSEY
HIGHGATE
CROUCH END
HIGHGATE WOOD
HARRINGAY
HAMPSTEAD & HIGHGATE
HAMPSTEAD
HAMPSTEAD HEATH
FINSBURY PARK
CLISSOLD PARK
HOLLOWAY
HIGHBURY
BELSIZE PARK
KENTISH TOWN
BARNSBURY
SWISS COTTAGE
PRIMROSE HILL
CANONBURY
KING'S CROSS
ISLINGTON
MAIDA VALE
REGENT'S PARK
MARYLEBONE
PADDINGTON
EUSTON
ST PANCRAS
HYDE PARK
ST JAMES'S PARK
WATERLOO
VICTORIA
Bistro Aix
Florian's
The Bull
The Parsee
St John's
The Wells
The Magdala
Junction Tavern
The Hill
Eriki
Bradley's
Le Petit Train
Sardo Canale
The Queens
Odette's
La Collina
The Engineer
The Salt House
Rosmarino
L'Aventure
Prince Alfred & Formosa Dining Room
see "Central London"

The Parsee

Indian

Archway

34 Highgate Hill — Archway

N19 5NL — **H1**

(020) 72729091 – **Fax** (020) 76871139

Closed Christmas-New Year, Sunday and Bank Holidays – dinner only

Carte £17/24

Even the frosted glass and painted flame façade tells you that this is no ordinary Indian restaurant. Opened by Cyrus Todiwala of Cafe Spice Namaste fame, The Parsee celebrates all that is *Zoroastrianism,* one of the oldest religions in the world, by offering the most heart-warming Parsee home cooking.
The menu helpfully explains not only the content of the dish but also its history both culturally and personally (Cyrus's mother gets a few mentions). The dishes are great to share and the colours as vibrant as the Farohar Angel looking down over the simply furnished restaurant.
Cyrus has kept the prices commendably low so that over-ordering can be done without breaking the bank. You'll be grateful that the walk back to the Tube is downhill.

St John's

Gastropub 

Archway

91 Junction Rd — Archway

N19 5QU — **H2**

(020) 72721587 – **Fax** (020) 76872247

Closed 25-26 December, 1 January and lunch Monday-Thursday

Carte £20/30

If anywhere represents what can be achieved with imagination, enthusiasm and an eye for the bigger picture it is surely St John's. Not many years ago this was a dodgy old boozer into which only the big and the brave would venture. It still looks pretty scruffy from outside but inside it is a lively and very successful gastro-pub, whose fans include writers and actors from the smarter houses up the hill in Dartmouth Park.
The front half is a busy bar but go through to the back and you'll discover a vast and animated dining room, with a blackboard menu offering a selection of gutsy dishes, chatty staff, artwork and an atmosphere of relaxed conviviality.
Any more of this and they'll start calling it Archway Village.

The Hill

Gastropub

Belsize Park

94 Haverstock Hill — ⊖ Chalk Farm

✉ NW3 2BD — **G2**

✆ (020) 72670033

e-mail thehill@geronimo-inns.co.uk

VISA · MC

Closed 25 December

Carte £18/25

Another old Victorian boozer given the make-over, but happily this one avoids swapping dingy for that ubiquitous gastropub look favoured by the majority of updated pubs. Instead it ploughs its own design furrow with a twinkling and idiosyncratic style, combining gilded mirrors, a bit of velvet, black and white photographs, old sofas and ornate chandeliers. The menu is equally *à la mode*, offering a balanced selection with some Mediterranean influence, as well as a popular end-of-week brunch menu.

Quite a crowd is drawn in the evenings thanks to the atmosphere, which is both energetic and fun and helped along by the chatty enthusiasm of the young staff. In the summer, the large terrace proves a popular local hangout.

Philpott's Mezzaluna

Italian

Child's Hill

424 Finchley Rd

✉ NW2 2HY — **F2**

✆ (020) 77940455 – **Fax** (020) 77940452

Web www.philpotts-mezzaluna.com

A/C · VISA · MC

Closed 25-26 December, 1 January, Saturday lunch and Monday

Menu £20/29.50

The eponymous Mr. Philpott has established a loyal local following since opening here in 2000. Most of the heavy traffic has turned off by the time you reach this part of the Finchley Road and it is handily placed to attract customers from across North London. They come here for the robust and unpretentious cooking, which uses assorted influences from across Italy. Menus are priced according to the number of courses you take.

The service is undertaken by Mr Philpott's fellow partner in the business who has mastered that relaxed and imperturbable style which helps create a welcoming air.

The room mixes a traditional feel with some modern touches. The tiled flooring and colours add to the light and inviting feel.

Florian's

Italian

Crouch End

4 Topsfield Parade, Middle Lane
N8 8RP **H1**
(020) 83488348 – **Fax** (020) 82922092
Web www.floriansrestaurant-crouchend.co.uk

Carte £28/31

Don't panic when you first enter - you're in the bar which always seems to be this busy, mostly, apparently, with the same crowd every time. Just head through it and up the few steps and you'll get to the restaurant at the back. Don't, however, sit in the first section which seems a rather disconnected spot betwixt and between bar and restaurant.
The dining room is a bright affair, relaxed and informal, with rough white-washed brick and assorted paintings of varying aptitude available for purchase. The ebullient owner oversees the service, which is undertaken by the young team. The reliable Italian cooking comes in satisfyingly generous portions and the daily changing blackboard specials are always a good option.

Bistro Aix

French

Crouch End

54 Topsfield Parade, Tottenham Lane
N8 8PT **H1**
(020) 83406346 – **Fax** (020) 83487236
Web www.bistroaix.co.uk
Closed 26 December, 1 January and Monday

Carte £15/35

The location may be Crouch End, the chef owner may be American but for a couple of hours this little bistro will whisk you off to the verdant French countryside. The high ceiling, mustard coloured walls, dressers, plants and mirrors all add to that rustic feel, while two specially commissioned paintings of cooks and pastoral scenes tell you this is a place run by, and for, those with a genuine love of food.
Francophiles will find plenty of contentment in the vast majority of the menu, which features all the favourites from classic onion soup or seared *foie gras* to *steak frites* or rack of lamb, but there are other dishes whose origins owe more to Italian cooking. Look out for the good value weekday set menu.

The Wells

Gastropub 

Hampstead

30 Well Walk ⊖ Hampstead Heath

✉ NW3 1BX **G2**

✆ (020) 77943785 – **Fax** (020) 77946817

e-mail info@thewellshampstead.co.uk

Closed 1 January

A/C · VISA · MC

Menu £15.95/28.50 – Carte £17/22

So, when is a pub a restaurant and when is a restaurant a pub? Well, you won't find the answer here, because The Wells lies somewhere in between but is all the more satisfying because of that. Its location is certainly a big plus, either for those strolling on the Heath or shopping in Hampstead's swanky high street, and its attractive 18th century façade draws in passers-by exploring the village atmosphere.
The ground floor is the pubbier part, with an interesting selection of light dishes and snacks, but it can be a bit of a bun-fight for village people at weekends. Upstairs is an altogether more composed affair but one that still has considerable charm. Here, the kitchen produces dishes that are flavoursome, refined and respectful of the seasons.

The Magdala

Gastropub 

Hampstead

2A South Hill Park ⊖ Belsize Park

✉ NW3 2SB **G2**

✆ (020) 74352503 – **Fax** (020) 74356167

VISA · MC · AE

Carte £20/25

Hampstead Heath covers nearly 800 acres of north London, so it is hardly surprising that there are a few strategically placed pubs for those seeking sustenance. Whether it was a stroll, an amble or a full-scale hike, The Magdala is just the sort of pub you'll want to come across after your exertions and is usefully positioned just off South End Green.
There are two bars, both with a hassle-free and welcoming atmosphere and the open-plan kitchen dispenses honestly prepared dishes using well sourced ingredients. There is a more formal dining room upstairs which is used primarily at weekends. All great pubs should have a secret and The Magdala was where Ruth Ellis, the last woman to be hanged in Britain, shot her lover in 1955.

The Bull

Gastropub 

Highgate

13 North Hill ⊖ Highgate

⊠ N6 4AB **G1**

✆ (0845) 4565053 – **Fax** (0845) 4565034

e-mail info@inthebull.biz

VISA

Closed Monday lunch

Menu £17.95 – Carte £27/40

Up and over the top of Highgate brings you to The Bull, a good-looking pub spread over two floors with a large front terrace.

Apparently there's been a pub here since 1765 but its current incarnation, with the emphasis firmly on the food, very much captures the zeitgeist. Cream walls, wood flooring, modern art and mix of furnishings give it an urbane and uncomplicated feel. There's a self assured swagger about the service and equal confidence about the menu which tells you the people behind this pub (and their other place, The House) have gained experience at some fairly lofty establishments. The cooking cleverly combines classical French with British, so you can have your Sunday roast but also your *foie gras parfait* beforehand.

The Greyhound

Gastropub 

Kensal Rise

64-66 Chamberlayne Rd ⊖ Kensal Green

⊠ NW10 3JJ **F2**

A/C

✆ (020) 89698080 – **Fax** (020) 89698081

e-mail thegreyhound@needtoeat.co.uk

VISA

Closed 25-26 December, 1 January, Sunday dinner and Monday

Carte £16/27

So, what do you do when you've bought a rather striking painting of a greyhound and have nowhere to hang it? You simply buy a derelict old boozer in an area hitherto starved of dining options, knock through to next door, do it up with some friends, hang your painting and rename the pub in the hound's honour.

The place is split down the middle, with a bar on one side with leather chesterfields and an easy-going atmosphere, and on the other side, a dining room setting a slightly more formal tone with reclaimed tables, leather banquettes and thoughtful and efficient service. The menu captures the essence of gastro-pubbery, with a mix of modern and unfussy cooking using decent, fresh ingredients.

And the painting looks good too.

Odette's

Modern European XX

Primrose Hill

VISA

130 Regent's Park Rd — ⊖ Chalk Farm

⊠ NW1 8XL — **G2**

✆ (020) 75865486 – **Fax** (020) 77225388

e-mail odettes@vpmg.net **Web** www.vpmg.net

Closed 24-31 December, Sunday dinner and Monday

Menu £21.95/40 – Carte £26/44

A new Odette's but still very much *la grande dame* of Primrose Hill. To compete with its increasingly well-groomed neighbourhood and the growing number of local dining choices now available, Odette's was re-opened and re-launched in October 2006 with an arresting new look and obvious aspirations. The mirrors have all gone, to be replaced by strikingly bold wallpaper and there's an elegance and warmth to the place – especially the front room - that has been missing for some time. Service is undertaken seriously but not solemnly.
An ambitious kitchen is at work here, with set menus at prices loftier than one usually sees in these parts. Classical in technique, the food is considered, serious-minded and elaborate.

Sardo Canale

Italian XX

Primrose Hill

A/C

VISA

AE

42 Gloucester Ave — ⊖ Chalk Farm

⊠ NW1 8JD — **G2**

✆ (020) 77222800 – **Fax** (020) 77220802

e-mail info@sardocanale.com **Web** www.sardocanale.com

Closed 25-26 December and Monday lunch

Carte £23/33

Baby sister to Sardo's near Warren Street, Sardo Canale is a relaxed, neighbourhood Italian restaurant boasting a warm and familiar ambience which acts as something of a counterpoint to the recent racy reputation afforded to Primrose Hill, thanks to the exploits of its more recognisable locals.
The place is divided into four different rooms, as well as the summer terrace, three of which are contemporary in style with the fourth being the most interesting place for star crossed lovers and which was originally an access tunnel to the canal. The cooking is appetisingly rustic, with a proud Sardinian theme running through the menu that's supplemented by daily changing specials. Post-prandial strolls along the canal are optional.

Le Petit Train

French XX

Primrose Hill

A/C
VISA
MC

40 Chalcot St — ⊖ Chalk Farm
✉ NW1 8LS — **G2**
✆ (020) 74830077

Closed 25-26 December and Sunday – dinner only and Saturday lunch – booking essential

Menu £14.75 – Carte £23/32

Spare a thought for the local celebrities who have made Primrose Hill such a favourite for the gossip columns - every time a new restaurant opens here all everyone wants to know is "has Jude Law been in yet?"
The Petit Train, so named as steam trains used to be turned for Euston close by, is the most recent incarnation in a spot that has seen various nationalities of restaurant over the years. Its new owner, who also operates a catering company, re-opened it at the end of 2005 as a French restaurant, offering all the classics from snails to *Chateaubriand*, accompanied by an exclusively French wine list. Service is polite and friendly but just make sure you get a table downstairs rather than on the entrance level.

La Collina

Italian XX

Primrose Hill

VISA
MC

17 Princess Rd — ⊖ Camden Town
✉ NW1 8JR — **G2**
✆ (020) 74830192

Closed Bank Holidays – dinner only and lunch Friday-Sunday

Menu £22.50

"The Hill" arrived in early 2006 to continue the trend of there being an Italian restaurant at this address. It comes divided between the ground floor and the basement, with the former brighter and the latter more intimate. Decorated in a suitably rustic style, with its artwork for sale, it has a pleasant little garden terrace at the back. Service makes up in efficiency what it may lack in personality.
The chef hails from Piedmont, so expect some hearty specialities from this region to feature on the menu of Northern Italian cooking. There's ample choice, the portions come sensibly sized and it's all good value – being priced per course, the more you eat the cheaper it seems. The exclusively Italian wine list is also commendably affordable.

The Queens

Gastropub

Primrose Hill

49 Regent's Park Rd — ⊖ Chalk Farm

✉ NW1 8XD — **G2**

✆ (020) 75860408 – **Fax** (020) 75865677

e-mail mail@thequeen49.fsnet.co.uk

Closed 25 December

Carte £20/26

The Queens will have a place in the annals of gastropub history, as it was one of the pioneers in bringing decent food into an environment hitherto resistant to change and proved that a local with good food was not a contradiction.
Its location on the main drag and alongside the Hill is clearly another attraction and the balcony terrace is a sought after summer spot. The whole place was stripped down and done up in 2006.
The narrow bar remains an established local meeting point, with the footie on the TV on the corner, but head upstairs and you'll find a warm and welcoming dining room. Here, gutsy gastropub staples are on offer; main courses come with a good choice of side dishes and there's a daily special for two to share.

The Engineer

Gastropub 

Primrose Hill

65 Gloucester Ave — ⊖ Chalk Farm

✉ NW1 8JH — **G2**

✆ (020) 77220950 – **Fax** (020) 74830592

Web www.the-engineer.com

Closed 25-26 December

Carte £18/45

The pub dates from around 1850, has plenty of character and is close to the Canal but The Engineer's greatest pull is that it seemingly fits perfectly into the fabric of Primrose Hill life - those who have to drive here can often be spied looking forlornly in estate agent windows. The front bar has a relaxed local feel, albeit without much elbow room, while the dining areas have a very convivial atmosphere, helped by the chatty and fun servers. Mirrors and contemporary art decorate the walls and the back garden is a delightful spot in summer.
The kitchen shows a keen respect for the provenance of its meats and balances modern influences with pub favourites. The fabulous Baker fries enjoy something of a local reputation and are well worth ordering.

Bradley's

Modern European XX

Swiss Cottage

25 Winchester Rd — ⊖ Swiss Cottage
✉ NW3 3NR — **G2**
✆ (020) 77223457 – **Fax** (020) 74351392
e-mail ssjbradleys@aol.com

Closed Christmas, Monday, Sunday dinner, Saturday lunch and Bank Holidays

Menu £13.95 (lunch) – Carte £24/36

A number of menus are available from which to choose dishes that come neatly presented and with a decidedly classical base. There is an 'early bird' for those who missed lunch, a pre-theatre for attendees at the nearby Hampstead Theatre and a full *à la carte* for diners under no time or dietary restraints. The eponymous owner, who supervises the cooking, runs a smooth operation and is helped out by a young but efficient team, all smartly kitted out in black.
The room is sophisticated and contemporary in its tone but without the impersonal feel one often encounters in the West End. Extra warmth comes courtesy of the high count of loyal locals, who all seem to know one another, and the genuine neighbourhood feel that this generates.

Eriki

Indian XX

Swiss Cottage

4-6 Northways Parade, Finchley Rd — ⊖ Swiss Cottage
✉ NW3 5EN — **G2**
✆ (020) 77220606 – **Fax** (020) 77228866
e-mail info@eriki.co.uk **Web** www.eriki.co.uk

Closed 25-26 December and Saturday lunch

Carte £14/19

You'll see it just at the moment you realise you're in the wrong lane. Eriki's location may not be the greatest, bang on the permanently busy Finchley Road, but once seated all is calm and the traffic outside gets quickly forgotten. The decoration certainly helps in this regard - the vivid red and orange walls, carved wooden screens and smart table setting make the room smart yet unstuffy and the cutlery, imported from Rajasthan, is certainly original. Furthermore, the conscientious and obliging waiters, all in smart tunics, ensure that everyone is attended to. The menu takes diners on a culinary trail around India and the carefully prepared dishes come with a level of refinement usually associated with more expensive establishments.

Junction Tavern

Gastropub 

Tufnell Park

101 Fortess Rd ⊖ Tufnell Park
✉ NW5 1AG **G2**
VISA
(020) 74859400 – **Fax** (020) 74859401
Web www.junctiontavern.co.uk
Closed 24-26 December and 1 January

Carte £20/30

Halfway between Tufnell Park and Kentish Town - which is a location, not a line from a '60's troubadour - sits the Junction Tavern. This grand Victorian pub was 'gastro'ed' a few years back, but still retains the look and atmosphere of a venerable old dame. You can sit anywhere to eat - the main dining room, with the mismatched chairs and the open kitchen; the more casual bar with an adjoining conservatory or the secluded little garden. The staff are all eager and chatty and the menu offers something for everyone, with the influences stretching from the Med to the occasional touch of something Asian. Those who judge their food more by weight will be pleased to find that the dishes come generously proportioned.

Sabras

Indian vegetarian 

Willesden Green

263 High Rd ⊖ Dollis Hill
✉ NW10 2RX **F2**
(020) 84590340 – **Fax** (020) 84590541
Closed 25-26 December and Monday – dinner only

Carte £15/22

Sabras will certainly never win any awards for its interior design, but it has won plenty of prizes for the quality of its food. Many of these have since been framed and now line the walls of this sweet little place.

Apart from a rather glitzy sign outside, the restaurant treads an uncompromisingly straightforward path in its decoration and the feel is decidedly homespun. The husband and wife team share the responsibilities of the kitchen and the serving.

The food is certainly what attracts the customers here, as well as the more than generous pricing policy. The menu is quite extensive, offers a comprehensive selection of vegetarian specialities from the Gujarat and is another example of the variety in Indian cooking available these days.

Sushi-Say

Japanese

VISA

Willesden Green

33B Walm Lane ⊖ Willesden Green
✉ NW2 5SH **F2**
✆ (020) 84592971 – **Fax** (020) 89073229

Closed Christmas, Easter, 1 week August and Monday – dinner only and lunch Saturday-Sunday

Menu £19.80/31 – Carte £13/35

Decoratively spartan and, with due deference to the delights of Willesden Green, situated on a pretty drab street, it is unlikely that Sushi-Say attracts many passers-by solely with its looks. However, when you do walk past the place you'll often find it full, testament to the esteem in which it is held by the assorted regulars.

There is no doubt that the sweet natured, almost coy service is very appealing and hard to fault, while the owner's pride in his operation is manifestly there for all to see - he will be the man in control at the sushi counter at the front of the restaurant. Lovers of Japanese food will find much to savour from the extensive choice, and set menus make sharing an easy option.

The Green

Gastropub 

Willesden Green

110 Walm Lane ⊖ Willesden Green
VISA ✉ NW2 4RS **F2**
✆ (020) 8452 0171 – **Fax** (020) 8452 0774
e-mail info@thegreennw2.com

Closed 1 January

Menu £17.50 – Carte £25/40

Everything about The Green says gastropub, everything except the fact that this was never actually a pub in the first place - it was the snooker room of the local Conservative Club which, presumably, never got close to ever being this busy or, indeed, this much fun.

The only queue now will be at the bar, which attracts all manner of local and has its own menu. The main dining area is a roomy yet relaxed affair, with high ceilings and an open hatch into the kitchen. That kitchen sends forth dishes that are both robust in flavour and generous in size, from a menu that showcases, along with modern staples, a number of Caribbean inspired dishes, a reflection of the chef-owner's heritage.

C. Barrely/MICHELIN

North-East London

C. Eymenier/MICHELIN

A wellspring of champagne socialism, **Islington** enjoyed a rejuvenation in the late 1980s which has made it less a marked area on a map and more an aspirant lifestyle. Symptomatic of this escape from geography is the Islington within Islington - while the name might technically encompass an entire London borough, it is the gentrified Georgian enclave around **Upper Street's** irrepressible liveliness which has made it synonymous with fashionable theatre crowds, media darling dinner parties and hanging out in bars, looking like you really can't help being that cool.

Although Islington's half-suburban homeliness prevents it from being part of central London proper, it is the district's habit to suggest that it can match anything the rest of the capital cares to offer - indeed, that real London is to be found in N1, not Westminster or the West End. To an extent, it has a point; after all, it was in an Upper Street restaurant that Blair and Brown made their infamous power-sharing pact, while the scene-stealing **Almeida Theatre** frequently eclipses more central venues in combining artistic daring with glamour and commercial success. What is more, this is where many of British society's powerhouses live, as well as play. Shopping in the Sainsbury's Local by **St Mary's Church** can require you to steer your basket round a who's who of popular comedians and television news readers.

Upper Street itself is an intriguing journey from beginning to end, starting with the odd mix of chain stores and antiques arcades around **Angel**, going past the cosmopolitan headiness of **Islington Green**, before reaching the esoteric music venues, lounge bars and furniture sellers closer to **Highbury Corner**. To the west lie the handsome squares of **Barnsbury**, where an imaginative one-way system leaves strollers to enjoy the streets in peace - though many prefer to duck into some of the most atmospheric old-man pubs in zone one. To the east, **Canonbury** is even prettier, with some drinking taverns boasting that most prized of urban assets: a beer garden. Head north and the lovely leafy space of **Highbury Fields** leads on to the Victorian cosiness of **Highbury** itself, where the arresting Art Deco of the old **Arsenal Stadium** has now been superseded by the Gunners' new space-age ground at **Ashburton Grove.**

But if the gentrification of Islington's slums would have appeared remarkable to bygone residents like George Orwell, who turned **Canonbury Square** into the squalid Victory Mansions in *Nineteen Eighty-Four*, neighbouring **Hackney's** turnaround seems properly in the realm of science fiction. Up against decades of neglect, parts of Hackney are beginning to blossom - literally, in the case of the **Columbia Road Flower Market.**

Some of this is overspill from Islington's success, with first-time buyers forced further out, moulding **Stoke Newington's Church Street** into a calmer, slightly more bohemian version of Upper Street. In general, however, Hackney's rise has a flavour all of its own. **Shoreditch** became London's edgiest clubland, where mainstreamers still don't quite fit in and some venues open only after dawn begins to break. Meanwhile, nearby **Hoxton** was invaded by the Young British Artists, shocking the establishment with unmade beds and sharks pickled in formaldehyde. Soon, City financiers were also moving in, with derelict warehouses converted into luxury loft apartments, alongside the garrets and studios.

Now the boundaries of trendy living are being pushed ever northwards, up **Kingsland Road** and right into **Dalston**. The area is likely to be one of the big winners when the Olympics come to town, close to the main venues. What's more, the underground is extending into Hackney - a sure sign of London's own estimation of this district's rising star.

Trafalgar Square, 2002 de Xavier Pick/Bridgeman-Giraudon

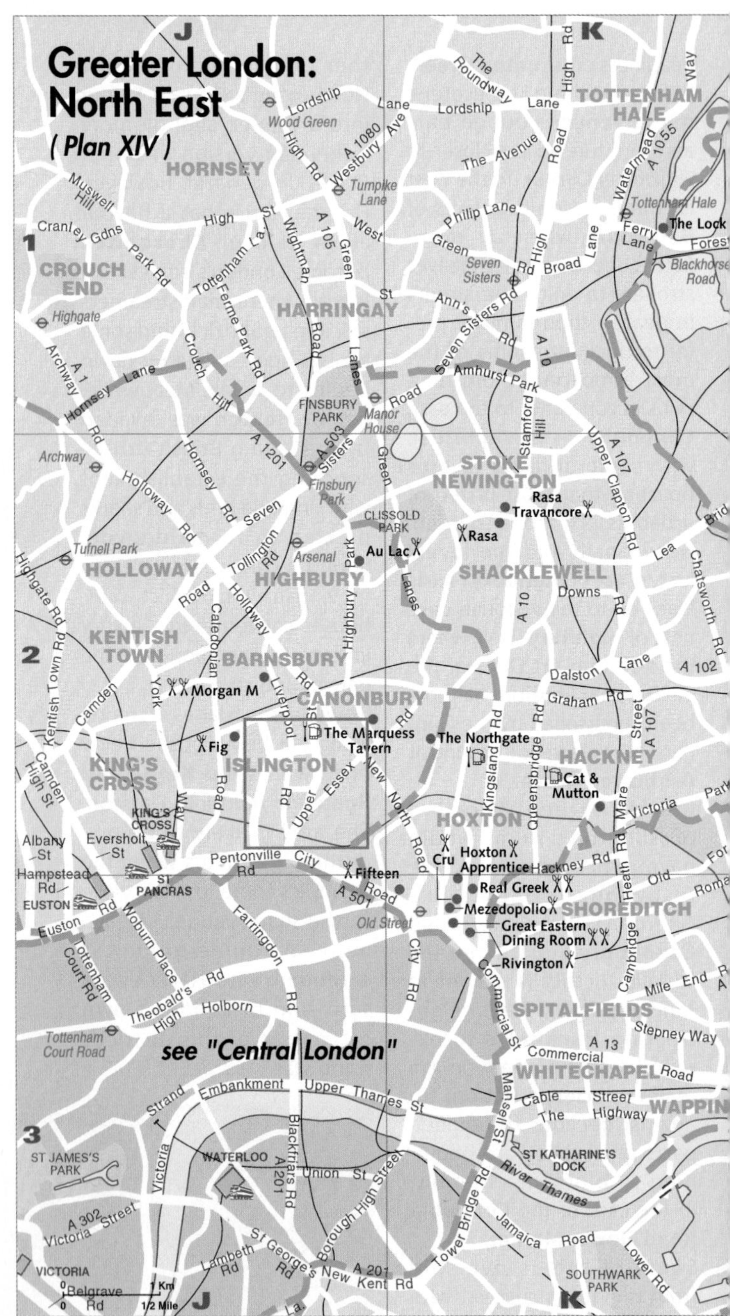
Greater London: North East
(Plan XIV)
HORNSEY
CROUCH END
HARRINGAY
TOTTENHAM HALE
STOKE NEWINGTON
HOLLOWAY
HIGHBURY
SHACKLEWELL
KENTISH TOWN
BARNSBURY
CANONBURY
ISLINGTON
KING'S CROSS
HACKNEY
HOXTON
SHOREDITCH
SPITALFIELDS
WHITECHAPEL
ST PANCRAS
EUSTON
WATERLOO
VICTORIA
ST JAMES'S PARK
ST KATHARINE'S DOCK
SOUTHWARK PARK
FINSBURY PARK
CLISSOLD PARK
The Lock
Rasa Travancore
Rasa
Au Lac
Morgan M
Fig
The Marquess Tavern
The Northgate
Cat & Mutton
Fifteen
Cru
Hoxton Apprentice
Real Greek
Mezedopolio
Great Eastern Dining Room
Rivington
see "Central London"
River Thames
J
K
1
2
3

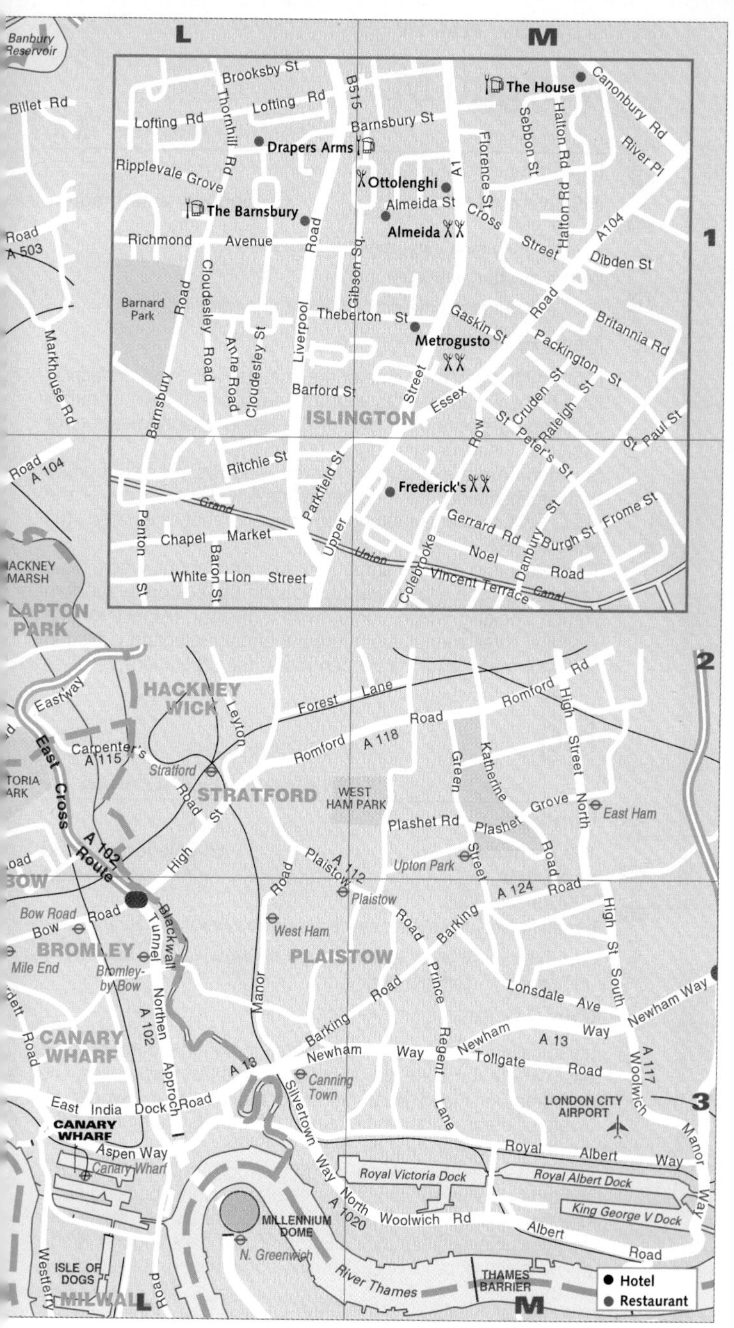
L
M
1
2
3
The House
Drapers Arms
Ottolenghi
The Barnsbury
Almeida
Metrogusto
Frederick's
ISLINGTON
HACKNEY WICK
STRATFORD
WEST HAM PARK
PLAISTOW
BROMLEY
CANARY WHARF
LONDON CITY AIRPORT
MILLENNIUM DOME
THAMES BARRIER
ISLE OF DOGS
MILWALL
Royal Victoria Dock
Royal Albert Dock
King George V Dock
River Thames
Hotel
Restaurant

Morgan M

French XX

Barnsbury

489 Liverpool Rd ⊖ Highbury and Islington
✉ N7 8NS **J2**
✆ (020) 76093560 – **Fax** (020) 82925699
Web www.morganm.com

Closed 24-30 December, lunch Tuesday and Saturday, Sunday dinner and Monday

Menu £23.50/32

M is for Meunier, the name of the chef patron of this endearing little place which radiates warmth and goodwill from its rather challenging position on one of the less enchanting streets of Islington, where lifestyle gurus fear to tread.
Shielded from the outside by frosted windows, the bright white and green dining room comes embellished with some of the chef's own colourful artwork and shelves of that celebrated little red guidebook.
The reassuring service stops you worrying about where your car's parked and allows you to focus on the elaborate, modern French cooking which comes with a healthy respect for the seasons. Three menus are offered: the main selection, a tasting seasonal menu and the Garden menu for vegetarians.

Fig

Modern European X

Barnsbury

169 Hemingford Rd ⊖ Caledonian Road
✉ N1 1DA **J2**
✆ (020) 76093009
e-mail figrestaurant@btconnect.com **Web** www.figrestaurant.co.uk

Closed 22 December-3 January, last 2 weeks August, Monday and Tuesday – dinner only and Sunday lunch – booking essential

Carte £19/29

It's so called because there's a fig tree in the little garden at the back, where there are also four tables on a first come basis. The restaurant changed hands in 2006 but the new owners are aware of the importance of keeping the locals happy by retaining the sweet and friendly feel.
There's a somewhat colonial feel to the room, enlivened by some spirited art. With just ten tables, it's always worth booking first.
The Danish chef owner has an international CV but his weekly changing menus keep things European. He does, though, like to throw in the occasional challenging combination to keep diners on their toes.
The Aussie co-owner gets the tenor of the service just right.

The House

Gastropub 

Canonbury

63-69 Canonbury Rd
⊠ N1 2DG
✆ (020) 77047410 – **Fax** (020) 77049388
e-mail info@inthehouse.biz **Web** www.inthehouse.biz

⊖ Highbury and Islington
M1

VISA MC ①

Closed Christmas and Monday lunch

Menu £17.95 (lunch) – Carte £45/66

When Islingtonians arrange to meet you back at 'the house', more than likely they mean at this coolly sophisticated pub, tucked away in a residential part of the borough. It effortlessly combines a laid back vibe at the bar, which adjoins a triangular shaped terrace at the front, with a more urbane atmosphere found in the nattily attired dining room.
Just reading the menu provides evidence that The House has loftier culinary ambitions than many a gastropub. Indeed, a number of the kitchen's carefully composed dishes would not look out of place in restaurants sporting a much higher brow and a more prosperous postcode.
Pleasingly, it also remembers its roots and still knows how to do a decent shepherd's pie.

The Marquess Tavern

Gastropub 

Canonbury

32 Canonbury St
⊠ N1 2TB
✆ (020) 73542975
Web www.marquesstavern.co.uk

⊖ Highbury and Islington
J2

VISA MC AE

Carte £22/28

This marquess is a handsome old chap who fell on hard times but is now once again standing proud. The Victorian character is still there, just sympathetically updated for our age and everything now seems to fit just so.
The owners' haven't just focused on the food and wine – beer and whisky enjoy equal billing with the former the perfect accompaniment to the offerings at the bar, like cheese sandwiches or pork pie and pickles. The dining room is at the far end, with high ceilings and a period feel, although the blackboard menu can be enjoyed anywhere. The cooking is resolutely and laudably British and suits the pub perfectly. There's nothing twee about the dishes - all are satisfyingly hearty and some come designed for sharing.

Cat & Mutton

Gastropub

Hackney

76 Broadway Market — Bethnal Green
E8 4QJ — **K2**
(020) 72545599
e-mail info@catandmutton.co.uk
Closed 25-26 December, Sunday dinner and Monday lunch

Carte £19/29

Standing outside the Cat and Mutton you'd think nothing much has changed here over the years. The large sign, the Victorian façade and the huge windows etched with "Toby and Carrington" convey a certain tradition but, when inside, it's the one single huge space of the room which seems so striking.
Exposed brick, panelled ceiling, wood top tables and old school chairs account for the decoration, with the large windows on two sides making it all seem so open. The daily changing menu is chalked on a slate board, with snackier items at lunch and gutsier fare for the evening, with an admirable selection of wines available by the glass.
A DJ plays on Sunday evenings - information which will either attract you in or frighten you off.

Au Lac

Vietnamese

Highbury

82 Highbury Park — Arsenal
N5 2XE — **J2**
(020) 77049187 – **Fax** (020) 77049187
Closed 25 December and Bank Holidays – dinner only and lunch Thursday and Friday

Carte £12/16

On a busy road boasting a number of dining options, several of them Vietnamese and some of questionable quality, Au Lac manages to stand out from the crowd and pull in plenty of regulars. Its draw is perhaps not in its decoration, which has a simple but curiously comforting modesty about it, but in the tangy Vietnamese cooking and the extensive choice available. The brothers who run the place are eager to please and the charming nature of the staff helps guide those unfamiliar with the zesty delicacies. Vegetarians will find many appealing dishes and there are set menus available for larger parties. Perhaps best of all, the generous pricing allows for unabashed experimentation and unselfish sharing.

Great Eastern Dining Room

South-East Asian XX

Hoxton

54 Great Eastern St ⊖ Old Street

✉ EC2A 3QR **K3**

✆ (020) 76134545 – **Fax** (020) 76134137

Web www.greateastern-restaurant.com

Closed Christmas and Sunday

Carte £24/37

Will Ricker's flourishing group of hip restaurants came into its own here in Great Eastern Street and coincided with Hoxton's own emergence onto the fashion radar.

The format here is similar to the others in the group: the bar, given equal billing as the restaurant, occupies most of the front section and it's usually so packed a sardine would think twice. The noise spills into the restaurant, adding a lively vibe to the place. It's all great fun. The kitchen's influences spill across South East Asia, with *dim sum*, curries, roasts and *tempura* all carefully prepared. Helpfully, the reverse of the menu carries a glossary of Asian culinary terms.

The serving team are a sassy and well-informed bunch.

Real Greek

Greek XX

Hoxton

15 Hoxton Market ⊖ Old Street

✉ N1 6HG **K3**

✆ (020) 77398212 – **Fax** (020) 77394910

e-mail admin@therealgreek.co.uk **Web** www.therealgreek.co.uk

Closed 25-26 December, Sunday and Bank Holidays

Carte £23/34

There haven't been Greeks as upwardly mobile as this since Icarus. Housed in a 1913 Christian Mission, the Real Greek opened in 1999, adding to the buzz surrounding Hoxton as a fashionable address for the creative and artistic. And those who work in The City.

The restaurant has one of those vibes that relaxes everyone - just watch the suited hurriedly remove their ties as they head toward their table.

The open-plan kitchen offers a wide choice of Greek country cooking. The menu, written in Greek and English, is divided into four: *meze* combinations, *mezedes* and *fagakia* which are small dishes perfect for sharing and *kirios piata*, the main courses. Order a bowl of large, juicy olives as you select something from the exclusively Greek wine list.

Fifteen

Italian

Hoxton

13 Westland Pl — Old Street

N1 7LP — **K3**

(0871) 3301515 – **Fax** (020) 72512749

Web www.fifteenrestaurant.com

Closed 25 December- 1 January

Menu £25/60 – Carte £34/42

Jamie Oliver's rise to sainthood began in earnest in 2002 with "Jamie's Kitchen", a TV programme which followed the traumas and ultimate triumphs of setting up a training kitchen and restaurant for disadvantaged youngsters. Fifteen is that established restaurant, with other branches of this most laudable charitable foundation being set up elsewhere.

There are two dining options: the downstairs restaurant, with its open plan kitchen, where you can watch the chefs prepare dishes with Italian and Mediterranean influences using carefully sourced ingredients, and the ground floor Trattoria which offers a more relaxed and less expensive dining option.

If you're undecided whether to have that third course, remember that all profits go to the foundation.

Cru

Mediterranean

Hoxton

2-4 Rufus St — Old Street

N1 6PE — **K3**

(020) 77295252 – **Fax** (020) 77291070

e-mail info@cru.uk.com **Web** www.cru.uk.com

Closed 25-30 December and Monday

Carte £19/25

The flowering of a neighbourhood can often be put down to the seeds planted by pioneering local restaurants and artistic endeavours. Virtually opposite The White Cube Gallery, you'll find the restaurant Cru.

Great use has been made of the 19th century warehouse in which it is housed. At the front there's a bar and small all-day deli. The restaurant is at the back, divided by the open kitchen. The vibe is animated and the service relaxed but in control.

The Mediterranean provides the influence to the menu and the sunny colours clearly suit the place. Many of the dishes are designed for sharing. Smaller, lesser-known vineyards are a feature of the interesting wine list and many unfamiliar wines are also available by the glass.

Hoxton Apprentice

Modern European 

Hoxton

16 Hoxton Sq. ⊖ Old Street
N1 6NT **K2_3**
(020) 77492828
Web www.hoxtonapprentice.com

Menu £13 (lunch) – Carte £21/32

Despite the severe parking restrictions, Hoxton Square has become quite a dining quarter and Hoxton Apprentice stands out from others for two reasons. Firstly, it was set up by a charity, Training for Life, to give opportunities to the unemployed or homeless with all the profits going back into the charity and, secondly, the cooking is rather good.

This is not merely a restaurant for the community minded - the restaurant stands up in its own right. The apprentices work alongside pros and the kitchen uses decent, seasonal ingredients; the wine is competitively priced and the service is both conscientious and considerate.

Housed in a former Victorian school, the room retains a relaxed and easy feel, with French windows opening out onto the terrace.

Mezedopolio

Greek 

Hoxton

15 Hoxton Market ⊖ Old Street
N1 6HG **K3**
(020) 77398212 – **Fax** (020) 77394910
Web www.therealgreek.co.uk

Closed 25-26 December, 1 January, Sunday and Bank Holidays – bookings not accepted

Carte £10/17

The popularity of The Real Greek led to an expansion of the business within the same Victorian building and two years after its opening came its baby sister, the more informal Mezedopolio, which specialises in small tapas-style Greek dishes.

The large semi-circular bar acts as the centrepiece of the room and tells you this is a relaxed spot where the drinks menu is just as important as the food menu. That latter menu, however, has plenty on offer, from *mezedes* and *souvlaki* to salads and grills and all boasting a zingy freshness. Most plates are designed for sharing which adds to the overall geniality of the place, as does the wine list which is exclusively Greek and has some real bargains. Plenty of staff are on hand to offer sound advice.

Frederick's

Modern European XX

Islington

Camden Passage ⊖ Angel

N1 8EG **M2**

(020) 73592888 – **Fax** (020) 73595173

e-mail eat@fredericks.co.uk **Web** www.fredericks.co.uk

Closed 25 December-1 January, Easter, Sunday and Bank Holidays

Menu £17 (lunch) – Carte £28/37

It feels as though Frederick's has been around for as long as some of the antiques being sold in the surrounding shops and stalls of Camden Passage. Its laudable longevity comes down to a successful formula of providing a popular little bar for the after-work crowd and, once you've pushed past them, a large airy dining room. The room glows with warmth in winter and shimmers in light in summer thanks mainly to the large conservatory, with its big vaulted glass roof, which leads out onto the delightful terrace.
The kitchen is reliable and honest, balancing perennial favourites with more refined specialities from sunnier European climes, matched in colour by the bold and striking artwork on the walls.

Almeida

French XX

Islington

30 Almeida St ⊖ Angel

N1 1AD **M1**

(020) 73544777 – **Fax** (020) 73542777

Web www.almeida-restaurant.co.uk

Menu £17.50/27

What better way of attracting the pre-theatre crowd than by taking the same name as the theatre, which is also, in turn, the name of the street on which they're both located. The Almeida Theatre is certainly one of the jewels of North London and attracts audiences from across London, so it's right to have a restaurant opposite which combines a local buzz with sophisticated surroundings and reliably good food.
This being a Conran restaurant means the design element is in the bag, with a modern yet warm feel to the room. Meanwhile, the kitchen wisely leaves the risk-taking to the theatre opposite and sensibly concentrates on providing dependable French regional cooking with many classic favourites.

Metrogusto

Italian

Islington

13 Theberton St — Angel

N1 0QY — **M1**

(020) 72269400 – **Fax** (020) 72269400

Web www.metrogusto.co.uk

Closed 25 December, 1 January, Easter, Sunday and Bank Holidays – dinner only and lunch Friday and Saturday

Carte £23/32

Just looking in the window tells you that this is no ordinary Italian restaurant. One rarely sees interesting artwork in local restaurants - maybe some chefs feel threatened by the presence of someone else's creativity - but Metrogusto shows that having interesting pieces of art can, at the very least, provide diners with a conversation piece. The menu, too, shows an unwillingness to merely go with the flow and offers four courses of carefully prepared dishes, where the vitality of the ingredients is very much to the fore and where hints of originality are subtle and well judged. The pricing structure sensibly allows those who have come for an occasion or for a simple, quick bite to do so without breaking the bank.

Ottolenghi

International 

Islington

287 Upper St — Highbury and Islington

N1 2TZ — **M1**

(020) 72881454 – **Fax** (020) 77041456

e-mail upper@ottolenghi.co.uk

Closed Christmas-New Year, Sunday dinner and Bank Holidays

Carte £26/31

Ottolenghi provides further evidence of the current trend for more spontaneous dining and less structured menus. A hugely appealing display of tempting pastries, unusual salads and mouth-watering desserts greet you as you enter. Behind this, one finds the restaurant, decorated as white as celestial purity, where two long communal tables dominate. Waiting staff will explain the 'concept' which involves ordering an assortment of small dishes, some of which display certain Mediterranean leanings while others may exhibit subtle Eastern spicing. The breads and puddings are particularly good.
Takeaway is a large part of the business and lunch is an altogether simpler affair, with mostly salads and quiches.

Drapers Arms

Gastropub

Islington

44 Barnsbury St — Highbury and Islington

N1 1ER — **L1**

(020) 76190348 – **Fax** (020) 76190413

e-mail info@thedrapersarms.co.uk **Web** www.thedrapersarms.co.uk

VISA MC AE

Closed 24-28 December

Carte £22/35

Tucked away in a corner of Islington lies The Drapers Arms, one of the area's many gastropubs giving local restaurants a run for their money.

It makes an ideal local because you can eat casually in the downstairs bar but you also have the choice of going up to the slightly more formal dining room. It has the relaxed feel of a re-born pub, with sofas and original floorboards, tables and booths all in a room with an altogether cleaner, brighter and more contemporary palette. The outside courtyard terrace is a charming spot.

It is to the Mediterranean that the menu looks for influence and inspiration, but balances that with what those closer to home would call pub classics. They also offer a decent selection of wines by the glass.

The Northgate

Gastropub

Islington

113 Southgate Rd — Highbury and Islington

N1 3JS — **K2**

(020) 73597392 – **Fax** (020) 73597393

e-mail thenorthgate@hppubs.co.uk

MC

Closed 25 December – dinner only and lunch Saturday and Sunday

Carte £18/24

The Northgate is a large, square Victorian pub located on a corner of, paradoxically, Southgate Road. It may look fairly unremarkable from the outside but it was one of the first of many Islington pubs to blossom into a gastropub. There's an honesty about the place which engenders a relaxed and welcoming vibe, even when it is full-on busy which appears to be most evenings.

The front section comes decked out with the gastropub uniform of mismatched furniture, modern art and a large central bar. There's a separate dining room at the back with a skylight and the terrace is a big draw.

From the blackboard menu comes liberally sized plates of satisfying wholesome gastropub staples, like tiger prawns and lamb shank.

The Barnsbury

Gastropub

Islington

209-211 Liverpool Rd ⊖ Highbury and Islington

✉ N1 1LX **L1**

VISA

✆ (020) 76075519 – **Fax** (020) 76073256

e-mail info@thebarnsbury.co.uk **Web** www.thebarnsbury.co.uk

AE

Closed 24-26 December and 1 January

Carte £21/30

It may have been spruced up a few years back but The Barnsbury is still your proper local. Hence, you'll find it on down-to-earth Liverpool Road rather than glossier Upper Street which runs parallel.

The more traditional features of restored wood panelling and a large central counter contrast with contemporary touches, such as the chandeliers made from crystal wine glasses and the regularly changing local artwork. It's all very relaxed and the young staff are helpful and competent.

The owner, an acolyte of the Conran empire, clearly knows what he is doing. The menu will satisfy the appetites of both those who like to see recognisable British ingredients, as well as those who prefer more of an Italian connection to their food.

Rivington

British

Shoreditch

28-30 Rivington St ⊖ Old St

VISA

✉ EC2A 3DZ **K3**

✆ (020) 77297053

Web www.rivingtongrill.co.uk

AE

Closed 25-26 December and 1 January – brunch at weekends

Carte £25/36

Well judged English cooking is the draw here, using oft forgotten ingredients to make Mrs Beeton proud, such as haslet, mutton, turnips and pilchards, all prepared with today's lighter and more nimble touch.

The converted warehouse, with its well worn floorboards, paper menu-as-placemats, school chairs and playful 'neon-art' embellishments, provides the coolly contemporary backdrop for this everyman fare. It even attracts all manner of customer, from business-type to local - even the odd hoodie has been known to venture over the threshold.

Serving staff all have their skates on, particularly at lunch when delivery from the kitchen is swift, but those in even more of a hurry can grab something from the next door deli.

The Princess

Gastropub 

Shoreditch

76-78 Paul St (1st floor) ⊖ Old Street
✉ EC2A 4NE **PLAN page 165 M1**
(020) 77299270

Closed 24 December-8 January, Saturday lunch and Bank Holidays

Carte £22/26

How exactly did a dodgy old boozer full of villains turn into a gastropub run by antipodeans? Social historians can explain but we should just be grateful that it did, as The Princess now ticks all the right boxes.
The downstairs remains loyal to its Victorian roots, except with better food, but ascend the spiral staircase and you'll find yourself in an unexpectedly stylish dining room. A little art deco, oil paintings, floral wallpaper, mirrors and a fireplace all set the tone. The kitchen is skilled at producing flavoursome and robust dishes of assorted influences, but with a pronounced seasonality.
The name of the place is not, sadly, in honour of East End vernacular but is a shortened version of the original, The Princess Royal.

The Fox

Gastropub 

Shoreditch

28 Paul St ⊖ Old Street
✉ EC2A 4LB **PLAN page 165 M1**
(020) 77295708

Closed 23 December-3 January, Easter, Saturday, Sunday and Bank Holidays – booking essential

Menu £21.50

Friday lunchtime and it'll be like a rugby scrum at the bar, but head upstairs for the contrasting serenity of the first floor dining room, where you'll also find a delightful roof terrace.
Four choices per course form the set menu, although there's no pressure exerted to have the full three-courser. Dish descriptions are refreshingly concise and this no-nonsense simplicity is reflected in the rustic cooking with specialities of either a British or Mediterranean persuasion.
The dining room boasts an appealingly thrown-together quality and, in between their constant sprints up and down the stairs from the kitchen, the waiting staff pitch the tone of service perfectly.
There are rumours of a revamp and a change in ownership.

Rasa

Indian vegetarian

Stoke Newington

55 Stoke Newington Church St

VISA ✉ N16 0AR **K2**

✆ (020) 72490344 – **Fax** (020) 76370224

Web www.rasarestaurants.com

AE Dinner only and lunch Saturday and Sunday – booking essential

Menu £16 – Carte £9/12

It's easy to spot because of the liberal use of the trademark pink paintbrush, both inside and outside.
Stoke Newington has been proudly extolling the virtues of Rasa for many a year and, with branches popping up elsewhere, they can rightly claim to have played host to the original.
Rasa means "taste" in Sanskrit and the menu celebrates the vibrancy and colour of the state of Kerala, on the South West coast of India. Wholly vegetarian, the 'feast' menu is a perfect way for the uninitiated to become familiar with the specialities of the region. The snacks, pickles and chutneys are all prepared with care and are well worth sampling, while the main courses feature all of Kerala's wondrous produce such as bananas, cardamom and cashews.

Rasa Travancore

Indian

Stoke Newington

56 Stoke Newington Church St

VISA ✉ N16 0NB **K2**

✆ (020) 72491340

Web www.rasarestaurants.com

AE Dinner only and Sunday lunch

Carte £16/21

Virtually opposite Rasa is its sister Rasa Travancore. It also offers specialities from the Kerala region of India, but this time carnivores are catered for as it celebrates the unique cooking found within the Christian Syrian communities. Meat and fish play a large part and the menu offers a balanced selection, from steamed prawns to chicken stews and lamb curries. Despite having a basement kitchen, the dishes arrive piping hot and portions are in manageable sizes, so be sure to try some of the pre-meal snacks.
Ornamentation within the two dining rooms is relatively limited but the delightful and charming service more than compensates. Everyone involved in the restaurant hails from Kerala and they're all rightly proud of their cuisine.

The Lock

Mediterranean XX

Tottenham

VISA

Heron House, Hale Wharf, Ferry Lane — ⊖ Tottenham Hale

MC

✉ N17 9NF — **K1**

AE

✆ (020) 8885 2829 – **Fax** (020) 8885 1618

Web www.thelock-diningbar.com

Closed 1-8 January, 28 May-6 June, Saturday lunch, Sunday dinner and Monday

Menu £14.50 (lunch) – Carte £22/32

Full marks to The Lock for opening in Tottenham and doing their bit for the regeneration of this part of London. It's in the big yellow industrial looking building on your left as you approach from the west and, while the address may hint at a rather charming lock-side setting, the Norfolk Broads it ain't.

It is, though, a very sweetly run place, with two keen young owners. The room's quite spacious, with a bar and sofas on one side and the restaurant, with its mismatched tables and chairs, on the other. With much of the produce coming from Walthamstow market, the open kitchen offers up a menu of French and Italian influences, with the odd idiosyncratic twist, and several vegetarian choices. Let's hope Tottenham is ready.

RAIN DANCE

Designer water may be all the rage these days, but perhaps it has been ever thus among the metropolitan elite. Just ask savvy C17th entrepreneur Richard Sadler who, discovering a well in his garden, claimed the water could solve all sorts of distempers and drew custom from London's most fashionable hypochondriacs. True, rival wells soon sprang up and stole his business - but Sadler's Wells has proved more than a damp squib in the long run.

C. Barrely/MICHELIN

GREATER LONDON

South-East London

C. Eymenier/MICHELIN

The rest of the world may once have relied on **Greenwich** to keep the clocks ticking, but down in the historic centre, you'd be forgiven for thinking time had stopped. Greenwich has succeeded in the miraculous trick of preserving its heritage without becoming just a museum piece. There are museums, of course, the **Royal Observatory** and the **National Maritime Museum** among them. But despite Greenwich's designation as a World Heritage Site, life carries on in the pubs and the playhouse, the tea rooms and the market, albeit at a steady pace.

Visitors are well advised to maintain that relaxed speed as they scale the heights of **Greenwich Park** in the direction of neighbouring **Blackheath,** one of the most pleasant examples of London's village-suburbs. You may be tempted immediately to cross the heath towards the striking **All Saints Church** and the lovely hanging-basketed streets behind. But turn around and the view could change your mind - for beyond the picture-postcard perfection of Wren's **Naval College** you'll see the glistening towers of **Canary Wharf**, with the rest of the **Docklands** spread out like a toy town below. The scale of the project to redevelop London's derelict dockyards really hits you from this vantage point, but its success is even more overwhelming down among the glass canyons.

There was a time - until really quite recently in fact - when Londoners looked on this crystal and chrome landscape with little but suspicion, as if the CBD of a second-tier North American city had been plonked in the capital. Yes, these office buildings reaching for the sky, reflected in the water, were all very impressive. But where was the life? And where was London?

Today, Canary Wharf is not only an established fixture of the skyline, but also - with the Tube whisking you to **Westminster** in roughly 10 minutes - an integrated part of the city. With that, it's found the confidence to develop its own personality. There's still something of the Toronto about it, but funky quayside bars, signature bridges, subterranean shopping malls and surprising vistas of the **Gherkin** and the **Dome** all give character. Sure, the place is quieter at the weekends, when the financiers, journalists and advertisers go home - but since many now live in the plush residential developments nearby, the beat goes on.

And on we go too, to **Wapping**, which - although part of the Docklands - has been revitalised in a different way. Here, after an initial stage of demolishing warehouses and filling in docks, the decision was made to try to pursue projects that were in sympathy with the existing architecture. The result is a rather high-class Dickensian feel - appropriate enough since the great man was a regular in some of the local pubs.

Still, it was **St Katherines Dock** on Wapping's edge which was the initial showpiece and proved that redevelopment could produce atmosphere where most original buildings had been destroyed. The marina might now be more St Tropez than smugglers' den, but somehow it still evokes the mastmakers, victuallers and pirates of the not too distant past.

But for dark undercurrents, you can't beat the adjacent **Whitechapel**, with its Jack the Rippers, Elephant Men and general East End edginess. Emerging from the relatively clean-cut Docklands, the gothic vibe is actually rather refreshing. What's more, the gigs here are great and the pubs nicely bohemian. Local markets such as **Spitalfields**, meanwhile, tread the line the area also walks: between lovably tatty and madly hip.

S. Ollivier/MICHELIN

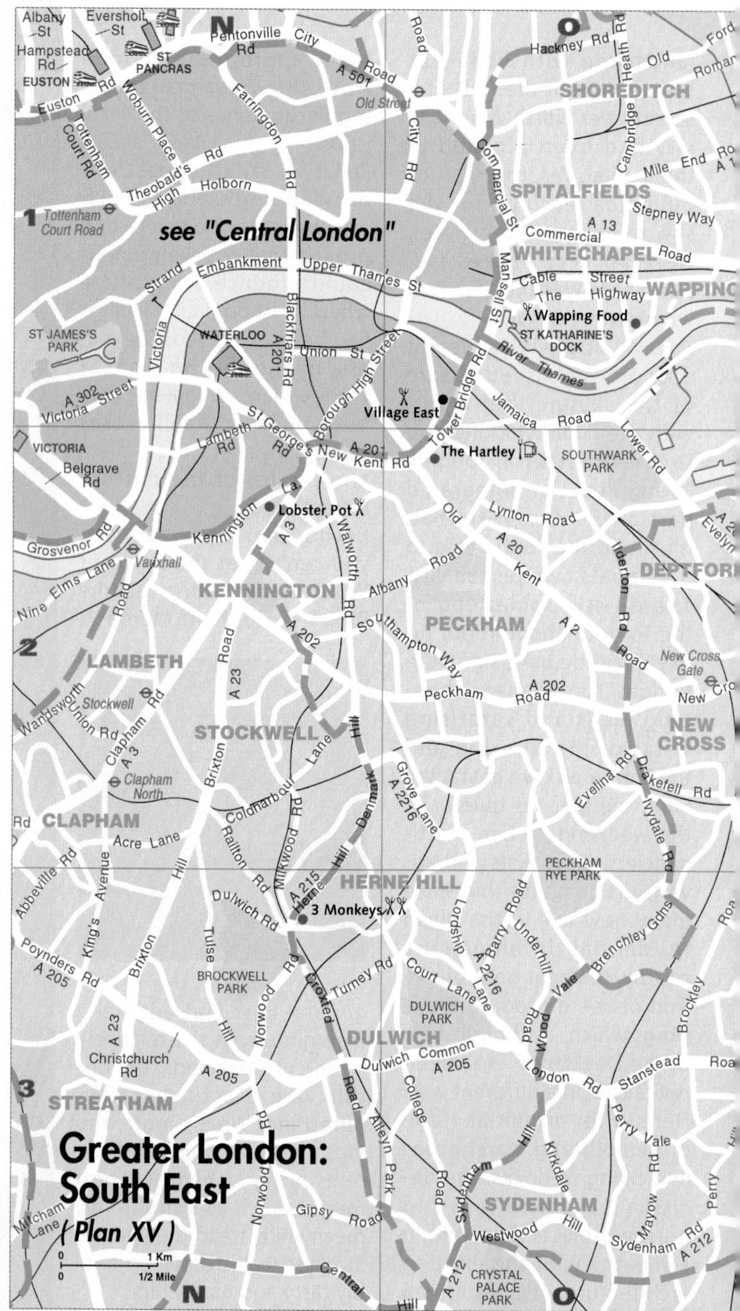
Greater London: South East
(Plan XV)
see "Central London"
Wapping Food
Village East
The Hartley
Lobster Pot
3 Monkeys
SHOREDITCH
SPITALFIELDS
WHITECHAPEL
WAPPING
ST KATHARINE'S DOCK
WATERLOO
ST PANCRAS
EUSTON
VICTORIA
ST JAMES'S PARK
SOUTHWARK PARK
KENNINGTON
PECKHAM
DEPTFORD
LAMBETH
STOCKWELL
NEW CROSS
CLAPHAM
HERNE HILL
PECKHAM RYE PARK
BROCKWELL PARK
DULWICH PARK
DULWICH
STREATHAM
SYDENHAM
CRYSTAL PALACE PARK
River Thames
0 1 Km
0 1/2 Mile

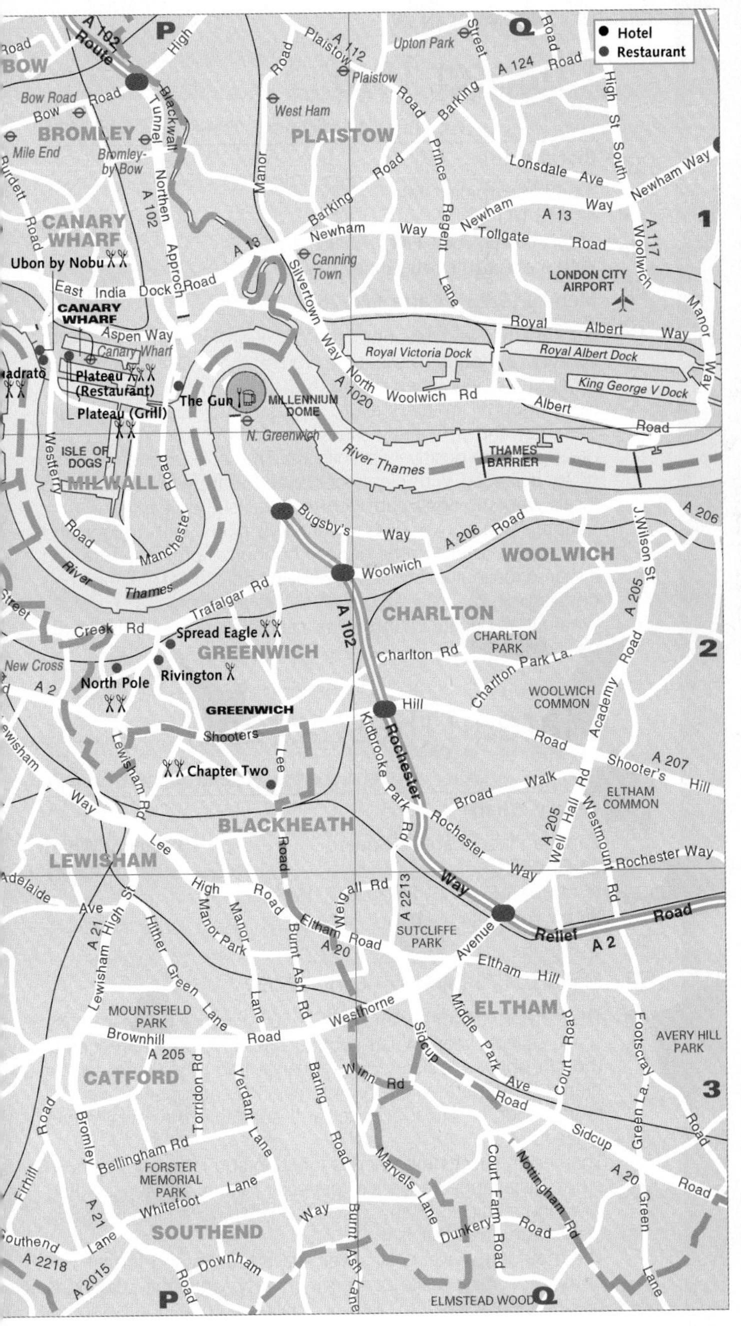

Hotel
Restaurant
P
Q
1
2
3
BOW
BROMLEY
Bow Road
Bow
Mile End
Bromley-by-Bow
CANARY WHARF
Ubon by Nobu
East India Dock Road
CANARY WHARF
Aspen Way
Canary Wharf
Plateau (Restaurant)
Plateau (Grill)
The Gun
MILLENNIUM DOME
N. Greenwich
ISLE OF DOGS
MILWALL
Westferry Road
Manchester Road
River Thames
PLAISTOW
Plaistow
West Ham
Upton Park
Canning Town
Newham Way
Barking Road
Tollgate Road
Lonsdale Ave
LONDON CITY AIRPORT
Royal Albert Way
Royal Victoria Dock
Royal Albert Dock
King George V Dock
North Woolwich Rd
Albert Road
THAMES BARRIER
Bugsby's Way
A 206 Road
WOOLWICH
CHARLTON
CHARLTON PARK
Charlton Rd
Charlton Park La.
WOOLWICH COMMON
Trafalgar Rd
Creek Rd
Spread Eagle
GREENWICH
New Cross
North Pole
Rivington
GREENWICH
Shooters Hill Road
Chapter Two
Lewisham Way
Lewisham Rd
BLACKHEATH
Rochester Way
Kidbrooke Park Rd
Shooter's Hill
ELTHAM COMMON
Well Hall Rd
Westmount Rd
Rochester Way Relief Road
LEWISHAM
Lee High Road
Manor Park
Eltham Road
Weigall Rd
SUTCLIFFE PARK
Eltham Hill
ELTHAM
Middle Park Ave
Court Road
Footscray Road
AVERY HILL PARK
MOUNTSFIELD PARK
Brownhill Road
Westhorne Avenue
Sidcup Road
Winn Rd
CATFORD
Torridon Rd
Verdant Lane
Baring Road
Bellingham Rd
FORSTER MEMORIAL PARK
Whitefoot Lane
SOUTHEND
Downham Way
Burnt Ash Lane
Marvels Lane
Dunkery Road
Court Farm Road
Nottingham Rd
Green Lane
ELMSTEAD WOOD

Chapter Two

Modern European XX

Blackheath

43-45 Montpelier Vale
SE3 0TJ **P2**
(020) 83332666 – **Fax** (020) 83558399
Web www.chapterrestaurants.co.uk

A/C VISA MC AE

Menu £19/23 – Carte £20/26

Blackheath was a favoured spot for highwaymen in the 18th century, although these days you're more likely to witness daylight robbery when dining in the West End.
Here, though, in Blackheath, you can now eat thoughtfully prepared and eminently satisfying modern European food at prices that are positively munificent. The set price menus come nicely balanced, with plenty of choice to satisfy the demanding locals who still don't part with their wallets too easily.
Chapter Two comes divided into two floors, with a light and breezy feel thanks to the general bonhomie of the service and a shared feeling of satisfaction of being able to eat well on one's doorstep.
Where it all began, Chapter One, can be found in Farnborough, near Bromley.

Plateau (Restaurant)

Modern European XXX

Canary Wharf

Canada Place, Canada Square — Canary Wharf
E14 5ER **P1**
(020) 7715 7122 – **Fax** (020) 77157110
Web www.conran.com

A/C VISA MC AE

Closed Sunday

Menu £24.75 (dinner) – Carte £27/37

The corporate wonderland that is 100 acres of Grade A office space called Canary Wharf continues to develop. Until recently though, anyone looking for sustenance had to make do with a branded high street chain. But then Plateau opened, on the fourth floor of Canada Place, and suddenly the cavalry had arrived.
The design successfully blends function and form and its modernist glass appearance sits perfectly within the surrounding towering edifices. If any part of London feels like midtown Manhattan, then this is it.
The moulded swivel chairs, well spaced tables and formal, unobtrusive service make conversation easy, while the cooking is predominantly modern, with underlying European influences.

Ubon by Nobu

Japanese XX

Canary Wharf

34 Westferry Circus ⊖ Canary Wharf
✉ E14 8RR **P1**
✆ (020) 77197800 – **Fax** (020) 77197801
Web www.noburestaurantlondon.com

A/C VISA MC AE

Closed 25-26 and 31 December, 1 January, Saurday lunch, Sunday and Bank Holidays

Menu £55/90 – Carte £35/51

Harder to find but, ironically, easier to get into, Ubon by Nobu is the lesser known sibling of the celebrity-studded Mayfair joints. First of all, you have to locate the lift that'll bring you up to the fourth floor of this modern building. You'll then find yourself in a room with floor to ceiling windows and spectacular views of the river and city skyline, which virtually merit a bill of their own.

Decoratively, it's not too dissimilar to the Nobu restaurants, with simple tables in a fairly minimalist setting. Here, though, the clientele is a little more corporate and a little less showbiz. The menu is largely the same too, with bento boxes for those on a schedule and the familiar mix of Japanese specialities with South American touches.

Quadrato

Italian 

Canary Wharf

at Four Seasons H., ⊖ Canary Wharf
Westferry Circus ✉ E14 8RS **P1**
✆ (020) 75101999 – **Fax** (020) 75101998

A/C VISA AE

Carte £34/50

The Four Seasons hotel was the first luxury hotel to pitch up in Canary Wharf. Not only did they foresee the demand for top-notch accommodation but they also understood the need for a decent restaurant and one that appealed to a wider audience than merely hotel guests.

Quadrato was the result and it's located just off the atrium. What's more, it has a terrific terrace, with views over the river. It's equally plush inside, with floor to ceiling windows and well-dressed, well-spaced tables.

The kitchen seeks its influence from the more northerly parts of Italy and dishes are prepared with care and a fair degree of flair. Lunch is understandably more of a corporate event but the pace in the evenings is gentler and the service a little less frantic.

Plateau (Grill)

Modern European XX

Canary Wharf

Canada Place, Canada Square ⊖ Canary Wharf
✉ E14 5ER **P1**
✆ (020) 77157000 – **Fax** (020) 77157110
Web www.conran.com

Closed 25 December, 1 January and Sunday dinner

Menu £20/24.75 – Carte £27/37

The Grill is sufficiently different from the main Plateau Restaurant to stand separately in its own right. Even though it shares the fourth floor, with its own dedicated lift, it's just a bit louder, slightly more casual and informal and, with it, a little bit more fun. The opening times are also somewhat less structured, allowing for those who prefer a later lunch.

The food comes from the same semi-open kitchen as the restaurant but is a tad more rustic and earthy. There is also the addition of a number of grilled dishes, as well as some rotisserie choices which are a popular option.

No corners have been cut with the service which demonstrates the same levels of attentiveness and courtesy that you'll find in the restaurant.

The Gun

Gastropub 

Canary Wharf

27 Coldharbour ⊖ Blackwall (DLR)
✉ E14 9NS **P1**
✆ (020) 75155222 – **Fax** (020) 75154407
e-mail info@thegundocklands.com
Web www.thegundocklands.com

Closed 26 December

Carte £22/35

The Gun is glorious proof that not everything in this part of London is big, new and shiny. Dating back to the 18th century, the pub's history is entwined with that of the surrounding docks and it was here where Lord Nelson conducted his trysts with Lady Emma Hamilton.

Today, painstakingly restored after a fire, The Gun has been brought up to date, but without compromising its colourful heritage. The charming decked terrace looks over the Dome while the interior is warm and inviting, with separate areas for drinkers and eaters.

With specials on the blackboard and much of the fish from Billingsgate, the cooking is contemporary in style and exact in execution. The only thing missing is a room full of dockers and smugglers.

North Pole

Modern European XX

VISA MC AE D

Greenwich

131 Greenwich High Rd ⊖ New Cross

✉ SE10 8JA **P2**

✆ (020) 88533020 – **Fax** (020) 88533501

e-mail north-pole@btconnect.com

Web www.northpolegreenwich.com

Menu £25 (dinner) – Carte £21/35

North Pole sits on the summit of a converted pub, above a hip bar, but has its own street entrance for those not wishing to expose their corduroy to the fashion police downstairs.
It's divided into two rooms and has a cosy feel and a twinkly warmth to it. There's a fireplace in the smaller of the two rooms, while those in the larger, airier room have the benefit of a nightly playing pianist to accompany their dinner and add to the general bonhomie. The tables are all neatly laid, the candlelight supplies extra intimacy and the service is well organised.
The cooking is modern with a fairly classical base to it. Dishes come with unfussy and straightforward presentation, allowing the quality of the ingredients to come to the fore.

Spread Eagle

French XX

A/C VISA MC

Greenwich

1-2 Stockwell St ⊖ New Cross

✉ SE10 9JN **P2**

✆ (020) 88532333 – **Fax** (020) 82931024

e-mail goodfood@spreadeagle.org **Web** www.spreadeagle.org

Closed January

Carte £25/35

Forming part of a 17th century coaching inn, the Spread Eagle in its current incarnation has been part of the Greenwich dining scene since 1966 and, in that time, has remained proudly impervious to changing design and decorative tastes.
There are a number of different sitting areas, the best being the two semi-private booths on the ground floor, but the more able-bodied should try upstairs, via the original spiral staircase. On a winter's night the place really comes into its own with its log fire, panelling, antiques and dim lighting all adding to the well-mannered atmosphere.
The kitchen attempts a modern interpretation of rustic French cooking and offers tasting menus, one of which is a vegetarian, accompanied by chosen wines.

Rivington

British X

Greenwich

178 Greenwich High Rd ⊖ New Cross

✉ SE10 8NN **P2**

✆ (020) 82939270 – **Fax** (020) 82939271

e-mail office@rivingtongrill.co.uk **Web** www.rivingtongrill.co.uk

Closed 25-26 December and 1 January

A/C VISA MC AE D

Menu £16 – Carte £19/33

Perhaps all independent cinemas should have an adjacent restaurant so that the Pavlovian effect of watching *Babette's Feast* or *Big Night* (but perhaps not *Life is Sweet*) can be satisfied by nipping next door after the credits. Rivington, sister to the original Shoreditch branch, takes this further by offering cinemagoers an extra 10% discount.

The menu features classic British dishes using classic British ingredients but executed in more contemporary style. Meanwhile, the dining room, with a galleried level overlooking the bar, sets the right tone with its hassle-free atmosphere.

Service is switched on and the place is open early for appealing breakfasts and also offers a set lunch menu at a compassionate price.

3 Monkeys

Indian XX

Herne Hill

136-140 Herne Hill

✉ SE24 9QH **N3**

✆ (020) 77385500 – **Fax** (020) 77385505

Web www.3monkeysrestaurant.com

A/C VISA MC AE D

Carte £19/29

A busy road junction in Herne Hill may not be the obvious place in which to open a stylish and adventurous Indian restaurant, but Herne Hill it is and the locals must be very pleased. The only design feature that's not so understated is the bright neon sign outside which curiously includes the word 'vintage' to describe the cuisine.

Once inside, you cross a bridge between the front door and the dining room, with tables beneath you. The bright white walls and plenty of windows lend a freshness and sense of vitality. Service is thoughtful and diligent.

The open-plan kitchen delivers fragrant and attractively presented dishes, using influences and techniques from all corners of India. A very busy takeaway service is operated from the small shop.

Lobster Pot

French

A/C VISA MC AE

Kennington

3 Kennington Lane — ⊖ Kennington
⊠ SE11 4RG — PLAN XV **N2**
(020) 75825556
Web www.lobsterpotrestaurant.co.uk
Closed 24 December-8 January, Sunday and Monday

Menu £21.50/43.50 – Carte £26/40

Kennington Lane may not necessarily evoke scenes of seafaring adventure and fishermen's catches - and there is certainly little in the way of salty sea air around the Elephant and Castle - but come to the Lobster Pot and you'll be instantly transported to a Breton fishing village, complete with the sound of seagulls. Portholes, fishing nets, shells and aquariums complete a scene so nautical you'll need to find your sea legs before ordering.
There is, however, much more to this place that its highly eccentric but undeniably endearing décor. The husband and wife team know what they're doing and serve authentic and expertly timed French accented seafood, supplemented by the daily specials depending on the day's catch.

Bengal Trader

Indian

A/C VISA MC AE

Spitalfields

44 Artillery Lane — ⊖ Liverpool Street
⊠ E1 7NA — PLAN IX **N2**
(020) 73750072 – **Fax** (020) 72471002
e-mail mail@bengalclipper.co.uk **Web** www.bengalclipper.co.uk

Carte £13/23

The renewal of this part of town continues apace, but you'll find the Bengal Trader down a little lane that's positively Dickensian in its character.
Sister restaurant to the Bengal Clipper in Butler's Wharf, the Trader comes divided into two, with ten tables on the ground floor but the main event is the cavernous downstairs area, where larger parties are entertained.
The place may be lacking a little in personality but regulars seem to appreciate the consistency of the cooking and the earnest service. The menu journeys across India, from Goa to the Bay of Bengal and those who never like to stray too far from more traditional Anglo-Indian dishes will also find many recognisable favourites, to which the kitchen has added its own touches.

Les Trois Garçons

French XX

Spitalfields

1 Club Row — ⊖ Shoreditch
✉ E1 6JX — **PLAN page 165 N1**
✆ (020) 76311924 – **Fax** (020) 70121236
e-mail info@lestroisgarcons.com **Web** www.lestroisgarcons.com

Closed Sunday – dinner only

Menu £28 (Monday-Wednesday) – Carte £34/44

The decoration is so gloriously theatrical and eccentric, you can't fail to feel just a little bit better about life. The three friends who own the place have antique shops and the room is practically bursting with everything from stuffed and mounted animals to elaborate chandeliers and beads - even a display of evening handbags hang from the gold coloured ceiling. Despite being a converted pub, it also has something of the French brasserie about it, with waiters kitted out in the traditional style.
The cooking is not as unconventional as the menu suggests and there is clear ability in the kitchen but at prices which are certainly high for the area so there should be. There is, though, a less expensive set menu on offer early in the week.

Canteen

British X

Spitalfields

2 Crispin Pl. — ⊖ Liverpool Street
✉ E1 6DW — **PLAN page 165 N2**
✆ (0845) 6861122
e-mail info@canteen.co.uk **Web** www.canteen.co.uk

Closed 25 December

Carte £17/29

This glass enclosed modern cube, juxtaposed next to the old Spitalfield market, has come up with a terrific idea which, like all great concepts, leaves you wondering why no one else had thought of it before. The clue's in the name.
It has adopted the all-day menu and shared refectory table look but then serves well priced, decidedly British food. So, whether it's a morning bacon sarnie, a lunchtime pie or an evening stew, there's something for everyone and every appetite. The daily roasts and fish are favourites but all flavours are natural and all produce conscientiously sourced.
If you're a team of four you may snag one of the outer tables with cushioned seats. Otherwise, just hunker down with your fellow man and rediscover some classics.

St John Bread and Wine

British

A/C

Spitalfields

94-96 Commercial St — ⊖ Shoreditch

VISA ⊠ E1 6LZ — **PLAN page 165 N2**

MC ✆ (020) 72510848 – **Fax** (020) 72478924

Web www.stjohnbreadandwine.com

AE Closed Christmas, Sunday dinner and Bank Holidays

Carte £19/32

This offshoot of the Smithfield St John is a slightly less structured affair, with all day opening and, as the name implies, bread and wines – in this case French – available for take-out. In contrast, the cooking looks to this side of the Channel and follows the style of the mother ship by using unusual cuts and rediscovered recipes and, by doing so, celebrates Britain's somewhat neglected culinary heritage. So, settle down for kippers for breakfast or a lunch of ox heart or pig's cheeks.
Housed within a sturdy looking former bank, the restaurant fits rather well into this bourgeoning neighbourhood. The open kitchen and easy-going staff contribute to the relaxed atmosphere that makes it such a local favourite.

Wapping Food

Modern European 

Wapping

Wapping Wall — ⊖ Wapping

VISA ⊠ E1W 3ST — **PLAN page 290 O1**

MC ✆ (020) 76802080

e-mail info@wapping-wpt.com

AE Closed 24 December-3 January, Sunday dinner and Bank Holidays

Carte £24/33

Tate Modern isn't the only former industrial edifice put to good use. The Wapping Project also opened in 2000 and is an art and restaurant complex housed within an 1890's hydraulic power station. The vast industrial space looks remarkably unchanged, from the rough brick walls to the pumps and machinery. There are exhibitions, an outside cinema, assorted performances and this most unique of restaurants. If you want to see all the action, ask for a table on the 'plinth'.
As expected, the cooking has its own vitality and comes with a mostly European feel, with the odd Asian accent. In deference to the owner's homeland, the wine list is exclusively Australian. For those after something a little different, Wapping Food certainly fits the bill.

Cafe Spice Namaste

Indian XX

Whitechapel

16 Prescot St — ⊖ Tower Hill
✉ E1 8AZ — **PLAN page 165 N3**

✆ (020) 74889242 – **Fax** (020) 74810508
e-mail info@cafespice.co.uk **Web** www.cafespice.co.uk

A/C VISA MC AE D

Closed Christmas-New Year, Saturday lunch, Sunday and Bank Holidays

Carte £22/34

This red bricked Victorian building was once a magistrate's court. That information hardly prepares you for the sheer vivaciousness of the interior. Cyrus Todiwala's vibrant and ebullient restaurant has been going strong now for over a decade, having been at the vanguard of the new wave of Indian restaurants.
It comes divided into two large, high-ceilinged rooms separated by the bar. If there is a colour that hasn't been used in the fabrics or on the walls it's because it hasn't yet been created. Don't be surprised to see game and other classic British ingredients on the menu - the cooking here has moments of real innovation. All dishes come fragrantly spiced and nicely balanced, but look out for the Parsee specialities.

WAITING IN VAIN

We all know that the Great Fire of London started in Pudding Lane, but its connection to food doesn't stop there. The first local building to be rebuilt was the Ye Olde Cheshire Cheese pub, which provided the inspiration for George Augustus Sala's note on "furious waiters" who never get to sample the delicious "steaks... floury potatoes and fragrant green peas" they serve. Stumped, he wondered: "where do waiters dine, and when, and how?"

C. Barrely/MICHELIN

South-West London

TIPS/PHOTONONSTOP

South West London is perhaps best defined by the Thames, which coils through the districts and former villages that make up the outer reaches of the metropolis. However, although the river is central to SW – from sleepy pubs dappled with shifting light to the cries of birds and the hum of insects at the London Wetland Centre in Barnes – it's not the only thing the area has to offer.

If you're of a sporting bent you can catch national and international rugby union matches at **Twickenham**, while football-mad **Fulham** is home to Premiership rivals Fulham FC and Chelsea FC. The University Boat Race takes place on the river in spring, starting at **Putney Bridge** and ending up at **Mortlake**: spectators line the banks to cheer on the light and dark blues. As summer ripens, sports fans head down to **Wimbledon** for strawberries and cream, and world-class tennis.

For those who prefer their entertainment to come with a little less physical exertion, SW is equally rich in television and film associations. **Ealing** not only gave its name to the film comedies, most of which are set in the area, but the studios have played a part in the making of films from *Star Wars* to *The Importance of Being Earnest*. BBC Television Centre is a stone's throw away from **Hammersmith** and a great place for a free evening's entertainment: check out the website for the chance to be part of a studio audience. Down the road **Earl's Court Olympia** not only holds exhibitions such as the Ideal Home Show, it's also one of London's top concert venues. **Battersea Arts Centre** already offers an eclectic programme of theatre and music, however, it could soon be joined by a local rival: Sir Giles Gilbert Scott's **Battersea Power Station** is being redeveloped as a residential and creative hub.

For the obligatory London green spaces and historical ambience, head down to the magnificent botanic gardens at **Kew** and the deer park at **Richmond**. If this leaves you feeling a little out of the loop then check out **King Henry VIII Mound**, where a specially protected sight line offers a clear view all the way to **St Paul's Cathedral**. However, tranquil appearances can be deceptive: **Bushy Park** in **Teddington** may seem serene, but it was General Eisnehower's base when he planned the D-day invasion in 1944. All in all SW has seen its fair share of less happy times – from the all too real bombings of the blitz to the Martian destruction of **Sheen**, chillingly imagined by HG Wells in *The War of the Worlds*.

Today SW is particularly popular as a home for City workers and the influx of money has resulted in a roaring night life in **Clapham** and **Tooting**, with pubs, bars and restaurants lining the streets: although there's plenty to choose from it can be difficult to find a seat on a weekend night. Alternatively head over to **Chiswick**, where discerning residents throng to the smorgasbord of dedicated foodie shops. **Wandsworth** has long been a fan of letting the good times roll: it's home to Young's Brewery where beer has been brewed on the same site since the 16C. Neighbouring Smithfields has a more sober history: an abstinence law prevented pubs from being built in the so-called grid until it was repealed in the 1990s. Perhaps it's only fitting that SW's mixture of creative talent and suburban surrounds has resulted in some genuine rock'n'roll legends: Pete Townshend was born and bred in **Acton**; John Lydon, formerly Jonny Rotten, comes from Fulham; while the ill-fated Marc Bolan was born in **Putney** and met his untimely end in Barnes.

R. Booth/akg-images

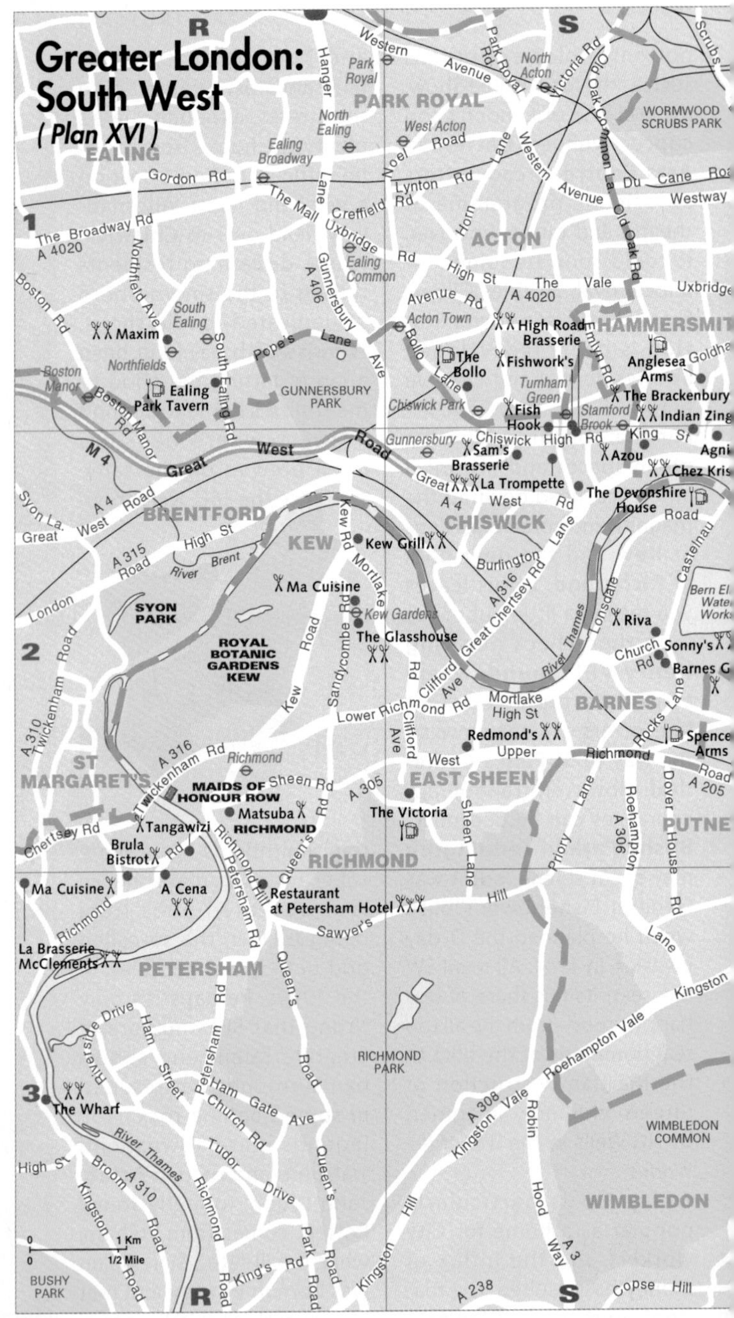
Greater London: South West
(Plan XVI)
R
S
1
2
3
EALING
PARK ROYAL
North Acton
WORMWOOD SCRUBS PARK
ACTON
HAMMERSMITH
Maxim
Ealing Park Tavern
High Road Brasserie
The Bollo
Fishwork's
Anglesea Arms
The Brackenbury
Indian Zing
Fish Hook
Azou
Sam's Brasserie
Chez Kristof
La Trompette
The Devonshire House
GUNNERSBURY PARK
BRENTFORD
KEW
CHISWICK
Kew Grill
Ma Cuisine
The Glasshouse
SYON PARK
ROYAL BOTANIC GARDENS KEW
Riva
Sonny's
Barnes Grill
BARNES
Redmond's
Spencer Arms
ST MARGARET'S
MAIDS OF HONOUR ROW
Matsuba
RICHMOND
EAST SHEEN
The Victoria
PUTNEY
Tangawizi
Brula Bistrot
Ma Cuisine
A Cena
Restaurant at Petersham Hotel
La Brasserie McClements
PETERSHAM
RICHMOND PARK
The Wharf
WIMBLEDON COMMON
WIMBLEDON
BUSHY PARK
0 1 Km
0 1/2 Mile

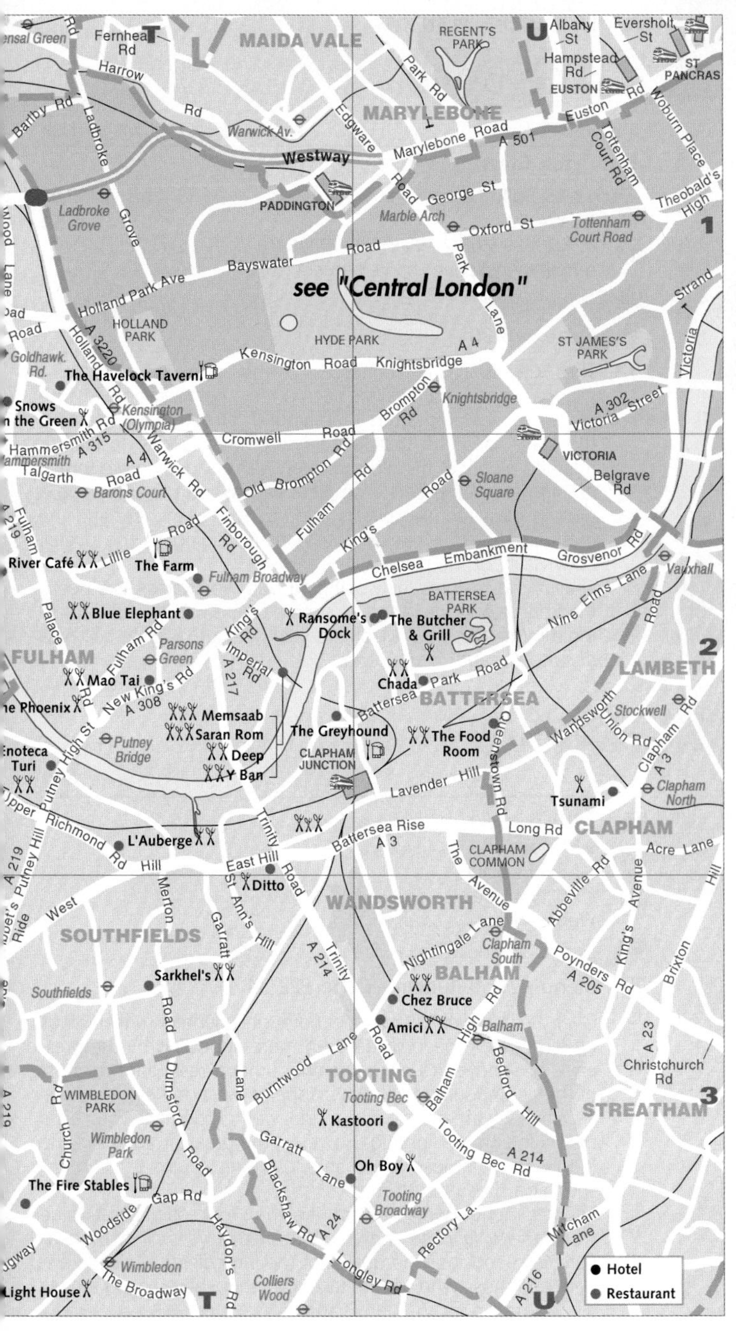

see "Central London"
MAIDA VALE
MARYLEBONE
PADDINGTON
HOLLAND PARK
HYDE PARK
ST JAMES'S PARK
VICTORIA
FULHAM
BATTERSEA
LAMBETH
CLAPHAM
WANDSWORTH
SOUTHFIELDS
BALHAM
TOOTING
STREATHAM
WIMBLEDON PARK
The Havelock Tavern
Snows on the Green
River Café
The Farm
Blue Elephant
Mao Tai
The Phoenix
Memsaab
Saran Rom
Deep
Ban
Enoteca Turi
L'Auberge
Ransome's Dock
The Butcher & Grill
Chada
The Greyhound
The Food Room
Tsunami
Ditto
Sarkhel's
Chez Bruce
Amici
Kastoori
Oh Boy
The Fire Stables
Light House
Hotel
Restaurant

The Bollo

Gastropub

Acton Green

13-15 Bollo Lane ⊖ Chiswick Park
✉ W4 5LR **S1**
✆ (020) 89946037 – **Fax** (020) 87435810
e-mail thebollopub@btinternet.com

Closed 25 December

Carte £18/30

The Bollo is a large, handsome corner pub and this grand Victorian local landmark has been given a new lease of life. One of its best features is the wrap-around terrace which is clearly the place to be for that languid summer's Sunday. Inside, it's retained plenty of the old character, with a slightly more formal dining area at the back, complete with wood panelling and a domed glass roof. Hospitality, though, is the key here and the menu is served wherever you want it, adding to the overall conviviality of the place.
That menu features fairly standard pub workhorses, like deep-fried brie, alongside others of a more gastro nature and displaying a more ambitious Mediterranean heritage, such as sea bass *al cartoccio* and *panna cotta*.

Sonny's

Modern European

Barnes

94 Church Rd
✉ SW13 0DQ **S2**
✆ (020) 87480393 – **Fax** (020) 87482698
Web www.sonnys.co.uk

Closed Sunday dinner and Bank Holidays

Menu £21.50 (lunch) – Carte £22/34

Over the last twenty years, the thoroughly genteel surroundings of Barnes have been made even more appealing by the presence of Sonny's. It's a true neighbourhood restaurant as most of the neighbourhood appear to spend most of their time here. It's all very light and modish inside, with modern artwork, glass bricks and subtle lighting. However, the greatest appeal is the highly genial atmosphere, thanks to the restaurant attracting all sorts and sizes of customer.
The set menus, which run during the week, offer great value while the *à la carte* shows off the kitchen's skill in modern European cooking. The quality of the ingredients is clearly evident and those who wish to take something home need merely to pop next door to Sonny's shop.

Riva

Italian

VISA MC AE

Barnes

169 Church Rd
SW13 9HR **S2**
(020) 87480434 – **Fax** (020) 87480434

Closed last 2 weeks August, 24 December-4 January, Sunday lunch and Bank Holidays

Carte £27/40

There are two Riva restaurants for two types of Riva customer. The first Riva is for the regulars - the famous and the celebrated who treat the place like home and boast of never even seeing a menu. The rest of us know the other Riva, where we order hearty Northern Italian dishes from an appetising menu and dream of the day when other diners recognise us.
The proprietor, Andrea Riva, is a proper, old school restaurateur who's always in his restaurant, doing the rounds of the tables. This goes someway towards accounting for the place's longevity and continued popularity.
The cooking will certainly satisfy most appetites and the style of the room is modest yet warm, with seating for about fifty which keeps it all quite intimate.

Barnes Grill

Beef specialities

A/C VISA MC AE

Barnes

2-3 Rocks Lane
SW13 0DB **S2**
(020) 88784488
Web www.awtonline.co.uk

Closed Monday lunch – booking essential

Carte £22/45

There are a number of rather affluent suburbs around the edges of London wholly devoid of decent restaurants. Barnes is not one of them because here the locals have always been very supportive of any local endeavours and it only takes one good restaurant to succeed for others to follow.
Barnes Grill is a relative new boy but comes with an established format which was developed in Notting Hill and Kew and comes courtesy of Antony Worrall Thompson, TV chef and champion restaurant-opener.
That format is relatively simple: bright and casual surroundings with a few eye-catching decorative touches and a generally relaxed atmosphere coupled with an appealing menu of classic British dishes, with the emphasis on well hung steaks.

The Food Room

French XX

A/C VISA MC

Battersea

123 Queenstown Rd
✉ SW8 3RH **U2**
✆ (020) 76220555 – **Fax** (020) 76275440
e-mail info@thefoodroom.com

Closed 1-3 January, 25-26 December, Sunday and Monday – dinner only

Menu £26.50

Having wowed them in Surbiton with The French Table, owner Eric Guignard was able to open a second restaurant, The Food Room, in Battersea in 2004. As he edges closer to Central London, you can but marvel at the admirable honesty of the chosen names for his restaurants for they do exactly what they say they do.

The clean and simple decoration of The Food Room is inoffensive, unremarkable but pleasant, with mirrors and cream walls. It shifts the focus of the customers onto the plates in front of them. Fortunately, these plates come filled with expertly executed cooking, from a nicely balanced set price menu. France is the major influence, with the odd nod to the Mediterranean and the occasionally taste bud tweak from a North African spice.

Chada

Thai XX

A/C VISA MC AE

Battersea

208-210 Battersea Park Rd
✉ SW11 4ND **U2**
✆ (020) 76222209 – **Fax** (020) 79242178
e-mail enquiry@chadathai.com **Web** www.chadathai.com

Closed Sunday and Bank Holidays – dinner only

Carte £16/37

It's nice to see that some of the early pioneers who brought Thai cooking to London are still going strong. Chada has not only celebrated its twentieth anniversary, but that longevity has been achieved in the altogether less enchanting surroundings of Battersea Park Road.

The extensive menu offers a comprehensive selection of authentic and prettily presented Thai cooking, while the warm-hearted service is overseen by the owner.

The dining room is quite a spacious affair, with tiled floor, neatly laid tables, ornate mirrors and Thai influenced decorative touches. It has a warm and welcoming feel and the atmosphere is friendly and relaxed.

Ransome's Dock

Modern European

Battersea

35-37 Parkgate Rd
SW11 4NP **U2**
(020) 72231611 – **Fax** (020) 79242614
e-mail chef@ransomesdock.co.uk **Web** www.ransomesdock.co.uk

Closed Christmas, August Bank Holiday and Sunday dinner

VISA MC AE

Carte £21/42

Many wine lists in London are like Aston Martins: nice to look at but prohibitively expensive to mere mortals. The wine list at Ransome's Dock, however, is more your Alfa Romeo: fun, more affordable and made for enjoyment. The mark-ups are low and the range terrific.
The owners, Martin and Vanessa Lam, have had the place since 1992. Martin's passion is reflected in the wine list but he also knows his onions in the kitchen. The menu is *à la mode* in its simplicity and European in its posture.
The setting is a little different - a converted warehouse in a dockside development.

The Butcher & Grill

Traditional

Battersea

A/C

39-41 Parkgate Rd
SW11 4NP **U2**
(020) 79243999 – **Fax** (020) 72237977
Web www.thebutcherandgrill.com

Closed 25-26 December, 1 January and Sunday dinner

VISA MC AE

Carte £21/48

The name really says everything - this is all about carnivores and all about meat. What better way is there of providing customers with provenance assurance than by having your own butcher's shop, complete with a Master Butcher, forming part of your restaurant? Simply pick your meat of choice, get it grilled to your liking, decide what "stuff on the side" you want and tuck in with your Rambo hunting knife. Even the napkins are man-sized tea towels.
A converted warehouse provides just the right surroundings for this clever concept, with everything exposed and spread over two levels. Prices are kept realistic, while the atmosphere is contagiously enthusiastic.
There is one fish dish available for those who came by accident.

The Greyhound

Gastropub 

Battersea

136 Battersea High St

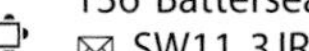

✉ SW11 3JR **T2**

✆ (020) 79787021 – **Fax** (020) 79780599

Web www.thegreyhoundatbattersea.co.uk

Closed Christmas, New Year, Sunday dinner and Monday

VISA MC AE

Menu £31 (dinner) – Carte £14/16

There was a time when the only wine served in pubs was warm, probably corked and invariably German. When the current owner took over The Greyhound he brought with him his passion and knowledge of wine gained from his previous career as a sommelier and now this attractive pub boasts a terrific list with great breadth of choice and super prices. The pub's not bad too.

The bar is quite a stylish little number and, behind it, sits the restaurant which continues the theme of being casual yet contemporary. It, in turn, opens out onto a courtyard.

The kitchen does its bit to compete with the wines. The set price dinner menu (with the more limited lunchtime choice) reads like a gastropub manifesto, with influences aplenty.

La Trompette

French 

Chiswick

5-7 Devonshire Rd ⊖ Turnham Green

✉ W4 2EU **S2**

✆ (020) 87471836 – **Fax** (020) 89958097

e-mail reception@latrompette.co.uk **Web** www.latrompette.co.uk

Closed 24-26 December and 1 January

A/C VISA MC AE

Menu £29.50/35

Like its two siblings, The Glasshouse and Chez Bruce, La Trompette gives the discerning Chiswick local an opportunity of experiencing West End sophistication, without having to journey east.

The smart looking glass and canopy façade reflect the style of the interior, which uses fawn and mushroom colours and softer textures to create a space which is not only comfortable but surprisingly soft. The large French windows add light to the room and opens onto the little terrace at the front.

Set menus allow the kitchen to show off their repertoire of French influenced dishes and you can hear many a local ordering their favourite. The wine list not only offers great depth and variety but also provides plenty of choice at decent prices.

High Road Brasserie

Mediterranean XX

Chiswick

162 Chiswick High Rd — ⊖ Turnham Green

⊠ W4 1PR — **S2**

✆ (020) 87427474

Web www.highroadhouse.co.uk

A/C VISA MC AE

Carte £28/36

The name says it all. It's a brasserie and it's on the High Road. With French windows opening onto a terrace, mirrors, pewter topped tables, leather seats and tiled flooring, all the ingredients are in place to create that genuine brasserie feel. But it also manages to avoid being an art nouveau Parisian pastiche - there's not an Alphonse Mucha poster to be seen.

Chiswickians have clearly taken to the place because there's often a snake of people queuing to get in. Maybe they should consider staggering their arrival times, because it all starts at breakfast, the menu is served all day and weekend brunches are a big hit. The menu will float everyone's boat, with classics like potted shrimp and eggs Benedict to casseroles, grills and salads.

Sam's Brasserie

Mediterranean 

Chiswick

11 Barley Mow Passage — ⊖ Turnham Green

⊠ W4 4PH — **S2**

✆ (020) 89870555 – **Fax** (020) 89877389

e-mail info@samsbrasserie.co.uk **Web** www.samsbrasserie.co.uk

Closed Christmas

Menu £15 (lunch) – Carte £20/32

Sam's Brasserie burst into life in 2005 and proved such an instant hit that now when people talk about going 'up west' for dinner they may well mean Chiswick.

The Barley Mow Centre is a red brick former paper mill and the restaurant uses its sparse semi-industrial surroundings to good effect. There's a big bar which pulls in the crowds and the 100 seater dining area is bright and open, with large circular ceiling lamps and exposed girders and vents.

Most heartening of all is that it takes the role of a neighbourhood restaurant to its logical conclusion by offering a flexible menu to appeal to all comers, from mussels to red mullet and salads to sea bass. The omnipresent young owner ensures cheerful service.

Fish Hook

Seafood

Chiswick

6-8 Elliott Rd — Turnham Green
W4 1PE — **S1_2**
(020) 87420766 – **Fax** (020) 87423374
Web www.fishhook.co.uk

Closed Christmas

Menu £18.50 (lunch) – Carte £24/34

What was previously a South African restaurant called Fish Hoek became the more straightforward Fish Hook in the end of 2005 and it's been pulling in the locals from day one.
It has kept the unusual device adopted by the previous owner whereby virtually every dish is available as either a starter or a main course – it's merely a matter of size. This works to a degree, although some dishes just sound more of one course than the other. Nevertheless, there is plenty of choice available; the chef owner clearly has ability and he handles his fish with dextrous aplomb.
The room's simply dressed with wood-backed banquettes, mirrors and black and white photos. It has a cheery atmosphere, thanks to the closely set tables.

Fishworks

Seafood

Chiswick

6 Turnham Green Terrace — Turnham Green
W4 1QP — **S1_2**
(020) 89940086 – **Fax** (020) 89940778
e-mail chiswick@fishworks.co.uk **Web** www.fishworks.co.uk

Closed 25 December-5 January, Sunday dinner, Monday and Bank Holidays – booking essential

Carte £26/41

The Chiswick branch of this bourgeoning chain was the first to open in London and you can see why there are others now popping up everywhere. The formula is wonderfully simple: an open fishmonger on the street level (although the passing traffic rather spoils the scent of the sea), then up a few steps into a bright, sunny restaurant. On warm days head straight for the charming decked terrace at the back, where diesel belching buses seem a world away. Freshness is the key here and all the fish is delivered daily, mostly from Devon or Cornwall. The choice is considerable, from shellfish platters to fisherman's stew, but there can be few things in life more pleasing that a simply grilled piece of fish with some hollandaise on the side.

The Devonshire House

Gastropub

Chiswick

126 Devonshire Rd ⊖ Turnham Green

VISA ✉ W4 2JJ **S2**

MC ✆ (020) 89872626 – **Fax** (020) 89950152

Web www.thedevonshirehouse.co.uk

AE Closed 24-30 December and Monday lunch

Carte £15/26

When a pub changes its name from Manor Tavern to The Devonshire House you can be pretty sure it has also turned itself into a gastropub. Strolling from the high street, past all the pretty terrace houses of Devonshire Road and just when you're wondering if anything is down here you'll come across The Devonshire, with its tell-tale modern sign and lettering. The interior has retained a sense of its Victorian heritage but with the addition of some leather furniture and a general feeling of openness. The shaded garden terrace provides a very pleasant little spot in the summer.
The daily changing menu is refreshingly concise and balanced, hints at the Mediterranean and proves that the owners here know their onions.

Tsunami

Japanese

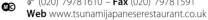

Clapham

Unit 3, 5-7 Voltaire Rd. ⊖ Clapham North

✉ SW4 6DQ **U2**

MC ✆ (020) 79781610 – **Fax** (020) 79781591

Web www.tsunamijapaneserestaurant.co.uk

AE Closed 25-26 December and Easter – dinner only and Saturday and Sunday lunch

Carte £16/40

The restaurant certainly doesn't make life easy for itself. We all now sadly understand the name and the location is on the uninspiring side but, thanks to this Japanese restaurant's coolly minimalist interior, you'll forget soon enough where you are.
Tsunami attracts a younger clientele and proves that one doesn't have to be in the West End to sample good food in stylish surroundings. While the menu will easily satisfy the more traditionally minded, it is those willing to try the more exotic specialities and original combinations who will get most out of the experience. Indeed, the knowledgeable staff positively encourage you to try something different. Dishes arrive from the kitchen as and when they are ready, so sharing is encouraged

Maxim

Chinese (Peking) XX

A/C VISA MC AE

Ealing
153-155 Northfield Ave ⊖ Northfields
✉ W13 9QT **R1**
✆ (020) 85671719 – **Fax** (020) 89320717
Closed 25-28 December and Sunday lunch

Menu £15/35 – Carte £17/30

Obviously that maxim is 'if it ain't broke, don't fix it'.
This Ealing stalwart has been run by Mr and Mrs Chow for over thirty years and today all the members of their extended family appear to be involved in the business. If a place is providing good food to a loyal band of regulars, then it's great for everyone to see it staying put for a long time.
Mrs Chow is responsible for the cooking, which includes specialities from Peking. Freshness is the key to the popularity of her cooking and the reason why the place is always so busy.
Tables are all a good size and the room is peppered with assorted Oriental ornaments. The red neon sign may attract the odd passer-by, but inside you'll find the usual crowd of locals.

Ealing Park Tavern

Gastropub

VISA MC AE

Ealing
222 South Ealing Rd ⊖ South Ealing
✉ W5 4RL **R1**
✆ (020) 87581879 – **Fax** (020) 85605269
Closed 25-26 December and Monday lunch except Bank Holidays

Carte £20/25

This corner Victorian pub underwent its full makeover a few years back and has been extremely popular ever since. It looks big from the outside and seems equally vast once you're inside. It comes divided into two, with a bar and a dining area; plenty of light comes flooding through the large windows. Even the outside terrace area is big.
The open plan kitchen knows what the locals want and provides it in spades: a regularly changing menu that mixes the modern with the more rustic and robust. Service is a lot friendlier and chattier than one encounters in many a city gastropub.
The M4 may hurtle along nearby but the Ealing Park Tavern feels like a genuine local pub, with a genuine local atmosphere.

Redmond's

Modern European XX

East Sheen

170 Upper Richmond Rd West
✉ SW14 8AW **S2**
✆ (020) 88781922
e-mail pippa@redmonds.org.uk **Web** www.redmonds.org.uk

Closed Christmas, Sunday and Bank Holidays – dinner only

Menu £15.50 (weekdays)/32

Celebrating their tenth anniversary this year, Redmond's should be cherished for two reasons: it is family owned and run - sadly all too rare a thing these days – and it is waving the flag of gastronomy away from the bright lights of Central London.
The Hayward's are the family, with Pippa overseeing the service and Redmond the kitchen. Whether they ever considered calling it "Pippa's" is a question for them.
His cooking is deft and defined, with a clarity to the flavours. The set price menu is appealingly balanced and those happy to eat earlier can benefit from the excellent value early evening menu. The restaurant is as spick as it is span, with neutral colours and wood flooring. The clientele is made up largely of contented locals.

The Victoria

Gastropub

East Sheen

10 West Temple Sheen
✉ SW14 7RT **S2**
✆ (020) 88764238 – **Fax** (020) 88783464
e-mail bookings@thevictoria.net **Web** www.thevictoria.net

Closed 24-27 December

Carte £25/35

The Victoria is squirreled away in a leafy residential street but is also just moments away from the vast, regal expanse of Richmond Park, where over 600 deer roam free.
Venison may not be on the menu but what will be is fresh, seasonal produce and a mix of British cooking alongside splashes of continental colour. Consistency comes from having as your chef one of the owners of the pub, while the addition of helpful menu notes is a lesson for all those chefs who try to bamboozle their diners with the muddled lexicon of modern cookery.
It's a sizeable place, with a roomy bar and a terrific conservatory. Children are positively encouraged, by virtue of the play area and the coffee-and-cake mornings which have proved a hit with local mothers.

Saran Rom

Thai XXX

Fulham

The Boulevard,
Imperial Wharf,
✉ SW6 2UB
✆ (020) 77513111
e-mail info@saranrom.com **Web** www.saranrom.com

⊖ Fulham Broadway

T2

Carte £29/38

Imperial Wharf is giving Chelsea Harbour a run for its money. In February 2006 Saran Rom opened, with a look based on a Thai Royal summer palace. It's so impressive you think you're gazing across the Chao Phraya River rather than The Thames. Elaborately decorated with carved teak, it's divided into a series of large rooms, including a very attractive bar and pretty terrace, but it still manages to feel quite intimate, despite its size.
The menu prudently treads a traditional path and does so with aplomb, with the cooking executed with care and attention.
The charming girls are reminders of how nothing beats sweet and eager service and how can you not love a place which has tuk-tuks on hand outside to ferry you to the local station?

Memsaab

Indian XXX

Fulham

The Boulevard, Imperial Wharf
✉ SW6 2UB
✆ (020) 77360077 – **Fax** (020) 77315222
Web www.memsaabrestaurant.co.uk

⊖ Fulham Broadway

T2

Closed 25 December

Menu £9.95 – Carte £23/35

No restaurant development is complete without Indian representation and so it is that, in among all the matching façades on the boulevard of Imperial Wharf, one finds Memsaab.
It's occupies the same amount of square footage as its neighbours. A love of white emulsion paint has been thoughtfully balanced by colourful silks and large pictures of spice baskets; the room is certainly light and open in its feel. Larger parties should try for one of the four booths beneath the central palm tree.
There's ample choice on the menu, with the nucleus exhibiting a fair degree of originality and impressive presentation, although those who prefer more familiar dishes are not forgotten. A takeaway service is available for locals.

Yi-Ban

Chinese XX

A/C VISA MC AE D

Fulham

The Boulevard, Imperial Wharf ⊖ Fulham Broadway
✉ SW6 2UB **T2**
✆ (020) 77316606 – **Fax** (020) 77317584
Web www.yi-ban.co.uk

Closed Sunday – dinner only

Menu £15/45 – Carte £30/60

Yi-Ban completes the roll call of international cuisines found at Imperial Wharf by offering Chinese cooking. The decorative style is seductively nocturnal - appropriate as the restaurant does not open at lunchtime - with billowing sheer drapes, moody lighting and dark, polished tables.

The menu comes clearly laid out and covers a number of bases by offering contemporary dishes alongside more traditional specialities and, curiously, some Japanese sushi. Efforts are made with the presentation, portion size is creditably generous and service comes courtesy of a young team in traditionally inspired outfits.

It's divided into three main areas: a smart cocktail bar, a grill and sushi counter and the main dining area.

Deep

Seafood XX

A/C VISA MC AE

Fulham

The Boulevard, Imperial Wharf ⊖ Fulham Broadway
✉ SW6 2UB **T2**
✆ (020) 77363337 – **Fax** (020) 77367578
e-mail info@deeplondon.co.uk **Web** www.deeplondon.co.uk

Closed first 2 weeks January and August, Monday, Sunday dinner and Saturday lunch

Menu £17.50 (lunch) – Carte £25/78

Apart from pavement terraces clouded with exhaust fumes, the choice of where to eat on a summer's day is not altogether overwhelming. Fortunately, Deep is at hand. It not only has a great terrace but also offers river views from its spot on this revived riverside wharf.

Inside it's all very slick and contemporary, with immaculate napery and comfortable armchairs making it all a relaxing experience. It is also very big, which is presumably why it was used as the setting for Gordon Ramsay's "F Word" TV programme.

The bar is quite an attraction. It has its own terrace and the UK's largest selection of Aquavit. Seafood is the speciality of the house and comes with a delicate Scandinavian touch, reflecting the owners' nationality.

Blue Elephant

Thai XX

Fulham

4-6 Fulham Broadway ⊖ Fulham Broadway
✉ SW6 1AA **T2**
✆ (020) 73856595 – **Fax** (020) 73867665
e-mail london@blueelephant.com **Web** www.blueelephant.com

Closed Saturday lunch – booking essential

Menu £15 (lunch) – Carte £29

There are now Blue Elephants stretching from Dubai to Moscow but the Fulham branch has had a twenty year head start and is still as busy as ever.
The façade gives nothing away but, then again, no façade could do justice to what's going on inside. It's a cross between a tropical forest and a film-set with a decent budget. There are plants and flowers, water gardens, streams, bridges, barges and pergolas. No, really, it's a jungle in there.
Fortunately, they realise that the surroundings won't distract the diners forever and put just as much effort into the cooking. Those relatively unfamiliar with Thai could do worse than head for the Royal Banquet menu, while the main menu offers an intriguing mix of the familiar and the more original.

Mao Tai

Chinese XX

Fulham

58 New Kings Rd, Parsons Green ⊖ Parsons Green
✉ SW6 4LS **T2**
✆ (020) 77312520
e-mail info@maotai.co.uk **Web** www.maotai.co.uk

Closed 25-26 December

Carte £22/31

We all have our local Chinese restaurants, but in you live in the well-heeled environs of Parsons Green then your Chinese restaurant is going to be just that little bit posher than most.
Mao Tai has been a favourite in these parts for many a year and it's easy to see why: the place has a bright and sunny disposition and is contemporary in its style without threatening to be trendy.
The menu comes clearly laid out and offers a choice which is extensive without being worryingly vast. It also proudly announces the complete absence of monosodium glutamate in any of the dishes. Those who missed their *dim sum* at lunch will find it remains available until 8pm and the dumplings, steamed or grilled, are clearly something of a house speciality.

The Farm

Gastropub 

Fulham

18 Farm Lane — ⊖ Fulham Broadway

✉ SW6 1PP — **T2**

✆ (020) 7381 3331

e-mail info@thefarmfulham.co.uk **Web** www.thefarmfulham.co.uk

VISA · MC · AE · 🍷

Closed 25 December

Carte £18/35

Style and sophistication are words not usually associated with the pub, but then The Farm is not your typical pub, gastro or otherwise. It certainly does what pubs usually do, with a large bar and a separate dining room at the back, but this one comes with a higher degree of class and, through its use of woods, leathers, glass and thoughtful lighting, a greater appreciation of comfort and design.

The kitchen also assumes some degree of sophistication on the part of the customer by offering a modern take on brasserie favourites, combined with a certain amount of Mediterranean vibrancy.

Lovers of spit-and-sawdust may cry foul, but The Farm highlights the resourcefulness and potential of the modern city pub.

ROLL OUT THE BARREL

Horatio Nelson is celebrated by one of London's best-known landmarks; however he was not always treated with such respect. When he fell at the Battle of Trafalgar in 1805, his body was transported back to England preserved in rum or brandy. The story goes that when the ship arrived home the crew had drunk half the spirits from the barrel: although of dubious truth, the tale has given rise to the slang 'tapping the Admiral', for illicit drinking.

Hammersmith – South-West

River Café 

Italian XX

Thames Wharf, Rainville Rd
W6 9HA
(020) 73864200 – **Fax** (020) 73864201
e-mail info@rivercafe.co.uk **Web** www.rivercafe.co.uk

Barons Court
T2

Closed Christmas-New Year, Sunday dinner and Bank Holidays – booking essential

Carte £42/57

Ian Heide

Their cookbooks don't just sell by the boatload because they've got colourful covers and look good on a coffee table – they've been a marketing phenomenon because the River Café is more than just a great restaurant: it offers a culinary philosophy that we would all do well to follow.

Rose Gray and Ruth Rogers opened the River Café in 1987, with the aim of proving that sourcing the best ingredients is the cornerstone of all good cooking - give second rate ingredients to a talented chef and his cooking will be second rate. Thus, the Italian food here is seasonal, regional, fresh and vigorous and, as with most things in life, the relative simplicity of it all belies the skill and dedication involved and the depth of knowledge.

Just like the cookbooks, the restaurant is user-friendly, accessible and fresh feeling. The style of the room and tone of the service add to a feeling of dining egalitarianism, although the fact that it's off the beaten track and there's a high celebrity count among the regulars increases the exclusivity reading.

All this and they gave us Jamie Oliver too.

A LA CARTE

FIRST COURSE
- Chargrilled squid with rocket and red chilli.
- Split and roasted langoustines with garlic, parsley and lemon.

MAIN COURSE
- Wood roasted turbot with capers, fennel and marjoram.
- Wood-roasted partridge with thyme, sage and Savoy cabbage with pancetta.

DESSERT
- Chocolate "nemesis".
- Lemon, polenta and almond cake.

Indian Zing

Indian XX

Hammersmith

236 King St ⊖ Ravenscourt Park
✉ W6 0RF **S1_2**
✆ (020) 87485959 – **Fax** (020) 87482332
e-mail indianzing@aol.com **Web** www.indianzing.co.uk

A/C · VISA · MC · AE

Carte £21/26

As the name implies, this is a sophisticated and urbane Indian restaurant, which opened in 2005. The kitchen presents a selection of the more traditional and recognisable fare one usually expects from an Indian restaurant but accompanying them are dishes of an altogether more vibrant and modern persuasion. It is these dishes, such as jumbo prawns in pomegranate seeds and dill, which make a visit to Indian Zing worthwhile and show the kitchen's creativity alongside its respect for the traditions and craft of Indian cooking.
The interior is appropriately bright and crisp, with assorted pictures of life on the subcontinent mixed with some striking architectural pieces, such as elaborately carved doors.
The service is thoughtful and efficient.

Chez Kristof

French XX

Hammersmith

111 Hammersmith Grove, Brook Green ⊖ Hammersmith
✉ W6 0NQ **S1**
✆ (020) 87411177
e-mail info@chezkristof.co.uk **Web** www.chezkristof.co.uk

A/C · VISA · MC · AE

Closed Christmas

Menu £15 (lunch) – Carte £23/30

From the people who brought you the Eastern European restaurants, Baltic and Wódka, comes Chez Kristof, a restaurant so celebratory in its Frenchness that it could only be the brainchild of a non-Frenchman.
You'll find all the classics on the menu and, in this age where culinary identities are becoming interestingly blurred, that can be a reassuring sight. So, if your favourites include such standards as *escargots, steak tartare* or *pot au chocolat* you've come to the right spot.
The place really comes into its own in the summer with its large, appropriately French, windows opening onto a bamboo framed terrace.

Snows on the Green

Mediterranean

Hammersmith

166 Shepherd's Bush Rd, Brook Green ⊖ Hammersmith

W6 7PB **T1**

(020) 76032142 – **Fax** (020) 76027553

Web www.snowsonthegreen.co.uk

A/C VISA MC AE

Closed 24-28 December, Saturday lunch, Sunday and Bank Holiday Mondays

Menu £17.50 (lunch) – Carte £25/28

The eponymous Mr Snow was one of the first of a troupe of chefs who decided to pitch their culinary tent in greener and leafier surroundings than Central London. Neighbourhood restaurants are the lifeblood of a healthy eating-out scene and Snows on the Green has now been doing its bit in this part of town for over 15 years. This part of town is Brook Green and the locals appear pleased to have this place in their armoury when jousting with their Notting Hill neighbours.

It has a fresh and sunny feel and the undeniable challenges of being a neighbourhood joint are reflected in the varyingly priced menus available. The constant is the cooking which embraces both France and the Med. It's fresh, flavoursome and executed with care.

The Brackenbury

Modern European

Hammersmith

129-131 Brackenbury Rd ⊖ Ravenscourt Park

W6 0BQ **S1**

(020) 87480107 – **Fax** (020) 87486159

VISA MC AE

Closed August Bank Holiday, Christmas, Saturday lunch and Sunday dinner

Menu £14.50 (lunch) – Carte £24/33

Local estate agents may still insist on calling the area Brackenbury Village but, for most of us, it's just the place we looked up in the A-Z to find The Brackenbury restaurant all those years ago.

It's changed hands a couple of times over the years but for many it remains a firm favourite and is still the type of place we'd all like on our own street.

It's simply furnished but adequately comfy and comes divided into two rooms with a bold colour scheme. There's a popular heated terrace at the front.

The daily changing menu focuses on primary ingredients, in dishes ranging from the modern and eclectic to more traditional European and British. It still gets busy and the lively atmosphere remains one of the attractions.

Azou

North African

Hammersmith

375 King St — ⊖ Stamford Brook

✉ W6 9NJ — **S2**

(020) 85637266 – **Fax** (020) 87481009

e-mail info@azou.co.uk

Closed 25 December and 1 January – dinner only

Carte £15/24

Morocco, Tunisia and Algeria are the main countries whose cooking features most at this sweet little neighbourhood restaurant, although other North African and Middle Eastern influences occasionally find themselves on the menu.

The husband and wife team run a cosy little place with only ten tables and the room is simply but decoratively furnished with draped silks and Moroccan lanterns. Specialities of the house include *brik*, rich *tagines* and assorted *couscous* dishes which will all satisfy the heartiest of appetites. It is certainly worth leaving room to sample the gloriously sweet pastries, especially when accompanied by mint tea, although they do also offer a well chosen selection of wines and beers.

Agni 

Indian

Hammersmith

160 King St — ⊖ Ravenscourt Park

✉ W6 0QU — **S2**

(020) 88469191 – **Fax** (0870) 1996940

e-mail info@agnirestaurant.com **Web** www.agnirestaurant.com

Closed 25 December and 1 January

Carte £14/22

Many of us have found ourselves getting used to the *ghee* based dishes of traditional Indian restaurants, but Agni makes its pitch by offering a consciously healthy angle to their cooking, by using natural ingredients of dietary importance. Here, you can sip on a colourful fresh juice and choose from the exotic and original temptations on the menu, from Hyderabad *biryani* pots to the nutritional balanced *thalis*.

The philosophy is captured by the desserts which include *'paan' kulfi* - home made betel leaf ice cream which is a natural digestive and blood purifier.

The room is long and narrow, with further space available upstairs; the service is helpful and conscientious and, most commendably, the prices are wallet-friendly.

Anglesea Arms

Gastropub 

Hammersmith

35 Wingate Rd ⊖ Ravenscourt Park
✉ W6 0UR **S1**
✆ (020) 87491291 – **Fax** (020) 87491254

Closed 1 week Christmas – bookings not accepted

Menu £12.95 (lunch) – Carte £20/35

The best thing about the Anglesea Arms is that it's a proper pub. Granted, it was one of the pioneers of the gastropub movement, but it has managed to retain the looks, feel and atmosphere of a corner local and is all the more popular for that.

This popularity does have a downside: if you have come to eat then take note that reservations for tables are not taken, so be prepared to wait. Fortunately the bar is a welcoming spot at which to pass the time.

Another reason for the pub's continuing prosperity is the food. The open kitchen offers a decent selection of robust and full flavoured fare and at prices that remain on the right side of reasonable. Service makes up in endeavour what it lacks in alacrity.

The Havelock Tavern

Gastropub 

Hammersmith

57 Masbro Rd ⊖ Kensington Olympia
✉ W14 0LS **T1**
✆ (020) 76035314 – **Fax** (020) 76021163
Web www.thehavelocktavern.co.uk

Closed 22-26 December and Easter Sunday – bookings not accepted

Carte £21/26

Recovered and re-launched following a serious fire, The Havelock Tavern has stuck firmly to its roots as a 'proper' pub, just one that happens to do good food.

It still looks quite imposing on the corner, and inside it remains not a million miles away from paid up membership of the spit-and-sawdust brigade. Don't bother booking: it is all done on a strictly first-come-first-serve basis and you can leave your plastic at home – they only take the readies, although irritatingly that means paying at the bar with each order.

However, it's all about the food which is good enough and well-priced enough to overlook these inconveniences. The daily changing menu lobs up a selection of balanced, hearty dishes, in fittingly pub-like portions.

The Glasshouse 

Modern European XX

14 Station Parade ⊖ Kew Gardens
✉ TW9 3PZ **R2**
✆ (020) 89406777 – **Fax** (020) 89403833
Web www.glasshouserestaurant.co.uk.

Closed 24-26 December and 1 January

Menu £23.50/35

The Glasshouse

Within stone throwing distance of Kew Gardens, The Glasshouse comes from the stable that bought you Chez Bruce. It manages the same trick of satisfying the locals as well as encouraging outsiders into venturing over.

Two sides of glass wall may not necessarily be enough to justify the name but light certainly does infuse the room and the stylish padded ceiling adds a note of warmth. Tables are not set too far apart - there's nothing like listening to your neighbour's conversation to make you feel part of the community. Those tables come neatly laid and the room has a contemporary feel but without the ache of trendiness.

The atmosphere remains welcoming and genial, thanks to the urbanity of the customers and the confidence of the well informed serving staff.

The cooking, though, is largely why this restaurant succeeds when so many in monied suburbs fail. It is precise without being pernickety, sure of its roots and considered in its influences, which remain within Europe. Last, without being least, it is sensibly priced and has a wine list boasting admirable depth and range.

A LA CARTE

FIRST COURSE
- Warm salad of duck magret with deep-fried truffled egg.
- Endive, apple and celeriac salad with blue cheese, beetroot and walnuts.

MAIN COURSE
- Slow roast belly of pork with apple tart, choucroute and crispy ham.
- Baked organic salmon with Charlotte potatoes and shellfish bisque.

DESSERT
- Vanilla yoghurt with exotic fruit salad and ginger crumble.
- Chocolate brownie with chocolate chip ice cream and hot chocolate sauce.

Kew Grill

Beef specialities XX

A/C VISA MC AE D

Kew

10b Kew Green
TW9 3BH
(020) 89484433 – **Fax** (020) 86053532
e-mail kewgrill@aol.com

Kew Gardens
R2

Closed 25-26 December and Monday lunch – booking essential

Menu £14.95 – Carte £25/43

This was the second branch of Antony Worrall Thompson's bourgeoning restaurant empire to open and follows the same guiding principles as the original in Notting Hill. It offers diners plenty of choice with the emphasis on classic dishes from prawn cocktail to beef Stroganoff and with a special feature on steaks, which are all Prime Aberdeen Angus and aged for 35 days.
The restaurant is on the eastern side of Kew Green and boasts a relaxed and friendly neighbourhood feel, helped along by some personable service. Sturdy tables line the exposed brick walls, brightened by large photos and the exposed kitchen adds a little theatre to the operation. Booking is necessary as capacity isn't as large as the apparent demand.

Ma Cuisine

French X

VISA MC

Kew

The Old Post Office, 9 Station Approach
TW9 3QB
(020) 83321923
Web www.macuisine.kew.co.uk

Kew Gardens
R2

Menu £15.50 (lunch) – Carte £18/24

This informal French bistro, set in a red bricked former post office, certainly delivers the goods for a neighbourhood restaurant - the prices are fair, the service friendly and the cooking rustic and regional.
The French theme is hard to avoid, from the period posters and pictures to the gingham tablecloths, while the menu offers a comprehensive selection of robust dishes from across France, including some of the classics. A blackboard marks that day's seasonal special, while those without much time can take advantage of the lunchtime *menu rapide*.
Staff all welcome their regulars by name and, as it's quite a small place, it fills very quickly, particularly at weekends. There's another branch in nearby Twickenham.

L'Auberge

French XX

VISA MC

Putney

22 Upper Richmond Rd
SW15 2RX **T2**
(020) 88743593
Web www.ardillys.com

Closed 1-15 January, 2 weeks August, Sunday and Monday – dinner only

Carte £23/30

This is what those of a certain maturity would call a 'proper' restaurant - it's run by a husband and wife team, provides authentic and traditionally prepared French cuisine and is decorated in a rustic and homely style which makes the countryside feel that little bit closer. The L-shaped dining room comes with yellow walls of heavily textured artex, tiled flooring and even Edith Piaf makes the odd appearance on the soundtrack to add to the Gallic character.
The owners provide service that is reassuringly gracious and warm hearted while the menu is decidedly old fashioned but in the very best sense. Just make sure you leave room for a dessert, the speciality of the house, as the chef owner originally trained as a *patissier*.

Enoteca Turi

Italian XX

A/C VISA MC AE

Putney

28 Putney High St ⊖ Putney Bridge
SW15 1SQ **T2**
(020) 87854449 – **Fax** (020) 87805409
e-mail enoteca@aol.com **Web** www.enotecaturi.com

Closed 25-26 December, 1 January and Sunday

Menu £16.50 (lunch) – Carte £24/36

Along with the river, Giuseppe Turi is one of Putney's greatest assets. The High Street may have adopted the bland façade of unthreateningly familiar chains, but Enoteca Turi still proudly stands there in the middle, waving the flag for individuality and bringing something wholly lacking from nearly every High Street – a sense of pleasure.
This Italian restaurant boasts enthusiastic and well organised service, a bounteous selection of regional dishes all using well-sourced ingredients and, thanks to a full refurbishment a couple of years back, a bright and sunny spot in which to enjoy it all. Evenings are particularly busy and the mood is always contagiously friendly.
So why can't every high street have one of these?

The Phoenix

Italian influences

Putney

Pentlow St
✉ SW15 1LY **T2**
✆ (020) 87803131 – **Fax** (020) 87801114
Web www.sonnys.co.uk

Closed 25-26 December and Bank Holidays

Menu £15.50 (lunch) – Carte £23/30

The entrance to the restaurant may be on Pentlow Street but that's the Lower Richmond Road's traffic outside, which only slightly diminishes the enjoyment of sitting on the otherwise charming terrace.
The inside, though, is even more attractive and is bright and neat, with splashes of colour from the assorted artwork. It also feels very clean - the *sine qua non* of any restaurant.
There is also brightness and cheer in the menu, which journeys through the Mediterranean with a particularly beguiling detour through Italy. The set menu at lunch offers excellent value, while the *à la carte* has something for everyone.
The owners also have Sonny's in Barnes, which proves they know what they're doing.

Spencer Arms

Gastropub

Putney

237 Lower Richmond Rd
✉ SW15 1HJ **S2**
✆ (020) 87880640 – **Fax** (020) 87800816

Closed 25-26 December

Carte £20/28

This Victorian pub sits on the edge of Putney Common and is close to the river which is exactly where you'd want to find a gastropub. It even has a pavement terrace for summer days. Etched glass and a lick of paint have brightened the exterior, while the inside has been sympathetically updated and divided into two. On your left as you enter is an area with leather sofas, a fireplace and plenty of books and games, while on the other side you'll find a rustic bar-cum-restaurant, with the ubiquitous hardwood floor, pine scrubbed tables and mix and match chairs. The semi open-plan kitchen delivers a well-balanced menu of dishes that are as hearty as they are heart warming, from a blackboard menu which focuses on seasonality and changes daily.

Restaurant at Petersham Hotel

French XXX

Richmond

at Petersham H.,
Nightingale Lane ✉ TW9 6UZ **R3**
✆ (020) 89391084 – **Fax** (020) 89391002
Web www.petershamhotel.co.uk

Closed 25-26 December

Menu £25 (lunch) – Carte £34/46

From its vantage point on Richmond Hill, the Petersham Hotel, built in 1865, offers wonderfully unspoilt vistas of the Thames at its most majestic and, thanks to its large windows, diners at virtually all the tables in its restaurant can enjoy this great view.
The advantages of dining within a hotel include the considerable elbow and leg-room: tables are well spaced for added privacy and there's a comfortable lounge and bar, with its own terrace. Those understandably hesitant about dining within a hotel can rest assured that the room does have its own personality.
The cooking displays a classical French education, but will also please those who prefer their culinary ambitions to be a little closer to home.

Matsuba

Japanese 

Richmond

10 Red Lion St
✉ TW9 1RW **R2**
✆ (020) 86053513
e-mail matsuba10@hotmail.com **Web** www.matsuba.co.uk

Closed 25-26 December, 1 January and Sunday

Carte £35

The sleek and contemporary interior of this Japanese restaurant on the High Street, with its panelled walls, polished tables and high-backed leather chairs, provides a perfectly comfortable environment in which to enjoy their delicately prepared specialities. However, with only eight tables in the restaurant, those without reservations may find themselves having to wait.
It's family run which adds to the relaxed and friendly mood. A small counter is also on hand from where an impression selection of *sushi* and *sashimi* is offered. Lunchtime visitors will find particularly good value Bento Boxes in assorted variations, as well as various 'rice bowl' options which come with appetiser, soup, pickles and fruit.

South-West

Sarkhel's

Indian XX

Southfields

199 Replingham Rd ⊖ Southfields
✉ SW18 5LY **T3**
(020) 88701483
e-mail info@sarkhels.co.uk **Web** www.sarkhels.co.uk

Closed 25-26 December and Monday

Menu £9.95 (lunch) – Carte £13/23

Udit Sarkhel opened his eponymous restaurant ten years ago with his wife, having gained experience with Taj Hotels in India before making his name as Head Chef of the Bombay Brasserie in South Kensington. Over the decade, and thanks to his winning formula and the ensuring popularity of the place, the restaurant has steadily developed and been forced to expand to cope with demand.
Sarkhel's is now a smart and contemporary Indian restaurant, with an inviting luminous glow, warm terracotta tiles and some vivid artwork.
Traditional Indian cooking - the kind served in Indian homes - is the draw here, with the influences stretching across the diverse regions of India. The prices are kept admirably reasonable and service is sweet and sincere.

The Wharf

Modern European XX

Teddington

22 Manor Rd
✉ TW11 8BG **R3**
(020) 89776333 – **Fax** (020) 89779444
e-mail the.wharf@walk-on-water.co.uk

Closed 25-26 December, first week January, Sunday dinner and Monday

Menu £16/19 – Carte £23/32

The Wharf is a delightful converted boathouse on the banks of the Thames, overlooking Teddington Lock, and reminds us how little we sometimes make of this great river. On warm summer days the whole place becomes one vast terrace and many will leave a July lunch wishing they had a little something to navigate towards the landing stage next time.
Weekends and Twickenham match days are naturally the busy periods and the upstairs floor is ideal for private parties. Those coming during the weekdays are rewarded with keenly priced menus.
The chef owner, a protégé of Anton Mosimann, offers modern European cuisine, coupled with some Asian touches. Waiting staff catch the mood with their competence and courtesy.

Kastoori

Indian vegetarian 

Tooting

188 Upper Tooting Rd — ⊖ Tooting Bec
✉ SW17 7EJ — **U3**
✆ (020) 87677027

Closed 25-26 December and lunch Monday and Tuesday

Carte £13/16

There are over 9,000 Indian restaurants in the UK, the majority of which are actually Bangladeshi and seemingly content to merely churn out the same old anglicised favourites. Thanks, therefore, are due to places like Kastoori which offers something both original and authentic.

The Thanki family spent some time in Uganda and their extensive vegetarian and vegan menu features both Gujarati specialities as well as flavours from East Africa. The result is a unique blend of fresh and exhilarating tastes, full of such vitality that even the most rabid carnivore will not notice the lack of meat. The room is neat and tidy, if unremarkable, but the service is proud and thoughtful, as you would expect from a real family operation.

Oh Boy

Thai

Tooting

843 Garratt Lane — ⊖ Broadway
✉ SW17 0PG — **T3**
✆ (020) 89479760 – **Fax** (020) 88797867

Closed Christmas and Monday – dinner only

Carte £14/19

One of London's greatest strengths is in the variety, choice and diversity of its restaurants - not only is virtually every nationality of cuisine represented but also for every David Collins' designed sleek new gastro-dome there's a place like Oh Boy, in a nondescript road in Tooting.

Oh Boy has never been fashionable, but any slick West End restaurant would willingly swap their hip-ness in return for this kind of longevity. Opened in 1984, it was one of the first Thai restaurants in the country. Today, it's still pulling in the locals and the decorative style remains proudly understated. We may all now be a little more familiar with the cooking but the charming, traditionally dressed girls are more than willing to offer guidance.

La Brasserie McClements

French XX

Twickenham

2 Whitton Rd
TW1 1BJ **R3**
(020) 87449598
e-mail johnmac21@aol.com **Web** www.labrasserietw1.co.uk

Closed 1 January, Sunday and Monday

Menu £20 (lunch) – Carte £28/35

John McClements has revamped his restaurant a few times over the years but the latest incarnation is probably the best. He has successfully captured that Parisian brasserie look with dark wood, a bit of brass and touches of art deco. The only thing missing from a truly authentic experience is some Gallic insouciance but the staff here seem determined to remain smiley and friendly.
Classic cuisine bourgeoise is the feature of the menu – there can't be many places in London with a Frenchier menu than this. You'll find everything from *grenouilles* and *escargots* to *canard* and, for the more adventurous, *tête de porc*, all prepared with genuine understanding.
Those who failed their O level need not worry as all dishes have English translations.

A Cena

Italian XX

Twickenham

418 Richmond Rd Richmond
TW1 2EB **R3**
(020) 82880108 – **Fax** (020) 89405346
Web www.acena.co.uk

Closed last 2 weeks August, Sunday dinner and Monday

Carte £21/36

Just as Italy is now an established participant in the Six Nations Rugby, so it is appropriate that an Italian restaurant, A Cena, has built a reputation among the assorted dining options available in the vicinity of Twickenham, home of English rugby.
Italian for "to eat", A Cena succeeds by combining flavoursome cooking, a well chosen all-Italian wine list, grown-up service and calming, stress-free surroundings. Decorated with church pew style chairs and scrubbed floorboards, with large mirrors adding to the feel of light and space, the room also benefits from having a stylish bar offering an extensive cocktail list to those making it more of an occasion.
Odds on an English restaurant opening in Rome remain long.

Brula Bistrot

French

Twickenham

43 Crown Rd, St Margarets

VISA ✉ TW1 3EJ **R3**

(020) 88920602 – **Fax** (020) 88927727

e-mail info@brulabistrot.com

AE Closed 25-26 December and 1 January – booking essential

Menu £14.50 (lunch) - Carte £21/34

The stained glass windows and the old church pews lend a somewhat blessed feel to this corner bistro and the locals clearly regard it as somewhere sacred.

The parquet flooring, mirrors and paintings help achieve what all bistros around the world attempt – that full-on Gallic experience. Where this one works is not only in the classic French cuisine, with all the favourites from snails to chocolate pots, but also in their pricing policy. This is generous enough to allow regular visits and thus avoids the curse of the suburban restaurant - being considered a place reserved for that 'special occasion'.

Little wonder that the atmosphere is decidedly secular in its jollity. It also helps when the service is personable and attentive.

Ma Cuisine

French 

Twickenham

6 Whitton Rd

✉ TW1 1BJ **R3**

(020) 86079849

Web www.macuisinetw1.co.uk

Closed Sunday

Menu £15.50 (lunch) - Carte £18/24

Londoners have always appreciated that dining out should be part of every day living. This does, in turn, call for plenty of affordable restaurants and here Ma Cuisine fits the bill nicely. By keeping prices low, it has proved a real local draw and makes us wish we had one of these at the end of our street.

For starters, it's a bistro, with the sort of informality that makes dining out a relaxing, stress-busting experience. Secondly, it serves reassuringly rustic and recognisable French classics like onion soup, *coq au vin* and lemon tart. The French theme continues in the decoration, in the posters and the music, gingham table covers and plenty of cries of "*bon appétit*" from the staff. You get all this without breaking the *banque*.

Tangawizi

Indian

Twickenham

A/C VISA MC AE

406 Richmond Rd, Richmond Bridge — Richmond
TW1 2EB — **R2**
(020) 8891 3737 – **Fax** (020) 8891 3737
e-mail tangawizi-richmond@hotmail.com
Closed 25 December and 1 January – dinner only

Carte £15/22

London has not only witnessed vast improvements in the quality of Indian cooking in the past decade, but is also now seeing greater individuality and flair in Indian restaurant design and decoration. Tangawazi is proof that these developments are not merely confined to the West End; the general atmosphere here may be of a genuine neighbourhood restaurant but it is one whose contemporary style, attention to detail and sense of originality would once only be found in a more central location. The silky colours of the room are matched by the sartorial elegance of the staff, and the keenly priced menu successfully mixes the tried and tested with monthly changing specials and specialities from more northerly provinces of India.

THE HALF MONTY

Londoners love a good English breakfast, as demonstrated by Peckham-born performance artist Mark McGowan, who in 2003 made the headlines by spending a week in a bath of baked beans (handily located in a south London gallery), with chips up his nose and sausages wrapped around his head. McGowan claimed to be defending the Great British fry up from a bad press - but without eggs, bacon and toast, the effort was perhaps a bit half-hearted.

Chez Bruce ✿

French XX

2 Bellevue Rd
SW17 7EG
(020) 86720114 – **Fax** (020) 87676648
e-mail enquiries@chezbruce.co.uk **Web** www.chezbruce.co.uk

⊖ Tooting Bec
U3

Closed 24-26 December and 1 January – booking essential

Menu £23.50/37.50

Chez Bruce

The clue is in the name - a bit of French followed by a good Celtic name. It says "we may serve French-inspired food but don't expect anything poncey here". This is a place for anyone who likes their food and its Wandsworth location just seems so right. Opposite, you'll see that's a common, designed for public use - not a park or a green or a garden.
Bruce Poole is the man responsible for this ever popular restaurant which proves that great food doesn't have to come with a fanfare of liveried staff doing ridiculous things with silver cloches. But neither does this no-nonsense approach to food mean a lack of precision or care. First rate ingredients yield bold and well-defined flavours and, along with the regional French, come influences from the Southern Mediterranean. The set menu offers something for everyone and, decoratively, the plates come refreshingly restrained. The wine list is wise and reasonable.
The simple lay out of the restaurant, with the tables set quite closely together, and the lack of affectation in the service, ensures that the atmosphere is warm and sociable.

A LA CARTE

FIRST COURSE	MAIN COURSE	DESSERT
• Tuna ceviche with king prawn tempura, pine nuts. lime and coriander.	• Roast pigeon with foie gras, Savoy cabbage and caramelised onions.	• Cherry and almond croustade with almond ice cream.
• Foie gras and chicken liver parfait with toasted brioche.	• Fillet of sea bream with mushroom duxelle, oysters and potato pancakes.	• Chocolate and brazil nut brownie, rum and raisin ice cream.

Amici

Italian XX

Wandsworth

35 Bellevue Rd ⊖ Balham

✉ SW17 7EF **U3**

✆ (020) 86725888 – **Fax** (020) 86728856
Web www.amiciitaly.co.uk

Closed 25-28 December

Carte £19/26

To be called a genuine 'neighbourhood' restaurant requires more than just a leafy location – the restaurant has to be part of the local community. Amici does its bit by holding cookery demonstrations, courtesy of local resident and cookery writer Valentina Harris who is the consultant here. The fact that some of those classes are for kids and teenagers is proof than local families make up an important part of the clientele here.
It's a brightly decorated place, with an appealing and easy-going charm, relaxing and informal service. The Italian cooking is equally uncomplicated and unfussy, and comes with a slight Tuscan influence.
The attractive bar at the front, overlooking the Common, is open all day and offers up its own snack menu.

Ditto

Mediterranean 

Wandsworth

55-57 East Hill

✉ SW18 2QE **T2**

✆ (020) 88770110 – **Fax** (020) 88750110
e-mail will@doditto.co.uk **Web** www.doditto.co.uk

Carte £17/28

Wandsworth's one-way system appears to have been designed to bamboozle the out-of-towner, so it's hardly surprising that Ditto enjoys a lively, and very local, atmosphere. It comes divided into two, with a roomy bar down one side with assorted sofas, and an informal restaurant on the other. The menu jumps around, from Spain to Italy via France, but it all works well; there's something for everyone, including small snacks for sharing like tempura and some original touches like dessert cocktails. Meals can be taken in the bar or restaurant and the serving team are all helpful and obliging.
How can you not take to a place that turns its private dining room into a crèche to encourage mums to meet up for lunch?

Light House

International

VISA MC AE

Wimbledon

75-77 Ridgway
SW19 4ST
(020) 89446338 – **Fax** (020) 89464440
Web www.lighthousewimbledon.com

⊖ Wimbledon
T3

Closed 25-26 December, 1 January and Sunday dinner

Menu £16.50 (lunch) – Carte £23/32

Those expecting a tall, tubular building with a light on the top will be disappointed. The name refers to the time when this was a shop selling lights and light fittings. Nowadays it provides an illuminating insight into our more adventurous dining habits by offering cooking unfettered by national boundaries. On any one day you may find influences ranging from a bit of Italian, Greek or Tunisian to the odd Asian twist. The fact that it seems to work speaks volumes for the quality of the ingredients. The pricing is also eminently sensible, especially for the set lunch menu.
The restaurant itself is a relatively simple affair, with plenty of light wood, a semi-open kitchen and a roomy bar area. The atmosphere is one of contented bonhomie.

The Fire Stables

Gastropub

A/C VISA MC

Wimbledon

27-29 Church Rd
SW19 5DQ
(020) 89463197 – **Fax** (020) 89461101
e-mail thefirestables@thespiritgroup.com

⊖ Wimbledon
T3

Menu £15.50 (lunch) – Carte £22/33

'Gastropub' is a somewhat nebulous term to describe anywhere serving decent food in fairly casual surroundings and The Fire Stables proves that not all gastropubs were once old boozers. This may have originally been where the horses to pull the old fire engines were stabled but nowadays it calls itself a 'pub and dining room'. Whatever it is, it seems to work.
You'll find a separate bar area with its own menu and a long dining room at the back. Lunchtimes appear popular with those with young children, while noise levels become more boisterously adult in the evenings. The menu covers all bases, from Caesar salads and burgers to more adventurous fare like belly of pork and rack of lamb.
That tennis club is just down the road.

Where to **stay**

WHERE TO STAY WHERE TO STAY WHERE TO STAY WHERE TO STAY WHERE TO STAY

www.purestockx.com

Alphabetical list of hotels

Dorchester

Park Lane
⊠ W1A 2HJ
✆ (020) 76298888 – **Fax** (020) 74090114
e-mail info@thedorchester.com
Web www.thedorchester.com

⊖ Hyde Park Corner
PLAN page 36 G4

200 rm – **£423** **£617**, £28 – 49 suites
China Tang (See restaurant listing)

The Dorchester

The Dorchester was built in 1931 and has been a byword for glamour, discretion and comfort ever since. Indeed, its guest list would read like a veritable who's who of the rich, famous and successful, although the hotel is far too discreet to actually let anyone see that list.

The hotel occupies a commanding position looking over the park, but the reason its reputation remains as high as ever is that it continues to evolve and to pre-empt the expectations and needs of its clients. The bedrooms are certainly one of its great strengths and its suites some of the most sought after rooms in London. Standards of housekeeping are exemplary, as one would expect, and the bathrooms are particularly luxurious. The Promenade, famed for its light meals and afternoon tea, is the most recognisable feature of the hotel; The Grill Room has been given an exuberant makeover, with acres of tartan and vast murals of dancing Highlanders and retains a certain Britishness in its cooking. For a truly glamorous Chinese restaurant, try China Tang downstairs.

The Dorchester is clearly one of London's finest hotels and its continued development shows no signs of abating.

The Ritz

150 Piccadilly
✉ W1J 9BR
✆ (020) 74938181 – **Fax** (020) 74932687
e-mail enquire@theritzlondon.com
Web www.theritzlondon.com

⊖ Green Park
PLAN page 37 H4

116 rm – 🛉£294/470 🛉🛉£352/470, ☕ £30 – 17 suites
🍴 ***The Restaurant*** (See restaurant listing)

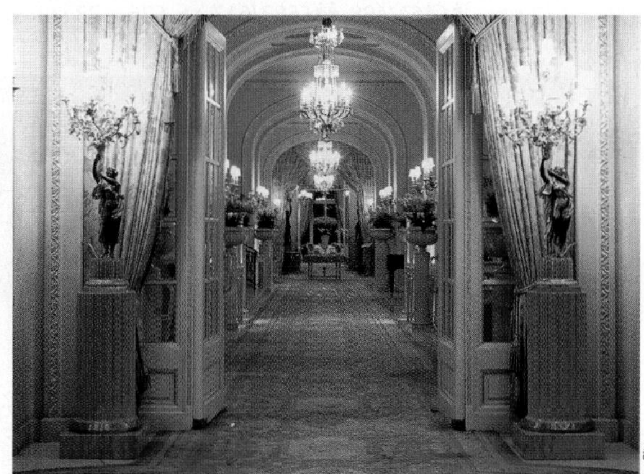

The Ritz

The Ritz was open in 1906 and conceived by Cesar Ritz, that most celebrated of hotelier. It is fitting to his memory that, one hundred years later, the hotel is back in private ownership and has been restored to its former majesty.

In the style of a French chateau, with Louis XVI furnishings, The Ritz has always been more than just a byword for glamour and luxury: it has set standards by which we judge others and its roll-call of admirers reads like a who's who of the last century. Afternoon tea in the magnificent surroundings of the Palm Court is as much a London institution as the Changing of the Guard. The Ritz Restaurant is unquestionably the grandest dining room in the country and the dazzling Rivoli Bar rightly celebrates its art deco origins.

Peach, pink, blue and yellow are the distinctive Ritz colours used in the bedrooms. Antique furniture and gold leaf enhance the Louis XVI feel and the elegance of the suites makes them highly desirable.

However luxurious the bedrooms or ornate the decoration, a grand hotel's reputation will always rest on the quality of the service. At The Ritz you'll find a veritable battalion of liveried staff to attend to every whim.

Mandarin Oriental Hyde Park

66 Knightsbridge
SW1X 7LA
(020) 7235 2000 – **Fax** (020) 7235 2001
e-mail molon-reservations@mohg.com
Web www.mandarinoriental.com

Knightsbridge
PLAN page 199 F4

177 rm – £464/488 ££587/617, £26 – 23 suites
Foliage (See restaurant listing)

Spa · VISA · MC · AE

Mandarin Oriental Hyde Park

The façade of this grand hotel, built in 1889, must be one of the most impressive in London and, when you've got Hyde Park as your own garden, the view at the back isn't bad either.

It opened as a Gentleman's Club before becoming a hotel and its links to the Royal Family go back many years. At the beginning of this new century, the hotel underwent a comprehensive refurbishment which brought it straight up to date and further work is already under way.

The liveried doorman and the marbled steps up to the lobby prepare guests for the luxury which lies within. A spa offers a huge variety of treatments for all types of stress, while the ultra slick Mandarin Bar is a destination in its own right.

There are two restaurants, both of which look out over the park and the Household Cavalry as they ride pass: the accomplished and skilled cooking of Foliage and the less formal Park restaurant, whose menu traverses the world.

Every conceivable luxury can be found in the bedrooms which combine a sense of Victorian decorum with a subtle Asian gracefulness. The mod cons are carefully concealed amid the rich fabrics and antique furniture and there is a manager on duty for every floor of the hotel.

Savoy

Strand
WC2R 0EU
(020) 78364343 – **Fax** (020) 72406040
e-mail info@the-savoy.co.uk
Web www.fairmont.com/savoy

Charing Cross
PLAN page 88 J3

236 rm – £246/457 ££269/480, £25 – 27 suites
The Savoy Grill (See restaurant listing)

VISA AE

The Savoy/Fairmont Hotels

The Savoy opened in 1889 and the electric lighting and sheer number of bathrooms were enough to impress the first guests. Its art deco splendour has never been in doubt but its reputation was really cemented when Cesar Ritz and Auguste Escoffier were engaged as manager and chef. Today, the hotel can lay claim to one of the most recognisable hotel names in the world (and trivia enthusiasts will know that it's on the only stretch of tarmac in the UK where you drive on the right).

The hotel has managed the clever trick of being the Establishment's favourite hotel while also appealing to the next generation of hotel-stayers.

The American Bar enjoys legendary status among hotel bars, while The Thames Foyer provides everything from afternoon tea to a late snack, all with musical accompaniment. The River Restaurant is now only used for breakfast and private parties and there can be few better views in the morning. Serious dining happens in the reinvigorated Savoy Grill, while Banquette is a take on the American diner.

All the bedrooms are unquestionably elegant and mix traditional mores with contemporary expectations. Book a river room to experience the views which inspired Monet.

Claridge's

Brook St
W1A 2JQ
(020) 76298860 – **Fax** (020) 74992210
e-mail info@claridges.com
Web www.claridges.co.uk

Bond Street
PLAN page 36 G3

143 rm – £480/562 £598/621, £27 – 60 suites
Gordon Ramsay at Claridge's (See restaurant listing)

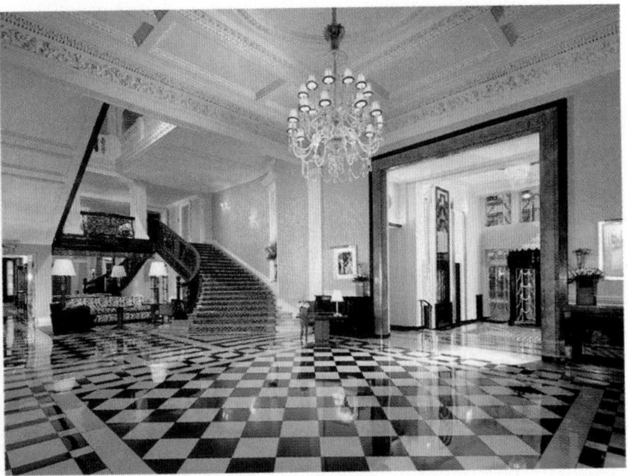

Claridge's

If there is one hotel in London which represents the city and its history, then it must surely be Claridge's. Built in 1898, it has remained a favourite with Kings, Queens, statesmen and world leaders throughout its history and is the hotel most closely associated with the Royal Family. Just enter the Front Hall and you'll know you are somewhere special; the art deco, the marble, the staircase and the fireplace transport you to an age of elegance and discretion. An accompanying harpist makes afternoon tea a popular occasion, which is served in the Foyer beneath the striking light sculpture.
Into such genteel surroundings came the more bullish figure of Gordon Ramsay, but he has managed to update and improve the restaurant while still respecting its traditions. The bar shows how to skilfully add contemporary glamour to complement the original art deco design. This updating of the traditional continues in the bedrooms; the Brook Penthouse suite manages to retain its 1930's fittings and features, yet also still feels fresh and vibrant. The smart and confident staff all know exactly what they're doing and do it very well.

The Berkeley

Wilton Pl
SW1X 7RL
(020) 72356000 – **Fax** (020) 72354330
e-mail info@the-berkeley.co.uk
Web www.the-berkeley.co.uk

Knightsbridge
PLAN page 100 G4

189 rm – £539 £598, £29 – 25 suites
Pétrus (See restaurant listing)

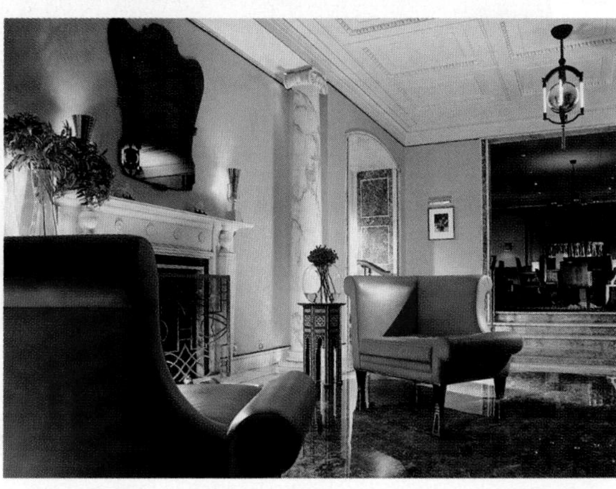

The Berkeley

The Berkeley is so called because the original hotel was on Berkeley Street - it wasn't until 1972 that it re-opened at its new, far smarter, address opposite the park in Wilton Place. The warm and welcoming lobby sets the tone for the hotel, with concierge and porters desk on either side of the entrance and a couple of steps up to the reception area.
One of the hotel's most striking features is the rooftop swimming pool, complete with a retractable roof and terrific views of Hyde Park. Those who prefer more spirit-based relaxation should head for the ice cool Blue Bar, which has become one of the most fashionable destination bars in London.
New bedrooms have been seamlessly added to the hotel in recent years which are more contemporary in their styling, but all the rooms are very smart and extremely comfortable; the first to get snapped up are the conservatory suites which all have their own outside terrace. Gordon Ramsay has taken control over Boxwood Café, located to the side of the hotel, which has a relaxed and breezy feel and a menu to match. For some seriously indulgent dining, make reservations at Marcus Wareing's opulent restaurant, Pétrus.

The Lanesborough

Hyde Park Corner
SW1X 7TA
(020) 72595599 - **Fax** (020) 72595606
e-mail info@lanesborough.com
Web www.lanesborough.com

⊖ Hyde Park Corner
PLAN page 100 G4

86 rm - £370/511 £511, £28 - 9 suites

VISA MC AE

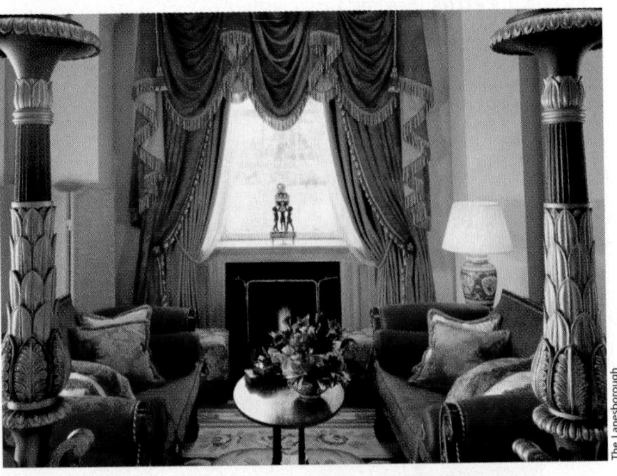
The Lanesborough

The original Lanesborough House was built in 1719, became St.George's Hospital in 1733, was demolished and rebuilt in 1827, and continued to operate as a hospital on this spot until 1980. Now, as one of the city's premier luxury hotels, it still dominates this part of Hyde Park Corner with its strikingly bright exterior and no doubt some of its more health conscious guests benefit as much from the fresh air of the park as did the patients over the years.

Never knowingly understated, the bedrooms are decorated with a bold Regency opulence and all technological mod cons have been incorporated in an unobtrusive manner. Travelling corporate types will appreciate the mobile phone and business cards printed on arrival and all guests enjoy the services of a butler. The Royal Suite must surely be one of the most lavish and luxurious suites in London. The ornate glass-roofed Conservatory restaurant has a striking Chinoiserie theme and serves an internationally influenced menu, while the Library Bar boasts a distinctly masculine and clubby feel. Service levels are all that one would expect from a hotel of this calibre.

Four Seasons

Hamilton Pl, Park Lane
⊠ W1A 1AZ
✆ (020) 74990888 – **Fax** (020) 74931895
e-mail fsh.london@fourseasons.com
Web www.fourseasons.com

⊖ Hyde Park Corner
PLAN page 36 G4

193 rm – †£394/429 ††£458, ☕ £25 – 26 suites

VISA MC AE

Four Seasons

For the many years this was the only Four Seasons hotel in Europe and, in an understandable bid for independence and individuality, went by the name of the 'Inn on the Park'. Nowadays, in our world of brands and 'corporate identity', it falls more into line among the international portfolio of hotels that cover a considerable number of the major cities around the world. Purpose built over thirty years ago, what it may lack in architectural character it makes up for in space and size - the bedrooms are on average 430 square foot, which is considerably larger than most in the city.

A majority of the suites have balconies or little terraces and the corner suites are particularly capacious. The lobby is overseen by separate concierge and reception areas, while the lounge at the far end of the ground floor is a popular spot for snacks and afternoon tea. Upstairs on the first floor one finds 'Lanes', the hotel dining room which is colourfully decorated with plenty of glass and has an easy, appetising menu. Overlooking the park, it occupies a pleasant spot, as does the clubby bar adjacent.

Landmark London

222 Marylebone Rd
✉ NW1 6JQ
✆ (020) 7631 8000 – **Fax** (020) 7631 8080
e-mail reservations@thelandmark.co.uk
Web www.landmarklondon.co.uk

⊖ Baker Street
PLAN page 118 F1

290 rm – †£217/288 ††£247/305, ☕ £25 – 9 suites

Landmark London

Those Victorians certainly knew how to build hotels. The Landmark was originally called the Great Central and was one of the last of the great railway hotels; the façade today still reflects the architectural style of that age. Once inside, however, you quickly realise you're in the company of an international hotel corporation, where size, comfort and facilities fit the exacting standards demanded by your average 21st century traveller.

The most striking feature of the hotel is the vast glass-roofed atrium, under which the Winter Garden restaurant serves breakfast and an international menu at lunch and dinner. Those after something a little more traditional should head downstairs to the wood panelled Cellar Bar, while the Mirror Bar is an altogether more sophisticated spot for cocktail hour.

The bedrooms, many of which face inwards into the atrium, are all generously proportioned and have every mod con you need. Bathrooms are also a good size and the majority have separate showers and double washbasins. Those looking for even greater levels of relaxation will be more than happy with the well equipped Health Club.

Connaught

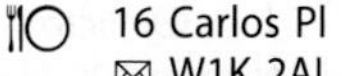

16 Carlos Pl
✉ W1K 2AL
✆ (020) 74997070 – **Fax** (020) 74953262
e-mail info@the-connaught.co.uk
Web www.the-connaught.co.uk

⊖ Bond Street
PLAN page 36 G3

68 rm – 🚹£363/480 🚹🚹£504, ☕ £29 – 24 suites

🍴 ***Angela Hartnett at The Connaught*** (See restaurant listing)

Connaught

The Connaught opened in 1897, but was then called The Coburg Hotel, changing its name during the Great War. Of all of the London hotels who have tried to create the feeling of a private house, albeit an immensely grand private house, few have been as successful as The Connaught. From the discreet lobby and the striking mahogany staircase to the 'English country house' style of the bedrooms, everything here shouts Englishness, although no one actually shouts anything here - it would be more of a gentle whisper.

The sound of teaspoon on bone china can be heard each afternoon in the charming setting of the Connaught Bar, with its thoroughly genteel atmosphere, while the American Bar provides slightly more clubby surroundings. The restaurant is a serious affair, with exquisite food, and is run by Gordon Ramsay and his protégé, Angela Hartnett.

The hotel will be closed for an extended period in 2007. A huge injection of funds will be used to add more facilities and up-to-date features and extras, as well as more bedrooms. There will also be a full refurbishment of the existing rooms but they'll retain that Edwardian character for which the hotel is famed.

The Goring

15 Beeston Pl, Grosvenor Gdns
SW1W 0JW
(020) 73969000 – **Fax** (020) 78344393
e-mail reception@goringhotel.co.uk
Web www.goringhotel.co.uk

⊖ Victoria
PLAN page 100 H5

65 rm – 🛉£347/405 🛉🛉£541, ☕ £24 – 6 suites

VISA MC AE

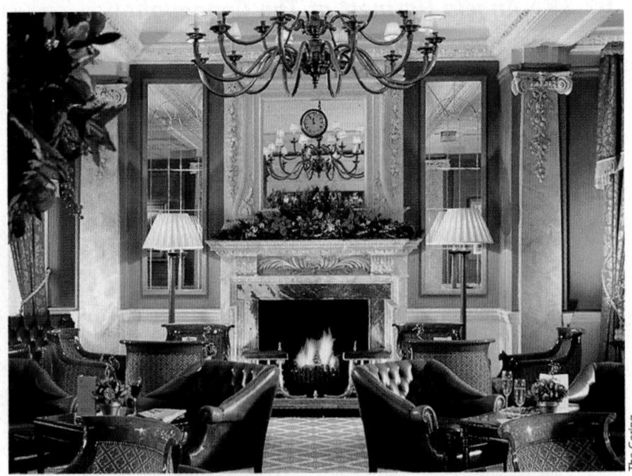

The Goring

The Goring celebrates proper old school hospitality and is all the more admirable for that. It opened in 1910, when it could proudly boast of being London's first hotel to offer private bathrooms and central heating in all its bedrooms, an achievement of uncommon innovation at that time. Today, it is one of the few hotels that have stayed in private hands. Even more remarkable is that those hands all belong to the same family, as it is now being overseen by the fourth generation of the Goring family.

The style is very much English country house in the city (it even has a garden) and the housekeeping standards are never less than exemplary. The atmosphere is discreet and thoroughly courteous.

The Goring, commendably, never merely rests on its considerable laurels but it still looks for ways of improving and developing; the restaurant was recently redesigned by David Linley in an understated yet contemporary way which perfectly complements the proudly British fare on offer.

If you see someone in morning dress in the lobby don't assume they're the manager - they're just as likely to be one of the guests about to pop over the road to collect a gong.

The Soho

4 Richmond Mews — ⊖ Tottenham Court Road
W1D 3DH — PLAN page 37 I3
(020) 75593000 – **Fax** (020) 75593003
e-mail soho@firmdale.com
Web www.sohohotel.com

83 rm – £282 £346, £19 – 2 suites

The Soho

Amazing what you can do with an old NCP car park, imagination, and an eye for detail and design. The Soho opened late 2004 and the ten foot bronze cat by the entrance tells you this is no ordinary hotel.

For one thing, it proves that style need not compromise comfort and that size does sometimes matter - the bedrooms here are more than generously proportioned and the Penthouse and Soho suites are both handsome and vast. Modern art and sculptures are found throughout the rooms and no detail has been overlooked in their design.

'Refuel' is half bar, half restaurant, with an enormous mural paying ironic homage to this site's former life as one of those architectural carbuncles known as multi-storey car parks. The menu treads a sunny path through warmer climes and offers something for everyone. The adjoining bar will be a welcoming sight after a long day, as will the two sitting rooms which both have a soothing and relaxed quality about them.

The young staff are confident and knowledgeable about their hotel. Even with Soho just outside the door and a youthful clientele, the bedrooms somehow manage to be relatively quiet.

Brown's

Albemarle St — ⊖ Green Park

✉ W1S 4BP — PLAN page 37 **H3**

(020) 74936020 – **Fax** (020) 74939381

e-mail reservations.browns@roccofortehotels.com

Web www.roccofortehotels.com

105 rm – £364 £723, £27 – 12 suites

The Grill (See restaurant listing)

Brown's

Few hotels can match Brown's for its sense of history, its atmosphere of discretion and its atmosphere of true Englishness. Originally opened in 1837 by James Brown, Lord Byron's butler, and extended by the Ford family later that century, Brown's quickly established itself as the favoured choice of the gentry, nobility and royalty. It was here that Alexander Graham Bell first demonstrated his telephone.

The hotel reopened at the end of 2005, having spent a million pounds for every one of the 20 months it was closed for refurbishment, and now takes its place back as one of Mayfair's best addresses. The new look Brown's is both updated but also respectful of the past, so long standing guests will not feel threatened while newer ones will find much to enjoy. Afternoon tea is still hugely popular but now so is the more contemporary Donovan Bar, named after the celebrated photographer, Terence Donovan. For classic British cooking and a traditional style of service, book a table at The Grill restaurant.

Bedrooms have also managed the trick of being contemporary in look but traditional in feel, with all the gadgets discreetly concealed.

Great Eastern

Liverpool St
✉ EC2M 7QN
✆ (020) 76185000 – **Fax** (020) 76185001
e-mail info@great-eastern-hotel.co.uk
Web www.great-eastern-hotel.co.uk

⊖ Liverpool Street
PLAN page 165 M2

264 rm – ♦£118/370 ♦♦£118/370, ☕ £22 – 3 suites
Aurora (See restaurant listing)

Great Eastern

This is a large, red bricked, classic Victorian railway hotel, in the heart of the City, but don't expect to find a correspondingly classic interior, because inside it's all very stylish and design orientated.

What also sets it apart is that just as more and more hotels offer nothing more than a breakfast room, The Great Eastern has gone the other way and provides enough choice of restaurant to satisfy the pickiest of eater and the most capricious of diner. The choice is staggering: you can have classic comfort food in George, the quintessentially British wood-panelled pub; Terminus is a homage to the hotel's railway connections and offers modern European food; lovers of Japanese food should head for the minimalist surroundings of Miyabi; Fishmarket, as the name implies, is the place to go for seafood and has a great Champagne Bar, while Aurora is the grand flagship of the operation. There's also a room service menu.

All the bedrooms are individual in style, size and shape. Some are in the style of a 'loft living', while all the rooms retain a sense of warmth and comfort - something that not all 'designer' hotels can boast.

The Bentley Kempinski

27-33 Harrington Gdns
✉ SW7 4JX
✆ (020) 72445555 – **Fax** (020) 72445566
e-mail info@thebentley-hotel.com
Web www.thebentley-hotel.com

⊖ Gloucester Road
PLAN page 200 D6

52 rm – 🚹£340/458 🚹🚹£458, ☕ £20 – 12 suites
🍴 ***1880*** (See restaurant listing)

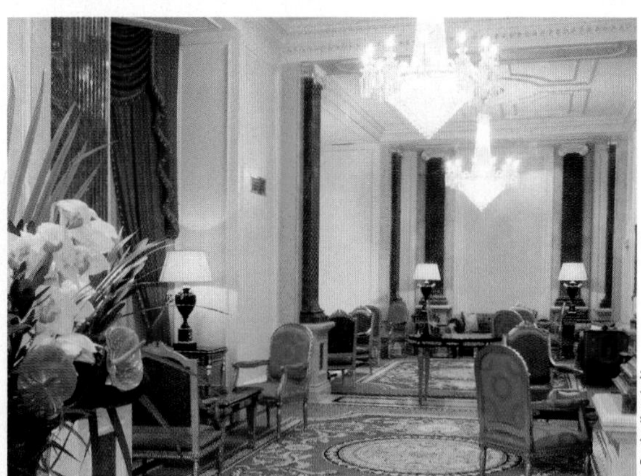

The Bentley Kempinski

Over six hundred tons of imported marble were used during the conversion, in 2003, of a series of grand stuccoed houses into what is the Bentley Kempinski Hotel. Understated it ain't.
The lavish reception hall and lobby used up quite a bit of that tonnage and, along with the crystal chandeliers, provide suitably ornate surroundings for those who like a slice or two of grandeur with their morning coffee.
Breakfast and lunch are served in the bright Peridot restaurant, which boasts a striking mosaic floor and a sensibly light midday menu, while those who like their dinner served in altogether more luxurious surroundings should head downstairs to 1880. Cigar smokers will enjoy their own clubby den and the more health conscious will find relaxation in the spa which includes an impressive Turkish bath. If any expense was spared, it certainly wasn't spared in the bedrooms which continue the luxury theme with silk lined walls, gold leaf and exquisite fabrics. The bathrooms are particularly ornate and come with walk-in showers and plenty more of that marble.

The Waldorf Hilton

Aldwych
⊠ WC2B 4DD
(020) 78362400 – **Fax** (02) 78367244
e-mail waldorflondon@hilton.com
Web www.hilton.co.uk/waldorf

Covent Garden
PLAN page 88 J3

289 rm – £233/375 £233/375, £22 – 10 suites

The Waldorf Hilton

The Waldolf Hilton awoke in 2005, following a £35 million refurbishment and this Grande Dame of London hotels was able to reclaim its reputation, having spent rather too many years looking a little tired and frail. The striking Edwardian façade can still instil a sense of awe in visitors and a sense of pride in Londoners. Inside, the designers have tried to marry that sense of tradition with a more updated feel, so bedrooms now have a more stylised look and come with flat-screen TV's and all the other communication and electronic paraphernalia that the modern traveller demands.

In the original 1908 Grill Room one now finds 'Homage', the hotel restaurant that seeks to recreate the feel of a Grand European Salon, and its menu offers something for everyone. Not many central London hotels can boast a 14 metre swimming pool, while theatre-goers will find fewer hotels better placed for a short amble back after the final curtain. What a shame, though, that the Palm Court, once one of the most famous of spots for afternoon tea dances, is now used purely for private parties.

Langham

1c Portland Pl, Regent St
⊠ W1B 1JA
(020) 76361000 – **Fax** (020) 73232340
e-mail lon.info@langhamhotels.com
Web www.langhamlondon.com

⊖ Oxford Circus
PLAN page 119 H2

409 rm – †£411 ††£411, ☕ £25 – 20 suites

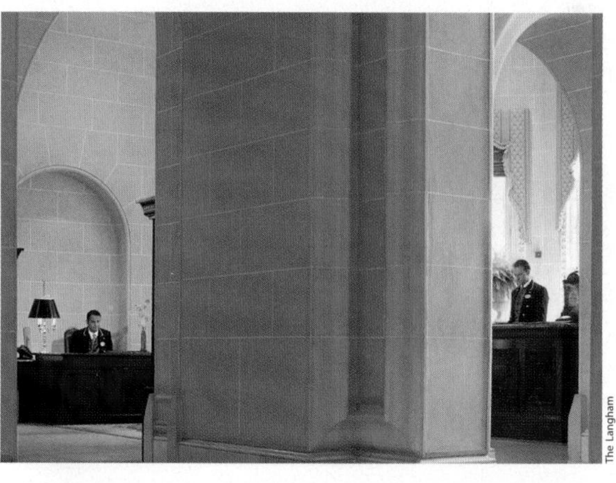

The Langham

1865 was when this strikingly grand building was first opened but its current appearance owes more to the comprehensive restoration and refurbishment that occurred in the 1990's.
The marbled lobby, with steps up to the reception area, sets the tone. The Palm Court, with its elaborate coving and glass canopy, provides decidedly glamorous surroundings for light meals and afternoon tea and the restaurant, with its high, ornate ceiling and pillars, is a popular choice for assorted BBC employees with some licence-fee money to spend. The bars are roomy and masculine.
Bedrooms are very much the strength here. All are decently proportioned and are being given a more contemporary makeover. The Infinity Suite lives up to its name by seemingly going on for ever and must surely be one of the biggest in London. Leisure facilities will satisfy the most active of guest and are housed within what was once the next door Natwest Bank. The swimming pool is in the old money vault.
The Langham Hotel Club is a hotel within a hotel, where guests enjoy extra services and their own lounge where their breakfast is served.

Sofitel St James London

6 Waterloo Pl
NW1Y 4AN
(020) 77472200 – **Fax** (020) 77472210
e-mail h3144@accor-hotels.com
Web www.sofitelstjames.com

Piccadilly Circus
PLAN page 37 I4

179 rm – **£417/464 £493,** **£21** – **7 suites**
Brasserie Roux (See restaurant listing)

VISA MC AE

Sofitel St James London

Another hotel with a great location, this one overlooking the John Nash designed Waterloo Place, on the corner with Pall Mall and within strolling distance of many of the city's most familiar attractions. It is housed, commendably discreetly, within the sensitively restored Grade II listed former home of the Cox and Kings Company and was built in 1923.

The hotel opened as a Sofitel in 2002 and offers the level of comfort one associates with today's more demanding international traveller; the bedrooms come with all the communication gadgets we now expect, there's a choice of colour schemes and the general style is one of sleek, contemporary design lines, refreshingly free from chintz.

Yin and Yang come courtesy of the bar and lounge; the bar is a decidedly masculine room, furnished with plenty of wood and leather and with a decidedly clubby atmosphere, while the Lounge is an altogether more florid affair, which exuberantly celebrates the rose in all its splendour and serves that altogether more genteel event: afternoon tea. For classic French specialities head to Brasserie Roux, found in the former banking hall.

One Aldwych

1 Aldwych
✉ WC2B 4RH
✆ (020) 73001000 – **Fax** (020) 73001001
e-mail sales@onealdwych.com
Web www.onealdwych.com

⊖ Covent Garden
PLAN page 88 J3

96 rm – 🚹£400 🚹🚹£423, ☕ £22 – 9 suites
Axis (See restaurant listing)

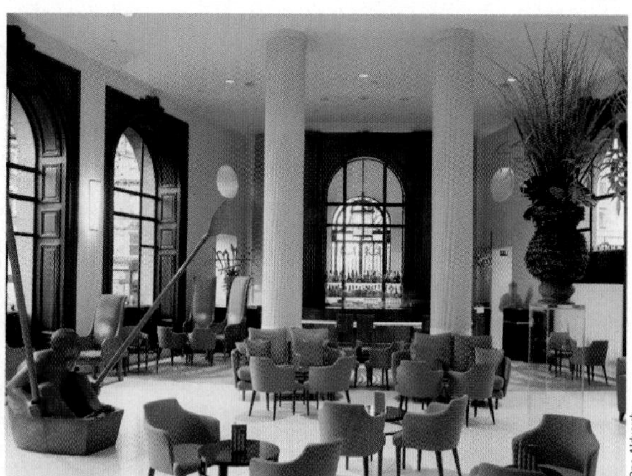

One Aldwych

A grand 19th century bank in a great position on a corner of The Strand was converted into One Aldwych in 1998. It set a new standard in terms of contemporary styling and up-to-the-minute facilities and forced other luxury hotels to raise their game. Once past the omnipresent doorman you'll find yourself in a stunning lobby which doubles as a hip bar, with striking works of contemporary art and sculpture for which the hotel is celebrated and which are also displayed throughout the hotel. Considerable care and thought has gone into every detail of the bedrooms, from the bespoke furniture and daily delivery of fresh fruit and flowers to the mist-free mirrors and mini TV's in the bathrooms. All the rooms have individual works of art and some of the suites come with a private gym or a little terrace attached.

There are two restaurants; Indigo overlooks the bar and offers an easy-going modern European menu while Axis is an altogether glitzier affair with a separate identity. The health club is equally state-of-the art with an 18 metre swimming pool, complete with music piped underwater.

Capital

22-24 Basil St
SW3 1AT
(020) 75895171 – **Fax** (020) 72250011
e-mail reservations@capitalhotel.co.uk
Web www.capitalhotel.co.uk

⊖ Knightsbridge
PLAN page 201 **F5**

49 rm – †£247/335 ††£385, ☕ £19
The Capital Restaurant (See restaurant listing)

Capital

Even those with the heaviest shopping bag will be able to manage the short walk from Harrods to The Capital. This is a very British hotel, still run by the same family who opened it in 1971 and still flying the Union Jack outside.

The entrance is pleasingly discreet and you find yourself in a charming little lobby, complete with fireplace, where the uniformed staff are always eager to assist, a hallmark of this particular hotel. To the right is the neat little bar which leads into the acclaimed and elegant restaurant while the drawing room, where afternoon tea is served, evokes the style of a country house.

The bedrooms are all also unashamedly British in their style and decoration, albeit in an updated and rejuvenated style, and all come with their own individual furniture and artwork, much of which comes from the owner's own private collection. Needless to say, mattresses are hand-made and sheets Egyptian cotton, ensuring that the most fundamental purpose of any hotel, namely providing a decent night's sleep, is virtually guaranteed. The junior suites are always the first to go and come with an impressive array of extra touches.

Charlotte Street

15 Charlotte St
W1T 1RJ
(020) 78062000 – **Fax** (020) 78062002
e-mail charlotte@firmdale.com
Web www.charlottestreethotel.co.uk

Goodge Street
PLAN page 119 I2

44 rm – £229/240 £335, £19 – 8 suites
Oscar (See restaurant listing)

Charlotte Street

It's not just the location, within strolling distance of Soho, or that the hotel has its own private screening room that attract the media types, film industry sorts and arty souls who have made this hotel their own, but the stimulating way in which it has been decorated and the prevailing vibe.

This one-time dental warehouse has been deftly transformed into a very chic hotel and proves that comfort and design can be equal bed fellows and that something good has come from British dentistry. Using a combination of abstract art, sculpture and paintings from artists of the neighbouring Bloomsbury set, the hotel manages to be also quite English in tone. The drawing rooms are tranquil, stress-free areas, in contrast to the bustle of the bar and Oscar restaurant.

Dotted among the bedrooms are one-off pieces of furniture combined with top drawer fabrics and fittings, all supported by a maintenance programme of virtually constant refurbishment. Staff all appear to be enthusiastic and confident. The loft and penthouse suites will stir emotions of envy and desire or, if you've got one, glee.

The Halkin

5 Halkin St ⊖ Hyde Park Corner
SW1X 7DJ PLAN page 100 **G5**
(020) 73331000 – **Fax** (020) 73331100
e-mail res@halkin.como.bz
Web www.halkin.como.bz
Closed 25-26 December and 1 January

35 rm – £288/411 £370/500, £25 – 6 suites
Nahm (See restaurant listing)

VISA

AE

Once upon a time, having an en-suite bathroom in your hotel room was considered the very apotheosis of luxury but just as comforts improved in the average home so the expectations of those staying in hotels grew. The Halkin was the first in the new breed of hotel to recognise that design and aesthetics could play a key role and to challenge the traditional idea of what makes a luxury hotel.

Today, through constant refurbishment and refreshment, it remains one of the city's most chic addresses, offering understated English elegance matched with Italian design flair, while effortlessly complementing the very charming Georgian surroundings of Belgravia. You know you're somewhere special when even the staff are wearing Giorgio Armani.

The lobby is a relatively discreet affair, with the bar to one side then its through to Nahm for artful Thai cuisine. The accommodation, spread over five floors, offers guests all the latest hi-tech facilities but, more importantly, uncluttered and unfussy rooms with lean, straight lines and top of the range materials.

Covent Garden

10 Monmouth St
✉ WC2H 9HB
✆ (020) 78061000 – **Fax** (020) 78061100
e-mail covent@firmdale.com
Web www.coventgardenhotel.co.uk

⊖ Covent Garden
PLAN page 138 I3

56 rm – 🛉£258/311 🛉🛉£358/364, ☕ £20 – 2 suites

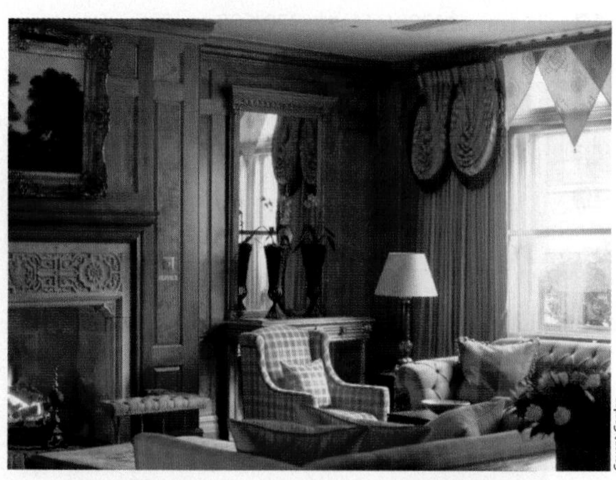

Covent Garden

This was once a hospital and you can still see the words 'dispensary' etched into the red brickwork. Now a very stylish hotel, it continues to care for the welfare of visitors by offering a complimentary neck and shoulder massage to all arrivals, ensuring that even the brusquest of guest will soon be switched to relax mode.

To the right of the entrance one finds Brasserie Max, a casual, easy restaurant that boasts plenty of local followers and offers an extensive selection of modern dishes with European influences, as well as doubling as the breakfast room. It's upstairs to the charming wood panelled drawing room, open only to residents, which offers a calming oasis when not being used for a photo shoot.

Those whose pastime or profession involves cinema can arrange a private viewing in the hotel's own screening room, with its soft Italian leather seats. Bedrooms continue the theme of understated elegance and thoughtful design and are all very comfortable and individual. Those on the Monmouth Street side tend to benefit from larger windows and of the two top floor suites, one has its own library, the other its own terrace.

The Pelham

15 Cromwell Pl,
SW7 2LA
(020) 75898288 – **Fax** (020) 75848444
e-mail pelham@firmdale.com
Web www.pelhamhotel.co.uk

South Kensington
PLAN page 201 E6

50 rm – £188/229 £294, £18 – 2 suites

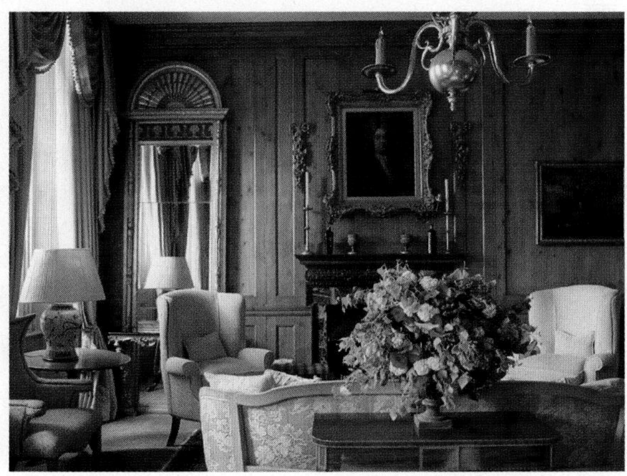

The Pelham

The Pelham is a charmingly individual townhouse, decorated in a quintessentially English country house style. The period feel surrounds you the minute you enter and the two drawing rooms, one with pine panelling the other with mahogany lined bookcases and both with fireplaces, are a delight.

Downstairs you'll find Kemps, the cosy restaurant decorated with original works of art which becomes a very romantic spot in the evenings. The menu offers a satisfying selection of dishes with either a British or Mediterranean bent.

All the bedrooms are individually decorated and continue the theme of a country house in the city. Those on the first and second floors benefit from higher ceilings and many share some of the original features of the house. Techno-extras are discreetly blended into the decoration to ensure that that business types have all the facilities they require, without the feeling of sleeping in an office. South Kensington tube station is literally across the road so, if the plethora of attractions nearby is not enough, reaching those around the city could not be easier.

Blakes

33 Roland Gdns
SW7 3PF
(020) 73706701 – **Fax** (020) 73730442
e-mail blakes@blakeshotels.com
Web www.blakeshotels.com

Gloucester Road
PLAN page 200 D6

45 rm – £206/323 £417, £25 – 3 suites

VISA

AE

Blakes

Before they applied to hotels like Blakes, words like "daring" and "dramatic" were mostly used to describe the more eccentric of guest, when the poor loves had nowhere to stay that really understood them. The opening by Anouska Hempel of Blakes in 1981 not only provided London with its first strikingly theatrical hotel, but it also blazed a trail in hotel design in which all subsequent boutique hotels and townhouses were to follow.
The lobby sets the tone with oriental boxes, bamboo, birdcages and idiosyncratic little design touches, which all tell you this is no ordinary hotel. The Chinese room and bar, which adjoin the basement restaurant, have become popular nightspots and this fusion of east meets west continues in the specialities on the menu.
It is in the bedrooms where the uniqueness and sheer individuality is most evident. Stencils, shutters, prints, period furniture, ethereal drapes and *trompe d'oeils* make every room a true original. Suite 007 is one of the most striking bedrooms in London. Many hotels boast of not having two rooms alike, but few can really claim to boast of differences as conspicuous as Blakes.

The Milestone

1-2 Kensington Court
W8 5DL
(020) 79171000 – **Fax** (020) 79171010
e-mail bookms@rchmail.com
Web www.milestonehotel.com

High Street Kensington
PLAN page 238 D4

52 rm – £235/294 £235/294, £22 – 5 suites

R.Burr/Michelin

It may be on quite a busy road, but the location of this charming Victorian hotel is pretty impressive as it's opposite Kensington Palace and allows great views across Kensington Gardens. Inside, it's much bigger than one realises but it still manages to retain a sense intimacy and affability.

Afternoon tea is served in the Park Lounge, a charming wood panelled room with comfy sofas, while Cheneston's is the sweet little dining room, offering a menu which balances contemporary dishes with the more traditional. If you're a bigger group try booking the Orangery, a cosy area attached to the restaurant, which was originally the prayer room of the house. The bar is at the back of the house and is called Stables - this was where the original owner of the house kept his horses and the equine theme is continued with the paintings and collection of jockey silks.

Bedrooms are all attractively furnished, have a discernible sense of individuality and all offer plenty of modern extras. The suites are particularly charming; some are split level and several have four poster beds.

Stafford

16-18 St James's Pl
SW1A 1NJ
(020) 74930111 – **Fax** (020) 74937121
e-mail info@thestaffordhotel.co.uk
Web www.thestaffordhotel.co.uk

Green Park
PLAN page 37 H4

75 rm – £282/323 £376/393, £20 – 6 suites

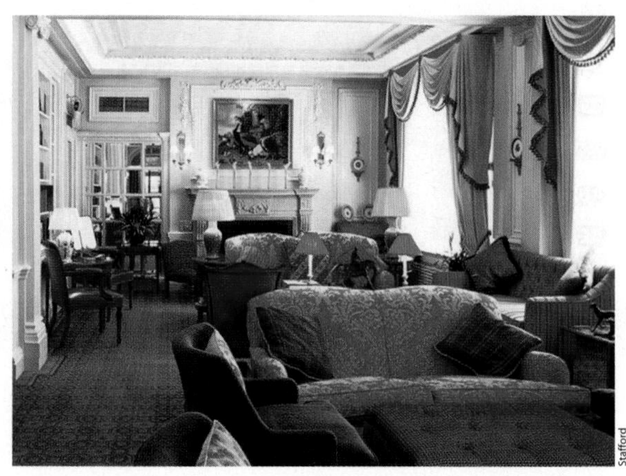

Stafford

The Stafford seems to fit its surroundings of St James's like a glove, a leather glove from Gieves and Hawkes. It has that ageless English feel that comes from having once been a private residence and offers a standard of accommodation that is refined yet practical. Antiques and period furniture grace the ground floor, from the quiet and thoroughly genteel drawing room to the spacious, traditionally furnished dining room. Those who feel the world is spinning too quickly can get off here and enjoy classic British cooking from Beef Wellington to Dover Sole, all in a room where gentlemen are still required to wear a jacket. The hidden gem that is the American Bar trumps others of the same name in its exuberant decoration of assorted memorabilia, donated by the customers, which provides a potted history of the last century.

The majority of the bedrooms are in the main house, where they are decorated in a traditional English style, enlivened with colourful patterned wallpaper and top quality fabrics. Those after something a little different should book a room in the Carriage House, delightful converted 18th century stables.

Sanderson

50 Berners St
✉ W1T 3NG
✆ (020) 73001400 – **Fax** (020) 73001401
e-mail sanderson@morganshotelgroup.com
Web www.morganshotelgroup.com

⊖ Oxford Circus
PLAN page 119 H2

150 rm – †£264/441 ††£294/499, ☕ £22

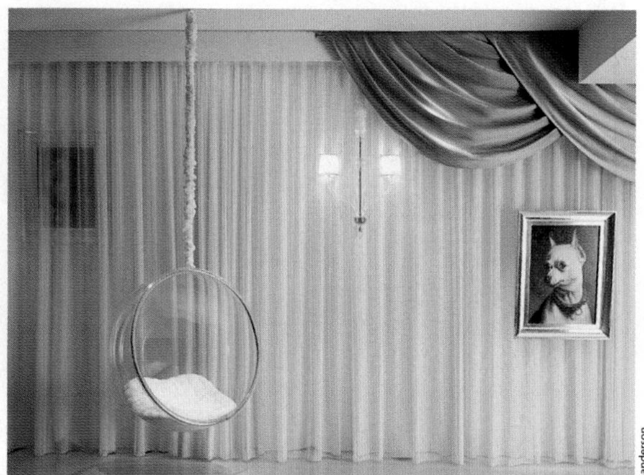

Sanderson

Oil paintings of pastoral scenes hang in all the bedrooms. The difference is that at The Sanderson they hang on the ceiling. Welcome to the world of Philippe Starck.

The celebrated French designer's touch is evident everywhere, reflecting his love of the playful, the whimsy, the clean and the uncluttered. The dream-like style of the lobby alone sets the tone for this most fashionable hotel, which takes its name from the building's previous incarnation as HQ of the famous wall-paper company.

The Purple Bar is as exclusive as it gets and uses fabrics of every shade of purple to create a theatrical and mysterious vibe. In contrast, the Long Bar rejoices in light and freshness. Spoon is the name of the dining concept where the customers can customize their own dishes, a course of action that requires more thought that you think. The spa is draped with white and offers some serious pampering, while those who prefer more active therapy should head to the billiard room, with its striking John Piper stained glass.

Modernity and originality continue in the bedrooms which come with glass enclosed bathrooms, sleigh beds, bright white walls and sheer drapes.

Draycott

26 Cadogan Gdns
SW3 2RP
(020) 77306466 – **Fax** (020) 77300236
e-mail reservations@draycotthotel.com
Web www.draycotthotel.com

Sloane Square
PLAN page 201 F6

31 rm – £147/206 £288/347, £20 – 4 suites

Draycott

The Draycott is actually three Edwardian houses (numbers 22, 24 and 26) knocked together, and occupies an enviable spot just yards from Sloane Square. The drawing room is one of the hotel's most charming features and looks out over the communal gardens. It is here where complimentary afternoon tea is served, as well as early evening drinks, giving the more sociably inclined the opportunity of meeting one's fellow guests.

All the rooms are named after writers or actors, although whoever decided that Peter O'Toole would be an appropriate name for the breakfast room is clearly unfamiliar with the great man's reputation.

Bedrooms are all individual in their size and styling; those in house number 22 tend to be slightly bigger and first floor rooms have higher ceilings. There are nice little touches, like a teddy bear in each room and a memento, such as a book or photograph, relating to the person after whom the bedroom is named and some of the rooms have a fireplace. There is no dining room but a room service menu provides an adequate selection for those not wishing to venture outside.

The Metropolitan

Old Park Lane
✉ W1K 1LB
✆ (020) 74471000 – **Fax** (020) 74471100
e-mail res.lon@metropolitan.como.bz
Web www.metropolitan.como.bz

⊖ Hyde Park Corner
PLAN page 36 G4

147 rm – 🕴£376/411 👥£411, ☕ **£25 – 3 suites**
🍴 ***Nobu*** (See restaurant listing)

The Metropolitan

Welcome to the world of the beautiful people. If you've seen paparazzi shots of a star – of the real or reality firmament - leaving a bar in a tired and emotional state then more than likely those snaps were taken outside the Met Bar, a nightspot considerably smaller in size than in reputation. For some, getting guaranteed access to the Met Bar is, in itself, reason enough to check into the Metropolitan Hotel but this is more than just a hang out for the achingly trendy.
The rooms are chic in an understated way and come with the full range of technological gizmos. For those staying in rooms at the front of the hotel, the large windows frame the wonderful views of Hyde Park and the penthouse suite – and its wonderful shower - is certainly one of the most striking in the city. All this and you've got Nobu on the first floor.
As one would expect, this is a popular hotel with the music and film businesses and those who use words like agent, stylist and wardrobe. So look carefully, because the seemingly confused troglodyte sharing the lift with you may well be someone who brushes up exceedingly well.

Westbury

Bond St
W1S 2YF
(020) 76297755 – **Fax** (020) 74951163
e-mail sales@westburymayfair.com
Web www.westburymayfair.com

Bond Street
PLAN page 36 H3

230 rm – £152/311 £152/311, £24 – 19 suites

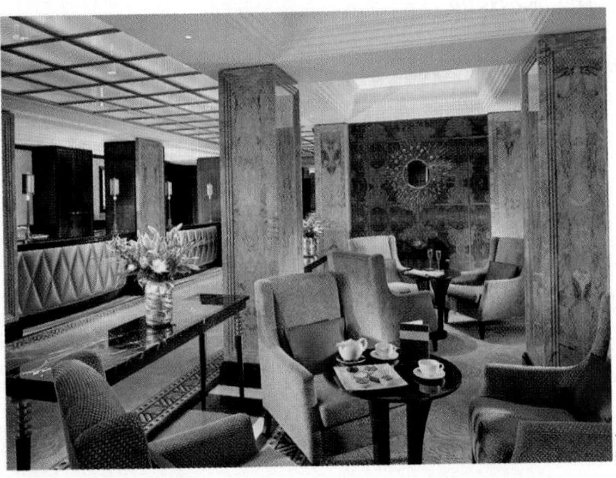
Westbury

If, by any chance, shopping has become an Olympic sport by 2012 then Bond Street will be the venue for the finals. You get all the labels and all the latest collections here and if you've heard of a glamorous designer or famous jeweller then they'll have a shop here too. It is, therefore, entirely appropriate that there's a rather smart hotel in the middle of it all, providing competitors with a chance to recuperate before their next boutique assault.

Restorative liquids can be best enjoyed in the legendary Polo Bar, which not only does a roaring trade in afternoon teas but is one of the smartest cocktail bars around. The Westbury was built in 1955 and the bar caused quite a stir at the time with its American swagger.

The hotel has recently been showered with money for a comprehensive programme of refurbishment and redecoration. The smart new restaurant uses a combination of natural light and sparkling chandeliers to create a warm yet contemporary feel, with an equally modern menu to match.

More contemporary styling continues in the bedrooms, which benefit from the full range of services. Most of the suites have balconies and the penthouse is certainly eye-catching.

The Cadogan

75 Sloane St
✉ SW1X 9SG
✆ (020) 72357141 – **Fax** (020) 72450994
e-mail reservations@cadogan.com
Web www.thesteingroup.com/cadogan

⊖ Knightsbridge
PLAN page 201 F5

62 rm – 🚹£347 🚹🚹£347, ☕ £20 – 2 suites

The Cadogan

The Cadogan owes much of its lasting fame to two of its most renowned residents; Lillie Langtry, actress and royal mistress, and Oscar Wilde, who was famously arrested here in 1895 (it was in room 118, which is, in reality, quite a lot smaller than it was depicted on stage in *The Judas Kiss*).

120 years after its opening, the hotel still has a very English, even Edwardian, feel, while still managing to offer the comforts and standards expected by today's traveller. The bedrooms are divided roughly half and half between a contemporary and a more traditional style, both with their own appeal. All the rooms are reached via a wonderful old-fashioned lift which, no doubt, causes palpitations for your average Health and Safety inspector. The ground floor wood panelled drawing room is a charming place for afternoon tea or afternoon napping, leading into the clubby bar. The restaurant is a fairly intimate affair, popular with local groups and societies, and offers a menu of assorted international influences.

Outside, one of the city's most exclusive shopping streets awaits your credit card.

Knightsbridge

⊖ Knightsbridge
PLAN page 199 F4

10 Beaufort Gdns
SW3 1PT
(020) 75846300 – **Fax** (020) 75846355
e-mail knightsbridge@firmdale.com
Web www.knightsbridgehotel.com

44 rm – £176/212 £306, £17

A/C SAT VISA AE

Knightsbridge

The assertion "whoever said money can't buy happiness simply didn't know where to shop" has been attributed to several people, but whoever it was would love the Knightsbridge Hotel. Being so close to all the great shops, department stores and boutiques of London it's hardly surprising that every guest returning to the hotel late in the day appears weighed down with shopping bags. The hotel re-opened in 2002, was originally converted from a row of Victorian terrace houses and the pretty little cul-de-sac provides relatively quiet surroundings considering the central location.

Featured in the centre of the lobby is an original sculpture resembling a stalagmite of slate and you'll find further artwork in the drawing room, summing up the general style of the place. There's a library which, surprisingly for a hotel, actually contains books, as well as an honesty bar for residents. There is no restaurant but breakfast and a 24 hour menu are served in the rooms.

The bedrooms themselves offer the perfect balance between style and practicability, with the three junior suites being particularly attractive. This is a cool and altogether rather sophisticated London address.

The Zetter

86-88 Clerkenwell Rd
EC1M 5RJ
(020) 73244444 – **Fax** (020) 73244445
e-mail info@thezetter.com
Web www.thezetter.com

Farringdon
PLAN 164 K1

59 rm – £176 £176/264, £17

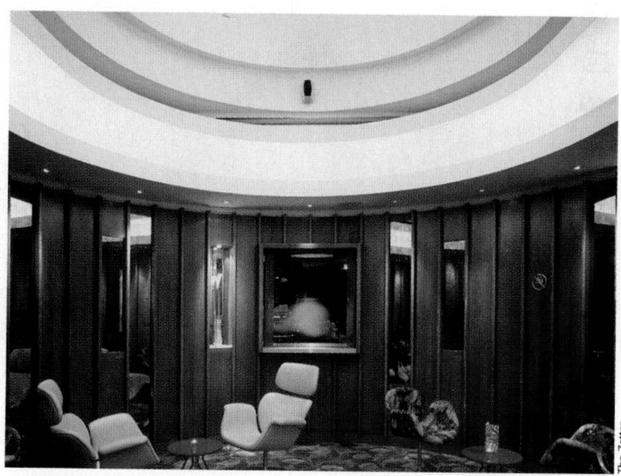
The Zetter

Housed in a converted 19th century warehouse and with a reputation for style, design and laid-back urban chic, The Zetter mirrors the fashionable reputation of its Clerkenwell surroundings. The building's origins are evident in the exposed brick walls but there are also a number of original design aspects to set this hotel apart, from the striking atrium to the 7 studio bedrooms with their own patios.
Within the subtly lit bedrooms you'll find modern techno services, such as LCD televisions with a vast library of music tracks available, have been nicely juxtaposed with homely touches, such as a selection of classic Penguin paperbacks. Vending machines on each floor provide anything from disposable cameras to champagne and the building's air conditioning uses water pumped from the hotels own bore-hole.
The general carefree vibe of the crescent-shaped restaurant, with its large sash windows overlooking the cobbled St John's Square, also bears little resemblance to a typical hotel dining room. Here the cooking is Italian in influence, with a welcome flexibility in both menu and opening hours to suit all comers.

Number Sixteen

16 Sumner Pl
SW7 3EG
(020) 75895232 – **Fax** (020) 75848615
e-mail sixteen@firmdale.com
Web www.numbersixteenhotel.co.uk

⊖ South Kensington
PLAN page 201 E6

42 rm – £118/206 £300, £13

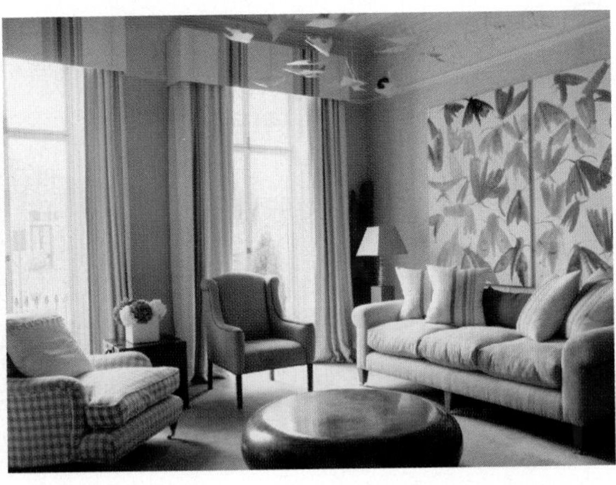

Number Sixteen

Actually, it's numbers 14 – 17 but whose counting? Anyway, Number Sixteen is a snappier name. The hotel is made up of four lustrously bright white houses in a mid Victorian terrace, located in a very charming street with all the museums, shops and restaurants you'll need within walking distance. Unlike many a recent conversion from private house to intimate hotel, this one has ensured that everyone has plenty of room. On the ground floor there are two delightful drawing rooms, overlooking Sumner Place and decorated with interesting modern British artwork.

The conservatory breakfast room leads out into a pretty private garden, which is surprisingly large given the South Kensington location, and indeed four of the bedrooms open out onto this very restful space.

All the bedrooms combine a sense of Englishness with a modern freshness and vitality. Roberts radios are in all the rooms, along with granite bathrooms and top of the range fabrics and the housekeeping department is clearly on top of its game. This is one of those hotels which doesn't feel too much like a hotel and is all the more special for that.

Durrants

26-32 St George St
W1H 5BJ
(020) 79358131 – **Fax** (020) 74873510
e-mail enquiries@durrantshotel.co.uk
Web www.durrantshotel.co.uk

Bond Street
PLAN page 119 G2

VISA MC AE

88 rm – £105/155 ££175, £15 – 4 suites

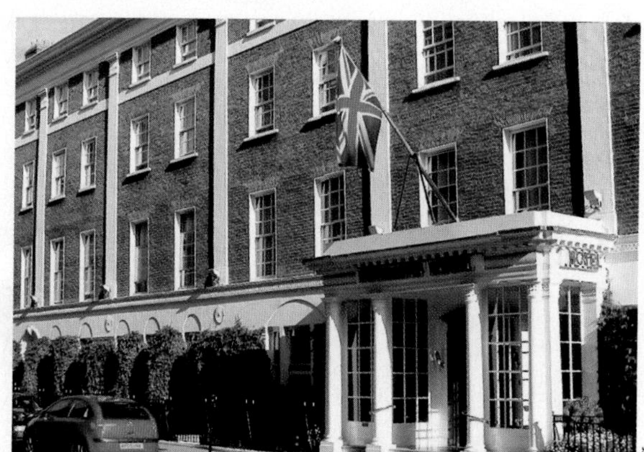

Durrants

This Georgian townhouse has been under the same family ownership for over eighty years and is as English as warm beer and understatement. Enter the lobby and you're likely to see traditionally attired staff polishing the brass, or stroll down the hallway to one of the drawing rooms and what looks like your Great Aunt will be taking afternoon tea in surroundings resembling one of the more established country house hotels. The timeless feel of Durrants is particularly evident in the bar which is divided into two rooms and has muskets hanging on the walls and a warming fireplace.

The wood panelled dining room offers a full range of classics from smoked salmon to grilled lamb cutlets, supplemented by the daily changing dishes on the trolley, although there are also nods to more contemporary cuisine. A separate dining room is used exclusively for breakfast.

Traditionalists and technophobes will be pleased to know that bedrooms are still opened by an actual key - this is no place for plastic cards and flashing lights. The rooms themselves are also traditionally English in a simple and unassuming style.

Dorset Square

39-40 Dorset Sq
NW1 6QN
(020) 77237874 – **Fax** (020) 77243328
e-mail reservations@dorsetsquare.co.uk
Web www.dorsetsquare.co.uk

Marylebone
PLAN page 118 F1

37 rm – £176/258 £306/411, £16

A/C SAT VISA AE

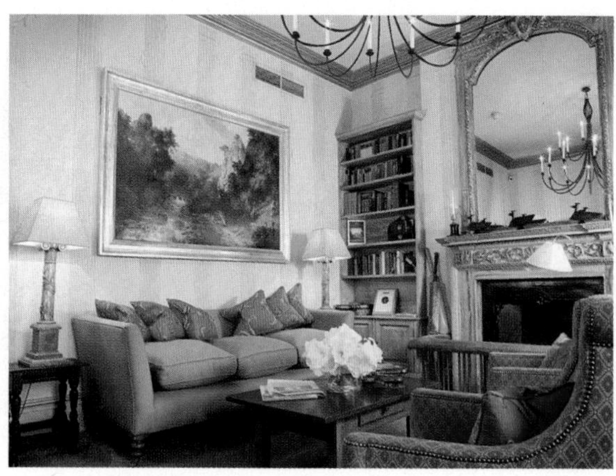

Dorset Square

This is a charming Regency house in a square where Thomas Lord originally laid out his cricket ground in 1787 before it moved up the road in 1814 to what is now Lord's, the undisputed HQ of world cricket. Indeed, England's most idiosyncratic gift to the sporting world is celebrated in the hotel through many of its pictures and paintings; on test match days expect to see a few chaps sporting the egg-and-bacon tie. The hotel itself feels just as English and a charming and friendly atmosphere prevails, helped by very pleasant and eager-to-please staff.

The drawing room overlooks the square but downstairs you'll find the Potting Shed restaurant, a delightfully sweet and distinctive little place decorated with pots and watering cans and a large mural of a cricket match. Jazz evenings are held on Fridays and the menu is divided between British favourites and lighter Mediterranean dishes.

The age of the house means that lintels slope and rooms come in various shapes and sizes. Room 3 is on the lower ground floor and has a four-poster bed and a terrific skylight.

Dorset Square is a perfect antidote to the plethora of faceless international chain hotels.

K + K George

1-15 Templeton Pl
SW5 9NB
(020) 75988700 – **Fax** (020) 73702285
e-mail hotelgeorge@kkhotels.co.uk
Web www.kkhotels.com

Earl's Court
PLAN page 200 C6

154 rm – £182 £217

K&K George

K+K hotels are a small, privately owned chain, all of whose hotels seem to blend seamlessly into the fabric of the assorted European cities in which they are located. London is no exception, as the K+K George is set within an imposing stucco fronted and luminously white Georgian terrace and is in a useful location for both tourists and attendees of exhibition halls and trade fairs nearby.

In contrast to the period façade, the hotel's interior is colourfully contemporary in style, with clean lines and a refreshing lack of chintz. Those who struggle to lift their mood first thing in the day will appreciate the bright and comfortable breakfast room as it looks out onto the hotel's own private garden - a charming and, considering the location, surprisingly decent size and clearly the envy of surrounding houses.

A simple bistro style menu is served in the friendly and less structured surroundings of the bar while corporate guests will find all the kit they need for any homework. Bedrooms all come in relatively decent dimensions and have a certain Scandinavian feel and freshness about them.

The Gore

190 Queen's Gate
✉ SW7 5EX
(020) 75846601 – **Fax** (020) 75898127
e-mail reservations@gorehotel.co.uk
Web www.gorehotel.com

⊖ Gloucester Road
PLAN page 200 D5

50 rm – **🚹£170/235 🚹🚹£211/235,** ☕ £17

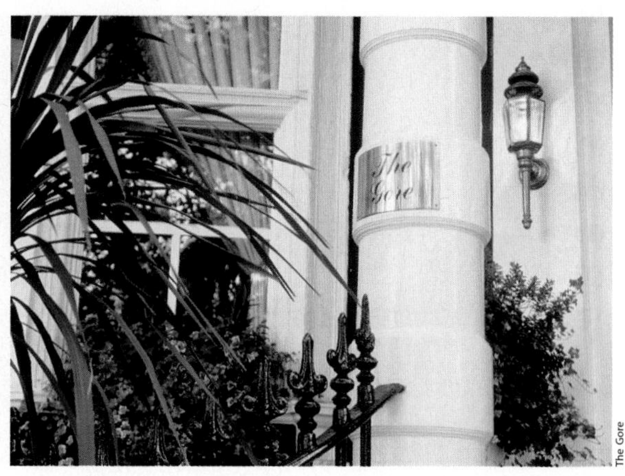

The Gore

The Gore feels considerably smaller and more intimate than its number of bedrooms suggests, has considerable idiosyncratic charm and its location, in a pleasant tree lined avenue within walking distance of so much, cannot be faulted. The tone is set by the charming hallway and reception, where the walls are covered with pictures and paintings of Queen Victoria, highly appropriate considering this is a late Victorian building and the neighbourhood is so closely linked to her reign.

The restaurant lies somewhere between a bistro and a brasserie and is a fun and lively spot, with a Euro friendly menu. The wood panelled bar opposite has proven to be a destination in itself (and benefits from being the nearest one to the Albert Hall).

An on-going refurbishment programme ensures that the rooms and bathrooms are kept up to scratch, although there has been a reduction recently in the vast number of paintings and pictures which once covered virtually every space. The style of the bedrooms remains theatrical, original and, at times, mildly eccentric with many a story behind the furniture: the Venus Room boasts Judy Garland's old bed.

The London Outpost

69 Cadogan Gdns
✉ SW3 2RB
✆ (020) 75897333 – **Fax** (020) 75814958
e-mail info@londonoutpost.co.uk
Web www.londonoutpost.co.uk
Closed 23-27 December

⊖ Sloane Square
PLAN page 201 F6

A/C

VISA

AE

11 rm – †£235 ††£273/387, ☕ £17

R.Burr/Michelin

Until recently the full moniker was 'The London Outpost of Bovey Castle' but when the owner, Peter de Savary, sold off his hotel in deepest Devon the name of his London hotel changed to its current shorter version.

The London Outpost is his charming little townhouse hotel with just eleven bedrooms, all of which are named after writers or artists who have some local connection to this part of Chelsea. 'Turner' is the best room, with a four poster bed, high ceiling and a fireplace, but all the bedrooms are individual in character, with busts, antiques and prints adding to the period feel.

Being so small, the hotel encourages a certain house-party mood and guests are invited each evening to share a glass of champagne with the manager and a chance to meet fellow guests in the very charming drawing room. Afternoon tea is served in the downstairs library, as are an extensive selection of malt whiskies later in the day.

The hotel will also supply a key for access to the gardens opposite and will willingly organise a picnic on summer's days.

22 Jermyn Street

22 Jermyn St
✉ SW1Y 6HL
(020) 77342353 – **Fax** (020) 77340750
e-mail office@22jermyn.com
Web www.22jermyn.com
Closed 24-25 December

⊖ Piccadilly Circus
PLAN page 37 I3

5 rm – 🚹£258 🚹🚹£258/364, ☕ £13 – 13 suites

22 Jermyn Street

Running between Regent Street and St James's Street, Jermyn Street dates back to 1664 and is one of Central London's most celebrated streets, thanks largely to the roll call of famous shops and outfitters, providing all manner of sartorial finery to the well dressed gentleman. Number 22 was reconstructed at the turn of the 19th century and has been in the Togna family since 1915, with Henry Togna, the current owner, responsible for transforming it into the luxury townhouse it is today.
While there are no public areas to the hotel, the bedrooms are of sufficient size for this not to matter; of the 18 rooms, 13 are suites and who can complain when breakfast in bed is the only option. A full 24-hour room service menu is also available but the beauty of this central London location is the innumerable dining options within strolling distance and assorted hostelries within sloping distance. The hotel is more than willing to help with reservations.
All the bedrooms are elegantly decorated, with additional sofa beds in the suites and all have plenty of extras, from DVD players to bathrobes.

Knightsbridge Green

159 Knightsbridge
SW1X 7PD
(020) 75846274 – **Fax** (020) 72251635
e-mail reservations@thekghotel.co.uk
Web www.thekghotel.com

Knightsbridge
PLAN page 199 F4

Closed Christmas

16 rm – £105/160 £140/160, £12 – 12 suites

Knightsbridge Green

Those who enjoy shopping, jogging or sightseeing, or indeed all three, will find little wrong with Knightsbridge Green's location: it's on the doorstep of all the best shops, a road crossing away from Hyde Park and a short bus ride away from all the attractions.

Spread over six floors, it offers clean and comfortable accommodation at a price that must be thought reasonable when one considers the position and the neighbourhood. Decoration is inoffensively neutral and unfussy, with decent sized single rooms found on the top floor. Bedrooms 34 and 24 are perhaps the pick of the rooms in size and are also quieter than most.

What makes Knightsbridge Green stand out is the care shown to customers, consequence of it being relatively small and privately owned. It also helps that many of the staff, from manager to maid, have been with the hotel for many years so regulars are recognised and any special requests catered for.

Complimentary teas and coffees are provided throughout the day and breakfast is served in the bedrooms until 10am for those impervious to the attractions of early morning exercise.

The Rookery

A/C

12 Peters Lane, Cowcross St
⊠ EC1M 6DS
✆ (020) 73360931 – **Fax** (020) 73360932
e-mail reservations@rookery.co.uk
Web www.rookeryhotel.com

⊖ Barbican
PLAN page 164 L2

VISA MC AE

32 rm – 🚹£205 🚹🚹£240/288, ☕ £10 – 1 suite

The Rookery

For an area of London so obviously steeped in history, it is entirely fitting to find a hotel that positively exudes character and whose very name was used colloquially to describe the surrounding streets once known for their rather raffish reputation.

The Rookery is a hotel housed in a row of restored 18c houses and is decorated with a unique blend of period furniture, ranging from the restored Victorian bathrooms - whose grandeur gives meaning to the expression "sitting on the throne" - to wood panelling, stone flag flooring, oil paintings and open fireplaces.

Bedrooms are named after those who have lived at the address over the last 250 years and the fact that no two of the 33 bedrooms are the same can go without saying. What appeals most is the cosy and seductively secretive atmosphere that prevails, which is aeons away from the modern purpose-built bed factories that seemingly spring up overnight. This is a place for those who wish to feel like a genuine Londoner and you spent half your time expecting a camera crew to turn up to start filming a period drama.

Hazlitt's

A/C

6 Frith St — ⊖ Tottenham Court Road
✉ W1D 3JA — PLAN page 37 I3
(020) 74341771 – **Fax** (020) 74391524
e-mail reservations@hazlitts.co.uk
Web www.hazlittshotel.com

SAT VISA MC AE

22 rm – †£206/240 ††£240 – 1 suite

Hazlitt's

Named after the essayist and critic William Hazlitt who lived and died here in 1830, Hazlitt's is a delightfully idiosyncratic little hotel made up of three adjoining town houses dating from 1718. The 23 bedrooms are spread over three floors (there are no lifts) and are all named after writers from the 18th and 19th century who were either residents or visitors to the house. Today, the hotel is still attracting its fair share of writers, artists and those of a bohemian bent. Each room is full of character, from everything from wood panelling, busts and antique beds to Victorian bathroom fittings and fixtures.

The Earl of Willoughby is the largest room and comes with a small sitting room. The ground floor sitting room is the only communal area and breakfast is served in the bedrooms as there's no restaurant. Being in very heart of Soho, however, means that if you can't find a restaurant here then you really shouldn't be allowed out.

The staff match their surroundings in their wit and self-assurance which clearly comes from having pride in their hotel. As Hazlitt himself said "the art of pleasing consists in being pleased".

Miller's

111A Westbourne Grove (entrance on Hereford Rd) — ⊖ Bayswater

VISA ✉ W2 4UW — PLAN page 154 **C2**

MC ✆ (020) 72431024 – **Fax** (020) 72431064

e-mail enquiries@millersuk.com

AE **Web** www.millersuk.com

7 rm ☕ – 🚹£176/194 🚹🚹£217/270

Miller's

Many hotels boast of being a home from home but stay at Miller's and you genuinely feel as though you are staying in a private house with friends, albeit friends who have enough treasures to warrant their own series of "Antiques Roadshow". This is hardly surprising when you consider that this 18th century house is owned by Martin Miller, he of the eponymous antique guide.

The place revolves around the delightful drawing room which is filled with candles, period pieces, pictures and ornaments and is often used for film shoots or private parties. This is also the room where guests are served breakfast and, during the rest of the day, complimentary sherry and fruit.

The seven bedrooms are named after poets, with Browning and Tennyson being the rooms with four poster beds and Keats being the grandest, although Wordsworth comes close and boasts an added dash of theatricality in the decoration. The general bohemian air is aided by the staff who are all young and seemingly imperturbable. Guests are all given their own front door key, adding to that sense of relaxed familiarity.

Twenty Nevern Square

Nevern Sq
⊠ SW5 9PD
✆ (020) 75659555 – **Fax** (020) 75659444
e-mail hotel@twentynevernsquare.co.uk
Web www.twentynevernsquare.co.uk

⊖ Earl's Court
PLAN page 200 C6

19 rm – †£99/110 ††£175/270, ☕ £9

R.Burr/Michelin

There can be few things more irritating for hoteliers who have spent buckets of money on marketing than to read their hotel being described as a "well kept secret" but Twenty Nevern Square is just that. It's part of a very charming red bricked Victorian Square, overlooking gardens, with comes with a palpable sense of neighbourhood.
Through the arched entrance you'll find they've made the best of the available space with a small but cosy little lounge area which leads into the light of the conservatory breakfast room. Ten of the bedrooms overlook the gardens and that includes Room 5, the Pasha Suite, which is the best room in the house, with an elaborately carved four poster and is own private terrace. Indeed, much of the furniture comes hand-carved from Indonesia which adds to the slight exoticism of the hotel when combined with the elaborately draped curtains. Bathrooms all come with a clever light sensor which turns itself on when movement is detected. The regular guests all seem to know one another and the small number of rooms makes for a general air of friendliness.

Aster House

3 Sumner Pl
✉ SW7 3EE
✆ (020) 75815888 – **Fax** (020) 75844925
e-mail asterhouse@btinternet.com
Web www.asterhouse.com

⊖ South Kensington
PLAN page 201 E6

13 rm – £93/159 £128/182

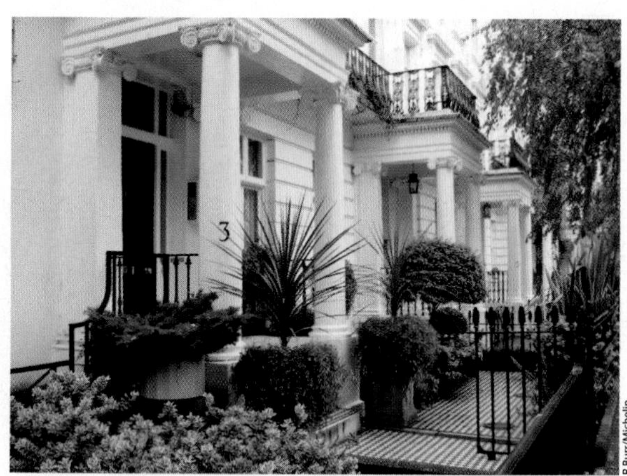

R.Burr/Michelin

Sadly, but realistically, few of us will ever be able to afford to buy a huge Victorian house, spread over four floors, in the Elysian Fields known as South Kensington. So staying in a Bed and Breakfast in a delightful and typically Kensington street, with restaurants, shops and attractions all within walking distance, is a great opportunity to live the dream.

Like all B&B's you get the distinct feeling you are staying in someone's house, particularly when you have to ring the doorbell to be let in. But it's not just its location where Aster House scores heavily; the house is immaculately kept, offers sizeable rooms and comes with rates that are a little more down to earth than many.

Three of the thirteen rooms are classified as "superior", including the particularly popular Garden Room which, as the name suggests, leads out onto a small garden. Breakfast is served in a very charming conservatory on the first floor which doubles as a bright and comfortable sitting room, overlooking Sumner Place and your fellow Kensington residents below.

Mayflower

26-28 Trebovir Rd
✉ SW5 9NJ
✆ (020) 73700991 – **Fax** (020) 73700994
e-mail info@mayflower-group.co.uk
Web www.mayflowerhotel.co.uk

⊖ Earl's Court
PLAN page 200 **C6**

VISA

AE

47 rm – 🚹£65/99 🚹🚹£89/109, ☕ £9

Mayflower

A few years back if you mentioned you were staying in a hotel in Earl's Court everyone would have assumed you were sharing a leaky room with half a dozen Aussie backpackers. Just as the area is smartening itself up, so is the accommodation on offer. The Mayflower has had a lot of money spent on it and now provides both comfort and style; it's also accessible and affordable. The reception area is quite swish and adjoining it is a little juice bar for the health conscious. Following the wholly understandable trend these days, there is no restaurant in the hotel but a decent and sustaining breakfast can be had in the basement room.

The bedrooms have been nicely done up, with some personal design touches lending a sense of individuality. Hand carved bed heads and wardrobes, along with ceiling fans, add a subtle Eastern note, while the bathrooms are well lit and attractive. Some of the rooms can be a little on the small size but bear in mind the prices charged. Five of the rooms are on the ground floor and several on the first floor have their own balcony.

B+B Belgravia

64-66 Ebury St
⊠ SW1W 9QD
(020) 72598570 – **Fax** (020) 72598591
e-mail info@bb-belgravia.com
Web www.bb-belgravia.com

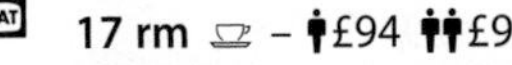

17 rm – £94 £99

VISA

⊖ Victoria
PLAN page 100 G6

R.Burr/Michelin

Affordable accommodation in London is rarer than hen's teeth so when B&B Belgravia opened in 2004 it proved to be an instant hit. The formula is straightforward: clean, simple but very well priced bedrooms in the heart of the city. The downside of this success is that, with only seventeen rooms, actually getting one of those rooms can be challenging.

The entrance is quite discreet which adds to the feeling that you're staying with friends rather than in a faceless edifice in hoteldom. Don't, though, let the name confuse you: this is not your Mrs Miggins type of B&B with candlewick bedspreads and a pervading smell of soup but an altogether rather stylish and contemporary place.

Two terrace houses have been knocked together and there is a welcoming lounge on the ground floor decorated in black and white with a complimentary coffee machine available all day, as well as local information and DVD's. Breakfast is served in a bright and sunny room which overlooks the little garden terrace. Bedrooms have a Scandinavian freshness and simplicity and provide perfectly comfortable accommodation.

Hart House

51 Gloucester Rd
⊠ W1U 8JF
✆ (020) 79352288 – **Fax** (020) 79358516
e-mail reservations@harthouse.co.uk
Web www.harthouse.co.uk

⊖ Marble Arch
PLAN page 118 F2

15 rm – **£70/95 £95/110**

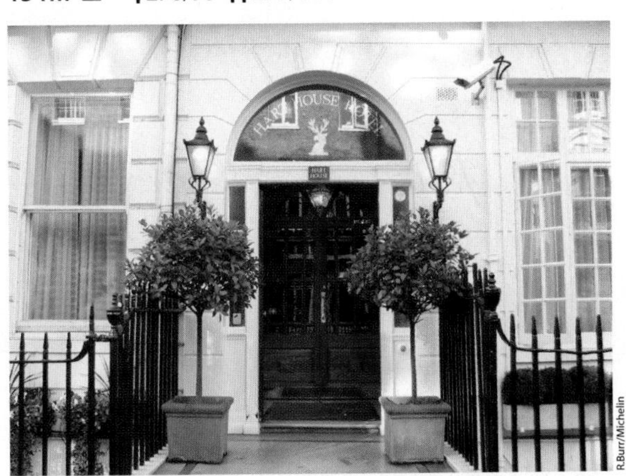

R.Burr/Michelin

Gloucester Place is a street made up almost entirely of large Georgian terrace houses, many of which are given over to the provision of accommodation of a budgetary nature and questionable standard. Hart House bucks the trend by proving that you can offer bedrooms that are clean, spacious and still competitively priced for those travelling on a budget or those looking for something a little less impersonal than your average overpriced city centre bed factory.

Run by the same family for over thirty-five years, Hart House has its bedrooms spread over three floors where the ceilings get lower the higher you climb, reflecting the time when the house's staff had their quarters at the top of the house. Rooms on the front of the house benefit from the large windows and they're fitted with double glazing which keeps the traffic noise outside at bay, so maybe those salesmen were telling the truth after all. Four of the fifteen rooms are decently priced single rooms and there are family rooms also available. There are no communal areas except for the small basement room where breakfast is served.

Index of maps